English IA
JAN. 25
7:30 - 9:30

Thurs.
12:30 - 2:30

Reading,
Writing,
Rhetoric

Reading, Writing, Rhetoric

WILLIAM HERMAN
The City College of
The City University of New York

HOLT, RINEHART AND WINSTON
New York   Chicago   San Francisco   Atlanta   Dallas
Montreal   Toronto

To Donna Ann Herman,
a demon reader,
a darling daughter

Library of Congress Cataloging in Publication Data

Herman, William.
  Reading, writing, rhetoric.
  1. English language—Rhetoric. 2. College
readers. I. Title.
PE1408.H466   808'.042   76-46546
ISBN: 0–03–017916–5

Printed in the United States of America
7 8 9 0   059   9 8 7 6 5 4 3 2 1

To the Instructor

Students learn to write well by reading well and by imitating the best writers. This idea has governed my work as a teacher of composition, and this book is based on it.

To help students read well, I chose the selections for their interest, brevity, completeness, plainness of style, and variety of subject matter. Most are whole essays, but a number are brief, freestanding units taken from larger works of prominent contemporary vitality. Thirty-two of the fifty-three essays included here have never before been anthologized.

Each essay appears in a separate chapter according to the rhetorical category to which it belongs. Each has a headnote giving the student relevant biographical information about the author and a brief lead-in to the selection. Footnotes explain possibly obscure references. Each selection is also provided with a three-part apparatus: *Questions for the Critical Reader*, which asks questions formulated to engage the student in meanings and values contained in the essay and to suggest their relevance to his own experience; *Rhetorical Technique*, which asks questions designed to sharpen a student's awareness of both the expository technique illustrated by the selection as well as other rhetorical techniques, such as point of view, emphasis, coherence, parallel structure, and so on; and *Diction and Vocabulary*, which takes up questions of diction, including figurative language, matters of connotation and denotation, tone, style, and the like.

The study questions have been prepared with a number of goals in mind: they are objective and offer the opportunity to train a reader's eye and mind; and they are open-ended, calling for broad discussion and thought—also appropriate for training the eye and the mind, but in a different way. Undoubtedly, there are more questions than some instructors can use.

To help students write well and understand the types of discourse and exposition, there are clear, brief explanations of each contained in nine chapter introductions. At the end of each chapter, there are writing assignments. The first of these is a general assignment appropriate to the subject matter of the chapter, that is, to the rhetorical type with which the chapter deals. The assignments that follow these are based on specific selections in the chapter and ask the student to use them as models. Thus instructors have a choice of assignment based on their individual preferences.

In addition to nine chapters organized in this manner, there is a tenth, which contains eight essays devoted to various aspects of the subject of language. Normally, selections on language appearing in a rhetoric/reader will fit easily into the category of *definition*. That is not the case with these, and the instructor is thus free to use this chapter either to deepen a student's ability to identify rhetorical types—for nothing in the headnotes to these selections identifies them as to type—or for a thematic study of language. The selections in this chapter have no apparatus, and there are no writing assignments at the end of it.

The section *To the Student* has been carefully designed to introduce the whole subject of the book to the student, in an easy way, before he or she reaches the introductory material of the various chapters. In it, the student will also find an annotated essay that is a good example of how methods of exposition are found mixed together in a single piece. The instructor may find it useful to stress reading this section before plunging into the main body of the text.

A *Glossary of Rhetorical Terms* is arranged at the back of the book for ease of access and includes those terms that seem most useful in analyzing the essays or most appropriate in illustrating the process of writing essays. Study questions that ask about these matters refer students to the Glossary.

The primary arrangement is, of course, by rhetorical category. Instructors may quarrel with my choice of categories, but I do not apologize for them. These, I think, are simple to teach, widely appropriate to what a student is likely to encounter in his reading, and richly justifiable on logical grounds. However, instructors are also provided with a *Thematic Table of Contents* and can easily design a different course from the one laid out here.

An *Instructor's Manual* is available to provide further opportunities for instructors to shape their courses in their own way.

In short, in all respects, the book has been designed for ease and flexibility of use.

I wish to express my appreciation for the helpful criticism and suggestions provided by friends and colleagues, but especially to Joanna

Pisello, Arthur Zeiger, James J. Greene, Edward Quinn, Karl Malkoff, Earl Rovit, Richard Goldstone, Arthur Waldhorn, and Leonard Kriegel. I would also like to thank my editor at Holt, Harriett Prentiss, for her unerring good taste and critical acumen and for the indispensable confidence she placed in me.

New York, N.Y.   W.H.
December 1976

Contents

To the Student

There are four basic kinds of communication—exposition, argument, narration, and description. If you will turn to the table of contents and look at the chapter titles, you will see all these and a few more. The others are major types of *exposition*, another term for which is *development*. Exposition is probably the most important of these because it is the most used. The type of development we call exposition has for its main function the *exposing* or conveying of information. As educated people—therefore, as people who have occasion to communicate in writing—we are more frequently called on to convey information than to tell a story (narration), describe a scene or a person (description), or convince somebody of the validity of our position (argument).

(If you are wondering why the chapter on argument comes first in the book if exposition is so important, the answer is that in writing an argument we always have to use a firmly stated main proposition. This is nothing but a main point, central theme, or thesis statement; and we begin with argument in order to acquire practice in controlling our writing with a firm central point.)

Now forms of exposition exist because different subjects and different purposes require that the writing take different forms. One form of exposition is called *process analysis*. If we wanted to write about how wheat gets planted and harvested, we would use *that* form of exposition (process analysis) for the purpose. Similarly, if we needed to write about competing candidates for a political office, we would use *comparison and contrast*. Your college reports and papers will take different forms, too. Your science report on the circulatory system of the frog will be a *process analysis*; your speech class on the virtues of Democratic fiscal policy will be an *argument*; your report on Cherokee Indian customs might be a *definition* of native American religion.

Each chapter introduction in the book explains each of the various methods in considerable detail; so we need not go into these matters here in great depth. For now, however, you should understand that few pieces of writing stick exclusively to one pattern of development. A particular pattern of development may be the principal one, but you will invariably find that other forms of exposition are also used to clarify particular points or emphasize some idea or other under discussion.

For example, look at the following piece. It is predominantly a story, the *narration* of a single episode in Murphy's classroom. But you will notice that there are other forms of exposition being used also. It is true that these are used to a limited extent, but they are present, nevertheless.

EDWARD F. MURPHY

Confessions of a Teacher

I feel guilty, all right, don't worry about that.

1 A kind of an *argument* occupies the whole paragraph.

1   I know I'm not supposed to have fun with my black and Spanish-speaking pupils. I'm there to help them with their mathematics, not to entertain them or enjoy them. That, surely, isn't a proper role for a fiftyish, fat, white, middle-class male in a Harlem school.

2   Education is, after all, a serious business. Grimness and high purposefulness is the order of the day. Not a minute must be wasted. Noses to the grindstone and pencils to the paper. No staring out the window. No kidding around, especially on my part. "Think of your professional dignity, man, think of your professional dignity."

2 All but the last sentence constitutes a *definition* of education.

Up and at those fractions!

Death to the multiplication facts for nine!

Don't let a single decimal get away alive!

3 This paragraph, in giving background information, is *describing* people—though not enough or in the kind of detail to make us *see* them.

3 All my students are retarded in their math. I myself am retarded, grossly so, in Spanish, black history and culture, the modern dance, golf and at least 16,000 other subjects. The range of my ignorance is vast, a shoreless sea. I have no reasonable hope of materially reducing its extent in whatever years are left to me to live.

4 So there I was in class today breaking into bits of song, mostly of my own making, and dancing a bit. Is that any way for a man of fifty to act before a group of students of elementary school age? Surely, I am not being paid, under Title I funds, to do that.

4 This is *storytelling*. It answers the question, "What happened?"

5 Again, a *description* of the times.

5 These are grim times. Blood or the threat of blood everywhere except on the moon, and who knows what a few years will bring there? Problems of staggering proportions at every hand. Subways so crowded that no self-respecting sardine will use them. I ride them at least twice a day, and find momentary salvation only in the pretty, though seldom smiling, faces of the young female passengers. (Roses they are in an urban desert.)

6 If we consider the preceding description as a series of *causes*, this is an *effect*.

6 Taxes and blood pressure up. No basic change for the better in sight.

7 Nevertheless, there I was celebrating life by dancing and singing and laughing, feeling a bit like a combination of St. Francis of Assisi and Danny Kaye. Enjoying myself. Enjoying the kids. Liking life. For-

7 More *narration*.

getting my middle-age melan-
cholia. Giving my phony image
of professional dignity a kick in
the pants. And teaching.

Make no mistake about that.
I was teaching. Not dutifully
but joyously. Digging the kids'
faces. Checking their work while
relishing their beauty. Not concerned about getting "respect"
from them. Instead, liking them
and showing it. Daring to let
my own humanity shine forth.
It's nice when you don't feel
compelled to pretend to be someone else, but are content to be
yourself.

8   *A causal
analysis* and an *ar-
gumentative
proposition* ("Test
scores have some
value, but . . .")

8   As a teacher, I know well
the American monomania for
getting results. I also know that
there is a kind of worshipful
attitude toward results which
virtually guarantees a poor har-
vest. Test scores have some
value, but they are as dung compared with the children whose
achievements they so imper-
fectly represent.

One of the occupational
hazards of teaching is that you
gradually deaden your respon-
siveness to the spontaneous
welling up of life. You become
a victim of lesson plans and
classroom routines. "Habit and
routine have an unbelievable
power to waste and destroy,"
wrote Henri de Lubac, S.J., in
"Paradoxes." Never is this more
true than in the joyless atmosphere of the average classroom.

9   Joy is not something you
can postpone. Nor is it something you can plan for. It comes
unbidden and will be served on
the instant. Teachers who are

9   Again, a
definition—first of
joy, then of
teachers.

overly concerned about their professional dignity will not scatter much sunshine. Unfortunately, teachers are not employed to scatter sunshine. Our primary task is to make kids work. Keep them busy in school, and give them an unconscionable amount of work to do at home. We load them down with books and notebooks. (I just weighed my 12-year-old daughter's bookbag. Twelve pounds of paper to be lugged back and forth five days a week.) We require them to absorb vast amounts of information. Apparently, our objective is to turn them into human data banks.

10   Again a *causal analysis* trying to answer the question "Why?"

10   I don't know why I broke into song and dance today in class. Perhaps it was because my supervisor had just visited me and found fault with many things. Initially, I felt depressed, discouraged, then angry. Life, at the moment, appeared to be more thorns than roses.

11   After she left, my gloom gave way to joy. I can't explain it. All I know is that I suddenly liked myself. Sure, I had faults and made mistakes, but so what? Life was still eminently worth living.

11   More *narration.*

True, I hadn't found any solution to raising math scores of the kids. I hadn't discovered how to bring them and the hundreds of thousands of children like them up to grade level.

12   Another piece of *causal analysis.*

12   All of the gross social injustices, which are, I think, at the root of the difficulties encountered by inner-city schools, still remained as massive as ever.

The world was still a stage where pain far exceeded pleasure.

Nevertheless, I felt good. Joy had come unbidden to me, and I had welcomed it.

13   More *narration*.   13   "Man, you look happy!" one of my kids said to me.

"I am, baby, I am!" I replied.

And I was.

You should be aware, then, that the selections in each chapter use one or another of the forms of exposition *predominantly*, but you should look in each for whatever other methods are present. At this point, you know what the various forms *are*—from having read this little introduction and looked at the table of contents—even though you are just learning how to use these forms in your writing. It is well just to learn to identify all these methods. And when you come to questions in the apparatus asking you what other methods of development you see, don't worry if you miss some of them. The practice in using your reading skills is more important than initial mastery.

Finally, you should also be aware that there are a good many opportunities in each selection to study general matters of rhetoric—good writing technique—and you should take advantage of these opportunities. Some of the writing assignments offer you the opportunity, for example, to use essays printed in that chapter as models. You might wish to try this exercise. Using the best of what other writers have to offer is an appropriate way to enrich your own skills. But the book is designed so that you can use it in a number of ways. You and your instructor will undoubtedly do so.

1

Building an *Argument*

Most of us think of an argument as a dispute involving people lined up on opposite sides of some question. Let's picture a street corner scene. Two automobile drivers have narrowly avoided a collision. They have both gotten out of their cars, however, and are arguing over who had the right of way. Another scene: this one in a living room, in front of a television set; a brother and sister are arguing over who's turn it is to do the dinner dishes. Frequently, these arguments begin with the parties trying reasonably to convince one another, but very often they take on a heated tone. In fact, as the argument fails to get resolved, the arguers can get more agitated and vehement. They stop using evidence to support their respective points of view; perhaps they accuse each other of lying. At this point, the original focus of the argument has been lost, and the arguers are very far from where they began.

The method of discourse we call *argument* differs from these everyday scenes in two important respects.

First, the formal argument may be passionate, even angry in its tone, but it never loses control, and it never resorts to personal attacks. In other words, unlike the personal arguments we have, the formal argument sticks to its point. We say that it steadily advances a *main proposition*. This may be a *proposition of fact*, a conclusion about some aspect of experience, such as "The United Nations has failed in its mission of keeping world peace"; or it may be a *proposition of action*, calling for something to be done, such as "National gun control laws should prohibit the private ownership of hand guns."

The second way in which a formal argument differs from the ordinary kind is that the formal argument always uses reason. Although in both kinds of argument the purpose is the same, that is, to convince our opponent of the rightness of our proposition, the methods of achieving that purpose are different. The informal arguer shouts down his opponent or resorts to personal attacks, but the writer of a formal argument supports his proposition with a chain of convincing evidence. Thus the writer wants to present logical proof; facts such as laws of nature, statistics, or undeniable historical events; authoritative opinion, such as a citation of the words of somebody who knows what he's talking about by virtue of his standing in his field: a Henry Kissinger in foreign policy, an O. J. Simpson in football; and reasoned consequences and antecedents, for example, "Since the UN was established, many wars have taken place" or "The greater the number of handguns, the more likely there will be fatal accidents."

But let's return to the two scenes we began with. Each of these informal arguments could have been settled by reason. For example, a witness might have been able to say whether it was the brother's or the sister's turn to do the dishes, and the laws of right-of-way for automobiles could have settled that dispute. Frequently, however, informal arguments take on their heated tones from the kinds of issues they begin with. Suppose, for example, we ran across a pair of arguers having at each other over the question of who makes better music, Ike and Tina Turner or the Rolling Stones. We would easily see that this argument has no chance of resolution because no amount of reason, fact, or authoritative opinion can settle the question. The issue is a matter of taste and cannot be settled by formal *or* informal argument. Because there are no means of convincing anybody that one kind of music is "better" than another, the whole question is unsuitable for argument.

Writers should take note of this fact and avoid choosing subjects like styles of clothing, people's motives, the entertainment value of one movie over another, and so on. Similarly, writers should avoid choosing propositions that draw no opposition because the purpose of argument is to convince and, if there's nobody to convince, there's no necessity to argue. For example, the proposition that swimming is a healthful and enjoyable activity will draw no opposition—not even from someone afraid of water. And although it may be true that you strongly believe that falling in love is wonderful—who will argue it with you? These are what we call self-evident propositions and should be avoided in choosing an issue to argue.

Once the writer has chosen a suitable proposition for a formal argument, he or she would do well to bear in mind the following important elements of the technique of argument:

1. A main proposition should be single in nature; that is, it may be true that "the UN has failed to keep world peace and its headquarters occupy valuable New York real estate," but there is no *necessary* connection between the two ideas. A reader can accept one as true without agreeing on the other, and arguing them in tandem can only weaken the force of both.

2. The structure of the formal argument is an arrangement of subordinate points supporting a main point or, in argumentative terms, a group of carefully arranged *minor propositions* supporting a *main proposition*. If the main proposition is that "national gun control laws should prohibit the private ownership of hand guns," then one minor proposition might be that "private ownership of hand guns leads to accidental death for innocent victims of inept handling." Another might be that "private ownership of hand guns leads to the possibility of a criminal's coming into possession of guns with great ease." Obviously, there will be many such possibilities. But these should be arranged carefully so as to have the greatest impact on a reader. (See Glossary: *emphasis*.)

3. A good argument always *anticipates* counterarguments by the opposition. Those who oppose gun control laws would counter the second minor proposition (stated in item 2) by asserting that "criminals can always gain access to illegal items like guns." A good way to anticipate this counter is to state it and then answer by acknowledging its partial truth, adding, "But do we have to make it *easy* for them to get the guns?" Anticipation of this kind is a very effective technique. It assures a reader that you are no fool, that you are thoughtful and thorough, and that your argument is, therefore, made with authority.

4. An effective argument is one that makes use of logic. But logic is a tricky thing. Check your chain of reasoning to be sure that your logic is not faulty.

GORE VIDAL

Drugs: Case for Legalizing Marijuana

Novelist, playwright, essayist, and critic, Gore Vidal has been a steadily productive writer since the appearance of his first novel, *Williwaw*, when he was just nineteen. He is also the author of, among other works, *Myra Breckenridge* and *Burr*; his latest novel is *1876*. "Drugs: Case for Legalizing Marijuana" was published in *The New York Times* on September 26, 1970, and is a firm but pessimistic argument for the legalization of the use of marijuana— and of other drugs. The authority of Vidal's minor propositions here makes for an interesting analysis.

1   It is possible to stop most drug addiction in the United States within a very short time. Simply make all drugs available and sell them at cost. Label each drug with a precise description of what effect—good or bad— the drug will have on whoever takes it. This will require heroic honesty. Don't say that marijuana is addictive or dangerous when it is neither, as millions of people know—unlike "speed," which kills most unpleasantly, or heroin, which is addictive and difficult to kick.

2   For the record, I have tried—once—almost every drug and liked none, disproving the popular Fu Manchu[1] theory that a single whiff of opium will enslave the mind. Nevertheless many drugs are bad for certain people to take and they should be told about them in a sensible way.

3   Along with exhortation and warning, it might be good for our citizens to recall (or learn for the first time) that the United States was the creation of men who believed that each man has the right to do what he wants with his own life as long as he does not interfere with his neighbor's pursuit of happiness (that his neighbor's idea of happiness is persecuting others does confuse matters a bit).

4   This is a startling notion to the current generation of Americans who reflect on our system of public education which has made the Bill of Rights, literally, unacceptable to a majority of high school graduates (see the annual Purdue[2] reports) who now form the silent majority—a

[1] *Fu Manchu theory.* Fu Manchu was the villain in a series of novels by Sax Rohmer (1883–1959). He was an absolute villain—no redeeming features—and one contact with him was all it took.

[2] The Purdue report that year revealed the results of a survey in which American high school graduates were asked if they favored the freedoms guaranteed by the Bill of Rights. The wording of the questions was altered so that the respondents would not recognize that they were being asked about a famous document. Nevertheless, a large majority were opposed to the first ten amendments to the Constitution.

phrase which that underestimated wit Richard Nixon took from Homer who used it to describe the dead.

Now one can hear the warning rumble begin: if everyone is allowed to take drugs everyone will and the GNP[3] will decrease, the Commies will stop us from making everyone free, and we shall end up a race of zombies, passively murmuring "groovie" to one another. Alarming thought. Yet it seems most unlikely that any reasonably sane person will become a drug addict if he knows in advance what addiction is going to be like.

Is everyone reasonably sane? No. Some people will always become drug addicts just as some people will always become alcoholics, and it is just too bad. Every man, however, has the power (and should have the right) to kill himself if he chooses. But since most men don't, they won't be mainliners either. Nevertheless, forbidding people things they like or think they might enjoy only makes them want those things all the more. This psychological insight is, for some mysterious reason, perennially denied our governors.

It is a lucky thing for the American moralist that our country has always existed in a kind of time-vacuum: we have no public memory of anything that happened before last Tuesday. No one in Washington today recalls what happened during the years alcohol was forbidden to the people by a Congress that thought it had a divine mission to stamp out Demon Rum and so launched the greatest crime wave in our country's history, caused thousands of deaths from bad alcohol, and created a general (and persisting) contempt for the laws of the United States.

The same thing is happening today. But the government has learned nothing from past attempts at prohibition, not to mention repression.

Last year when the supply of Mexican marijuana was slightly curtailed by the Feds, the pushers got the kids hooked on heroin and deaths increased dramatically, particularly in New York. Whose fault? Evil men like the Mafiosi? Permissive Dr. Spock?[4] Wild-eyed Dr. Leary?[5] No.

The Government of the United States was responsible for those deaths. The bureaucratic machine has a vested interest in playing cops and robbers. Both the Bureau of Narcotics and the Mafia want strong laws against the sale and use of drugs because if drugs were sold at cost there would be no money in it for anyone.

If there was no money in it for the Mafia, there would be no friendly playground pushers, and addicts would not commit crimes to pay for

---

[3] *GNP.* This is the gross national product, a standard measure of economic prosperity.

[4] *Benjamin Spock,* M.D., author of perhaps the most authoritative child care volumes ever printed in America. He advocated, in at least one of them, a permissive attitude toward child-rearing.

[5] *Timothy Leary,* Ph.D., professor of psychology at Harvard who advocated the use of LSD to achieve new levels of consciousness; Dr. Leary was, in the sixties, the guru of a whole generation of drug users.

the next fix. Finally, if there was no money in it, the Bureau of Narcotics would wither away, something they're not about to do without a struggle.

12   Will anything sensible be done? Of course not. The American people are as devoted to the idea of sin and its punishment as they are to making money—and fighting drugs is nearly as big a business as pushing them. Since the combination of sin and money is irresistible (particularly to the professional politician), the situation will only grow worse.

Questions for the Critical Reader

1. Do you agree with the assertion made in the first sentence? Justify your answer.
2. What underlying assumption is behind the argument in the first paragraph?
3. What is Vidal's purpose, in the second paragraph, in telling us of his personal experiences with drugs?
4. How does the last sentence in the same paragraph affect the point he makes in the first sentence?
5. Consider the phrase "as millions of people know" in paragraph 1: how effective is this statement as a piece of evidence?
6. Is the proposition in paragraph 3 a *legal* argument?
7. Does paragraph 5 effectively anticipate an opposing viewpoint? Justify your answer. (See Glossary: *point of view*.)
8. On what evidence do you suppose Vidal bases the point he makes in paragraph 7, that is, that Congress "launched the greatest crime wave in the nation's history"? How might you effectively validate or invalidate this proposition?
9. How do you evaluate the strength of the proposition in paragraph 9? Justify your answer.
10. Can you give any examples of our devotion to the idea of "sin and punishment" (last paragraph)?
11. Does the last paragraph tend to weaken or strengthen Vidal's whole argument? Justify your answer.

Rhetorical Technique

1. Where does Vidal state his main proposition?
2. a) Identify the minor propositions in the argument.
   b) Which of them is effective and which not? Justify your answers.
   c) Note Vidal's ordering of these propositions: Is it the most forceful and convincing arrangement possible?

3. Describe the technique common to paragraphs 6, 9, and 12. How effective is this technique?
4. In paragraphs 3, 4, 6, 7, and 12, Vidal makes parenthetical statements. How effective is this technique? Justify your answer.
5. Isolate two examples of parallel structure (see Glossary: *parallel structure*), and comment on their effectiveness.
6. Isolate two methods Vidal uses for emphasis. (See Glossary: *emphasis*.)
7. Compare the opening and concluding paragraphs: how do they relate to one another?

Diction and Vocabulary

1. Give two examples of figurative language employed here and comment on their effectiveness. (See Glossary: *figures of speech*.)
2. Consult the dictionary to be sure you understand the meanings of words like *exhortation* (par. 3) and *Mafiosi* (9).
3. Vidal is considered to be an excellent stylist:
   a) How would you describe the tone and style employed here?
   b) How do words like *Feds* (9), *Commies* (5), *zombies* (5), *mainliners* (6), and *kids* (9) contribute to the tone?
   c) Answer the same question with respect to *Demon Rum* (7) and *Fu Manchu* (2).

from <u>THE NEW YORKER</u>

Free the Banks

> The author of this piece is a staff writer for the magazine. Its policy
> is for him or her to remain anonymous. "Free the Banks" (whose
> title was supplied by the editor) was first printed in the Notes and
> Comment section of "The Talk of the Town," a regular feature of
> *The New Yorker* (November 24, 1975). Beneath its nearly absurd
> tone is a very serious argument.

1   A letter from a friend:

2   There is something President Ford can do that will enable him to go
down in history as the greatest American President since Abraham
Lincoln. He can free the banks. As everyone knows, banks have historically been second-class citizens in America. They are everywhere
hated, despised, reviled. The ordinary citizen would no more say a kind
word for a bank than he would bash his begonia plant over the head with
a chair. As early as 1908, Woodrow Wilson noted, "The banks in this
country are remote from the people and the people regard them as not
belonging to them but to some power hostile to them." See? Hostility.
Not-belongingness. It is time for a change.

3   Freeing the banks—"nationalizing" them, as it were—will have several
important consequences. The interest rates will go down. I suggest four
per cent, coming and going. That is, I pay a bank four per cent when I
borrow from it, and it pays me four per cent when it borrows from me.
That seems fair. The huge excess of money now generated by the banks
and placed by them in private hands (technically called "profit") will disappear. The important point here is that for the first time a bank will be
on a footing of equality with any other citizen. That the equality involves
an adjustment downward rather than upward on the financial scale is
logically no bar to the taking of this crucial step. Equality is equality.

4   Now, I am not against "profit" (sometimes called "profits," meaning,
I suppose, more than one). My old mother down in Georgia told me two
things; the first is unprintable and had to do with relations between the
sexes, and the second was "Screw every dollar out of the bastards that
you can." I believe in profit. Keeps the wheels whirling and all that.
This is called "incentive." A good thing. My one quibble is that from
what I hear around town the banks incentivize very few of their fellow-
citizens. *Very* few relative to the size of the population. Only a handful,
in fact. A bad thing. It is divisive, counterproductive, and not at all
sacred. Doesn't have to be that way.

5   A bank is fundamentally a device for moving money around. Sort of

a switchboard situation. Now, if you talk to a banker about this he'll say, No, no, you don't understand. And he's right, I don't understand. I don't understand nine hundred of the things banks do to earn their profits. If I mention this to the banker, he'll mumble something about "risk." And he's got a point. It is well known that banks are daredevil risk-takers, as brave as the famous diving horses of Atlantic City.[1] It is true that they like some kinds of risk better than other kinds of risk. The banks have a peculiar tendency to jump for what is called a "good risk." This may seem like a contradiction in terms to a layman, but to a bank it does not. Poor people, slum clearance, low-cost housing, and the City of New York are examples of "bad risks." But consider what would happen if the banks were freed (nationalized). *They could take any kind of risk they wanted to take!* "Bad" as well as "good"! They could be just like the rest of us, and make mistakes. Instant self-respect!

Now, it may appear to some that my proposal has what might be called a "Communist" or "Socialist" tinge. Not right. In point of fact, I met a Communist once and didn't like him at all. He was wearing clothes I didn't like, he was rude, and he ate his peas by picking up each individual pea with two fingers of his right hand. Anyhow, there is nothing Communist or Socialist about this proposal. I think of it as "nationalist." 6

A more serious question is: If the banks are nationalized, can the government handle this additional burden? I mean, can the government do anything efficiently? The recently reported incident wherein a U.S. spy submarine attempted to surface under the hull of a U.S.S.R. naval vessel during Soviet fleet maneuvers does not inspire super-confidence. But in fairness it must be said that the government does *some things* well. The Library of Congress. The Coast Guard. Whatever the difficulties, the moral issue is clear. We can and must rescue these poor banks from the intolerable weight of shame, discrimination, and (let us be plain) prejudice under which they have labored for centuries. We must enable them, and other free Americans, to say "Bank is beautiful." I call upon the President to act, immediately. 7

Questions for the Critical Reader

1. Comment on the irony in the first paragraph, where the author suggests by analogy that banks are slaves. (See Glossary: *irony; analogy.*)
2. Comment on the logic of paragraph 4.
3. In paragraph 5 a bank is defined as a "device for moving money around. Sort of a switchboard situation." Do you agree with this definition? Justify your answer.

[1] *the famous diving horses of Atlantic City.* A spectacular act featured at the Steel Pier, an amusement park in Atlantic City, New Jersey. The horses dove off a huge tower into a water tank.

4. In this same paragraph, the author claims not to know how banks earn their profits.
   a) Do you?
   b) How?
   c) Is the author's naïveté real?
   d) For what purpose is it designed?
5. Answer for yourself the question posed at the beginning of paragraph 7.
   a) Do you agree with the author's answer?
   b) Suggest some consequences if the government does take over the banks.
6. What is your attitude toward the profit motive?

Rhetorical Technique

1. What type is the main proposition of this argument?
2. What are the minor propositions?
3. For what reason does the author say he is putting forward the proposition?
4. What kinds of comic effects are being used here? What is the effect of the comic style? (See Glossary: *humor*.)
5. What is the author's real (serious) complaint about the banks? Is it justified? Why? Why not?
6. Consider the phrase with which this piece begins: Is this really a letter from the author's friend? How can you be sure? Can you think of some reason why the "friend" might have been invented?
7. Comment on the way the author anticipates his critics in paragraph 6.
8. How much do you know about the efficiency of the Library of Congress and the Coast Guard?
9. Cite two methods by which emphasis is achieved here. (See Glossary: *emphasis*.)
10. How much of the style of this piece depends upon its use of unusual syntax (in pars. 4 and 5, for example)? (See Glossary: *syntax*.)

Diction and Vocabulary

1. How much of the style of this essay depends on its diction? (See Glossary: *diction*.)
2. How much is matter of syntax? Select three examples of irregular syntax and comment on their purpose and effectiveness. (See Glossary: *syntax*.)

ROGER M. WILLIAMS

Away with Big-Time Athletics

Currently a contributing editor of *Saturday Review/World* magazine, Mr. Williams has been a writer for *Sports Illustrated* and a
bureau chief for *Time* magazine. "Away With Big-Time Athletics"
was published on March 6, 1976, in *Saturday Review/World*. The
argument Williams makes relies heavily and appropriately on a set
of solid educational values.

At their mid-January annual meeting, members of the National Col- 1
legiate Athletic Association were locked in anguished discussion over
twin threats to big-time college athletic programs: rapidly rising costs
and federal regulations forcing the allocation of some funds to women's
competition. The members ignored, as they always have, the basic issue
concerning intercollegiate athletics. That is the need to overhaul the
entire bloated, hypocritical athletic system and return athletics to a
sensible place in the educational process. ~ *Thesis statement*

A complete overhaul of the athletic programs, not the fiscal repair now 2
being attempted by the NCAA, is what is necessary. For decades now
big-time football, and to a lesser degree basketball, have commanded
absurdly high priorities at our colleges and universities. Football stands
at the center of the big-time system, both symbolically and financially;
the income from football has long supported other, less glamorous sports.

Many American universities are known more for the teams they field 3
than for the education they impart. Each year they pour hundreds of
thousands of dollars apiece into athletic programs whose success is
measured in games won and dollars earned—standards that bear no
relation to the business of education and offer nothing to the vast
majority of students.

The waste of resources is not the only lamentable result of the over- 4
emphasis of intercollegiate athletics. The skewing of values is at least as
damaging. Everyone involved in the big-time system—players, coaches,
alumni and other boosters, school officials, trustees, even legislators—is
persuaded that a good football team is a mark of the real worth of an
educational institution. Some of the most successful coaches elevate that
bizarre notion to a sort of philosophy. Woody Hayes of Ohio State has
said that the most important part of a young man's college education is
the football he plays. Jim Kehoe, athletic director at the University of
Maryland, has said of the games played by Maryland: "You do anything to win. I believe completely, totally, and absolutely in winning."

Reprinted by permission of Roger M. Williams.

5   Anyone doubtful of the broad psychic satisfaction provided by winning
teams need only observe who it is that shouts, "We're number one!" It
is seldom the players and only sometimes other students. The hard core
of team boosters is composed of middle-aged men—mainly alumni but
also legions of lawyers, doctors, and businessmen with no tangible connection to the school.

6   In the South, where football mania rides at a shrill and steady peak,
winning seems to offer a special reward: an opportunity to claim the
parity with other regions that has been so conspicuously lacking in more
important areas of endeavor. In Alabama in the late Sixties, when Coach
Bear Bryant was fielding the first of his remarkable series of national
championship teams, both Bear and team were the objects of outright
public adulation: that is, *white* public adulation. White Alabamians, reacting to the assaults on George Wallace and other bastions of segregation, took a grim, almost vengeful pride in "their" team. During those
years, when I covered the South as a reporter, one could hardly meet a
white Alabamian who didn't talk football or display, on an office or den
wall, a picture of Bryant and the Crimson Tide squad.

7   The disease of bigtime-ism seems to run rampant in provincial places
where there is little else to do or cheer for: Tuscaloosa and Knoxville,
Columbus and Lincoln, Norman and Fayetteville. But everywhere, always, it feeds on a need to win—not just win a fair share of games but
win almost all of them, and surely all of the "big" ones.

8   At the University of Tennessee last fall, coach Bill Battle nearly lost
his job because the Volunteers won a mere 7 of their 12 games. Never
mind that Battle's Tennessee teams had previously amassed a five-year
record of 46 victories, 12 defeats, and 2 ties and had been to a bowl in
each of those years. Although Batlte was eventually rehired, he received
no public support from a university administration which seemed to agree
with the fanatics that, outstanding as his record was, it was not good
enough.

9   Everyone knows something about the excess of recruiting high-school
players and something about the other trappings of the big-time system:
the athletic dormitory and training table, where the "jocks" or "animals"
are segregated in the interests of conformity and control, the "brain
coaches" hired to keep athletes from flunking out of school; the full
scholarships ("grants in aid"), worth several thousand dollars apiece,
that big-time schools can give to 243 athletes each year. (Conference
regulations restrict the size of football traveling squads to about 60,
while the NCAA permits 95 players to be on football scholarships. This
means that some three dozen football players at each big-time school
are getting what's called a full ride without earning it.)

10   What few people realize is that these are only the visible workings of
a system that feeds on higher education and diverts it from its true
purposes. The solution, therefore, is not to deliver slaps on the wrist to

the most zealous recruiters, as the NCAA often does, or to make modest reductions in the permissible number of athletic scholarships, as it did last year. The solution is to banish big-time athletics from American colleges and universities.

Specifically, we should: 11

(1) Eliminate all scholarships awarded on the basis of athletic ability *and* those given to athletes in financial need. Every school should form its teams from a student body drawn there to pursue academic interests.

(2) Eliminate athletic dormitories and training tables, which keep athletes out of the mainstream of college life and further their image as hired guns. Also eliminate special tutoring, which is a preferential treatment of athletes, and "red shirting," the practice of keeping players in school an additional year in the hope that they'll improve enough to make the varsity.

(3) Cut drastically the size and the cost of coaching staffs. Football staffs at Division I schools typically number 12 or 14, so that they are larger than those employed by professional teams. With practice squads numbering 80 or 50, the present staff size creates a "teacher-pupil" ratio that permits far more individualized instruction on the playing field than in the classroom. The salaries paid to assistant coaches should be spent to hire additional faculty members. The salaries of head coaches, who in some states earn more than the governor, should be reduced to a point where no head coach is paid more than a full professor.

(4) Work to eliminate all recruiting of high-school athletes. It has produced horrendous cases of misrepresentation, illegal payments, and trauma for the young man involved.

The worst of the abuses is the athletic scholarship, because it is central 12 to all the others. If members of a college team are not principally athletes, there is no need to lure them to the school by offering special treatment and platoons of coaches. They should be students to whom football or basketball is the season's major extracurricular activity.

What will happen if these changes are made? The games will go on. 13 In fact, they may well be more like real games than the present clashes between hired, supertrained, and sometimes brutalized gladiators. Will the caliber of play suffer? Of course, but every school will be producing the same lower caliber. Given a certain proficiency, which the best of any random selection of student-athletes always possesses, the games will be as competitive and as exciting for spectators as they are today. Is a 70-yard run by a non-scholarship halfback less exciting than the same run by Bear Bryant's best pro prospect? For spectators who crave top athletic performance, it is available from a myriad of professional teams. We need not demand it of students.

Certainly, the counter-argument runs, alumni and other influential 14 supporters would not stand for such changes. There would indeed be ill feeling among—and diminished contributions from—old grads who think of their alma mater primarily as a football team. Let them stew in their own pot of distorted values. Those legislators whose goodwill toward a state university depends on winning seasons and free tickets can stew with them. A serious institution is well rid of such "supporters." They may discover the pleasures of a game played enthusiastically by moderately skilled students who are not in effect paid performers.

15   Will athletic-program revenues drop? They undoubtedly will, at least for a while; not many people will pay seven dollars to see games of admittedly lower quality, nor will the TV networks pay fancy fees for the right to televise them. The fans and the networks will eventually return, because these will be the only college games available. And think of the financial savings, as the costs of the typical big-time athletic program drop by hundreds of thousands of dollars a year. If a revenue gap persists, let it be made up out of general funds. The glee club, the intramural athletic program, and innumerable other student activities do not pay for themselves. Why should intercollegiate athletics have to do so?

16   Supporters of big-time programs often say piously that, thanks to those programs, many young men get a college education who otherwise would have no chance for one. That is true. But there are even more young men, of academic rather than athletic promise, who deserve whatever scholarship money is available. If somebody has to pay an athlete's way to college, let it be the professional teams that need the training that college competition provides.

17   The president of a good Southern university once told me privately that he would like to hire outright a football team to represent his school and let the educational process proceed. George Hanford of the College Entrance Examination Board, who has made a study of intercollegiate athletics, would keep the present system but legitimize the preparation of players for professional sports. Hanford would have a college teach athletes such skills as selecting a business agent and would permit student-athletes to play now and return later to do the academic work required for a degree.

18   While Hanford's suggested changes would remove the mask of hypocrisy from big-time college athletic programs, they would not solve the fundamental problem: the intrusions the programs make on the legitimate functions and goals of an educational institution. For institutions with a conscience, this problem has been persistently vexing. Vanderbilt University football coach Art Guepe summed it up years ago, when he characterized Vanderbilt's dilemma as "trying to be Harvard five days a week and Alabama on Saturday."

19   Because of pressures from alumni and others who exalt the role of football, Vanderbilt is still attempting to resolve this dilemma; and it is still failing. Now it is time for all the Vanderbilts and all the Alabamas to try to be Harvard whenever they can and Small-Time State on Saturday.

Questions for the Critical Reader

1. Is Williams accurate when he says, in paragraph 5, that "it is seldom the players and only sometimes other students" who shout, "We're number one?" Justify your answer.
2. Is Williams being fair to the places he names for the reasons he names them in paragraph 7? Why? Why not?
3. Evaluate the argument given in the first sentence of par. 10: is it effective? Why? Why not? Are there *invisible* trappings that a reader would know about?
4. What is your attitude toward the athletic program at your college or university? How does it compare with Williams's?
5. Part of Williams's argument is based on certain assumptions he holds about education:
   a) What are these?
   b) Evaluate them. Which do you agree with? With which do you disagree?
   c) What *are* the "true purposes" (par. 10) of higher education?
6. Evaluate the racial argument in paragraph 6.

Rhetorical Technique

1. What is the main proposition of this piece?
2. How is it stated?
3. What reasons does Williams give for making this proposition?
4. Why does Williams set off a certain portion of his text from the main body under numbered headings (par. 11)?
5. What are the minor propositions? Comment on their effectiveness and on the effectiveness of the order in which they are arranged.
6. How much of this essay is analysis? Comment on its effectiveness. Which other methods of exposition are used here? (See introduction to the student.)
7. Beginning with paragraph 13, the author speculates on the consequences if his main proposition were to be adopted. Evaluate these speculations: are they effective arguments?
8. How does Williams anticipate a "counter-argument" in paragraph 14? In your opinion, is his anticipation effective?
9. Evaluate his anticipations of other arguments in paragraphs 15 and 16. Do his responses seem persuasive?
10. Consider and evaluate the solutions offered in paragraph 17.

Diction and Vocabulary

1. "Stew in their own pot": can you improve the accuracy of this idiomatic expression? Once you have, would you consider it too much of a cliché to use effectively? (See Glossary: *cliché*.)

2. Identify at least two examples of metaphor and comment on their effectiveness. (See Glossary: *figures of speech*.)

3. Consider the connotative value of the following words and phrases and then evaluate Williams's purpose in using them and their effectiveness: *big-time* (title); *bloated, hypocritical* (1); *absurdly* (2); *lamentable* (4); *bizarre* (4); *hard core* and *middle-aged* (5); *vengeful* (6); *"big"* (7); *fanatics* (8). (See Glossary: *connotation and denotation*.)

4. Consult the dictionary to be sure you know the meanings of the following words and phrases: *allocation* (par. 1); *fiscal* (2); *lamentable* and *skewing* (4); *legions* (5); *parity, adulation, bastions* (6); *rampant, provincial* (7); *zealous* (10); *trauma* (11); *myriad* (13); *vexing* (18).

MORTON CRONIN

The Tyranny of Democratic Manners

Morton [J.] Cronin was born in Ann Arbor, Michigan, in 1917 and received the Ph.D. in American Studies from the University of Minnesota in 1953. He is currently professor of English at California State University, Los Angeles, where he has taught since 1955. Professor Cronin's previously published work, on Hawthorne and on Currier and Ives, reflects his interest in American culture. This essay, first published in *The New Republic* in 1958, is both thoughtful and provocative, an argument that uses for evidence examples of our manners and gestures that could only have been gathered by a careful observer of the American scene.

I maintain that democratic manners—typified by the practice of calling the boss by his first name—have reached the point in our country where they conduce not to the preservation of personal dignity but to the abject submission of one man to another. These manners, gradually developed in colonial and post-revolutionary days, worked well in a society largely of self-sufficient farmers. But circumstances have changed, with the usual ironical result.

What happens on the job at the present time? An employee greets the boss by his first name, sits down in his presence, wears the same kind of clothes the boss wears, avoids the use of *sir*, and ostensibly comports himself in general as if he and the boss were as equal as two farmers. But of course he and the boss are not equal, and this inequality must be signalized. It must be signalized, first, because the employee is anxious to please the boss, who can advance or impede his fortunes; and, secondly, because the boss is anxious that his authority receive recognition, without which he cannot function with any confidence.

In the absence of overt and conventional methods of expressing deference, how then does the American employee acknowledge the boss's superior status? He does so by perfecting a subtle repertoire of body movements and vocal expressions. This repertoire includes the boyish grin, the deprecatory cough, the unfinished sentence, the appreciative giggle, the drooping shoulders, the head-scratch and the bottom-waggle. But there are employees, the truly gifted ones—as actors, they would adorn the Stanislavski school[1]—who can dispense with these definable

Originally published in *The New Republic*, January 20, 1958. Reprinted by permission of *The New Republic*.

[1] *the Stanislavski school.* A school of acting and a method invented by the Russian man of the theater Konstantin Stanislavski. The major tenet of the method is that the actor *lives* the part and thus establishes his sincerity to the audience.

maneuvers and simply *live* the part, their whole being radiating a kind of sweet eloquence of submission.

4   Now this body language, in both its definable and indefinable forms, is almost impossible to fake successfully, at least in any long-continued relationship. If it is not accompanied quite genuinely by the emotions appropriate to it, it will be contradicted and rendered sinister by involuntary movements and expressions which accord with the individual's true feelings. It is easy to execute a military salute, regardless of one's private thoughts, but the deprecatory cough—to say nothing of the Stanislavski method—requires great sincerity, else they appear villainous.

5   American manners, in short, decree egalitarian behavior in a hierarchical society. The result it that a subordinate, compelled to behave formally and superficially in a democratic way, is forced in making his adjustments to the facts of life to behave informally and profoundly in a hierarchical way. It should be just the opposite—the system of etiquette ought to furnish him with formal gestures of respect for his superiors and let his informal self work out its own salvation. It should be easier to render the boss what is the boss's without throwing in one's soul too.

6   Out of a doctrinaire devotion to palsy-walsy manners has sprung that misshapen, anomalous growth, the despotism of the nice guy. It is a truism that success on the job depends less on competence in performing one's duties than it does on ability to Get Along With People. But what is left out of this statement—it is no sporting to mention it—is that the word *People* refers to just one person—the boss. And the boss, barred from receiving any obvious obeisance, is commonly in a chronic state of insecurity—what he craves most of all is the assurance that he is really and truly the boss. The nice guy, with his fine talent for the right body language, provides this assurance better than the man who is merely efficient, is rewarded accordingly, and thus sets the pace for his clumsy fellows.

7   But the despotism of the nice guy reaches its fully convoluted luxuriance when, as happens, he himself is made the boss. He has not been soft-spoken, unassertive, accommodating and eager to please out of sheer masochism. However various the motives which explain his personality, ambition is one of them. Good Old Charlie likes the idea of being a boss. And if his underlings could give him a snappy salaam every day, all might be well. But Charlie would recoil from anything so Oriental in its disrespect for human dignity. All that he expects is that his subordinates will make the same sensitive, informal adjustments to his person which he used to make for the boss, a process which practically requires that they exchange their personalities for his. Only a few of them are capable of such virtuosity—Charlie's word for it is *loyalty*—but most of them do well enough to demonstrate that it is really the nice guy in authority, more than the rambunctious one, who has made America the natural habitat of the yes-man. Of course the situation is complicated by the fact that Charlie soon becomes pitifully dependent on his loyal sup-

porters, one of whom usually emerges as a split-personality and, like a skillful wife, sweetly dominates Charlie in all things.

Everybody complains that life is too competitive, but our national imagination is so limited that the principal remedies proposed for this or any other social disease are economic remedies—better jobs, better houses, and more social security. However justified on other grounds, these remedies, beyond a certain point, just hot up this particular fire, for life becomes not less competitive but decidedly more so as one moves up the ladder. Naturally. There is more to compete for. But still the fever could be brought down a few points by a modification of manners. Once men acquire everything they need—a condition soon reached in this country—they struggle primarily for recognition. But with manners as frustratingly egalitarian as they are, who knows when he has it made? Under present circumstances the ambitious can discern no resting place short of a crushing superiority of popular fame or material wealth. Hence, the devotion of many originally fine minds to Hollywood, Broadway and the medical profession. **8**

Consider, for instance, the folly of our disparagement of honorific titles. If a mayor were regularly addressed as *Your Honor*, and could count on this distinction after leaving office, he would be heartened in his efforts to remain honest. As it is, he must play it democratic, pooh-pooh his title, and prepare against the day when defeated for re-election, he must face the indifference of the public at large. Mayors are commonly corrupt, judges rarely. But judges are unfailingly objects of formal homage in office, and keep their titles for life. **9**

The sobriquets which used to attach to politicians—*Old Hickory, Tennessee Johnson, The Little Giant, The Plumed Knight*[2]—conferred distinction. They were titles of a sort and reflected a popular disposition to honor character, individuality and superior force in public men. But now the popular taste, encouraged by gee-whiz politicians who tutoyer one another in public is for first names and demure diminutives—*Ike, Dick, Stu, Bob, Estes* and *Foster*.[3] What makes these familiarities characteristic of our time is precisely that they ignore what is distinctive in **10**

[2] *Old Hickory, Tennessee Johnson, The Little Giant, The Plumed Knight.* These are names given, respectively, to Andrew Jackson (1767–1845), president of the United States, 1829–1837; Andrew Johnson (1808–1875), also a former president of the United States (1865–1869); Stephen A. Douglas (1813–1861), senator from Illinois who debated Lincoln (1858) and lost to him the presidential election of 1861; and James G. Blaine (1830–1893), unsuccessful Republican candidate for president in 1876. Blaine, too, was a U.S. Senator (from Maine, 1876–1881) and was later secretary of state.

[3] *Ike, Dick, Stu, Bob, Estes and Foster.* These are names given, respectively, to the following: Dwight Eisenhower (1890–1969), president of the United States, 1952–1960); Richard Nixon (b. 1913), vice-president under Eisenhower and later president himself; Stuart Symington, senator from Missouri (b. 1901; U.S. Senator); the late senator from Ohio, Robert A. Taft (1889–1953; U.S. Senator, 1939–1953); the late senator from Tennessee, Estes Kefauver (1903–1963; U.S. Senator, 1949–1963); and John Foster Dulles (1888–1959), secretary of state in the Eisenhower administration. All these figures were prominent at the time this essay was published.

either the personalities or the duties of the men they designate and thus suggest that government is best which is managed by Good Joes recently graduated from a basketball team. If Woodrow Wilson[4] were in politics today, he would probably have to submit to *Woody*—if not *Willie*—and wipe that purposeful and responsible look off his face.

11   But the avoidance of titles of respect is equally the fashion among highbrows. Professors in famous universities, for instance, make fun of their fellows in teachers' colleges because the latter often call one another *professor* or *doctor*, instead of plain *mister*, and are notorious for responding benignly when their students use these terms. But on this point it is the prominent professors whose perception is defective, for an examination of their total behavior reveals that they are much less democratic than those they smile at for putting on airs. Occupying positions in institutions of outstanding prestige—positions for which they have scrambled ferociously—they can afford to underemphasize their status, like wealthy men who insist that their limousines be inconspicuously black. The fact is that they maintain great distance between town and gown[5] and also between their students and themselves.

12   Many of them deplore their remoteness, but without an improvement of manners there is little they can do about it. Since they discourage formal acknowledgments of their status, any meeting between them and townfolk, or even between them and their own students, imposes on both sides such a strain on their respective capacities for the appropriate body language that it is almost unbearable. The man at Lower South Central Normal suffers his students to call him professor—doctor —sir—but he can often be observed chatting loftily and genially among them, snapping his suspenders the while, undisturbed by their politely impudent questions.

13   But the deprecation of titles and of formal manners in general characterizes all sorts of highbrows, not just those in universities. Yet no group in America complains so clamorously that it is not sufficiently respected and appreciated. And those among them who complain most bitterly are the ones who embrace the mucker pose passionately, not only in their speech and manners but even in their dress. This furious contradiction necessitates a furious resolution. Men who will not permit their attainments to be recognized conventionally and symbolically will seek such recognition radically and violently.

14   But democratic manners have not only promoted unnatural relations among men in their economic and professional careers. They have also corrupted relations between men and women in their romantic and domestic lives. Here, however, the democratization of manners has been

---

[4] *Woodrow Wilson* (1856–1924) was president of the United States, 1912–1920.
[5] *town and gown.* A term referring to those associated with a college (gown = academic gown) and those who live in the town in which the college is located.

one-sided. Many suitable formalities still govern the man's behavior—he follows a woman through a door, sashays around to the gutter-side of the street, etc., etc., in all of which he pays decorous tribute to her as a woman. But our culture has relieved her almost entirely of any reciprocal gestures of conventional tribute to him as a man. She does not curtsy, nor use respectful forms of address, nor stand at his shoulder when he has his picture taken. Her grandmother practiced a sweet, conventional smile. She grins, laughs uproariously, and talks in a loud voice. For her the emphasis is now completely on body language—but, unlike that used by men with their bosses, hers is *challenging* rather than deferential.

Since he does not receive from women any standard courtesies, cour- 15 tesies which, besides telling him that just being a man is a thing of some consequence, would remind him of his responsibilities, the American male gravitates in his dealings with women toward one of two roles— that of a little boy or that of a predator. Frequently he ricochets between the two. In the first role he simply abandons the effort to command respect as a male and, oddly enough, often becomes an abstract enthusiast for women, like a dull student whose every humiliation in class somehow increases his school spirit. In the role of predator he compels specific respect for himself as a man in the one decisive way that is still open. And, fortunately or unfortunately, such consolation has grown steadily more available. Women as well as men are symbolic creatures, and the radical elimination of ceremony reduces the human element in them and increases the animal part. Frustrated in her naturally human desire to express her feelings formally and stylistically, the American woman must express them directly and elementally.

But the inhuman effects of democratic manners afflict another funda- 16 mental relationship, that between parents and children. They spawn the ultimate in absurdity in those instances where parents, assuming the character of domestic politicians, encourage their youngsters to abjure the use of *mother* and *father* in favor of their parents' first names. The trouble with *mother* and *father* of course is that they suggest authority (as well as love), and thus strike an undemocratic note in the family. Often the parents' real motives, like those of tail-wagging politicians, are more complicated, for people who shun authoritative titles commonly shrink from responsibility too. But they could not persevere in this self-deception if our dedication to democratic manners did not furnish them with an exalted rationale.

Fortunately, this first-name business for parents is as yet limited. But 17 manners generally are primitive enough in American homes, as anyone knows who accepts invitations from his friends to dine *en famille*.[6] It is undemocratic to set up a children's table. It is also undemocratic to encourage children to listen to adult conversation. Parents and guests, con-

---

[6] *en famille*. French for "with the family."

sequently, listen to children's conversation. During intervals—when little mouths happen simultaneously to be stuffed up with food, for instance —the parents inevitably discuss the subject of children. Children, they tell you, are *people*. The children express themselves. The parents preen themselves. The only person who does not get a piece of this democracy is the guest. This lopsided egalitarianism even favors dogs and cats, with whom a guest must often cope with no assistance whatever from his host. They too, it seems, are *people*.

18 I have nearly finished. But I know that some fool—most likely, one with a Ph.D.—will read this article and forever after assert as a well-known fact that I yearn for a restoration of Tsardom,[7] for a reinvigoration of the Hindu caste system and for a truly Chinese subjugation of women and children. So let me recapitulate, in the course of which I shall add one or two points that I forgot to mention earlier.

19 A sensible system of manners, sensibly formal, performs various services. Besides acting as a constant reminder of some important facts of life, it affords human beings the distinctly human satisfactions of symbolic expression. Besides making collective living possible, it provides a person, thanks to its formalities, with protective armor against collective pressures. For these formalities allow the individual to acquiesce in the social order while reserving his final judgment of it. They enable him to pledge his loyalty to men in authority without making those fine adjustments whose long-term results are the same as those of brainwashing.

20 Democratic manners in America are eating the heart out of American democracy. With no impressive way of saluting the system and the position which a given official occupies in it, one must prostrate himself before the man. There is a country where such prostration is even more prostrate than in America. There the humblest citizen calls his mighty ruler *comrade*.

21 I suggest a prudent reform in American manners, not a revolution. If the only alternative to egalitarian manners is a nerveless society exhausted by protocol and ceremony, then this discussion is futile. But that is not the only alternative, except in the minds of latter-day Jacobins[8] for whom the stratifications of the *ancien regime*[9] are more real than the proletarianizations of their own time. There are in-between solutions, attuned to reality; however they resist simple and consistent formulation, as the English know, and as America, in her own fashion, can discover. Pedantic democrats presume to speak for wisdom, creative

---

[7] *Tsardom*. A reference to Russia. The tsar was the emperor of Russia before the Revolution of 1917 established the soviet system of government.

[8] *Jacobins*. The name given to radical republicans during the French Revolution; sometimes used abusively.

[9] *ancien regime*. Literally "the old regime," actually the name given to the political and social system before the French Revolution of 1789. Cronin means to reverse things and calls the Jacobins reactionaries in terms of social class.

ability and service, as against mere money in the bank. But without a rectification of manners most men would rather achieve a Cadillac than such virtues, for these virtues, unacknowledged in any regular way, do not show on a man, at least not conspicuously, whereas a Cadillac shows on anyone, conspicuously.

Questions for the Critical Reader

1. In the first part of the discussion, Cronin makes certain assumptions about the "boss," for example, that "the boss is anxious that his authority receive recognition, without which he cannot function with any confidence" (par. 2).
   a) What is your opinion of this assumption? Is it true? False? Why?
   b) Isolate any other assumptions about the motives of the boss and the worker and evaluate the truth or falsity of these.
2. Do you agree with Cronin's identification of *People* in the phrase "ability to Get Along With People" (par. 2) as the boss? Explain.
3. Do you know anybody who qualifies as what Cronin calls "the nice guy"?
4. Is Cronin's picture of Good Old Charlie an accurate one? Explain.
5. Consider the sentence in paragraph 8 that begins: "Once men acquire everything they need." Do you agree with this statement? Why? Why not?
6. Do you agree that the nicknames given to politicians "confer distinction" as the author says in paragraph 10? Explain.
7. In paragraphs 14 and 15, Cronin speaks of the status of women in a way that is remarkably close to that which has been articulated by the women's liberation movement today (the article, you may remember, was published in 1958). But how does his analysis of that status seem to you in the light of what we think now?
8. The whole question of democratic manners seems to Cronin a very *serious* matter. Cite the passages that seem to you to support this idea of his seriousness. Then evaluate it; that is, give *your* opinion: *is* it a serious matter? Explain why you think so or think not.
9. When Cronin calls them "democratic" manners, he gives a political cast to his argument. Should he have avoided this? Why? Why not?
10. Of all the manners detailed by Cronin here, which of them seem familiar to you from personal experience? That is, do you either find yourself behaving in ways he describes or do you observe the behavior he describes in others?
11. How would you compare the gestures described here as *manners* and the manifestations of "Dramatic Realization" that Erving Goffman describes in Chapter 2?

Rhetorical Technique

1. What is Cronin's main proposition?
2. List his minor propositions, and consider the order in which he deals with them. Are the minor propositions effective? Can you think of others he might have used that would have been more effective? What about the order of the discussion? Could this have been improved? How?
3. Of what does his "evidence" consist? How persuasive is this material? Can you think of better evidence? What is it?
4. How much of this argument consists of causal analysis (see Chapter 7)? How much of what he writes seems to you something other than argument?
5. How are paragraphs 2 and 3 similar in form? How effective is this form?
6. What standard types of introduction and conclusion are used here (See Glossary: *introductions; conclusions.*)? Are they effective? Explain.
7. Cite at least two methods by which Cronin achieves emphasis. (See Glossary: *emphasis.*)
8. Cite two examples of parallel structure, and evaluate their effectiveness. (See Glossary: *parallel structure.*)
9. Comment on the effectiveness of at least two methods of transitions between paragraphs. (See Glossary *transition.*)
10. What is Cronin's point of view? (See Glossary: *point of view.*) How does this affect his tone and style? (See Glossary: *style and tone.*)

Diction and Vocabulary

1. How are the tone and style (see Glossary: *style and tone*) affected by such language as *giggle* (par. 3); *bottom-waggle* (3); *palsy-walsy* (6); *nice guy* (6); *sashays* (7); *hot up* (8); *pooh-pooh* (9)? What would you call each of these examples?
2. Cite at least one example each of metaphor and simile, and evaluate their effectiveness. (See Glossary: *figures of speech.*)
3. What is the effect of the capitalization employed in paragraphs 6 and 7?
4. Cronin seems sharply aware of connotative values. (See Glossary: *connotation and denotation.*) Consider the following words and phrases: *abject submission* (par. 1); *subordinate* (5); *obeisance* (6); *prostrate* (20). Substitute a more denotative word for each, and then analyze what has been lost or gained thereby.
5. Consult the dictionary to be sure you understand the meanings of the following words and phrases: *abject submission* (par. 1); *con-*

duce (1); *ostensibly, comports, signalized, impede* (2); *deference, subtle repertoire, deprecatory, maneuvers, eloquence* (3); *egalitarian, hierarchical, etiquette* (5); *doctrinaire, anomalous, obeisance, chronic* (6); *convoluted, luxuriance, salaam, masochism, underlings, habitat* (7); *discern* (8); *disparagment, honorific* (9); *sobriquets, conferred, tutoyer, demure diminutives* (10); *notorious, benignly, defective, prestige, ferociously, underemphasize* (11); *deprecation, clamorously, mucker* (13); *sashays, gutter-side, decorous, curtsy, reciprocal, deferential* (14); *predator, ricochets, abstract enthusiast, humiliation, consolation, elementally* (15); *spawn, abjure, persevere, exalted rationale* (16); *reinvigoration, recapitulate* (18); *prostrate* (20); *protocol, stratifications, proletarianizations, pedantic, rectification, conspicuously* (21).

6. Consider the length of the word list just given: (a) Why are so many long and difficult words employed here? (b) Does it help or hinder your understanding of this piece? (c) What effect do these have on the tone of this piece? (See Glossary: *style and tone.*)

ROBERT M. HUTCHINS

The Limits of Dissent

Robert M. Hutchins (b. 1899), an important and innovative American educator, first became known for the revolutionary programs
he instituted at the University of Chicago during his presidency
there from 1929 to 1945. He has been a teacher and an administrator and a ceaseless promulgator of ideas. In 1974, he retired
as chairman of the Center for the Study of Democratic Institutions
in Santa Barbara, California. "The Limits of Dissent" was first published in November 1968 by *The Center Magazine*, a publication
of that organization. The essay was written at a time in American
life when the issue considered in it burned brighter than it usually
does.

1   Much of the talk about law and order goes on in a world of genteel
fantasy. That world is one in which all the channels of communication
are open to everybody. It is one in which all laws are ordinances of reason
directed to the common good, in which the law is easily discovered and
understood and justly and humanely enforced. It is one in which representative government represents all the people and in which the legislative process is truly deliberative. It is one in which all governmental
officers at every level are alert and attentive, eager to seek out injustice
and to rectify it. It is one in which the rights set forth in the First Amendment can be readily and effectively exercised by every citizen. It is one
in which political parties offer a significant choice of persons and programs and in which the voter can feel, when he is casting his ballot, that
he is having some slight effect on the course of history.

2   In such a world dissenters would have little reason for taking to the
streets and none at all for breaking the law.

3   In his recent book, *Concerning Dissent and Civil Disobedience*, Justice
Abe Fortas, a wise and experienced judge and one of the ablest lawyers
of his generation, accounts in the following way for the social revolution
of our time: "How wonderful it is that freedom's instruments—the rights
to speak, to publish, to protest, to assemble peaceably and to participate
in the electoral process—have so demonstrated their power and vitality!
These are our alternatives to violence. . . ."

4   Mr. Justice Fortas wrote these words with the report of the National
Advisory Commission on Civil Disorders before him. That report is a
detailed recital, in 581 pages of fine print, of the failure of freedom's instruments. There were evidently no effective alternatives to violence.

Reprinted with permission from *The Center Magazine*, a publication of the Center
for the Study of Democratic Institutions, Santa Barbara, California.

The Commission finds that the violence it describes resulted from the "frustrations of powerlessness," that is, from the inability of the Negro to move the society at a reasonable rate by means of the First Amendment and the electoral process. The present level of popular concern about minorities and the young would not have been reached if the dissenters had remained, as Mr. Justice Fortas says they must, within the law. The Civil Rights Act of 1968 would not have been passed without the push given Congress by Watts, Detroit, and Newark. The few changes that have been passed without the push given the country would not have taken place if the conduct of protesting students at such places as Berkeley and Columbia had always been perfectly legal.

The limits of dissent cannot be the limits set by law, because nobody 5 knows what the law is, and while the Supreme Court sits nobody will. What was illegal yesterday is lawful today, because the Court changes its composition or its mind. The only way to find out whether an ordinance, regulation, or statute is Constitutional is to violate it and see what happens. *Stare decisis*[1] does not apply in Constitutional cases, and not a term passes in which the Court does not overrule previous holdings, some of them very recent. Where the object of the infraction is to test the constitutionality of the law in question, and no illegal violence is done by the defendants, they should not be held to have passed the limits of dissent.

Since it is in the best interests of the community to promote the ex- 6 ercise of First Amendment rights, and not merely to tolerate it, the presumption must be against any official action, ordinance, regulation, or statute tending to restrict it. The prosecution should bear a heavy burden of proof that the defendants were not provoked by an excessive display of force, that they did not act in self-defence, and that what they did endangered human life.

There are laws and laws. Those designed for the convenience of the 7 public should not prevail against the First Amendment. The best analogy is the strike. What used to be regarded as a major crime is now a normal means of obtaining what the strikers regard as economic justice. The charge of "disruption" is often brought, and always fails. The highest paid laborers in the world, the airplane pilots, may tie up a vast country, simply to get more money, and there will not be a peep about law and order. People will complain, but even if they are stranded in a distant airport they will not say the strikers are subversive. Negroes or young people marching down the street because it is the only method of making a point about freedom and justice, on television or in the newspapers, are likely to be attacked by the police as a threat to the foundations of society.

We ought to try harder to make freedom's instruments work. At the 8 moment the cry for law and order has a hollow and hypocritical sound.

---

[1] *Stare decisis*. A doctrine or policy of following rules or principles laid down in previous judicial decisions unless they go against the ordinary principles of justice.

Questions for the Critical Reader

1. What is Hutchins's conception of "the law?"
2. What is his conception of the First Amendment?
3. In paragraph 4, Hutchins says, in effect, that lawlessness might be necessary in order to achieve social progress:
   a) Is the detailed argument he gives here effective?
   b) Do you agree? Justify your answer.
4. In paragraph 5, the last sentence asserts a principle that Hutchins would apply to an "infraction":
   a) Define *infraction*.
   b) Defiine *illegal*.
   c) Can there be such a thing as "illegal nonviolence" (as opposed to the phrase used here, "illegal violence")?
   d) Do you agree with the principle asserted? Explain.
5. Consider again the last sentence of paragraph 5: Is there any contradiction between this idea and the ones expressed in paragraph 4? Explain.
6. In paragraph 7 ,Hutchins contrasts,second sentence,the "public" and the "First Amendment." Can you clarify this opposition?
7. What is *your* position on "law and order"?
8. How can we "try harder to make freedom's instruments work"?

Rhetorical Technique

1. Locate Hutchins's main proposition.
2. What are his minor propositions?
3. Are these set out in an effective order?
4. Does he anticipate counterarguments?
5. Comment on the kinds of evidence presented.
6. What portion of his argument is analysis? Is it an effective one?
7. What illustrative examples does he use? How effective is each?
8. Which methods of emphasis are employed here? (See Glossary: *emphasis.*)
9. Comment on the effectiveness of the strike analogy (par. 7).

Diction and Vocabulary

1. Comment on the balance between *abstract* and *concrete* language in this essay. (See Glossary: *abstract and concrete.*)
2. Consult the dictionary to be sure you understand the meanings of the following words and phrases: *genteel* (par. 1); *rectify* (1); *hypocritical* (8).

3. How would you characterize the expression in paragraph 7, "there are laws and laws?"

Writing Suggestions for Chapter 1: *Argument*

I.

Bearing in mind that argument is a public and democratic form of discourse, develop your opinions about some community issue into a workable main proposition, either one of fact or one of action, and write an argument on it. Be thorough in doing the work of preparation. Work up your minor propositions. Check your logic and arrangement. Use an outline.

If you are having trouble beginning work, you may either use these propositions as they are or use some variation of one:

1. The grading system in this college does not accurately measure achievement.
2. The seniority system in the U.S. Congress is undemocratic.
3. The Equal Rights Amendment should be passed.
4. The depiction of antisocial behavior should be banned from television.
5. Radical action can change the American system of values.
6. A clean environment is the government's responsibility.
7. American democracy is based on economic distinctions.
8. The size of American cities should be limited to 250,000 residents.
9. Professional sports provide an inappropriate model for youth.
10. Marriage and divorce laws in this state favor males (or females).

II. A. Writing Assignment Based on "Free the Banks"

Write a tongue-in-cheek argument in which you propose some action that is not likely to be adopted but that you would personally wish were adopted anyway. Here are some suggestions for propositions of action and some suggested approaches for each:

Proposition: Your college should institute free tuition and free room and board.

Approach: Everyone knows that your college is fast gaining a reputation as a greedy business proposition. Faculty and administration are getting so involved in profits that they haven't time for education. You want to relieve them of this burden and make it possible for them to get back to teaching and research.

Proposition: TV programs should not be interrupted by commercials.

Approach: Advertisers, especially food advertisers, would have the satisfaction of knowing that they were responsible for many Americans losing weight. Nobody would go to the icebox during commercials. Advertising would thereby regain some of its lost prestige. Moreover, the average amount of TV watching done by Americans would be decreased —making the sociologists and educators happy.

B. Writing Assignment based on "The Tyranny of Democratic Manners"

Write an argument refuting Cronin's. That is, take as your main proposition that democratic manners *do* conduce to the preservation of personal dignity and *not* to the abject submission of one person to another. For evidence, look into the areas that Cronin discusses—love between men and women, political life, college communities, and especially work relations between an employer and the employed. If you are able to do so, look also at the situation in another society—perhaps a European one— where there are no democratic manners in force, and see if that situation can add to the persuasiveness of your case. Thinks of all the personal contacts you have where you are forced to use an honorific form of address—"Doctor," "Professor," "Sir," and so on—and see what evidence can be secured from that bit of experience. Then, when you have marshaled your evidence, make a careful outline and write your first draft.

C. Writing Assignment Based on "The Limits of Dissent"

Write an argument analyzing and arguing for or against one of the following amendments in the light of current conditions and issues: First (free speech); Fourth (illegal search and seizure); Sixth (right to counsel).

2

Using *Illustrative Examples*

One of the simplest forms of exposition is the use of illustrative examples to make clear a general idea or statement. Suppose you were explaining to your parents that you wanted to major in engineering because it was the best major course of study for you. Instead of just repeating that general statement, you would quite naturally give concrete examples of why you thought so: (1) you have a talent for mathematics, and you like to design and construct mechanisms; (2) engineers make a good salary; and (3) the engineering profession is a prestigious one. Your examples convey more and *clearer* information than the generalization alone. And you could go even further—and make things still clearer— by giving even more detailed examples, for example, by citing how productive a career engineering has been for your Uncle Peter, who is a structural engineer.

Good writers always use concrete examples to make clear and vivid whatever generalizations they wish to make. In fact, this method of exposition is perhaps the most basic one. It crops up in every form of discursive writing, and it derives from a natural tendency of the mind. It can always be seen in ordinary conversation.

For example, Joanna meets her friend Rose after work one evening and says, "I had a terrible day at the office today" (*generalization*). Rose naturally waits for an *example* of the kind of thing that happened to Joanna that day to make it so terrible. Joanna supplies it: "I had a fight with my assistant." But a whole day at the office can hardly be called "terrible" on the basis of a single unpleasant incident, and Joanna needs to supply more examples—perhaps even better ones. Rose might gain a clearer idea about this "terrible" day after Joanna adds that her vacation pay wasn't ready at the cashier's window, that the lunch she'd ordered sent in from the coffee shop never arrived, and that she tripped getting off the elevator and has a sprained ankle. In other words, the nature of the generalization will determine both the kind and the number of examples necessary to illustrate it fully, with vividness and clarity.

(Of course, it follows that if Joanna had only offered *one* example, such as, "I had a terrible day at the office [*generalization*]. I had to show up [*example*]," Rose would almost surely have snickered—or worse. And, although Rose *would* in this case have been informed about *something*—Joanna's dislike of going to her job—she would still be in the dark about *why* Joanna felt that way and would need an explanation for *it*.)

You can see that this note is itself a fair example of the method under discussion, but the writer judges that he or she needs to supply more examples.

Good examples have the virtue of making writing more interesting because they permit the reader to visualize something concrete—they *illustrate*. A good example of a fish is a herring; anyone who's ever seen that sleek, silver-scaled beauty, with its characteristically fishy dorsal fin, underhung jaw, and gill covers, would agree. But a good example of a car might *not* be a Cadillac *or* a Volkswagen. The former might not impress a reader who thinks initial cost and low gasoline efficiency take it out of the class of "good." Similiarly, a reader who values roominess and styling in an automobile over the virtues of good gas mileage and easy maintenance might object to the Volkswagen's being used as an example of a "good" car.

This brings us to a useful generalization about examples: the writer using them to illustrate a generalization should make sure that they are indisputable. For this, the writer needs to judge carefully not only the nature of the generalization, but also the audience to whom his or her presentation is being made. Examples may be good for one group of readers, but not another.

Finally, you should notice as you read essays in comparison and contrast or definition—in fact, essays in *all* the methods of exposition covered in this book—that illustrative examples are persistently used. Illustrative examples bring life to all kinds of writing.

JIM BOUTON

A Few World Series Sinkers

Jim Bouton, a popular TV sportscaster, was himself a series par-
ticipant during the early sixties, when he was an effective pitcher
for the New York Yankees. "A Few World Series Sinkers" appeared in *The New York Times* on October 10, 1970, the first day
of series play that year. Here Bouton gives us a clear example of
the use of illustration while managing a deflating, humorous tone.
Note that as the piece proceeds and the detailed examples get more
technical, the essay grades subtly into a kind of technical analysis
of the game of baseball.

The dedicated baseball fan is a man who likes to kid himself. He'll get   1
to a World Series game early, see a ballplayer yawning and take it as a
sign of nervousness. He'll see a nervelessly relaxed body leaning against
the batting cage and consider it merely feigned indifference. He'll watch
an outfielder casually scratching his nose and count it as a tic. He's
wrong. In fact, what looks like boredom on behalf of the people involved
in the World Series is most often just that.

In the years when I was involved in series competition, the only thing   2
that really got to me was the pennant race. A great deal of psychic energy
was expended while the pennant was being won. After that, there was
maybe a $3,000 difference between winning and losing.

Now things are even tougher. Winning a divisional title and the   3
World Series can be worth $20,000. Finishing second in the division or
losing the league playoff is worth virtually zilch. So the stakes are even
higher. Just watch the guys around the batting cage. If they were any
looser, they'd fall down.

Another thing you might keep your eye on is the baseball pants. It   4
tells a lot about a player. There is a new uniform in every locker as the
World Series begins. The trouble with new uniforms is that most often
the pants aren't tight enough. There are players who swear they can't
run if their trousers aren't skin tight. In the minor leagues there have
been instances of players refusing to take the field because a pencil
would fit between the cloth of their trousers and the skin of their thighs.

So what happens in the series is this: a lot of the players wear new   5
blouses and old trousers. Old trousers can be recognized because they've
been laundered many times and show evidence of fading. It's easier to
detect this in the grey road uniforms than the home whites. In any case,
a good pair of glasses and a keen eye can spot the tight pants men.

6   Another thing to watch during one of the little delays that make up such a big part of the game is what the pitcher is up to. I don't mean when he's looking in to get the sign, winding up, throwing the ball. I mean during the time he steps off the mound and seems to be looking out at his outfielders or into the stands at girls. What he's really doing is rubbing up the ball and under the latest rules he has to walk off the mound to do so.

7   This gives him some marvelous opportunities. He can, for one thing, stick a finger between his belt and trousers and come up with a gob of previously concealed vaseline. This while he has his back to the plate umpire. And what good is vaseline? Well, it's slippery like spit. This means you can throw the ball exactly as hard as you would a fastball and have it come off your hand behaving like a curve. This is **very** confusing for the hitter.

8   Sometimes the sharp observer will see the batter shouting out at the pitcher. He will wonder what the batter is saying, and well he might. Because chances are he's not saying anything to the pitcher at all; he's shouting at the umpire, probably because he didn't like the last called strike. The reason for the confusion is that umpires don't like to be showed up, which is their word for having a player arguing with them openly. So long as the batter looks out at the pitcher he can call the umpire almost every name in the book. Your best chance of getting the full flavor of this from the stands is to bring along a lip reader.

9   Finally, there is feet watching. Routine ground balls are not exactly the most thrilling things that ever happen in a baseball game. But a bit of spice can be added if you watch a good first baseman in action. The big thing is to catch him taking his foot off first base before the ball actually arrives in his glove. Gil Hodges, late manager of the Mets, was a master of this deception. It's an important move because the umpires watch the feet, too. But if the first baseman takes his foot off the bag with proper aplomb the umpire can easily delude himself into thinking he heard the sound of the ball in glove at the same time. Thus many runners who are actually safe at first base are called out.

10   There are other little cheats going on (like the umpire who sneaks into the dugout ostensibly to use the WC but actually to grab a smoke). But there are some things that are better left unsaid. Watch for them today.

Questions for the Critical Reader

1. What purpose is served by the information contained in paragraph 2, sentence 1?
2. Comment on the relationship between the last three sentences in paragraph 3.

3. How would you describe Bouton's attitude toward baseball? Toward its fans?
4. Compare your own attitudes with those he ascribes to fans.
5. In the spectacle of baseball, is anything lost by some disregard for rules on the parts of players and umpires? Is something gained? Explain.
6. How do Bouton's attitudes compare with your view of a baseball fan? A football fan?

Rhetorical Technique

1. What is Bouton's central theme? (See Glossary: *unity; subject.*)
2. Which of Bouton's examples are most effective? Which least?
3. Do Bouton's examples always give clear information about baseball? Justify your answer.
4. List several ways in which humor is achieved in this selection, and give specific examples of each. (See Glossary: *humor.*)
5. Isolate an effective example of parallel structure. (See Glossary: *parallel structure.*)
6. Find two of Bouton's transitional devices: are they effective? Justify your answer. (See Glossary: *transition.*)
7. Consider Bouton's opening and closing paragraphs. What general types of introduction and conclusion are these? (See Glossary: *introductions; conclusions.*)
8. Consider the tone of this essay. What has it to do with Bouton's central theme? (See Glossary: *style and tone; subject; unity.*)

Diction and Vocabulary

1. How much of the tone of this essay has to do with diction (see Glossary: *tone*)?
   a) Estimate the effect of words and phrases like *kid himself* (par. 1); *got to me* (2); *maybe a $3,000 difference* (2); *things are even tougher* (3); *zilch* (3); and *gob* (7).
   b) Why does Bouton use both *pants* and *trousers* in paragraphs 4 and 5?
   c) Can you improve on the phrase *on behalf of* (1) to make the whole statement more accurate?
2. Consult the dictionary to be sure you understand the meanings of the following words and phrases: *feigned indifference* (1); *virtually zilch* (3); *proper aplomb* (9); *ostensibly* (10); *WC* (10).

LARRY L. KING

Un-American Peeves

Larry L. King was born in Texas on New Year's Day of 1929. A free-lance writer, he is a former contributing editor on the staffs of both the *Texas Observer* and *Harper's*; he is currently occupying that position with the *Texas Monthly* and *New Times*, where this essay first appeared (July 25, 1975). He has also taught at both Duke and Princeton Universities. Mr. King's first novel, *The One-Eyed Man*, appeared in 1966, and he is currently working on a second novel as well as a nonfiction book about former President Lyndon Johnson. Mr. King's column in *New Times* is called "Fulminations" and "Un-American Peeves" is a perfect example of the fulminating tone. The essay shows no reticence in giving examples galore of its author's general statement.

1   There are certain things an American is not permitted to hate. Americans may, without social ostracism or penalty of law, hate their partisan or ideological opposites. They may hate someone because of race or religion or class so long as they show selective decorum and speak in coded euphemisms. It is permissible to hate anybody you accuse of beating you out of money or stealing your girl. You may hate your career rivals, former spouses or the neighboring town without losing public sympathy. You may hate the Hottentots[1] until you turn blue, especially if Dr. Kissinger[2] happens not to be getting along with them, and you'd damn well *better* hate the Godless communists, for who knows when or where the next Joe McCarthy[3] may appear. But there is a tyranny of the mind not permitting one to hate, for example, dogs.

2   I very much hate dogs. Some weeks ago in this space I made an excellent case for hating dogs. From the vituperative qualities of my mail, one might have thought I'd sold atomic secrets and repealed Mother's Day. Up with this I shall not put: if George Wallace[4] got the right to

[1] *Hottentots.* A people of southern Africa, apparently akin to both the Bushmen and the Bantus.

[2] *Dr. Kissinger.* Henry Kissinger (b. 1923), American secretary of state and national security adviser during the Nixon and Ford administrations.

[3] *Joe McCarthy* (1908–1957). Late United States Senator from Wisconsin (1947–1957), McCarthy gained notoriety and gave his name to a period of American history (roughly 1955–1960) by claiming to be able to identify Communists and Communist sympathizers in the highest levels of American government and starting a wave of anti-Communist witch-hunting. His name stands now for demagoguery.

[4] *George Wallace.* Twice governor of Alabama and candidate for president in 1968, Wallace was, at least during an early period of the 1960s, a staunch segregationist.

hate black folks and others got the right to hate George Wallace, then I got the right to hate dogs. Because the Constitution protects my First Amendment liberties, I hereby claim my right to be as honestly hateful as my nature allows. Fasten your seatbelts while I prepare to land four-square on some very un-American pet peeves:

The Star Spangled Banner. To avoid burdening you with terms of 3 expertise, trust me when I simply say that—musically—it's a piece of shit. No American, native-born or naturalized, has been discovered who properly can sing it. Instrumentally, it's perfectly suited to public executions. Its lyrics, when not bellicose, are nonsensical. I make the motion that we substitute in lieu thereof "Three Blind Mice." Plaintiff contends that it is as logical to get a chill up your spine on hearing "They all ran after the farmer's wife" as on hearing "O'er the ramparts we watched were so gallantly streaming."

Baseball. When the masses rise and restore me to my destined place, 4 justice quickly shall dictate that baseball fanatics draw stiffer terms than dope addicts; baseball players themselves will be dealt with more harshly than pushers. As a former sports writer I attest that the representative baseball player's I.Q. averages a full digit less than his hat size. The base-ball player alternately occupies himself by attempting to smite a cowhide spheroid with a wooden injector and preventing others from doing same. When he is unsuccessful, he sulks and kicks inanimate objects. The average baseball game consumes more than two hours. All but nine minutes consists of people standing around chewing tobacco and rubbing dirt on their hands. Once I am in power, baseball shall be abolished from the Little League up.

Little Kids. More expensive than yachts, more clamorous than street 5 parades, naturally grubbier than your average hobo, they rise at ungodly hours for the sole purpose of providing their parents a long day. In addition to encouraging dogs in the home and playing baseball, they keep far too many bad marriages going. They are permitted excessive holidays from school and spend perfectly good whiskey money on such fluff as dental work and bicycles. Even the Internal Revenue Service values the best of them at no more than $1,000. The outraged reader is reminded that Howard Cosell,[5] Spiro Agnew[6] and Jack the Ripper[7] began as little kids: The obvious moral lession is "Stomp 'em before they grow."

Public Prayer. The presumption of those who rise before audiences to 6 address Heaven is that God is so much at leisure He may trouble Himself

[5] *Howard Cosell.* A blunt-spoken sportscaster for ABC-TV, Cosell generated strong reactions in his viewers.
[6] *Spiro Agnew.* Vice-president under Richard Nixon until he was forced to resign from office in 1973. Like Cosell, he generated strong antipathies among certain portions of the American public.
[7] *Jack the Ripper.* An English mass murderer of the late Victorian period. He was never actually identified.

to assure the fates of football teams, Rotary Club[8] speakers, political condidates or beauty queens. Personally, I resent His being called away from keeping a wary eye on the North Koreans[9] and the John Birchers.[10] Besides, public prayer violates the civil rights of all us good atheists—especially if we've paid to get in.

7   *Vegetables.* Nobody respecting good health should eat anything green except quacamole. The prudent will be suspicious of all yellows. Red is not to be trusted when superimposed on tomatoes or radishes. Ditto for orange when applied to carrots and white as it influences cauliflower. Stick with browns and grays. As to liquids, don't drink nothing that won't make you giggle.

8   Space being short, you must trust me without explanations in being cautioned against TV sit-coms, suburban shopping centers, academicians, musical comedies, charities and foundations, neckties, women who keep cats, people who enjoy the telephone, the out-of-doors and any mother not your own. Don't question my Americanism, now. I'm a plumb damn fool about football and Mom's apple pie.

Questions for the Critical Reader

1. Is it, as King says, "a tyranny of the mind" that does not permit Americans "to hate, for example, dogs" or is it something else (par. 1)?
2. Comment on the valdity of King's analysis in paragraph 1.
3. If you could be as "honestly hateful" (par. 2) as *your* nature allows, what would you choose to express hatred about?
4. You can check the assertion King makes about baseball players' I.Q.'s by reading Jim Bouton's essay. What do you think?
5. Is King *serious* about his attitude toward *little kids*?
6. In paragraph 6, King assumes a "presumption." Is he right?
7. Would you have the author of this piece to dinner at your home?

Rhetorical Technique

1. Why does King use as his first example "The Star-Spangled Banner"?
2. Do all his examples qualify as "un-American" things to hate? Explain.
3. Which of the standard types of *introductions* and *conclusions* are used here? (See Glossary: *introductions; conclusions.*)

    [8] *Rotary Club.* One of a number of national clubs devoted to community service.
    [9] *North Koreans.* King is suggesting that this Communist country might have aggressive intentions toward the United States.
    [10] *John Birchers.* Extreme right-wingers in politics. Members of the John Birch Society.

4. Cite two methods by which *emphasis* is achieved. (See Glossary: *emphasis*.)
5. How is humor achieved in this essay? (See Glossary: *humor*.)
6. Are there examples here of *paradox*? Cite them. (See Glossary: *paradox*.)
7. Twice in his essay, King says, "Trust me." How does the request affect you? Why?
8. How much of this essay would you say is downright sarcastic? Or can you think of a more accurate term?

Diction and Vocabulary

1. Analyze the respective diction and syntax (see Glossary: *diction; syntax*) employed in paragraphs 2 and 4:
   a) How do they compare?
   b) How do they contribute to the style of the essay?
2. Isolate three examples of figurative language, and comment on their effectiveness. (See Glossary: *figures of speech*.)
3. Cite at least two examples of colloquial language. What are the effects of these? (See Glossary: *colloquial language*.)
4. Consult the dictionary if you do not know the meanings of the following words: *ostracism* (par. 1); *ideological* (1); *decorum* (1); *euphemisms* (1); *vituperative* (2); *bellicose* (3); *in lieu* (3); *plaintiff* (3); *spheroid* (4); *clamorous* (5); *guacamole* (7).
5. Can you think of a better, more accurate phrase than "wooden injector" (par. 4)?

JOANNA MERMEY

A Victim of the Consumer Crusaders

The author, who lives and works in New York City, is a television producer-director and film maker. Her forte is the TV documentary, of which she has made many. This essay was printed first in *The Soho News* (New York, February 19, 1976). Ms. Mermey has personally experienced the terrors of which she writes so wittily, and the concrete examples she offers make her point vividly.

1 I can't eat or drink anything. I can't go anywhere. I have become a victim of the consumer reporter. Ever since Ralph Nader[1] and his pals started investigating, I have gradually become an anorexia nervosa hermit. My friends warn me that I've been taking the news too seriously. But if you read the paper and watch television every night, you begin to get the feeling that if the mugger doesn't kill you—BOTULISM will!

2 I have ceased eating from a can. The tiniest dent sends me into fits of terror. After all, the *New York Times* said that seven ounces of botulism bacteria could kill the entire human race. Tuna fish is double jeopardy. You might avoid the toxic bacteria—but beware of maggots.

3 I started eating hamburgers instead of tuna for lunch, but then I read a story in the *New York Post* that hamburger meat tested around town showed particles of animal shit mashed in it, and the spices were spiked with rodent hairs. Hot dogs were banished from the luncheon fare following features of franks filled with cancerous chicken wings. If carcinogenic agents don't phase you, one doctor wrote that the nitrate in hot dogs inhibits one's sexual hormones.

4 Hormones are another horror. If you're afraid of blood clots and cancer from ingesting birth control or morning after pills—just think what happens when you devour a juicy steak from a cow chock full of hormones to fatten her up.

5 Sausage can cause trichinosis. It said so right on the package I bought at the D'Agostino Supermarket.[2] Eggs can give you a heart attack. If this story is making you nervous, don't take a drink—cirrhosis of the liver—and don't pick up that cigarette—you know what the Surgeon General said. It's on the side of the pack.

6 Reach for a tomato, and it's filled with gas and covered with DDT.

Reprinted by permission of the author, Joanna Mermey, and the publisher, *The Soho News*.

[1] *Ralph Nader.* America's leading consumer advocate, he and his associates alerted the nation to a host of defective and polluting consumer products.

[2] *the D'Agostino Supermarket.* A reliable chain of purveyors of fancy groceries.

The frozen food has preservatives and the milk you are feeding your baby could be watered down. And you know what they've been saying about the water in New Orleans. It might just be causing THE BIG C!

Mortal fear of the refrigerator drives me from the apartment. But I freeze at the elevator remembering too many tales of elevator rapes. I dash through the vestibule with visions of vestibule murders. Subways are out. Too much of a risk for a woman alone. I'm afraid to wait for a bus or a cab, because I might get mugged while I'm waiting or choke from the pollution. 7

The National Safety Council says someone dies in a car crash every nine minutes. There is no way I'm going to get on a plane after what happened in Guatemala, Venezuela, Tunisia and Paris. Even waving good-by to a daring traveller is fraught with perial. You never know where a Palestinian guerrilla will strike next. 8

So I'm lying under the covers in my apartment, freezing. I've turned off the steam heat, because it's bad for my complexion. I can't use the electric heater, because it might catch on fire. I'm lying flat on my back. I can't even get comfortable. I threw out my pillow last week. You see, it's because I read in a magazine that sleeping on a pillow gives you wrinkles on your neck. 9

So I turned over to watch the late movie on my color TV—and then I remembered—THE RAYS . . . THE RAYS . . . THE RAYS . . . 10

Questions for the Critical Reader

1. What is the relation between the humor in this essay and its subject matter? (See Glossary: *humor*.)
2. Do you consider a humorous treatment of a serious subject inappropriate? Explain.
3. Is there any information given here that you didn't know about? Explain.
4. How does this information affect you?
5. What course of action would be appropriate for someone who wished to avoid the dangers spoken of in this piece?

Rhetorical Technique

1. Locate the thesis statement illustrated by Mermey's examples. Comment on its placement in that paragraph. (See Glossary: *thesis statement*.)
2. How are the examples ordered? Why did the writer choose this pattern?
3. Comment on the examples:
   a) Which are the most effective? The least? Explain.

b) Are there some that you might have added but that Mermey does not give? What are they?

c) Isolate two examples that are clearly overstatements and comment on the effectiveness of the exaggerations. (See Glossary: *humor*.)

4. Consider the conclusion:
   a) Is it effective? Explain. (See Glossary: *conclusions*.)
   b) How does it relate to the introductory paragraphs? (See Glossary: *introductions*.)
   c) What is the effect of the final words being capitalized and the ellipsis (that is, the three spaced dots) between them?

5. Comment on the transition between paragraphs 6 and 7. (See Glossary: *transition*.)

6. Cite at least one method by which emphasis is achieved. (See Glossary: *emphasis*.)

Diction and Vocabulary

1. How would you characterize the language of this essay on the concrete/abstract scale? (See Glossary: *abstract and concrete*.)

2. What is the effect of Mermey's reference to *D'Agostino's Supermarket* instead of just *supermarket*?

3. Why does she name the newspapers instead of just using the word *newspapers*?

4. Why does she *not* give a brand name to the tuna fish?

5. Locate an example of paradox. (See Glossary: *paradox*.)

6. Consult the dictionary to be sure you understand the meanings of the following words and phrases: *anorexia nervosa* (par. 1); *botulism* (1); *toxic* (2); *carcinogenic* (3); *nitrate* (3); *trichinosis* (5); *cirrhosis* (5); and *DDT* (6).

RONALD BERMAN

Riding the Roller Coaster

Since 1971, Dr. Ronald Berman has been chairman of the National Endowment for the Humanities and concerned with the issue of values in America. Before that he was professor of Renaissance literature at the University of California, San Diego, to which he had come from teaching posts at Kenyon College and Columbia University. A former Naval Intelligence officer, Dr. Berman was associate editor of the *Kenyon Review* (1963–1970) and is the author of a number of books and articles. His last work, *America in the Sixties: An Intellectual History*, was published in 1970. The present essay was first published in *Newsweek* (January 5, 1976). Out of the contrast of two ideas, it makes a profusely illustrated general statement.

The first half of the '70s has been a battle between tradition and libera- **1** tion. This has been reflected in our politics and even more noticeably in our cultural life. For example, on prime time we see television programs that attempt to be ever more daring, that come as close as they can to the boundaries of what has been called the New Morality. But we see between these programs others that eulogize family life and fairly wallow in the values of the golden past. Alternation and uncertainty are thematic for a decade that has yet to shape its own character.

The same issue of any given magazine is likely to contain an article on **2** creative divorce or multiple love affairs—and another on keeping husbands perpetually contented. Even the *macho* magazines offer, in addition to their incredible cover stories, advice on how to stock wine cellars, appear impeccably dressed, and be ready to respond at the drop of a hat (or more basic item of wear) to questions of style and behavior. The opposing impulses of this decade are social responsibility and personal freedom, and no one in American culture is free of their operation. We are simultaneously expected to value our families, jobs and government —and to fulfill our personal desires in ways that few social systems can tolerate.

Changing Times

One thing suggested by changing times is that there will be less govern- **3** ment, or at least more talk of less government. Already in California, Massachusetts and New York, electoral strategies are evolving which reject the domestic imperialism of inflated budgets and which insist that national problems have to be solved by private ways and means. One detects in the media and on Capitol Hill a decrease in affection for regulation and subsidy. This may mean that family, church and community will once again exercise their rights of domain—or that they will have to compete with institutions of another kind.

4   I tend to think that the latter is more probable. Our love affair with Big Government may be over but that does not mean we can return to the America that many of us remember before the second world war. The lesson of democratic politics is pretty clear that government is unable to resist organized advocacy. Farmers, for example, are even now tempted to band together as members of agricultural unions or simply to regain control of prices and amounts of production. Certainly teachers and doctors on strike have shown them the way—as indeed have all those trades and professions that feel themselves unfairly treated by the present system.

5   The individual in the second half of the '70s will make his voice heard by belonging to a union, an association of consumers or lobby for his or her profession; in short, as a constituent of one or another movement involving sex, age, income and other broad distinctions. Women and minorities will continue to exert political pressure, and they will be joined by the aged, by white-collar workers and by those who, like doctors and lawyers, were once thought to be the individualists of capitalist culture.

The Adolescent Adult

6   I think it much more likely that our cultural responses will be shaped by schools and television than that the family will find its ancient authority restored. It is idle to think of shaping the minds of children who are absent from home physically for half the day and mentally for the other half. There is no great incentive, in fact, to have children at all in an age of inflation and taxation. Where the model for the middle class was once the nuclear family, it is now much more condensed: a childless husband and wife who are part of the national economy and style. There is now an extraordinary emphasis on self-fulfillment. Translated into practical terms, this means far more attention to the needs and desires of adults than to those of children.

7   Everywhere one looks, whether in the media, in the economy itself or even in personal experience, it becomes plain that the new norm involves what might be called the adolescent adult, the man or woman whose principal concern is self-development until long past maturity. Perhaps the best evidence for this is in the great American institution of media advertising, which relentlessly serves up to us the image of people well into their 30s whose interests are confined to the ways they can most enjoy and experience material things.

8   This kind of self-fulfillment occurs in a world increasingly less pleasant

and more dangerous. Over the past decade there has been both a higher incidence of crimes against the person and a new sense of their definition. It is now simply accepted that rape and assault happen to people who live in cities—just as it is accepted that police action can do very little about it. The effect has been to change these things from felonies to something very like misdemeanors. The entire onus has shifted to the victims, who are presumed to know better than to expose themselves to crimes of opportunity. The city, which is the habitat of the '70s, will become less hospitable as financial problems intensify human problems.

The cardinal rule of life in the big cities is the recognition of con-   9 stituencies; because of this we can pretty well bank on the balance of power that operates so noticeably in places like San Francisco and New York. Services will continue to be related not to productivity—and often not to needs—but to the demands of those interest groups that can best make claim to the distribution of taxes. The concept of equality will take on economic shape, unlike the '60s, in which it was an ideological issue.

Dynamic Prospects

We live in a decade of lowered expectations and in the midst of conflicting   10 social desires. Our domestic lives will be shaped by another conflict, that between the habits that made us what we are and the new facts that urge us to change our ideas and style of life. Brought up in abundance, we now face scarcity. Brought up with familiar moral institutions, we now face a kind of personal liberation that probably very few of us can sustain. The prospects for the rest of the '70s are dynamic in the literal sense of the word: it will be a roller coaster of a decade.

Questions for the Critical Reader

1. Do you agree with Berman's conclusion about the first half of the seventies as he expresses it in sentence 1?
2. a) What *is* the "New Morality"?
   b) How do TV shows "come as close as they can" to its "boundaries"?
3. What does the author mean by "social irresponsibility"? Does he illustrate this abstract idea anywhere? (See Glossary: *abstract and concrete*.)
4. Do you agree that "government is unable to resist organized advocacy"? (par. 4) Explain.
5. Consider the conclusion to paragraph 6 and the argument that leads up to it. Do you agree? Explain. (See Glossary: *conclusions*.)
6. Consider the media example in paragraph 7: Does it coincide with your experience? Explain.

7. Comment on the picture being drawn of life in the second half of the seventies:
   a) Does Berman seem to be making an accurate forecast? Why? Why not?
   b) Are there any factors he is not taking into consideration?

Rhetorical Technique

1. a) To what extent are comparison and contrast used in this essay? Cite specific evidence. (See Glossary: *comparison and contrast*.)
   b) Is it enough to reclassify the piece and shift it to Chapter 3? Explain.
2. What other types of exposition do you find here? (See Glossary: *exposition*.)
3. Locate the central theme or abstract statement being illustrated. (See Glossary: *central theme; abstract and concrete*.)
4. Which of the examples used to illustrate this are the most effective and which the least effective? Explain.
5. Comment on the balance between the abstract and the concrete in these examples. (See Glossary: *abstract and concrete*.)
6. Which general type of conclusion is employed? (See Glossary: *conclusions*.)
7. Comment on the *transitions* (see Glossary: *transition*) between at least two paragraphs.
8. Cite at least one example of parallel structure. (See Glossary: *parallel structure*.)

Diction and Vocabulary

1. Cite at least one example of paradox (see Glossary: *paradox*).
2. Give at least one example of metaphor (see Glossary: *figures of speech*), and evaluate its effectiveness.
3. Is there a word or expression here that to your ear qualifies as a cliché? (See Glossary: *cliché*)
4. Consider the connotative value of the word *cardinal* (par. 9). Why has Berman chosen it? (See Glossary: *connotation and denotation*.)
5. Consult the dictionary to be sure you understand the meanings of the following words and phrases: *eulogize* (par. 1); *impeccably* (2); *advocacy* (4); *constituent* (5); *nuclear family* (6); *onus* (8); *felonies* (8); *misdemeanors* (8); *constituencies* (9); and *ideological* (9).

ERVING GOFFMAN

Dramatic Realization

Erving Goffman was born in Canada in 1922 and came to the United States in 1945. Since 1968, Dr. Goffman has been Benjamin Franklin Professor of Anthropology and Sociology at the University of Pennsylvania. He has also taught at the University of California, Berkeley, and is the author of numerous books on the sociology of behavior, including *Encounters* (1961), *Asylums* (1961), *Behavior in Public Places* (1963), *Stigma* (1964), *Interaction Rituals* (1969), and *Relations in Public* (1971). This essay is adapted from his first book, *The Presentation of Self in Everyday Life* (1956), where he argues for a kind of normal theatricalism in the human character and personality—especially as these are manifested in social relations. The fascinating idea that Goffman illustrates here may at first be difficult to grasp, but it is worth the reader's time and effort to do so.

While in the presence of others, the individual typically infuses his 1 activity with signs which dramatically highlight and portray confirmatory facts that might otherwise remain unapparent or obscure. For if the individual's activity is to become significant to others, he must mobilize his activity so that it will express *during the interation* what he wishes to convey. In fact, the performer may be required not only to express his claimed capacities during the interaction but also to do so during a split second in the interaction. Thus, if a baseball umpire is to give the impression that he is sure of his judgment, he must forgo the moment of thought which might make him sure of his judgment; he must give an instantaneous decision so that the audience will be sure that he is sure of his judgment.

It may be noted that in the case of some statuses dramatization pre- 2 sents no problem, since some of the acts which are instrumentally essential for the completion of the core task of the status are at the same time wonderfully adapted, from the point of view of communication, as means of vividly conveying the qualities and attributes claimed by the performer. The roles of prizefighters, surgeons, violinists, and policemen are cases in point. These activities allow for so much dramatic self-expression that exemplary practitioners—whether real or fictional—become famous and are given a special place in the commercially organized fantasies of the nation.

In many cases, however, dramatization of one's work does constitute a 3 problem. An illustration of this may be cited from a hospital study where the medical nursing staff is shown to have a problem that the surgical nursing staff does not have:

> The things which a nurse does for post-operative patients on the surgical floor are frequently of recognizable importance, even to patients who are strangers to hospital activities. For example, the patient sees his nurse changing bandages, swinging orthopedic frames into place, and can realize that these are purposeful activities. Even if she cannot be at his side, he can respect her purposeful activities.
>
> Medical nursing is also highly skilled work. . . . The physician's diagnosis must rest upon careful observation of symptoms over time where the surgeon's are in larger part dependent on visible things. The lack of viability creates problems on the medical. A patient will see his nurse stop at the next bed and chat for a moment or two with the patient there. He doesn't know that she is observing the shallowness of the breathing and color and tone of the skin. He thinks she is just visiting. So, alas, does his family who may thereupon decide that these nurses aren't very impressive. If the nurse spends more time at the next bed than at his own, the patient may feel slighted. . . . The nurses are "wasting time" unless they are darting about doing some visible thing such as administering hypodermics.

Similarly, the proprietor of a service establishment may find it difficult to dramatize what is actually being done for clients because the clients cannot "see" the overhead costs of the service rendered them. Undertakers must therefore charge a great deal for their highly visible product —a coffin that has been transformed into a casket—because many of the other costs of conducting a funeral are ones that cannot be readily dramatized. Merchants, too, find that they must charge high prices for things that look intrinsically expensive in order to compensate the establishment for expensive things like insurance, slack periods, etc., that never appear before the customers' eyes.

4   The problem of dramatizing one's work involves more than merely making invisible costs visible. The work that must be done by those who fill certain statuses is often so poorly designed as an expression of a desired meaning, that if the incumbent would dramatize the character of his role, he must divert an appreciable amount of his energy to do so. And this activity diverted to communication will often require different attributes from the ones which are being dramatized. Thus to furnish a house so that it will express simple, quiet dignity, the householder may have to race to auction sales, haggle with antique dealers, and doggedly canvass all the local shops for proper wallpaper and curtain materials. To give a radio talk that will sound genuinely informal, spontaneous, and relaxed, the speaker may have to design his script with painstaking care, testing one phrase after another, in order to follow the content, language, rhythm, and pace of everyday talk. Similarly, a *Vogue* model, by her

clothing, stance, and facial expression, is able expressively to portray a cultivated understanding of the book she poses in her hand; but those who trouble to express themselves so appropriately will have very little time left over for reading. As Sartre[1] suggested: "The attentive pupil who wishes to *be* attentive, his eyes riveted on the teacher, his ears open wide, so exhausts himself in playing the attentive role that he ends up by no longer hearing anything." And so individuals often find themselves with the dilemma of expression *versus* action. Those who have the time and talent to perform a task well may not, because of this, have the time or talent to make it apparent that they are performing well. It may be said that some organizations resolve this dilemma by officially delegating the dramatic function to a specialist who will spend his time expressing the meaning of the task and spend no time actually doing it.

If we alter our frame of reference for a moment and turn from a particular performance to the individuals who persent it, we can consider an interesting fact about the round of different routines which any group or class of individuals helps to perform. When a group or class is examined, one finds that the members of it tend to invest their egos primarily in certain routines, giving less stress to the other ones which they perform. Thus a professional man may be willing to take a very modest role in the street, in a shop, or in his home, but, in the social sphere which encompasses his display of professional competency, he will be much concerned to make an effective showing. In mobilizing his behavior to make a showing, he will be concerned not so much with the full round of the different routines he performs but only with the one from which his occupational reputation derives. It is upon this issue that some writers have chosen to distinguish groups with aristocratic habits (whatever their social status) from those of middle-class character. The aristocratic habit, it has been said, is one that mobilizes all the minor activities of life which fall outside the serious specialities of other classes and injects into these activities an expression of character, power, and high rank.

> By what important accomplishments is the young nobleman instructed to support the dignity of his rank, and to render himself worthy of that superiority over his fellow-citizens, to which the virtue of his ancestors had raised them: Is it by knowledge, by industry, by patience, by self-denial, or by virtue of any kind? As all his words, as all his motions are attended to, he learns a habitual regard to every circumstance of ordinary behavior, and studies to perform all those small duties with the most exact propriety. As he is conscious of how much he is observed, and how much mankind are disposed to favor all his inclinations, he acts, upon the most indifferent occasions, with that freedom and elevation which the thought of this naturally inspires. His air, his manner, his deportment, all mark that elegant, and graceful sense of his own superiority, which

[1] *Sartre.* Jean-Paul Sartre (b. 1905), French philosopher, novelist, critic.

those who are born to inferior stations can hardly ever arrive at. These are the arts by which he proposes to make mankind more easily submit to his authority, and to govern their inclinations according to his own pleasure: and in this he is seldom disappointed. These arts, supported by rank and preeminence, are, upon ordinary occasions, sufficient to govern the world.[2]

If such virtuosi actually exist, they would provide a suitable group in which to study the techniques by which activity is transformed into a show.

Questions for the Critical Reader

1. Reread carefully the second sentence of the first paragraph. Try to rephrase it in your own words. Now discuss the truth of this assertion. In doing so, be sure to use concrete examples to illustrate your points.
2. Give examples of the "exemplary practitioners" cited in paragraph 2.
3. Is it true in your opinion that undertakers must "charge a great deal for their highly visible product—a coffin . . . because many of the other costs of conducting a funeral are ones that cannot be readily dramatized?" Explain.
4. Comment on Sartre's observation, quoted in paragraph 4.
5. Is it true that "individuals often find themselves with the dilemma of expression *versus* action?" (See par. 4.)
6. If it is, can you think of a reason why it may be necessary?
7. Think back to jobs you have held: how many required dramatization? How many just work?
8. The last sentence of paragraph 4 is a provocative one. Can you think of any such "specialists?"

Rhetorical Technique

1. Identify the thesis statement (see Glossary: *thesis statement*) that Goffman's piece goes on to illustrate. Can you put it into your own words more simply than he does?
2. Comment on examples given of workers who have no trouble dramatizing their roles. Can you think of better ones?
3. Do the same with the examples of those whose work is not of that type.
4. Consider the long quotations used as a single illustration (in paragraphs 3 and 5): Could something have been gained if the author had merely paraphrased them? Try the paraphrase yourself.

[2] Adam Smith, *The Theory of Moral Sentiments* (London: Henry Bohn, 1853), p. 75.

5. Is this piece entirely unified? If not, what elements do you find that challenge the unity? (See Glossary: *unity*.)
6. Is the introduction effective? What is the point of view taken there? Explain. (See Glossary: *point of view*.)
7. Comment on the balance between the concrete and the abstract in this essay. (See Glossary: *abstract and concrete*.)

Diction and Vocabulary

1. Comment on the special quality of Goffman's language. Does the language of the sociologist impede your understanding of this piece? Be specific in referring to words, phrases, sentences, or whole paragraphs.
2. Consult the dictionary to be sure you understand the meanings of the following words and phrases: *confirmatory* (par. 1); *interaction* (1); *status* (2); *dramatization* (2); *attributes* (2); *exemplary* (2); *intrinsically* (3); *compensate* (3); *divert* (4); *painstaking* (4); *delegating* (4); *frame of reference* (5); *encompasses* (5); *virtuosi* (5).

NOTE: For suggested writing assignments, see the end of this chapter.

Writing Suggestions for Chapter 2: *Illustrative Examples*

I.

Write an essay in which you use concrete examples to illustrate an abstract statement. In organizing your essay, collect your examples, and try to arrange them in emphatic order; that is, either work up to your best example by using it last, or use your best example first. (See Glossary: *emphasis*.) You may use one of the abstract statements listed below or one of your own devising:

1. Americans pamper their pets.
2. Sometimes it pays to be lazy.
3. Grading college students induces anxiety in them (*or* grading college students stimulates excellent performance).
4. My girlfriend/boyfriend doesn't understand me/understands me too well.
5. Reading daily newspapers is a depressing habit.
6. Jogging is great exercise.
7. Growing up in the city (country, suburbs) is an education.
8. Fast food is really slow poison.
9. It's hard/easy for a freshman to make friends.
10. Americans love scoundrels.

II. A. Writing Assignment Based on "A Victim of the Consumer Crusaders"

Write an essay from a point of view analogous to Mermey's; that is, you are, say, a victim for promoters of fads. Your abstract statement would be something like, "I respond perfectly to all the latest fads," and your examples would include showing how you (1) wear the latest clothes fad, (2) read the highly touted best sellers, (3) listen to the "in" pop records, (4) go on the latest diet, (5) watch the "in" TV shows and so on.

Or, you could take the opposite tack and use as a statement "I never respond to any fad" and choose appropriate examples to illustrate *that* statement.

B. Writing Assignment Based on "Riding the Roller Coaster"

Write an essay of the same type as Berman's, that is, one in which you make a statement about "what's happening" or what is likely to happen in our society in the near future. Use Berman's sources—the media; magazines and other popular literature; the situation in the rural areas and in the cities; the mood, as you perceive it, of various segments of the population—and make a list of examples that strike you as bearing significantly on the near future. When your list has a dozen or so examples, examine it critically, and see if you can find a general statement that can be illustrated by most (though not necessarily all) of the examples on the list. Discard the examples you can't use.

Then write an essay on the subject, using your best examples in an emphatic order.

3

Designing by *Comparison and Contrast*

If you have selected this college rather than another, chosen a dormitory room rather than some off-campus living arrangement, decided to pursue prelaw studies rather than teacher training—if you have made one or more of these choices, you have employed the mental operations called comparison and contrast. We call these basic mental operations fundamental to the process of thought, and Freud called thought *experimental action*. The advantages of such thought are obvious: instead of wasting the enormous energy involved in taking *action* on *both* possibilities, you try them out in your mind, weighing advantages and disadvantages. The mental operations of comparing and contrasting are employed every day, in deciding everything from which way to get to school (walk? take the bus?) to what we should order for lunch (a hamburger? grilled cheese?).

Sometimes these choices are made with little conscious planning, and so swiftly, in fact, that we are hardly aware that our minds are at work. When, however, we want to employ comparison and contrast as a formal method of organizing an essay, we need first to do some thinking and then some preparation.

The first thing to think about is that the kinds of pairs that can be used depend upon our purposes in making the comparison. For example, one purpose would be simply to explain a subject with which the reader is unfamiliar by placing it next to a subject he knows. Thus we could learn about the unfamiliar English parliamentary system by comparing it with the well-known American congressional system. We could do the same with Buddhism (unknown) and Christianity (known), African art (unknown) and American art (known), and so forth. Such a simple purpose, however, can frequently lead to deeper insights into *both* items. In the comparison of Buddhism and Christianity we might also illuminate the philosophies underlying Eastern and Western religions—in addition to explaining about Buddhism alone (our original purpose). T. Harry

Williams and Yi-Fu Tuan have achieved this in their respective essays.

Another purpose in making a comparison might be to establish which of the items is better than the other. When we want to convince the reader of the choice we have made, our purpose is also argumentative. We are being similarly argumentative when we choose to buy one notebook rather than another after comparing them for size, thickness, color, binding, and price. For rhetorical purposes, comparison that has the argumentative purpose can establish that one process of sewage recycling is more feasible than another, or that one course of foreign policy is more advantageous than its alternative. William Herman's essay in this chapter, comparing two methods of generating energy, has just this argumentative purpose.

A third purpose might be to determine what common theme is shared by both items. Thus the comparison of Christianity and Buddhism might produce an idea central to all *religion* and not just likenesses and differences. Michael Korda's essay produces an essential relationship between his ideas of work and power.

Whatever the purpose, however, the writer of an essay in comparison and contrast needs to keep several important things in mind:

1. Not everything is subject to an essay in comparison and contrast, and certain subjects that are may not be amenable to the writer's purposes. For example, one may compare the music of Joan Baez and Bob Dylan and learn a good deal about popular music in general. But if one doesn't know the music of one of these performers, it will be devilishly difficult—probably impossible—to learn about the other from the comparison. Moreover, even if one does know the music of both, it would be impossible to argue—by comparison and contrast—for the superiority of one or the other because the question is simply a matter of taste.

2. Comparison should be logical; that is, we need to select items that belong to the same class of things and compare them on similar points of significant interest within the context of the class. For example, it is logical to compare the English Parliament and the United States Congress on their respective methods of electing members, passing laws, and limiting debate, but it is illogical (and really uninformative) to compare the pomp and ceremony of the English system with, say, the barbershops and other personal amenities available to members of our House and Senate. Similarly, the country and the seashore are suitable as subjects to be compared for their relative merits as vacation spots, but not for their potential productivity as farm land.

3. Points of comparison must be evenly applied to both items in the comparison. In the consideration of a hawk and a jet aircraft, for example, the hawk's method of raising its young is an inappropriate point because it cannot be evenly applied to the aircraft. Because both are

members of the class of things that fly, wingspan in relation to body weight *is* an appropriate point of comparison.

4. The structure of a comparison takes three basic forms: (a) The writer can set out all the points with reference to one item and follow this by setting out all the points with reference to the second. This is appropriate where the points to be made are few, fairly broad, and fairly clear. Herman's essay proceeds in this way. (b) Or the items can be compared point by point, for example, the hawk's speed and the aircraft's, the hawk's method of takeoff and the aircraft's, the hawk's method of landing and the aircraft's, and so on. This method is appropriate where there are many points to be made. (c) The writer can mix these methods by exercising careful control. Note how it is done in T. Harry Williams's "Grant and Lee" and in the essay by Yi-Fu Tuan.

It is possible, however, to construct an essay in comparison and contrast by other plans. For example, the writer of an essay comparing Buddhism to Christianity might begin by defining religion and then go on to compare the two examples—by some one of the methods mentioned earlier. In any case, the writer must take into account the particular subject he or she has chosen and then carefully select the structure most suitable for his or her essay.

WILLIAM HERMAN

Solar Power versus Nuclear Energy

> William Herman, the editor of this volume, is a professor of English
> at the City College, CUNY, who has done research in the area
> under discussion. "Solar Power versus Nuclear Energy" was written
> especially for inclusion here and is thus printed for the first time.
> The method is clearly that of comparison and contrast, but the
> purpose is strongly argumentative and depends on the facts em-
> ployed to support the central theme.

1   Suddenly—we need energy.

2   After the most profligate expenditures of fossil fuels that man has ever
known—during the first three-quarters of the twentieth century—universal wisdom is that *we* have had it with such expenditures. Although
this knowledge was available long before 1973, the Arab oil boycott
initiated then has spread the word. Thus there is now a continuing debate
over the issue. In the United States, terms like *environmental impact*,[1]
energy self-sufficiency,[2] and *consistent energy policy*[3] are standard in
newspaper and magazine articles. Congress uses them to beat the president over the head. He uses them to strike back. Everybody now knows
that the so-called fossil fuels, coal, shale, and petroleum, are in finite
supply. Everybody also knows, even those who do not live in Los Angeles,
that burning fossil fuels causes shocking environmental pollution. It is
hard to believe that everybody does not also understand that prices for
fuel and energy-powered services are skyrocketing with no end in sight.

3   Given these aspects of the energy crisis, another common term nowadays, the question arises: what are we to do about all this?

4   One answer comes from a group already tagged by the official energy
establishment as the lunatic fringe, that is, the environmentalists. They
are calling for a large and serious commitment to the development of
solar power. The other answer is one that has underlain United States
energy policy since the end of World War II: nuclear energy.

5   Let us examine these alternatives by considering the previously men-

---

[1] *environmental impact.* The notion that any man-made structure—a housing
development, a mine, a manufacturing facility—has a measurable effect or impact
on the natural environment. Laws enacted in the late 1960s and early 1970s require
certain facilities to obtain statements measuring the environmental impact of a
proposed project before it can be built.

[2] *energy self-sufficiency.* The policy of generating our own energy rather than
relying on importation of energy resources, most notably petroleum.

[3] *consistent energy policy.* The policy of integrating plans and policies regulating
the use of energy and its production.

tioned aspects of their use, cost (including social cost), environmental pollution, and availability.

As Barry Commoner, professor of environmental sciences at Washington University in St. Louis, puts it, U.S. policy is that we shall be "saved by nuclear power." Yet twenty-one years after the first nuclear energy plant was built in this country, we now have all of fifty-eight such plants. They produce a full 8 percent of our electricity and a rousing 2 percent of the nation's entire energy demand. 6

The conventional nuclear power plant (as opposed to the breeder reactor, which we shall discuss in a moment) uses uranium ore that has been enriched with about 3 percent of U 235, the essential fuel in the fission process. Although this ore is plentiful and relatively cheap (though since 1973 the price has risen more than threefold), experts insist that by 1990–1995 both the dwindling supply and the high price of this ore would make conventional nuclear energy prohibitively expensive. The solution was to have been the breeder reactor. Unlike the conventional nuclear reactor, the breeder works is such a way as to produce plutonium 239. This highly toxic material can be separated from ordinary wastes and recycled as nuclear fuel. The trouble with this solution is that the economics and technology of the breeder reactor are in disarray. Capital plant costs and ore reprocessing costs are so high and technology so low as to make the whole scheme unlikely to reach the stage, according to the Energy Research and Development Administration, of "commercialization." 7

But these are only the beginnings of our nuclear problems. Even a breeder reactor will produce unrenewable wastes of deadly toxicity. And these wastes have an effective life of more than 150,000 years! So far, nobody has come up with an acceptable solution to this problem. At present, nuclear wastes are buried in concrete-lined containers on tracts of unused land, where they need monitoring for escaping radioactivity. They will continue to need this attention for 150,000 years, a nice gift for the succeeding 6,000 generations. 8

Moreover, even if the waste problem were solved, there would still be the possibility of accidents in nuclear energy plants and the fact that the entire complex nuclear system is widely scattered across the country. The latter fact means that enormous amounts of radioactive material will be crisscrossing our highways, from nuclear energy station to reprocessing plant, from mining complex to enrichment centers, increasing the possibility that some of this material will escape into the environment. 9

And if anybody doesn't know yet how deadly are these radioactive materials, let him consider this one fact: in a nuclear energy program based on the breeder, it is calculated that 130 million pounds of plutonium would be involved. If only four one-thousandths of this material were to escape into the environment, it is estimated that about 650,000 10 cancers might result. This is exactly double the present rate of cancer in the United States.

11   As for the possibility of accident at nuclear installations, we might leave those consequences to the imagination.

12   Yet the government has spent billions in nuclear energy research and development. By contrast and for reasons that can only be guessed at, as late as 1973 federal expenditures for solar power research constituted less than 1 percent of the total energy research budget. This, despite the fact that solar power is the most plentiful resource on the planet and the least used.

13   Solar power depends upon collection, on concentrating the sun's rays by means of mirrored surfaces, or retaining their heat by means of a black plate enclosed in a glass box (the so-called "greenhouse effect"). The advantage of this dependency is enormous. For, unlike other forms of energy production, all of which operate at wastefully high temperatures regardless of the many low-temperature tasks for which they are required, solar power can be concentrated at the exact temperature needed for the task at hand: space heating at 70°–80° F., hot-water heating at 140°–160° F., and cooking at 250° F. An oil burner heated to 500° F. just to deliver space heating at 75° F. is just one example of how one form of nonsolar power is wasteful.

14   By contrast with other energy fuels, especially with the uranium-plutonium fuels as their supplies diminish, sunlight is inexhaustible and cheap. It does not need reprocessing or enrichment, and conversion to solar power would not—as in the case of the breeder or conventional reactors of nuclear energy plants—require a huge outlay of capital costs. Space heating, hot water and electric power, perhaps 38 percent of the entire energy budget, could all be provided by basic solar collection and conducting devices hooked up to present household systems. Eight percent per year of the aluminum and glass needed for these devices could be made available if the huge number of throwaway containers we use were replaced by returnable bottles and if the size of our automobiles were somewhat reduced. The technology for this form of solar power is not in disarray but is readily available.

15   Moreover, the remaining energy tasks, those requiring portable liquid fuels (principally for transportation), could also be supplied by solar power with an engineering effort to make storable hydrogen (as plentiful in supply as sunlight) an easily produced commodity. This would also solve the problem of storing solar power during those periods when the sun does not shine.

16   Like so many other rational courses of action available to this country, the switch to solar power would require—energy, the energy of an enlightened and committed citizenry. The choice seems clear. The only question remaining seems to be this one: do we have the get up and go to reach for the sun?

Questions for the Critical Reader

1. Why is so much space given to nuclear energy and so little to solar power?
2. Why does the author refer *power* to the sun and *energy* to nuclear generation?
3. What is being suggested in paragraph 6?
4. Do you agree with this point? Explain.
5. What is your response to the numerical information given in paragraphs 8 and 10? Explain.
6. Is the news given in paragraph 10 really news to you?
7. The author does not refer to one general solution proposed by certain environmentalist groups, namely, that we must limit economic growth in order to conserve energy.
   a) What is your opinion of this proposal?
   b) Why has the author failed to mention it?
8. Can you comment on the validity of the author's analysis of solar power's capabilities?
9. How would one go about validating this information?
10. Do you believe, as the author suggests in his conclusion, that an "enlightened and committed citizenry" can make the choice?

Rhetorical Technique

1. What was the author's purpose in writing this essay? (See Glossary: *purpose.*)
2. Has he succeeded in that purpose? Explain.
3. Analyze the structure of the comparison. (See introduction to this chapter.)
4. A portion of this essay qualifies as process analysis (see Chapter 6).
   a) Identify these parts.
   b) Comment on their effectiveness: is the information given enough to enlarge your understanding? Explain.
5. Comment on the effectiveness of paragraph 1.
6. What general type of introduction is employed here? What type of conclusions? (See Glossary: *introductions; conclusions.*)
7. How does the author achieve emphasis? (See Glossary: *emphasis.*)
8. Identify an example of parallel structure, and comment on its effectiveness. (See Glossary: *parallel structure.*)
9. Identify at least two examples of verbal irony (see Glossary: *irony.*)

Diction and Vocabulary

1. In paragraph 2, the author cites three phrases as "standard."
   a) Are they so standard that you knew them without consulting his footnotes?

b) If you did have to consult the footnotes and if your conclusion is that the phrases are *not* standard—why would this author have said they were? In other words, what would his purpose be in making such a judgment?

2. Are there technical terms here that either helped or hindered your understanding? Name them. Explain.

3. What is the meaning of the reference to *Los Angeles* (par. 2)?

4. Consider words and phrases like *beat the president over the head* (2), *prices . . . are skyrocketing* (2), *tagged* (4), and *lunatic fringe* (4). Are they good colloquial usage? Cliché? Evaluate each expression by first consulting the appropriate Glossary entry: see *cliché; colloquial language*.

5. Consult the dictionary if you do not understand the meanings of any of the following: *profligate* (par. 1); *underlain* (4); *fission process* (7); *dwindling* (7); *toxic* (7); *disarray* (7).

T. HARRY WILLIAMS

Grant and Lee

T. Harry Williams was born in Vinegar Hill, Illinois, in 1909. He
has taught at the Universities of Wisconsin, Omaha, and West
Virginia and is currently professor of history at Louisiana State
University. Among his books are *Lincoln and the Radicals* (1941)
and *Romance and Realism in Southern Politics* (1961). "Grant and
Lee" was adapted from his book *Lincoln and His Generals* (1952).
It is a fine example of how comparison and contrast generate in-
formation.

Grant was, judged by modern standards, the greatest general of the Civil   1
War. He was head and shoulders above any general on either side as an
over-all strategist, as a master of what in later wars would be called
global strategy. His Operation Crusher plan, the product of a mind
which had received little formal instruction in the higher art of war,
would have done credit to the most finished student of a series of modern
staff and command schools. He was a brilliant theater strategist, as evi-
denced by the Vicksburg campaign, which was a classic field and siege
operation. He was a better than average tactician, although like even the
best generals of both sides he did not appreciate the destruction that the
increasing firepower of modern armies could visit on troops advancing
across open spaces.

Lee is usually ranked as the greatest Civil War general, but this   2
evaluation has been made without placing Lee and Grant in the perspective of military developments since the war. Lee was interested
hardly at all in "global" strategy, and what few suggestions he did make
to his government about operations in other theaters than his own
indicate that he had little aptitude for grand planning. As a theater
strategist, Lee often demonstrated more brilliance and apparent originality than Grant, but his most audacious plans were as much the product
of the Confederacy's inferior military position as his own fine mind. In
war, the weaker side has to improvise brilliantly. It must strike quickly,
daringly, and include a dangerous element of risk in its plans. Had Lee
been a Northern general with Northern resources behind him, he would
have improvised less and seemed less bold. Had Grant been a Southern
general, he would have fought as Lee did.

Fundamentally Grant was superior to Lee because in a modern total   3
war he had a modern mind, and Lee did not. Lee looked to the past in

war as the Confederacy did in spirit. The staffs of the two men illustrate their outlook. It would not be accurate to say that Lee's general staff were glorified clerks, but the statement would not be too wide of the mark. Certainly his staff was not, in the modern sense, a planning staff, which was why Lee was often a tired general. He performed labors that no general can do in a big modern army—work that should have fallen to his staff, but that Lee did because it was traditional for the commanding general to do it in older armies. Most of Lee's staff officers were lieutenant colonels. Some of the men on Grant's general staff, as well as the staffs of other Northern generals, were major and brigadier generals, officers who were capable of leading corps. Grant's staff was an organization of experts in the various phases of strategic planning. The modernity of Grant's mind was most apparent in his grasp of the concept that war was becoming total and that the destruction of the enemy's economic resources was as effective and legitimate a form of warfare as the destruction of his armies. What was realism to Grant was barbarism to Lee. Lee thought of war in the old way as a conflict between armies and refused to view it for what it had become—a struggle between societies. To him, economic war was needless cruelty to civilians. Lee was the last of the great old-fashioned generals, Grant the first of the great moderns.

Questions for the Critical Reader

1. What is the central theme of this essay? Identify the specific sentences that lead you to your answer. (See Glossary: *central theme; subject; unity.*)
2. Identify the larger issues that emerge from the particular comparisons and contrasts being made here. Which ones seem to interest Williams the most? (See introduction to this chapter.)
3. Do any of your answers to the above tend to deepen your insight into our Civil War? Explain.
4. How much does your understanding of this essay depend on your familiarity with the technical military terms used here?
5. Williams says at the beginning of paragraph 2 that the way in which "Lee is usually ranked" does not take account of "military developments" *after* the Civil War. Then he goes on to take such account in his own evaluation. Is this legitimate? Explain.
6. In the same paragraph, Williams says that Lee was often more audacious and brilliant than Grant as a theater strategist and then goes on to explain why he thinks so. Do you agree with the general principle he uses in his explanation? Justify your answer. Do you, in any case, see this principle operating in daily life? Explain.
7. Do you agree that war is "a struggle between societies"? Can societies struggle with one another without resort to war? Explain.

Rhetorical Technique

1. What would you say was the purpose of this comparison? (See Glossary: *purpose.*)
2. Describe the structure of this comparison essay by carefully analyzing the subject of each paragraph.
3. Apart from the fact that this piece is excerpted from a book, do you think that the structure is an effective one and holds together when viewed as a separate entity? Consult the introduction to this chapter for comments on the structure of a comparison essay.
4. What accounts for the coherence of this essay. Be concrete in your answer. (See Glossary: *coherence.*)
5. How does this author achieve emphasis (see Glossary: *emphasis*)?

Diction and Vocabulary

1. Identify the numerous adjectives used in this piece:
   a) Suggest a reason why there are so many?
   b) Are they effective in every case? Explain.
2. Consult the dictionary to be sure you understand the meanings of the following words and phrases: *strategist* (1); *global strategy* (1); *theater strategist* (1); *field and siege* (1); *tactician* (1); *perspective* (2); *aptitude* (2); *audacious* (2); *improvise* (2); *corps* (3); *legitimate* (3); and *barbarism* (3).

YI-FU TUAN

American Space, Chinese Place

> Yi-Fu Tuan is a professor of geography at the University of
> Minnesota and the author of *Topophilia* (Prentice-Hall, 1974).
> Appropriately enough, the title of his book means "love of place."
> "American Space, Chinese Place" was first printed in *Harper's* in
> July 1974. It is one of the purest examples of comparison and con-
> trast the reader is likely to come across and an eloquent statement
> about the distinctions between two cultures.

1   Americans have a sense of space, not of place. Go to an American home
in exurbia, and almost the first thing you do is drift toward the picture
window. How curious that the first compliment you pay your host inside
his house is to say how lovely it is outside his house! He is pleased that
you should admire his vistas. The distant horizon is not merely a line
separating earth from sky, it is a symbol of the future. The American is
not rooted in his place, however lovely: his eyes are drawn by the expanding space to a point on the horizon, which is his future.

2   By contrast, consider the traditional Chinese home. Blank walls en-
close it. Step behind the spirit wall and you are in a courtyard with perhaps a miniature garden around a corner. Once inside his private compound you are wrapped in an ambiance of calm beauty, an ordered
world of buildings, pavement, rock, and decorative vegetation. But you
have no distant view: nowhere does space open out before you. Raw
nature in such a home is experienced only as weather, and the only open
space is the sky above. The Chinese is rooted in his place. When he has
to leave, it is not for the promised land on the terrestrial horizon, but for
another world altogether along the vertical, religious axis of his imagination.

3   The Chinese tie to place is deeply felt. Wanderlust is an alien sentiment. The Taoist[1] classic *Tao Te Ching* captures the ideal of rootedness
in place with these words: "Though there may be another country in the
neighborhood so close that they are within sight of each other and the
crowing of cocks and barking of dogs in one place can be heard in the
other, yet there is no traffic between them; and throughout their lives
the two peoples have nothing to do with each other." In theory if not in
practice, farmers have ranked high in Chinese society. The reason is

[1] *Taoist*. In a manner of speaking, the Taoist writings have the same authority
with respect to Chinese culture as, say, the combined writings of the Founding
Fathers have to the American.

not only that they are engaged in a "root" industry of producing food but that, unlike pecuniary merchants, they are tied to the land and do not abandon their country when it is in danger.

Nostalgia is a recurrent theme in Chinese poetry. An American reader   **4** of translated Chinese poems may well be taken aback—even put off—by the frequency, as well as the sentimentality, of the lament for home. To understand the strength of this sentiment, we need to know that the Chinese desire for stability and rootedness in place is prompted by the constant threat of war, exile, and the natural disasters of flood and drought. Forcible removal makes the Chinese keenly aware of their loss. By contrast, Americans move, for the most part, voluntarily. Their nostalgia for home town is really longing for a childhood to which they cannot return: in the meantime the future beckons and the future is "out there," in open space. When we criticize American rootlessness, we tend to forget that it is a result of ideals we admire, namely, social mobility and optimism about the future. When we admire Chinese rootedness, we forget that the word "place" means both a location in space and position in society: to be tied to place is also to be bound to one's station in life, with little hope of betterment. Space symbolizes hope; place, achievement and stability.

Questions for the Critical Reader

1. Tuan's point about American homes, which he makes in paragraph 1, is based on the experience of visiting a suburban home. Would the same point hold good for a home in the city? Explain.
2. At the end of paragraph 2, Tuan says that "when he [the Chinese] has to leave, it is not for the promised land on the terrestrial horizon, but for another world altogether along the vertical, religious axis of of his imagination." In concrete terms, what exactly does this means?
3. In paragraph 3, Tuan says that the Chinese have been traditionally tied to the land. Why is this not true of Americans? What is it in our history that accounts for our being drawn by the horizon toward "the future"?
4. Is it true that our nostalgia for the home town is really a "longing for a childhood" to which we cannot return? In considering your answer, you should take into account how you define *nostalgia*.

   The whole question of Americans being attracted by childhood or things appropriate to youth keeps cropping up in the comments of our most thoughtful observers. Read Shana Alexander's "Kids' Country" (Chapter 7), and see if the perspective you gain from it helps to answer or alter your answer to the above.
5. Admired American ideals, Tuan says, are "social mobility" and "optimism about the future":

a) Give two examples of these traits as they are expressed in American life.

b) Are these among your own personal ideals? How so?

c) If you do not agree with Tuan that these result from our "rootlessness," what other sources can you suggest for them? If you agree, amplify the meaning of his statement.

6. What would you say is the central theme of this essay? (See Glossary: *subject; unity.*)

7. How would you describe the point of view here? (See Glossary: *point of view.*)

8. Tuan calls the horizon "a symbol of the future" for Americans. (See Glossary: *symbols.*) Do we have a corresponding symbol of the past? Explain.

a) What other symbols are used in this essay?

b) How would you describe their effectiveness?

Rhetorical Technique

1. Analyze the structure of this essay by deciding to which subject each paragraph is devoted. (See Glossary: *essay.*)

2. What was the author's purpose in making this comparison? (See Glossary: *purpose.*)

3. What was learned from this comparison?

4. Tuan uses a number of pairs of opposing terms, such as "American and Chinese" and "space and place":

a) Identify as many of these pairs as you can.

b) Comment on their effectiveness.

5. What other methods of exposition are employed here? (See introduction to the student.)

6. Which general type of conclusion is employed? (See Glossary: *conclusions.*)

7. Comment on the effectiveness of the quotation (par. 3).

Diction and Vocabulary

1. Why does the author use the word *exurbia* rather than a more common synonym? Is this a matter of connotation? (See Glossary: *connotation and denotation.*) Explain.

2. In paragraph 2, the author suddenly shifts—although the transition is a smooth one—to a second person voice; that is, instead of using "he" or "the American," as in paragraph 1, he uses the second person pronoun, "you." "Step behind the spirit wall," he invites, and then says "you are," "you have," and so on. What is the effect of this shift?

3. In paragraph 4, Tuan uses *sentimentality* and *sentiment*. Make a careful definition of each, and then comment on the precision of the author's diction. (See Glossary: *diction*.)
4. How would you describe the language of this essay on the scale of *abstract/concrete*? (See Glossary: *abstract and concrete*.)
5. Are there examples here of figures of speech? (See Glossary: *figures of speech*.) Account for what you find, both in number and kind, by relating them to the kind of essay this is (see Glossary: *essay*.)
6. Consult the dictionary to be sure you understand the meanings of the following words: *exurbia* (par. 1); *vistas* (1); *spirit wall* (2); *ambiance* (2); *terrestrial* (2); *wanderlust* (3); *pecuniary* (3); *recurrent* (4); *nostalgia* (4).

RICHARD ARMOUR

My Grandmother and My Grandfather

Poet, humorist, and professor emeritus of English, Richard Armour is the author of dozens of books. Born in San Pedro, California, in 1906, Professor Armour has a Ph.D. from Harvard and has taught at the University of Texas, Northwestern, College of the Ozarks, Scripps College, and the Claremont Graduate School. This essay is adapted from his *Drugstore Days* (1959), a richly humorous autobiography. In it, Professor Armour paints a vivid picture of his early days in Pomona—with the characters of his grandparents brightest in the foreground—while declaring forthrightly his own youthful preferences. All of it is done with considerable humor.

1   My grandfather and grandmother were named Elmer and Cora, respectively, and these names themselves suggest how long ago they lived. With a few unfortunate exceptions, the name Elmer has not been given to a boy baby since the turn of the century. Cora never did have much of a vogue. My grandmother used to refer frequently to the Women's Relief Corps, since she was president of the local chapter, and for a long time I thought it was the Women's Relief Cora, perhaps an organization for the relief of women who had to live with such a name as well as with a husband named Elmer.

2   My grandfather was the first of a short line of druggists in my family, a line which started with my grandfather and ended with my father. He had been a druggist, or pharmacist, in Ohio. After looking about for a better way of making a living when he got to Pomona,[1] he opened what was possibly the city's first drug store. Whether it was the first or the second is a fact which can be determined with a little research by anyone who really cares. I have always spoken of it as the first drug store, and as more and more people die off there is less and less chance of my being challenged. Actually, I have an uncomfortable feeling that it was the second.

3   But my grandfather did have the first telephone exchange, which was in the back part of the store near the prescription room, and his own phone number was 3. It could probably have been 1 if he had insisted, but he was not the sort of person to press for this sort of thing. It would have pleased my grandmother, however, and I suspect she made a try but was euchred out of it by the mayor and the chief of police. At any

[1] *Pomona.* A small town in California.

rate my grandfather and grandmother had no trouble remembering their phone number, and all the other numbers too, there being fewer than a hundred. My grandmother, who operated the switchboard and was in no hurry to disconnect herself after she had plugged in both parties, knew a good deal more than people's phone numbers. Most of her information she generously shared with others, especially if it was bad news.

"Give me 26," would come the voice of a telephone subscriber.   4

"There wouldn't be any use," my grandmother would say. "Herb   5
and Mary Westphall are over at her sister's."

"What did they go there for?"   6

"If you ask me, to get a free meal. Herb isn't doing so well these days.   7
Owes the wholesaler more than his store is worth. Has his house mortgaged up to the eaves. If they don't pay their phone bill pretty soon, you won't ever be able to get their number. Well, I can give you 43. That's the Andersons, and they're home tonight. Tom has a stomach-ache. Nervous indigestion, the doctor says, and no wonder, with that sister-in-law of his. . . ."

My grandfather was a shrewd businessman, but he was also exceed-   8
ingly sympathetic and kind. He was a man of slight build with soft brown eyes and a large, drooping mustache which made him look a little like Robert Louis Stevenson.[2] As the town's leading druggist, he attracted the ailing and the unhappy, who could get free medical advice along with a small purchase of cough syrup, sulphur and molasses, or mustard plaster. He also listened patiently to accounts of domestic and financial trouble, frequently being drawn to the front of the store, near the cigar counter, beyond earshot of my grandmother at the switchboard.

Pomona being too strait-laced in those days for bartenders, and it   9
being some years before the advent of psychiatrists, people who wanted to get something off their chest had to choose between their barber, their minister, and their druggist. The last named, available from 7:30 A.M. to 9 P.M., fortified by shelves full of mysterious medicines and unlikely to moralize or rebuke, was easily the most popular, especially when he was as understanding as my grandfather. He was honestly interested, but he also knew that good listening meant good selling. Many a customer came in for free advice and went out with a dollar bottle of Dr. Miles Nervine,[3] on which there was a profit of forty cents.

The distinguishing feature of my grandfather was his lameness. As a   10
boy, he had been scolded by his parents for walking along the precarious ledge of a picket fence. But he had persisted in the dangerous balancing act and had fallen, goring himself in the thigh on one of the pickets. Not wishing to let his parents know of his disobedience, he hid his injury for

---

[2] *Robert Louis Stevenson.* Scottish author (1850–1894). Photographs of Stevenson show him looking exactly as Armour describes.

[3] *Dr. Miles Nervine.* A patent medicine, a "nerve tonic," sold during those days.

several days, by which time it was too late for the doctor to prevent his having a stiff leg for the rest of his life. Actually, his lame leg lent him a certain distinctiveness and aroused sympathy, besides serving as a constant warning to me to keep off picket fences.

11 Gentle and kindly as my grandfather was, he was also a very determined man. Pomanans remember seeing him on his specially built bicycle, pumping away vigorously with one leg while resting his useless leg in a bracket at the side. His one-legged cycling won him a certain local fame when he pedaled in this fashion from Pomona to the Mexican border and back, a distance of three hundred miles, over difficult roads and up and down steep grades. My father inherited something of my grandfather's showmanship on a bicycle, if not his endurance, and could ride down a flight of steps on one wheel. (The back one, I believe.) However, this never caught the public fancy as much as my grandfather's riding on the level with one leg. The family flair for unusual cycling petered out before it got to me, since I have always preferred two wheels and, if possible, a motor.

12 My grandmother, who was nothing special on a bicycle, impressed everyone, and at every opportunity, with her intellectual attainments. She spoke several words of German, such as *ein, zwei, drei, die, der, das,* and *dummkopf,*[4] which she said was almost a swear word. Also she had read, or at least kept on display in her glass-front bookcose, the twelve volumes of *Stoddard's Lectures*[5] and the two-volume *Personal Memoirs of U. S. Grant,* by that eminent authority on the subject, U. S. Grant. Her knowledge of Grant was surpassed only by her knowledge of Shakespeare, whom she quoted whenever one of the half-dozen lines at her command could by any stretch of the imagination be considered appropriate.

13 "The quality of mercy is not strained," she might say, apropos almost anything. Immediately she would add, to be sure of getting literary credit, "That's Shakespeare." Sometimes she would refer to him as "the Bard," and bow her head reverently, the way she did when she came anywhere near the Flag on the Fourth of July. She had once been a schoolteacher, and for a brief period was temporary assistant principal, a height from which she never ceased to look down on ordinary people.

14 She was a large and in some ways handsome woman, with a Roman nose and a king-size (or queen-size) bust. The corseting of those days pulled her in at the middle and correspondingly spread her out above and below. Her bust formed a kind of ledge, on which she could place

---

[4] *words of German . . . ein, zwei, drei, die, der, das, and dummkopf.* That is, *one, two, three, the* (in masculine, feminine, and neuter forms) and *dumbbell.*

[5] *Stoddard's Lectures. John L. Stoddard's Lectures* (10 volumes, 1897–1898:5 supplementary volumes, 1901) by John Lawson Stoddard (1850–1931) were very popular in Armour's youth. They were mainly on travel subjects.

her glasses, her sewing materials, the morning paper, and a package of the large white mints which she ate incessantly.

Her hair in back curled in a series of regularly spaced waves. She was **15** especially proud of this symmetrical undulation and quick to tell everyone, after even a few minutes' acquaintance, that it was completely natural. Wetting her hair and pressing it between her fingers she considered no more than assisting nature in its work. Once, when a very small boy, I caught her using a curling iron, but she said it was unheated and offered to let me feel it, which I was too gentlemanly, or cowardly, to do.

A great many people were afraid of my grandmother, including my **16** grandfather. Perhaps he was not exactly afraid of her, but he liked to keep out of trouble and hated a scene. There was one room on the third floor of my grandparents' house in Pomona, reached by a narrow, steep flight of stairs. This was my grandfather's Refuge, to which he retreated when my grandmother was too much for him. How he spent his time there I do not know, but I suspect he sat brooding, with his head in his hands, or threw darts at a large picture of my grandmother on the wall.

Either because the stairs were so steep or because of a tacit agreement, **17** my grandmother never entered this third-floor sanctuary. In fact I believe all women were prohibited, and my grandfather swept and dusted it himself rather than have its privacy violated even by Jenny. Jenny was a thin, tubercular woman who was considered one of the family, which meant that she could work long hours without receiving adequate pay. This was an ideal arrangement for my grandmother, who managed to keep her busy with cooking and housework and doing things over that were not up to my grandmother's standard, which was just a little above perfection.

In the drug store, my grandfather had no such place of escape. My **18** grandmother would follow him into the prescription room and even to the door of the little wooden shed in the back yard, where she would shout at him through a knothole. He could stay for limited periods in the basement, which was reached by a rickety stairway that my grandmother considered too hazardous for herself and was none too easy for my grandfather, with his lame leg. But it was cold and damp down there, and after a while he would come up, shivering, and take the consequences.

It is no wonder my grandmother dominated my grandfather, in view **19** of her physical superiority in both height and, especially, weight. She was a good two inches taller and at least a hundred pounds heavier. My grandfather could do nothing about her height, but he kept her weight down somewhat with a preparation he compounded in the prescription room. What was in it only my grandfather knew. It may have been something with a gentle and continuous laxative action, or it may have been so nauseating that, after a dose, my grandmother lost all desire to eat. But it was unquestionably effective. While my grandfather lived, my grandmother was stout but not monstrous.

20   However, the formula for the reducing preparation, which might have made us wealthy, went to the grave with my grandfather, and his ample widow, on whom nothing else had the slightest effect, got ampler and ampler. She offered a reward to any clerk in the drug store who could find the formula, and I remember as a small boy how I searched through drawers and behind bottles in the prescription room as eagerly as if I had been hunting for the map of Treasure Island.[6] But the formula was never found, and my grandmother kept expanding, year after year, having tried everything but diet. Diet, after all, was newfangled and unproved, and it interfered with eating, a habit of long standing.

21   The greatest ambition of my youth was to discover how much my grandmother weighed. This should have been easy, except that she weighed only on her personal scales, which she kept in her bedroom closet. Whenever she weighed, she went into her closet with a box of matches and locked the door behind her. She was so secretive that she would not even turn on the light. Several times I stole into her room and put my eye to the keyhole, but through the small space around the key the most I ever saw, in the semi-dark, was a portion of my grand-mother's back.

22   My inability to find out what my grandmother weighed was one of the frustrations of my childhood that left its mark on my psyche.

23   Anyhow, whether because of her size or her force of character, my grandmother was unquestionably head of the house (all but the third floor) and, more important, head of the drug store. My grandfather might be the Proprietor, but she was in charge. As she sat at the switch-board, she could see all of the front part of the store, and could make herself heard by anyone in the prescription room. I have an old photo-graph of the drug store, taken in 1894; it shows my grandfather and two clerks standing behind showcases, as if waiting for customers, and my grandmother sitting at the switchboard, surrounded by wires. She looks like a spider spinning a web, and my grandfather and the clerks, though they smile bravely, are captive flies, held by invisible strands.

24   Nonetheless, my grandfather died a natural death in 1912. My grand-mother cried a great deal, especially in public, and said she wouldn't live very long, with Elmer gone. Somehow she managed to hold on for another thirty-eight years. What she was really crying about, besides the loss of that reducing formula, was the fact that she needed somebody to run the drug store. Not just anyone would do. It had to be someone who would run the drug store and let my grandmother run him.

25   My father, of course, was the very man.

---

[6] *Treasure Island*. The place in R. L. Stevenson's classic novel of that title.

Questions for the Critical Reader

1. Considering the information given in paragraphs 2 and 3, what would you say is the author's attitude toward his grandfather's accomplishments?
2. How much of the interest of this piece depends upon the author's detailed memory of his boyhood?
3. How much depends upon the fact that the period he is describing is near the turn of the century?
4. Consider some of the details given about his grandmother: what is his attitude toward her accomplishments?
5. In paragraph 9, the author suggests that bartenders and psychiatrists are the ones we go to when we want to get something off our chests. Comment on this.
6. What do you make of paragraph 22?
7. How would you describe the author's point of view? (See Glossary: *point of view*.)
8. Is there an element of tone that is something other than humorous? What is it? (See Glossary: *tone; humor*.)

Rhetorical Technique

1. What was the author's purpose in writing this piece? (See Glossary: *purpose*.)
2. Does he tend to use comparison to a greater degree than contrast or vice-versa? Be specific in referring to the text.
3. At what point in the essay does the author's central theme begin to emerge? Can you point to a thesis statement? (See Glossary: *subject; thesis statement; unity*.)
4. What *is* his central theme?
5. Consider the humor in this essay (see Glossary: *humor*):
   a) Who or what is being kidded the most?
   b) What are the other targets of Armour's humor?
   c) Select three examples of this humor, and analyze their bases.
6. Estimate the contribution to this essay of the author's use of dialogue.
7. Do the same for his descriptions of his grandparents.
8. What other forms of exposition do you find used to good effect here? Be specific in pointing to paragraphs in the text. (See introduction to the student.)

Diction and Vocabulary

1. In paragraph 1, Armour notes that the names Elmer and Cora suggest how long ago his grandparents lived. Can you find "typical" first names for your generation? Your parents?

2. Why, in paragraph 2, does the author say "druggist, or pharmacist"? Is the same principle at work as in the matter of people's first names?
3. Consider the colloquial expressions (see Glossary: *colloquial language*) *euchered out* (par. 3); *petered out* (11) and *beyond earshot* (8). Are any of these still current? Why are they used, and what is the effect of their use?
4. How would you characterize the expression *strait-laced* (11)?
5. What is the author's purpose in capitalizing *Refuge* (par. 16)?
6. Answer the same question with respect to the word *Proprietor* (par. 23).
7. Give one example of a metaphor and a simile. (See Glossary: *figures of speech*.)
8. Consult the dictionary to be sure you understand the meanings of the following words and phrases: *euchered* (par. 3); *advent* (9); *rebuke* (9); *precarious* (10); *strait-laced* (11); *apropos* (13); *incessantly* (14); *symmetrical* (15); *undulation* (15); *tacit* (17); *sanctuary* (17).

MICHAEL KORDA

(1) Work. (2) Power.

Michael Korda is the vice-president and editor in chief of Simon &
Schuster, the publishers. Born in London in 1933 and educated at
Oxford, he served two years in the RAF and moved to the United
States in 1958. He has written widely for national magazines and
is the author of *Male Chauvinism! How it Works*. The essay re-
printed here was adapted from his book *Power! How to Get It,
How to Use It* (1975). The comparison in this piece insists on a
close relation between the two terms in its title.

With the exception of skilled craftsmen—a vanishing breed—few people   1
work for pleasure. Most people don't *mind* working, but feel that it's
both indecent and wasteful to *enjoy* it openly.

Half the reason for working at all is the hold it gives us over other   2
people. In domestic situations, work can be used to justify almost anything: impotence, impatience, refusing to wash the dishes, falling asleep
on the sofa after dinner, a whole variety of excuses, demands, and
special pleadings.

Few men are inclined to come home from a day's work and say how   3
much they enjoyed it; there is more to be gained by affecting fatigue,
despair, and tension, as if the working day were a terrible sacrifice on
behalf of one's loved ones.

Women at home have their own way of exacting a tribute from others   4
for work performed: nobody has anything to gain from admitting that
they like their jobs.

Then too, there is always the suspicion that a person who enjoys   5
working may simply not be working hard enough.

It is safer to complain along with one's colleagues, and to hope that   6
the complaints will suggest that one's salary is being earned, and should
perhaps even be increased.

By contrast, people who are interested in power know how to work,   7
and usually work hard. They have a purpose beyond merely making
money or filling up time, because they want their work to lead somewhere, to reward them in terms of autonomy, independence, and self-
satisfaction.

There are three kinds of fool: those who think they can succeed by   8
playing power games without working; those who think they can succeed

by working hard without pursuing power; and those who think power and work are the same thing.

9   Only the person who understands power can extract the maximum benefit from his work, however skillfully it is performed.

Questions for the Critical Reader

1. Are work and power the true subjects of this essay? Explain.
2. Do you agree with the assertion made in the first sentence? In the second? Explain.
3. In your opinion, is it true that "nobody has anything to gain from admitting that they like their jobs"? (Par. 4.)
4. How would *you* define work?
5. Can you distinguish between *work* and *labor*?
6. What does Korda think *power* is? What do *you* think it is?
7. What is this author's point of view? (See Glossary: *point of view*.)
8. From your own work experience, can you provide examples of the three types of *fool* Korda describes in paragraph 8?

Rhetorical Technique

1. What accounts for the series of brief paragraphs employed here?
2. Comment on the balance of abstract and concrete material used in the section devoted to power. How would you improve this section? (See Glossary: *abstract and concrete*.)
3. What was the author's purpose in writing this comparison? (See Glossary: *purpose*.)
4. Identify other forms of exposition used here. (See Glossary: *exposition*.)
5. Account for the coherence of this essay by analyzing at least two transitional devices. (See Glossary: *coherence; transition*.)
6. Which methods of emphasis are employed here? (See Glossary: *emphasis*.)

Diction and Vocabulary

1. What technique is being used by the expression "exacting a tribute" (par. 4)?
2. In paragraph 8, Korda uses the word *fool*, a very strong term of disapprobation. What are the connotations of *fool*? Suggest two alternative words with the same denotative value, and consider why Korda chose *not* to use them? (See Glossary: *connotation and denotation*.)
3. Consult the dictionary if it is necessary to clarify the meanings of *affecting* (par. 3); *colleagues* (6); and *autonomy* (7).

Writing Suggestions for Chapter 3:
Comparison and Contrast

I.

Write an essay in comparison and contrast. In preparing the assignment, select a manageable number of points for comparison based upon your purpose in doing the job. Review the introduction to this chapter to see the possibilities for a structural plan, and then select the one that best suits your subject and approach. Below are listed some possible subjects to use, but you may use others if these are not suitable to your interests.

1. Foreign cars and American cars.
2. A vacation at the beach and a vacation in the woods.
3. A religious person and an atheist.
4. Democrats and Republicans: their respective policies regarding three or four aspects of American life.
5. Two novels, or two novelists.
6. Two movies or two television shows.
7. The styles of two salespeople you've dealt with.
8. Acid rock and folk rock.
9. Your present attitude toward a parent (or parents; or a brother or a sister) and your attitude toward the same person five years ago.
10. Two boyfriends or two girlfriends.
11. Living alone and living with your family.
12. Two bosses you've had.

II. A. Writing Assignment Based on "Grant and Lee"

Williams finds that one of his subjects is "modern" and the other a member of an older order though they both lived during the same period. Using this fundamental possibility, compare and contrast two leaders and see if you can emerge with a similar basic distinction. Your subjects can be the governor of your and another state, two United States Senators, two recent presidents, the current and the former president of your college, and so on.

B. Writing Assignment Based on "My Grandfather and My Grandmother"

Write a comparison between members of one of the pairs listed below. Take this opportunity to do as Armour has done and go back into the past. Ask the parties involved for their assistance in refreshing your memory. Use description, narration, or as much of any other form of exposition as you think necessary, but concentrate on writing a comparison and contrast. To keep things manageable, remember to limit the points of comparison.

a) Your grandmother and grandfather
b) Your sister and brother (or sister and sister, brother and brother).
c) Your aunt and your uncle.
d) Your mother and father.
e) Two of your cousins.

C. Writing Assignment Based on "(1) Work. (2) Power."

Write a comparison between *work* and *labor*. To begin with, you might reread Korda's piece, discuss it with fellow students, and try to come up with a definition of *work*. Then tackle *labor* by making a list of concrete examples of what you consider *labor*.

Select three or four points of comparison, such as compensation, satisfaction, levels of difficulty—or others that seem appropriate to you as you work (labor?) at the assignment.

4

Presenting a Subject
through *Classification*

Classification is still another fundamental way of organizing experience. The human impulse for order is realized chiefly through the appropriate use of categories. On the simplest level, for example, there are weekdays and weekends; classes meet on weekdays; and weekends are reserved for rest, play, and worship. We organize our homes in much the same way by classifying rooms: one for cooking and eating, one for sleeping, one for informal waking activities. We could hardly get through a meal if the kitchen weren't organized so that we could get our hands on pots, dishes, and silverware without a prolonged search. We even like and go to see movies by types—Westerns, thrillers, musicals, horror films.

But these are simple matters. We do not learn anything by making sure that knives, spoons, and forks are in the same place. A more complex and informative matter is the expository method of writing called *classification*. By organizing an essay in this manner, we not only organize experience for easy handling, but we also actually learn something.

This is because the classification of experience is not simply a matter of mechanical division. If we separate 200 people waiting to get into a movie into groups of fifty so that their tickets can be taken more conveniently, we have performed mechanical division. Nothing unites the members of any one group into a class. On the other hand, a real, if very simple, classification of the same group could be made after the show were over. Then the group might be divided according to who liked and who didn't like the movie. If 175 of the 200 liked it and twenty-five didn't, the producer of the film would learn that he probably had a big hit on his hands.

Another, more complex example, of how classification teaches: a town meeting is called for the purpose of discussing the rising crime rate in the town; those present are classified by age and location of their residences. The results show 68 percent of those attending are over sixty years old, and, of this group, 80 percent live in or near the central downtown area—a neighborhood with poor street lighting that is not well-patrolled by police during the nighttime hours. From this effort at classification, we would learn—because we could make the assumption —that older, more vulnerable people are the victims of the rising crime rate and that the principal area in which they live needs more police protection and better street lighting.

The specific system of classification used always depends upon the classifier's interests and purposes. The group we have assembled for that town meeting could be classified in other ways. A town politician might want to classify them according to party affiliation; a social psychologist attending the meeting might want to classify the same group into introverts, extroverts, and ambiverts; and someone in advertising or market research would probably classify them according to buying patterns; and the group could be classified according to any number of schemes, depending on who's doing the classifying and for what purpose.

Whatever system is used, however, a formal essay in classification demands that we use logic and consistency in our scheme. It would be illogical, for example, to classify certain kinds of popular music into jazz rock, acid rock, folk rock, and superstar sound, because doubtless there are many among the first three classes who could also qualify for the last. In other words, one of the categories in this scheme is inconsistent with the others. On the other hand, one could classify superstar sound into acid rock, jazz rock, folk rock—or even more categories.

A few paragraphs back we said that *mechanical* division was not a species of classification. Nevertheless, the word *division* is an appropriate one to use here. It is just the other side of the coin of classification. For example, in John Holt's essay, the subject of discipline is *divided* into three separate kinds; another way to look at it is to say that separate disciplining experiences are *classified* according to source and effect. Lewis Thomas *divides* medical technology into separate levels; another way to look at it is to say that separate varieties of health care are *classified* according to a fundamental principle. We can *classify* sculpture, painting, drawing, literature, music, drama, and the dance as fine art; we can *divide* fine art into sculpture, painting, drawing, literature, music, drama, and the dance.

We should also note that this process of classification/division can become elaborately informative. Hans Selye's essay is an example of this elaboration. To a lesser extent, so is Norman Runnion's.

Finally, the structural plan of an essay in classification depends upon planning and analysis; that is, you must first plan on your scheme of classification and then analyze it to see what kind of arrangement is most suitable for presenting the separate elements. In the matter of structure, the essays by Holt and Thomas are particularly instructive.

JOHN HOLT

Three Kinds of Discipline

> John Holt's book *How Children Fail* (1964) was a seminal work in
> the educational revolution of the 1960s. Since then, he has con-
> tinued to use his writings to turn America's attention toward its
> schools. His seventh and latest book, *Instead of Education*, is pub-
> lished by Dutton. He has taught English, French, and Mathematics
> in elementary and junior high schools and done educational re-
> search in several private schools. At present he is "writing, lectur-
> ing, playing the cello, and working out of a small Boston office with
> a small staff on large issues confronting society." This essay was
> adapted from *Freedom and Beyond* (1972). The subject classified
> here reveals a great deal about human psychology and reflects Mr.
> Holt's passionate interest in the humane education of the young.

The word "discipline" has more and more important meanings than just 1
this. A child, in growing up, may meet and learn from three different
kinds of disciplines. The first and most important is what we might call
the Discipline of Nature or of Reality. When he is trying to do something real, if he does the wrong thing or doesn't do the right one, he
doesn't get the result he wants. If he doesn't pile one block right on top
of another, or tries to build on a slanting surface, his tower falls down.
If he hits the wrong key, he hears the wrong note. If he doesn't hit the
nail squarely on the head, it bends, and he has to pull it out and start
with another. If he doesn't measure properly what he is trying to build,
it won't open, close, fit, stand up, fly, float, whistle, or do whatever he
wants it to do. If he closes his eyes when he swings, he doesn't hit the
ball. A child meets this kind of discipline every time he tries to *do* something, which is why it is so important in school to give children more
chances to do things, instead of just reading or listening to someone
talk (or pretending to). This discipline is a great teacher. The learner
never has to wait long for his answer; it usually comes quickly, often
instantly. Also it is clear, and very often points toward the needed cor-
rection; from what happened he can not only see that what he did was
wrong, but also why, and what he needs to do instead. Finally, and most
important, the giver of the answer, call it Nature, is impersonal, impartial, and indifferent. She does not give opinions, or make judgments;
she cannot be wheedled, bullied, or fooled; she does not get angry or
disappointed; she does not praise or blame; she does not remember

past failures or hold grudges; with her one always gets a fresh start, this time is the one that counts.

2   The next discipline we might call the Discipline of Culture, of Society, of What People Really Do. Man is a social, a cultural animal. Children sense around them this culture, this network of agreements, customs, habits, and rules binding the adults together. They want to understand it and be a part of it. They watch very carefully what people around them are doing and want to do the same. They want to do right, unless they become convinced they can't do right. Thus children rarely misbehave seriously in church, but sit as quietly as they can. The example of all those grownups is contagious. Some mysterious ritual is going on, and children, who like rituals, want to be part of it. In the same way, the little children that I see at concerts or operas, though they may fidget a little, or perhaps take a nap now and then, rarely make any disturbance. With all those grownups sitting there, neither moving nor talking, it is the most natural thing in the world to imitate them. Children who live among adults who are habitually courteous to each other, and to them, will soon learn to be courteous. Children who live surrounded by people who speak a certain way will speak that way, however much we may try to tell them that speaking that way is bad or wrong.

3   The third discipline is the one most people mean when they speak of discipline—the Discipline of Superior Force, of sergeant to private, of "you do what I tell you or I'll make you wish you had." There is bound to be some of this in a child's life. Living as we do surrounded by things that can hurt children, or that children can hurt, we cannot avoid it. We can't afford to let a small child find out from experience the danger of playing in a busy street, or of fooling with the pots on the top of a stove, or of eating up the pills in the medicine cabinet. So, along with other precautions, we say to him, "Don't play in the street, or touch things on the stove, or go into the medicine cabinet, or I'll punish you." Between him and the danger too great for him to imagine we put a lesser danger, but one he can imagine and maybe therefore want to avoid. He can have no idea of what it would be like to be hit by a car, but he can imagine being shouted at, or spanked, or sent to his room. He avoids these substitutes for the greater danger until he can understand it and avoid it for its own sake. But we ought to use this discipline only when it is necessary to protect the life, health, safety, or well-being of people or other living creatures, or to prevent destruction of things that people care about. We ought not to assume too long, as we usually do, that a child cannot understand the real nature of the danger from which we want to protect him. The sooner he avoids the danger, not to escape our punishment, but as a matter of good sense, the better. He can learn that faster than we think. In Mexico, for example, where people drive their cars with a good deal of spirit, I saw many children no older than five or four walking unattended on the streets. They understood about cars, they knew what

to do. A child whose life is full of the threat and fear of punishment is locked into babyhood. There is no way for him to grow up, to learn to take responsibility for his life and acts. Most important of all, we should not assume that having to yield to the threat of our superior force is good for the child's character. It is never good for *anyone's* character. To bow to superior force makes us feel impotent and cowardly for not having had the strength or courage to resist. Worse, it makes us resentful and vengeful. We can hardly wait to make someone pay for our humiliation, yield to us as we were once made to yield. No, if we cannot always avoid using the Discipline of Superior Force, we should at least use it as seldom as we can.

There are places where all three disciplines overlap. Any very demanding human activity combines in it the disciplines of Superior Force, of Culture, and of Nature. The novice will be told, "Do it this way, never mind asking why, just do it that way, that is the way we always do it." But it probably *is* just the way they always do it, and usually for the very good reason that it is a way that has been found to work. Think, for example, of ballet training. The student in a class is told to do this exercise, or that; to stand so; to do this or that with his head, arms, shoulders, abdomen, hips, legs, feet. He is constantly corrected. There is no argument. But behind these seemingly autocratic demands by the teacher lie many decades of custom and tradition, and behind that, the necessities of dancing itself. You cannot make the moves of classical ballet unless over many years you have acquired, and renewed every day, the needed strength and suppleness in scores of muscles and joints. Nor can you do the difficult motions, making them look easy, unless you have learned hundreds of easier ones first. Dance teachers may not always agree on all the details of teaching these strengths and skills. But no novice could learn them all by himself. You could not go for a night or two to watch the ballet and then, without any other knowledge at all, teach yourself how to do it. In the same way, you would be unlikely to learn any complicated and difficult human activity without drawing heavily on the experience of those who know it better. But the point is that the authority of these experts or teachers stems from, grows out of their greater competence and experience, the fact that what they do *works*, not the fact that they happen to be the teacher and as such have the power to kick a student out of the class. And the further point is that children are always and everywhere attracted to that competence, and ready and eager to submit themselves to a discipline that grows out of it. We hear constantly that children will never do anything unless compelled to by bribes or threats. But in their private lives, or in extracurricular activities in school, in sports, music, drama, art, running a newspaper, and so on, they often submit themselves willingly and wholeheartedly to very intense disciplines, simply because they want to learn to do a given thing well. Our Little-Napoleon football coaches, of whom we have too many and hear far too much, blind us to the fact that millions of children work hard every year getting better at sports and games without coaches barking and yelling at them.

Questions for the Critical Reader

1. Why does Holt think that the "Discipline of Nature" is "most important"?
2. He calls this discipline "a great teacher." Do you agree? Explain.
3. Is it appropriate to use the feminine pronoun for Nature, as Holt does? Explain and justify your answer.
4. While listing the positive characteristics of this "great teacher," Holt says "she does not praise or blame." Comment on this attribute: how does it affect learning?
5. In paragraph 2, Holt gives examples of his own experience of children's behavior in social situations. How do yours compare to his?
6. The author saves his disapproval for the third kind of discipline. Do you agree with this evalution? Explain.
7. Consider the example he gives of the children in Mexico City (par. 3): Is he implying that Mexican parents have devised some safe way to train children about the danger of automobiles and we have not? Explain.
8. What does Holt have to say about self-discipline?
9. How would *you* define self-discipline?
10. Do people either have or not have self-discipline as a result of the way they were brought up? To what degree is it possible to develop self-discipline as an adult?
11. How would you describe the tone of this essay? On what does it depend? (See Glossary: *style and tone.*)

Rhetorical Technique

1. What principle does Holt employ to classify kinds of discipline? Or do you believe this to be an essay in division? Explain. (See introduction to this chapter.)
2. The order of presentation of the three may seem to you logical or illogical. Comment on this order: can you think of a better arrangement?
3. Comment on Holt's paragraphing:
   a) Why are there only four paragraphs?
   b) Might he have more effectively created more paragraphs? How?
4. Identify other expository methods. (See introduction to the student.)

5. How does Holt achieve coherence? (See Glossary: *coherence.*)
6. Find two examples of parallel structure, and comment on their effectiveness. (See Glossary: *parallel structure.*)

Diction and Vocabulary

1. Consider the phrase "Our Little Napoleon football coaches." Does this qualify as an *allusion*? (See Glossary: *allusion.*)
2. Is there an example here of personification? (See Glossary: *figures of speech.*)
3. Consider the concrete language used in paragraph 1. Is it effective or overused? (See Glossary: *abstract and concrete.*)
4. The language of Holt's essay is unusually plain and clear, but occasionally he uses a word for its connotative value. Pick out at least one example, and substitute for it a word of similar denotative value. Then see what has been gained or lost. (See Glossary: *connotation and denotation.*)
5. Consult the dictionary to clarify the meanings of the following words: *impartial* (par. 1); *wheedled* (1); *autocratic* (4); *suppleness* (4); *novice* (4).

LEWIS THOMAS

The Technology of Medicine

Lewis Thomas, M.D., is a physician, biologist, educator, and administrator. Currently president and chief executive officer of the Sloan Kettering Cancer Center in New York, he has also engaged in fundamental research of his own. Dr. Thomas is a former dean of the medical schools of both Yale and New York Universities. His book, *The Lives of A Cell*, began as a series of essays in *The New England Journal of Medicine*. Published in 1974, it won the National Book Award the following spring. "The Technology of Medicine" is an entire chapter of *The Lives of a Cell* and reflects Dr. Thomas's interest in fundamental scientific truth.

1 Technology assessment has become a routine exercise for the scientific enterprises on which the country is obliged to spend vast sums for its needs. Brainy committees are continually evaluating the effectiveness and cost of doing various things in space, defense, energy, transportation, and the like, to give advice about prudent investments for the future.

2 Somehow medicine, for all the $80-odd billion that it is said to cost the nation, has not yet come in for much of this analytical treatment. It seems taken for granted that the technology of medicine simply exists, take it or leave it, and the only major technologic problem which policy-makers are interested in is how to deliver today's kind of health care, with equity, to all the people.

3 When, as is bound to happen sooner or later, the analysts get around to the technology of medicine itself, they will have to face the problem of measuring the relative cost and effectiveness of all the things that are done in the management of disease. They make their living at this kind of thing, and I wish them well, but I imagine they will have a bewildering time. For one thing, our methods of managing disease are constantly changing—partly under the influence of new bits of information brought in from all corners of biologic science. At the same time, a great many things are done that are not so closely related to science, some not related at all.

4 In fact, there are three quite different levels of technology in medicine, so unlike each other as to seem altogether different undertakings. Practitioners of medicine and the analysts will be in trouble if they are not kept separate.

5 1. First of all, there is a large body of what might be termed "non-technology," impossible to measure in terms of its capacity to alter either

the natural course of disease or its eventual outcome. A great deal of money is spent on this. It is valued highly by the professionals as well as the patients. It consists of what is sometimes called "supportive therapy." It tides patients over through diseases that are not, by and large, understood. It is what is meant by the phrases "caring for" and "standing by." It is indispensable. It is not, however, a technology in any real sense, since it does not involve measures directed at the underlying mechanism of disease.

It includes the large part of any good doctor's time that is taken up 6 with simply providing reassurance, explaining to patients who fear that they have contracted one or another lethal disease that they are, in fact, quite healthy.

It is what physicians used to be engaged in at the bedside of patients 7 with diphtheria, meningitis, poliomyelitis, lobar peneumonia, and all the rest of the infectious diseases that have since come under control.

It is what physicians must now do for patients with intractable cancer, 8 severe rheumatoid arthritis, multiple sclerosis, stroke, and advanced cirrhosis. One can think of at least twenty major diseases that require this kind of supportive medical care because of the absence of an effective technology. I would include a large amount of what is called mental disease, and most varieties of cancer, in this category.

The cost of this nontechnology is very high, and getting higher all the 9 time. It requires not only a great deal of time but also very hard effort and skill on the part of physicians; only the very best of doctors are good at coping with this kind of defeat. It also involves long periods of hospitalization, lots of nursing, lots of involvement of nonmedical professionals in and out of the hospital. It represents, in short, a substantial segment of today's expenditures for health.

2. At the next level up is a kind of technology best termed "halfway 10 technology." This represents the kinds of things that must be done after the fact, in efforts to compensate for the incapacitating effects of certain diseases whose course one is unable to do very much about. It is a technology designed to make up for disease, or to postpone death.

The outstanding examples in recent years are the transplantations of 11 hearts, kidneys, livers, and other organs, and the equally spectacular inventions of artificial organs. In the public mind, this kind of technology has come to seem like the equivalent of the high technologies of the physical sciences. The media tend to present each new procedure as though it represented a breakthrough and therapeutic triumph, instead of the makeshift that it really is.

In fact, this level of technology is, by its nature, at the same time 12 highly sophisticated and profoundly primitive. It is the kind of thing that one must continue to do until there is a genuine understanding of the mechanisms involved in disease. In chronic glomerulonephritis, for example, a much clearer insight will be needed into the events leading to the destruction of glomeruli by the immunologic reactants that now appear to govern this disease, before one will know how to intervene intelligently to prevent the process, or turn it around. But when this level of understanding has been reached, the technology of kidney replacement will not be much needed and should no longer pose the huge problems of logistics, cost, and ethics that it poses today.

13   An extremely complex and costly technology for the management of coronary heart disease has evolved—involving specialized ambulances and hospital units, all kinds of electronic gadgetry, and whole platoons of new professional personnel—to deal with the end results of coronary thrombosis. Almost everything offered today for the treatment of heart disease is at this level of technology, with the transplanted and artificial hearts as ultimate examples. When enough has been learned to know what really goes wrong in heart disease, one ought to be in a position to figure out ways to prevent or reverse the process, and when this happens the current elaborate technology will probably be set to one side.

14   Much of what is done in the treatment of cancer, by surgery, irradiation, and chemotherapy, represents halfway technology, in the sense that these measures are directed at the existence of already established cancer cells, but not at the mechanisms by which cells become neoplastic.

15   It is a characteristic of this kind of technology that it costs an enormous amount of money and requires a continuing expansion of hospital facilities. There is no end to the need for new, highly trained people to run the enterprise. And there is really no way out of this, at the present state of knowledge. If the installation of specialized coronary-care units can result in the extension of life for only a few patients with coronary disease (and there is no question that this technology is effective in a few cases), it seems to me an inevitable fact of life that as many of these as can be will be put together, and as much money as can be found will be spent. I do not see that anyone has much choice in this. The only thing that can move medicine away from this level of technology is new information, and the only imaginable source of this information is research.

16   3. The third type of technology is the kind that is so effective that it seems to attract the least public notice; it has come to be taken for granted. This is the genuinely decisive technology of modern medicine, exemplified best by modern methods for immunization against diphtheria, pertussis, and the childhood virus diseases, and the contemporary use of antibiotics and chemotherapy for bacterial infections. The capacity to deal effectively with syphilis and tuberculosis represents a milestone in human endeavor, even though full use of this potential has not yet been made. And there are, of course, other examples: the treatment of endocrinologic disorders with appropriate hormones, the prevention of hemolytic disease of the newborn, the treatment and prevention of various nutritional disorders, and perhaps just around the corner the manage-

ment of Parkinsonism and sickle-cell anemia. There are other examples, and everyone will have his favorite candidates for the list, but the truth is that there are nothing like as many as the public has been led to believe.

The point to be made about this kind of technology—the real high 17 technology of medicine—is that it comes as the result of a genuine understanding of disease mechanisms, and when it becomes available, it is relatively inexpensive, and relatively easy to deliver.

Offhand, I cannot think of any important human disease for which 18 medicine possesses the outright capacity to prevent or cure where the cost of the technology is itself a major problem. The price is never as high as the cost of managing the same diseases during the earlier stages of no-technology or halfway technology. If a case of typhoid fever had to be managed today by the best methods of 1935, it would run to a staggering expense. At, say, around fifty days of hospitalization, requiring the most demanding kind of nursing care, with the obsessive concern for details of diet that characterized the therapy of that time, with daily laboratory monitoring, and, on occasion, surgical intervention for abdominal catastrophe, I should think $10,000 would be a conservative estimate for the illness, as contrasted with today's cost of a bottle of chloramphenicol and a day or two of fever. The halfway technology that was evolving for poliomyelitis in the early 1950s, just before the emergence of the basic research that made the vaccine possible, provides another illustration of the point. Do you remember Sister Kenny,[1] and the cost of those institutes for rehabilitation, with all those ceremonially applied hot fomentations, and the debates about whether the affected limbs should be totally immobilized or kept in passive motion as frequently as possible, and the masses of statistically tormented data mobilized to support one view or the other? It is the cost of that kind of technology, and its relative effectiveness, that must be compared with the cost and effectiveness of the vaccine.

Pulmonary tuberculosis had similar episodes in its history. There was 19 a sudden enthusiasm for the surgical removal of infected lung tissue in the early 1950s, and elaborate plans were being made for new and expensive installations for major pulmonary surgery in tuberculosis hospitals, and then INH and streptomycin came along and the hospitals themselves were closed up.

It is when physicians are bogged down by their incomplete tech- 20 nologies, by the innumerable things they are obliged to do in medicine when they lack a clear understanding of disease mechanisms, that the deficiencies of the health-care system are most conspicuous. If I were a policy-maker, interested in saving money for health care over the long haul, I would regard it as an act of high prudence to give high priority

[1] *Sister Kenny.* Elizabeth Kenny (1886–1952) was an Australian nurse who became world famous for her treatment of polio. It consisted of stimulation and exercise of the affected muscles, but its value was limited.

to a lot more basic research in biologic science. This is the only way to get the full mileage that biology owes to the science of medicine, even though it seems, as used to be said in the days when the phrase still had some meaning, like asking for the moon.

Questions for the Critical Reader

1. Is it true, in your opinion, that what Thomas refers to as "non-technology" (par. 5) is "impossible to measure in terms of its capacity to alter either the natural course of disease or its eventual outcome"? Explain.
2. Evaluate Thomas's assertion with respect to "mental disease" (par. 8).
3. What "skill" is being referred to in paragraph 9?
4. Comment on the validity and persuasiveness of Thomas's argument in paragraphs 11 and 12. (See introduction to Chapter 1.)
5. How would you go about checking the validity of Thomas's position on basic medical research?
6. Could the statement in paragraph 17 have been made more effective by the use of examples? If you think so, give some. If you think not, explain.
7. Evaluate the validity and persuasiveness of the argument in paragraph 18.
8. List your experience as a patient of each class of medical technology Thomas describes. Now compare your experience with the points he makes. Does it agree? Disagree? Explain.

Rhetorical Technique

1. Describe the system of classification employed here. (See introduction to this chapter.
2. Do the names Thomas gives to the first two classes seem appropriate?
3. Can you give a name to the third?
4. What was Thomas's purpose in making this classification?
5. In a sentence or two give the central theme of this essay. (See Glossary: *subject; unity.*)
6. How does this theme relate to the purpose Thomas had in writing? (See Glossary: *purpose.*)
7. Which methods of exposition besides classification are used here? Isolate the paragraphs where you find them. Which is most important to Thomas's purposes? (See introduction to the student.)
8. What is gained or lost by Thomas's use of his particular personal

point of view? (See paragraphs 3, 15, 18, and 20 for use of the first person. Also, consult the Glossary: *point of view.*)

9. Give two examples of parallel structure, and evaluate their effectiveness. (See Glossary: *parallel structure.*)
10. Cite two methods by which Thomas achieves emphasis. (See Glossary: *emphasis.*)
11. Comment on the general types of introduction and conclusion. (See Glossary: *introductions; conclusions.*)

Diction and Vocabulary

1. Estimate the contribution to this essay of any slang or colloquial expressions you find here. (See Glossary: *colloquial language.*)
2. Is your understanding of this essay hampered by Thomas's use of technical medical terms that few people can understand, for example, *chronic glomerulitis, immunologic reactants, endocrinologic disorders?* Explain.
3. What is the effect of Thomas's juxtaposing the terms *highly sophisticated* and *profoundly primitive?* (Par. 12.)
4. Consult the dictionary to be sure you understand the meanings of the following words: *prudent* (1); *equity* (2); *intractable* (8); *incapacitating* (10); *therapeutic* (11); *sophisticated* (12); *immobilized* (18); *conspicuous* (20).

NORMAN RUNNION

Species of Students

Norman Runnion spent fifteen years as a newspaperman, starting with sportswriting for the Northwestern University campus paper and including assignments as a police reporter and financial writer on newspapers in Chicago. He has been a United Press International foreign correspondent and UPI bureau chief in Washington, D.C. Mr. Runnion has also served as an academic administrator at a "New England liberal arts college." This essay was adapted from his *Up the Ivy Ladder* (1969). It is an essay in classification that uses satiric exaggeration to make its sharp points, but it leaves the author vulnerable himself.

1   To be a successful teacher—and, later on, to be a successful administrator and college president—you must learn to like students. You do not necessarily have to reach the point where you insist that your daughter marry one, although you shouldn't object either, if she does, because the consequences are her problem, not yours. Your relationships with students should be such that you are not hesitant about inviting them to your house for dinner. Most of your neighbors will not object, particularly if you hold the dinner party at night, when you can draw the curtains. Even if the neighbors do object, the truly liberal professor—which, it is to be hoped, you are—will hold the dinner party anyway. Just bear in mind that segregation of students from the rest of academic society can only lead to deep and unjust divisions which will harm you and the college community.

2   The danger is that you will be so horrified by your initial encounter with students in the classroom that you will be prejudiced against them for the rest of your career. To help you avoid this, we have prepared brief summaries of various types of students that you will meet. To read about students is to understand them. The journey to the unknown is less fearful if the route is plainly marked.

The Student Revolutionaries

3   Everyone knows the characteristics of student revolutionaries. If perchance you don't, turn on the nearest television set and wait for the news broadcast. What you see may either frighten or anger you. This is because you haven't met any revolutionaries personally. Once you get to know them, you will discover they are just like other students except

that ideas are more firmly fixed in their heads. It is to get these ideas out of their heads that many college presidents call in the police with night sticks. This is not the constructive approach you should take to student revolutionaries.

These young radicals are deeply concerned with the state of the world. 4
Looking about them, they see nothing but violence and false ideals. They feel that the older generation has let them inherit a society that is polluted, crammed with social and racial injustices, and beset by totalitarianism and evil wars. They want to do something about it.

"Well," you tell the chief revolutionary on campus, "that's interesting. 5
I feel exactly the same. You and I think alike."

"You do?" he asks suspiciously. 6

"Sure I do. That's why I've gone into education. It's where, I think, 7
I can best make a contribution to the betterment of society."

"Yeah?" he pursues. "If that's so, why don't you join us in our demon- 8
strations?"

"Because," you say, "I don't think violence is the answer to violence." 9

"See!" he reports triumphantly to his friends. "I knew he was against 10
us and everything we stand for."

This will mark the end of the dialogue between you and the revolu- 11
tionaries. You will have been dismissed by them as a knee-jerk liberal, and you never will be able to influence their thinking.

Take this approach instead: 12

In your conversations with the chief revolutionary, agree that society 13
can be reconstructed only after it has been violently destroyed. Emphasize the need for widespread nuclear warfare. Call for the employment of bacteria and germs. Embrace the thought of a holocaust that will leave nothing but a few men and women living in caves. If you are going to reconstruct society to rid it of its injustices, you must start at the beginning rather than midway through.

The revolutionary will admire your grasp of the realities and consider 14
that your dialectical thinking is surprisingly close to his.

Next, wait until he makes a speech to his followers. Then, as he starts 15
to talk, scream "Fascist!" or "Pig!" Get it going in a good rhythm so that others in the crowd take it up. Combine the two words so that everyone is chanting, "Fascist pig, Fascist pig, Fascist pig!"

After a few minutes, pause and let him get a word in edgewise. This 16
is important. You must let him provide you with an excuse for further interruption. He is certain to say, "So this is your idea of free speech, is it?" Start yelling, "Free speech, free speech, free speech!" so that he can no longer make himself heard. Do this for at least five minues; then stop again. He will say, "Now my friends, you know what democracy is really like!" Chant, "Democracy, democracy, democracy!" until he is forced to abandon his speech in disgust.

The revolutionary will be delighted that you believe, as he does, that 17 the Right of Dissent should be both maintained and extended. Because of your actions, he will respect you both as a man and as a teacher. You will have won his confidence by using methods that are far less harmful than police night sticks.

The Intelligentsia

18   These students, according to most professors, bring joy to teaching. (A professor is likely to say this while enjoying a late-afternoon pipe somewhere on a beach with his family during the three-month-long summer vacation.) The intelligentsia are the ones who understand, who will absorb your wisdom with little effort and preferably with no back talk. This, however, is often the rub. The intelligensia can rebel as surely as the revolutionaries, but they do it in the classroom, where it can damage your ego. As bright young men and women, they feel the need to assert themselves at the professor's expense.

19   With an uncanny sense of timing, they can tell when you either have a hangover or are just rereading a lecture—for example, on the political justification of wars—which you had prepared years ago. Then they pounce.

20   "That's an interesting point, Doctor. But doesn't it conflict with what Hegel[1] said about the American Civil War?"

21   "Hegel?" you ask. "Did Hegel say anything about the Civil War?"

22   "Sure he did. It was in the required reading that you gave us last week."

23   It soon will turn out that Gustavius Hegel was an obscure Union private whose letters to his mother appeared in "Some Personal Tales of the Civil War," a book which you had assigned the class to read if anyone had the inclination, confident that no one would. And Hegel thought the army food was awful, which, you are now told, proves that all wars are hell.

24   Your immediate temptation might be to ask on the final examination: "Define Hegel's theories of war." The question would be aimed at only one member of the class, and you would blister him for his lack of logic, his weak grasp of the facts, and his bad spelling.

25   On the other hand you would find it far more productive to take an opposite approach. Open a line of communication with the young man, which needs only consist of walking with him to the student union and offering to buy a cup of coffee. It is quite possible that he will accept the coffee, thank you politely, and disrupt the class even more when he returns to it the next day.

26   If he does, ignore it and try once more to win him to your side. Buy him a coke instead of coffee. The intelligentsia are vital to your happiness, and efforts spent on getting them to like you are worth while.

[1] *Hegel.* Georg Wilhelm Friedrich Hegel, German philosopher (1770–1831).

Bright students can be turned into teaching assistants: they can read and grade freshman themes; freshman themes are the bubonic plague of academic life, and the quicker someone can be found to take them off your hands, the better you will enjoy your teaching career.

The Apathetic

Most of your colleagues will argue that these make up the majority of students at any college or university. Professors usually blame this state of affairs on the admissions office and the president, in that order. (The admissions department reverses this order; for further details, see chapter 6: Admissions.) 27

The apathetic are easy to spot. They affect a slouch in the chair so sharply angled that the student's rear end rests precariously on the very edge of the seat. His shoulders hand over the top. This is known as the bed position; it permits the student to sleep in relative comfort while at the same time occupying space in the classroom and not being marked absent. 28

Sometimes, on opening day of classes, you might mistake the apathetic for the intelligentsia. For instance, discussing philosophy, you ask a student in the rear of the room: "Name a philosopher." 29

"Can't." 30

"Kant?[2] Excellent." 31

If you are alert, you will not the sudden suspicion, the attitude of "What's he trying to pull on me?" that flits through the student's eyes, and you will know that he is a lost cause. 32

The apathetic do have one virtue. Few students are more adept at thinking up excuses for (a) not being in class, (b) not doing the assignment, or (c) missing the final examination. Many a luncheon in the faculty dining room has been enlivened by a barter of the latest excuses, such as, "I heard a new one today: He was skiing, and had to rescue someone, and they were marooned by the blizzard in a cabin overnight." 33

"Yeah," will come a snarl from the next table. "He was with my daughter." 34

Undoubtedly your temptation will be to pretend that the apathetic do not exist as human beings in your classroom. You will be encouraged in this attitude by some of your colleagues, who will tell you: "I've got fifty students, and only five of them have any brains. I aim all my lectures at those five, and the rest can go to hell." 35

You will discover that the argument has merit. If you had to teach to the lowest level of the class, you would provide only a mediocre education to those who deserve better. Sometimes, however, you will find that the apathetic are only scared—of both education and you. If you give them a little extra attention outside of class, you may be rewarded by a 36

[2] *"Kant?"* Immanuel Kant, German philosopher (1724–1804).

glimmer of interest in your lectures. In any case, it will not hurt to get the apathetic to like you and to trust you; once you have them firmly in your control, you can tell them that, for their own good and because you are concerned for their happiness, they should transfer out of your course into something complicated. This way you can both get rid of a hindrance to your teaching and do a disservice to another professor whom you don't like.

The Shaggies

37   A botanist was known recently to have staggered through the hall of a science building, eyes wide, exclaiming, "I saw a bush today."

38   "A bush? You always see bushes. Botanists are supposed to see bushes."

39   "This bush was in my class taking notes."

40   Beards, particularly those accompanied by pipes, always have been a mark of intellectual distinction. There is something about a neatly trimmed beard which implies that its owner has read a book. The hair and beard of a shaggy, however, implies only lack of a razor and a bath. It is unfortunate for those required to lecture in a small, stuffy classroom that cleanliness has become associated with the Establishment and the over-30s.

41   If you want to get a choral response from a roomful of shaggies, you can easily do so with certain phrases:

42   "Kennedy."

43   —"Beautiful."

44   "Pot is good for you."

45   —"Beautiful."

46   "Your thing."

47   —"Beautiful."

48   "Work is slavery."

49   —"Beautiful."

50   "Peanut butter is better than pot."

51   —"Ugly."

52   The shaggies are the great non-conformists of college and American society. You will discover that this is why they grow huge beards if they are men and long, straggly hair if they are women; dress in identical blue jeans and shawls; wear sandals; and talk alike. This not only sets apart their sharp identities but permits them to spot each other in a crowd.

53   Yet don't be alarmed by these creatures. Many shaggies are perceptive students and interesting conversationalists. They also flunk examinations and complain about grades as much as anyone. It is a cruel world, you will tell them. They will reply simply. "But it shouldn't be."

The Jocks

Jocks can be among the most interesting students in class, because 54
athletes can be great moralizers. Possibly this is because games signify
good fellowship and clean living. Jocks usually do not hesitate to make
their views known on many of the great issues of the day. Suppose you
are lecturing on the American Black Revolution, and you have emphasized, with feeling, that America has not done what it could for the
Negro.

"I think you're wrong," says the jock up in back. "The Blacks get a 55
lot of money."

"Oh?" you ask. "Like for example?" 56

The jock's face lights up in triumph. "Black basketball players get 57
higher pay than whites. You can look it up in *Sports Illustrated*."

Few students have more academic problems than the jocks, and it is a 58
situation not entirely of their own making. There have been, and are,
many academically brilliant athletes on college campuses. But some of
them have trouble with their professors simply because they are athletes.

Consider athletes. They are functionaries, as important a part of your 59
college's scene as student unions and fund-raising dinners. If they are
good enough, they will provide your college with prestige, money and
entertainment, for students and outsiders alike. No Phi Beta Kappa bookworm ever packed 50,000 persons into a football stadium. And if the
stadium doesn't hold 50,000 persons, the All-American halfback and his
playmates will be able to pay for a new one if they win the conference
title enough years in a row.

Who would ever think of holding homecoming in a science laboratory, 60
where straight-A chemistry majors performed on bunsen burners? Returning alumni would not be motivated to part with their annual giving
checks. Any normal college, therefore, sets aside money for athletic
scholarships knowing that its investment will be repaid in full.

Some of the money the jocks bring into the college may be used to 61
pay for the printing of the academic catalogue. This will describe the
virtues of a college education, such as having straight-A chemistry majors
performing on bunsen burners. Some professors will believe so firmly
in these ideals that they will be willing to flunk out the jock at the first
chance they get, since the jock represents a prostituting of the Educational Ideal.

They will do this after spending the previous evening shouting with 62
joy as the jock scores 44 points in a basketball game over the arch-rival.
Therefore, take this advice: either don't attend basketball games, or else
treat the jock like any another student.

Questions for the Critical Reader

1. What is Runnion's general attitude toward his students? Indicate what it was in his text that helped to form your opinion.
2. Is Runnion especially sympathetic or especially nasty to any one group?
   a) Is he being especially nasty toward "the Shaggies?" Explain.
   b) What is Runnion's attitude toward student athletes?
3. Paragraph 36 seems to express a mixture of attitudes and ideas:
   a) Do you agree with sentence 2? Explain.
   b) Does sentence 3 indicate the author's special qualities of sympathy? Explain.
4. Does Runnion mean to compliment revolutionaries when he says that "ideas are more fixed in their heads" (par. 3)?
5. Is there a serious point behind the humor of the last sentence in paragraph 17? (See Glossary: *humor*.)
6. Does Runnion's scheme of classification help you to determine the type of college at which he has taught?
7. If you were to construct a classification scheme for teachers, where would you put Runnion?

Rhetorical Technique

1. Analyze Runnion's classification scheme for logic and consistency. Is it complete? Does some class seem inconsistent with the others? Are some students left out?
2. Consider his order of presentation: can you isolate the principle by which he starts with "The Student Revolutionaries" and ends with "The Jocks"? Can you think of a better scheme?
3. To what audience is this essay directed? Be concrete in justifying your answer.
4. Which other method or methods of exposition are prominently used? (See introduction to the student.)
5. Irony and humor are plentiful here: Isolate two examples of each. With respect to the humor, on what do they depend? (See Glossary: *irony*; *humor*.)
6. Estimate the contribution made by Runnion's use of dialogue.
7. Which general type of introduction is this? (See Glossary: *introductions*.)

Diction and Vocabulary

1. Paragraph 17 is loaded with rather ordinary usage—for the period in which the book was written, 1969—but that now qualifies as sexist; that is, the use of masculine pronouns throughout, the reference to

"a man and . . . a teacher" (as if only men were members of that profession), and so forth.

    a) What is your response to such language now?

    b) How could the passage be rewritten to reflect the change in our attitudes?

2. How would you describe the tone of this essay? (See Glossary: *style and tone.*)

    a) How much depends upon the diction? (See Glossary: *diction.*)

    b) Isolate specific examples of word choices that contribute to the tone.

3. Estimate the contribution to the essay made by colloquial expressions. (See Glossary: *colloquial language.*)

4. Consult the dictionary if you do not understand the meanings of the following words and phrases: *perchance* (3); *knee-jerk liberal* (11); *holocaust* (13); *dialectical* (14); *bubonic plague* (26); *apathetic* (between 26 and 27); *botanist* (37); *moralizers* (54); *functionaries* (59); *bunsen burners* (60).

GREG JOHNSON

A Classification of Faith Healing Practices

Greg [Gregory R.] Johnson was born in 1946 and received the M.A. in American folk culture from State University College at Oneonta, Cooperstown Graduate Program, in 1974. The essay printed here was adapted from his master's thesis, "A Brief Survey of Non-medical Healing Practices," and was published first in *The New York Folklore Quarterly* (summer 1975). Johnson's essay necessarily makes much use of definition, but its essential purpose is to classify the various kinds of nonmedical healing. As such, it delivers insights into folk wisdom and culture.

1   Faith healing can be defined as any form of healing practice outside professional medical science which involves the use of faith on the part of the patient. The function of this kind of divine healing is the curing of earthly physical ills through the use of a power which supposedly originates from a divine intelligence rather than from human knowledge, an unnatural healing force directed from supernatural sources.

2   There are two key elements to the process of this supernatural event, the power and the faith. In a general sense both the faith of the patient and that of the healer flow toward the divine healing source. A flow of miracle healing power is believed to return from that source toward the healer and on into the faithful patient.

3   Today there are six levels of nonmedical healing in which this process holds true. They are primitive, emotional, charismatic, sacramental, spiritual, and psychic. Although each of these separate healing levels contains vastly diversified ceremonies, belief systems, and role expectations, on each level the force of faith runs one way and the force of healing power runs the other.

4   The easiest category in which to see this pattern forming is the primitive. Primitive healing encompasses two types: the elaborate, usually involving ceremonies of a tribal shaman or medicine man, and the simplistic, such as the neighbor-healer often found in a close-knit folk community. A good example of the latter is the thrash doctors and bloodstoppers interviewed in Eliot Wigginton's *Foxfire Book*.

5   In all forms of primitive healing the patient has complete faith in the power of either his shaman or his neighbor-healer, and also in the tradi-

From *The New York Folklore Quarterly* (Summer 1975). Reprinted by courtesy of the New York Folklore Society.

tion for which that healer stands. This faith is reinforced by the community's traditional belief system. The healer must also have total faith in his own god or gods and in his time-tested healing procedure. His faith is re-established by the community and tribal traditions of acceptance. All this makes for a very simple and direct line of healing theology, even though the healing ceremony, especially among primitive tribal people, can seem extremely complex. The pattern is one of faith flowing in a straight line one way and healing power steadily pouring back in the opposite direction, a simple up and back process.

On the next level, emotional healing has a more intricate pattern of flow, one that is almost circular. Most forms of nonmedical healing contain some elements of emotionalism, but the term emotional healing refers specifically to Pentecostal and revivalist church healings. Here the great intensity of emotion and anticipation are involved in building up to a spiritual release which supposedly can overcome both illness and sin. (Often in Pentecostal terms sin is the direct cause of illness; thus the release of sin becomes a cure.) 6

At this level of healing, the patient draws power from the emotions of the audience and the volatile goings on around him. The healer plays the role of orchestrating and directing the flow of this extremely vigorous emotional outpouring, which presumably originates from proximity to the divine spirit. Thus the flow of power, instead of being a straight line as in primitive healing, becomes a circle going faster and faster as the emotional velocity of the ceremony increases. The faster the circle spins, the stronger the power of healing appears to become. 7

Charismatic healing, as the name implies, functions through the power of the magnetic personality of the healer. Here, as in primitive healing, the flow of power and faith runs in a straight line. This arises from the many similarities between these two levels; primitive healers often rely on elements of strong charisma to accomplish their cures. However, in true charismatic healing the symbol representing the healer overshadows even that of the deity force, the source of the divine power, because the charismatic has a stronger and more immediate power which is reinforced by the faith of the audience and which often forms a type of "instant tradition." 8

Charismatic power functions as a strong magnet attracting the weaker elements of faith and belief. This is especially true in cases where the patient is depressed and frightened by his illness. In these instances, the lines of faith of the audience and the patient are frequently drawn *to* the charismatic healer rather than *through* him and on into the deity force. Of course the healer cannot stand alone. He needs a traditional belief system of divine and conferred healing power to give his power credibility. But the magnitude of the charismatic healer always appears much greater in the minds of the patient and audience than does that of any 9 deity. This may sound incongruous. How can an individual be greater than the thing that he stands for? But observation of human nature and a review of the history of man's beliefs reveal this strange trait to be a common phenomenon with civilized man.

10   Sacramental healing falls within the organized mainstream church. Today faith healing occurs in such established churches as the Roman Catholic, Episcopal, Methodist, and other denominations. Sacramental healing is characterized by a lack of emotionalism and by an emphasis placed on tradition, especially that of Christ's miracles. Here the deity symbol is all important, for it is the sole source of healing power and the singular focus of the faith of the healer, patient, and audience. On the sacramental level, the faith of the patient interacts with the faith of the audience and the healer. The holy traditions of the healing ceremony (compassion, love and mercy combined in prayer) augument the lines of faith and healing power flowing to and from the patient. On this level the healer (priest) plays a lesser role in the healing process. He often acts only as an encouragement to the patient. All the power is God's and none of it is an attribute of the healer-priest's personal magnitude.

11   Spiritual healing is a rather modern form of nonmedical practice and may be unfamiliar to some people. It is rooted in Spiritualism where it is believed that one can communicate with the dead via telepathy and seances. Here the healer (medium) can talk with departed spirits on behalf of the patient to determine what is physically wrong and what possible cures might be effective. In this type of healing the healer-medium uses a so-called spirit guide, a member of the afterlife world whose knowledge of healing and health is far greater than that of mere mortals. Each healer has one or more spirit guides to direct him.

12   The role of the spirit guide is to act as an emissary between the healer and the deity, a catalyst to the divine healing process. The direct flow of power is present here, but now there is an additional element. Two symbols represent the healer: one for the quick and one for the spirit guide. This inevitably dilutes the patient's power of faith, for he not only has to accept a divine healing power, he must also believe in the accessibility of an afterlife spirit omniscient in matters of good health. Thus in Figure 1 the line of faith does not extend beyond the spirit guide's symbol, because it is the spirit which is performing the actual healing. However, the spirit guide's vast healing knowledge and abilities supposedly originate from the deity force. Therefore, the line of power extends fully from the deity symbol to the patient. Spirit healing is not necessarily on an advanced cultural level; it also occurs in many primitive cultures.

13   Psychic healing is probably the most modern and most scientific of all nonmedical healing. It is also the most far removed from folk practices. In fact, it could almost be considered true medicine except for the small

Divine Force or Diety   ●   Healer   **X**

Patient   **O**   Audience   **D**

Line of Faith   ————   Line of Power   ————————

    The size of the symbol in the diagrams below indicates its importance in each particular healing category.

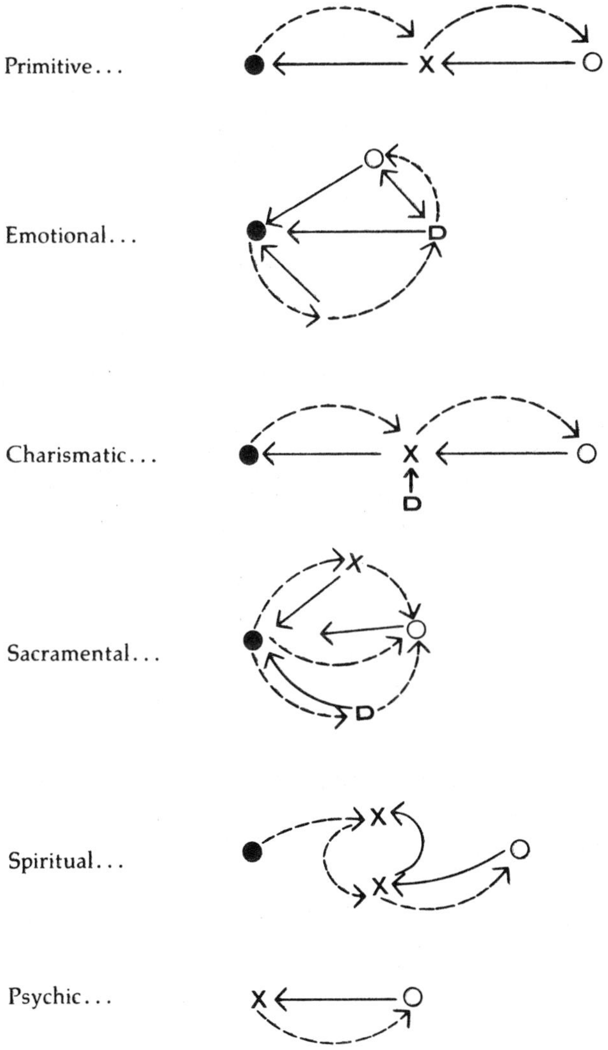

Primitive...

Emotional...

Charismatic...

Sacramental...

Spiritual...

Psychic...

Figure 1

aspect of faith involved. No one needs faith in penicillin to be cured of pneumonia. But in psychic healing, a degree of faith in the supranatural is necessary to effect a cure.

14　　Psychic healing, sometimes referred to as bioenergic healing, is one in which the healer (psychic) concentrates all his sensitive abilities into a state of superconsciousness. In this state he is able to visually observe the energy patterns surrounding the patient's body. These energy patterns, called auras, can rarely be seen by the naked eye, except by certain gifted healer-psychics who have a type of HSP (higher sensory perception). However, in recent studies this aura field around man has been photographed in what is known as Kirlian photography.[1]

15　　The aura field reflects both the mental and physical state of the human body. If anything is physiologically wrong with the patient, it shows up in his pattern of energy, usually as a type of energy blockage or as a weak spot in the pattern.

16　　Upon seeing this malfunction in the aura, the healer can place his hand on the damaged spot and pass higher charges of energy from his own field into the energy field of the patient. This outside energy jolt augments the patient's feeble energy level. In the case of a blockage the extra force helps break the obstruction. After several treatments, the patient's normal energy flow returns and his symptoms are relieved.

17　　The diagram of this pattern of healing lacks a deity symbol because the exponents of psychic healing believe the flow of energy around the human body is a natural force in the universe rather than something supernatural. In psychic healing the healing power (energy) is believed to be a tangible force, which flows from healer to patient, or more correctly from one human aura field into another. But there is also an element of faith, for the patient must believe in something he can't see. Faith makes the patient receptive to outside energy forces and plays an essential role, flowing from patient to healer. The pattern is simplistic, a straight line as in primitive healing but without the god force symbol.

18　　In our discussion of faith and healing power, we have yet to confront the problem of definition. How can they be defined? Can they be measured, seen, or in some manner evaluated? These and similar questions will never be fully answered without proper in-depth study directed at these problems, and at this point such studies are lacking.

19　　We do, however, have well documented accounts from individual healers, each describing how the healing force feels and the way in which the power of faith works. Healers on all levels have portrayed the force as "a cool stream coming from a cylinder in the solar plexus" or a

---

[1] *Kirlian photography.* Originated by two Russians, Semyon and Valentina Kirlian, in 1939, this technique requires neither camera nor lens—only a subject, an electrical current and unexposed film.

"penetrating heat flowing from the hands into the patient's body." Even Jesus describes healing as a tangible force. In Luke 8:43–45, when He is walking through a crowd and is unknowingly touched by a woman with a blood issue, she is instantly cured. At that point Jesus abruptly halts and turns to the crowd saying, "Someone halt touched me for I perceived that virtue is gone out of me." We also have descriptions from the patient's point of view which depict the healing force as "like being hit by lightning," "a thousand needles going through you all at once," "a cool breeze blows over you and then you're out," "an immense peacefulness."

The flow of healing power is induced by the power of faith which is   20
the other important element in the curative process. In general terms, faith can be explained as a confident belief in that which does not develop from pure logical or material evidence. This is one reason why faith healing can be interpreted as an illogical act within the boundaries of a rational environment.

Faith is, according to healers on all of these levels, the essential   21
element which the patient must bring to any healing ceremony. In some cases it is believed that the amount of faith a patient has is directly proportional to the cure he will receive. Thus only those of true faith are made well again.

Like healing power, faith can also be viewed as a tangible substance.   22
In the same chapter of Luke, Jesus speaks to the now cured woman, "Daughter, be of good comfort; they faith hath made thee whole (48)." Thus we see that at least in Christian terms, faith is strong medicine.

Strong faith, no matter where it is directed, can also erase anxiety, fear,   23
and doubt from the human soul. These are often direct causes of many modern illnesses both real and imaginary. Faith seems to have a calming and soothing effect on a troubled mind. Thus in a sense the patient often cures himself by his own strong faith, faith which is stimulated by the efforts of the healer and reinforced by the group traditions surrounding the healing ceremony.

Nonmedical healing, whether it be on the folk or mass culture level,   24
contains many more components than power and faith. There are always rudimentary elements of auto-suggestion, crowd hysteria, thought transference, and subtle forms of hypnotism lurking in these rituals, but the healing ceremony always centers on these two key ingredients. When the balance between the two is right, when the patient and audience exhibit deep, sometimes emotional, faith, then this strange power called healing begins to flow. What this force really is, modern science, psychology, and technology have not as yet determined. Perhaps it is a creation of man's imagination. Perhaps it is a substantial and measurable force. But whatever it is, it should be considered an intrinsic part of both popular and folk medical belief.

Questions for the Critical Reader

1. Consider the last sentence of paragraph 2. Johnson says in the first sentence of paragraph 3 that this "process holds true." Just exactly what does he mean? Is this a comment on the effectiveness of the healing?
2. From your own experience of recovery from illness, how would you evaluate the two elements, faith and power, that Johnson says are "keys" to the supernatural event?
3. To what extent is it useful, in trying to understand faith healing, to make an analogy between the "spirit guide" (pars. 11, 12) and a modern physician?
4. In paragraph 18, what kind of "in-depth" study could Johnson have in mind?
5. Explain more fully—if you can—the last sentence of paragraph 20.
6. Johnson says that the "healing" described in his essay is part of "both popular and folk medical belief." Do any of his assertions match your own beliefs or those of which you've heard?
7. If you haven't already done so, read Lewis Thomas's "The Technology of Medicine." What would be his attitude toward faith healing? Explain.

Rhetorical Technique

1. Read carefully the first three paragraphs, and then consider the title of the piece. Does the first sentence give the basis for the title? Explain.
2. The first sentence is a dangerous piece of definition. For example, it raises the question of whether there are forms of "healing practice outside professional medical science" that do *not* involve the use of faith on the part of the patient. Can you answer that question? Can you think of other ambiguous possibilities in the first sentence?
3. What is the structural principle behind the sequence of explanations? Why does Johnson begin with the primitive and end with the psychic?
4. Does the scheme of classification seem complete to you? Justify your answer. (See introduction to this chapter.)
5. Which explanation is clearest and most vivid? Justify you answer.
6. Which general type of introduction is employed? (See Glossary: *introductions*.)
7. How does Johnson achieve emphasis? (See Glossary: *emphasis*.)
8. What is the value of Johnson's reference to the Bible?
9. What is Johnson's purpose in using a diagram? How does it help your understanding? (See Glossary: *purpose*.)

Diction and Vocabulary

1. How would you describe the level of diction (see Glossary: *diction*) in this essay? Considering that and the source of this essay (that is, *The New York Folklore Quarterly*), what can you say about the audience for whom Johnson is writing? (See Glossary; *point of view*.)

2. In paragraph 3, why does Johnson use the word *levels* instead of *forms*? Is this a matter of connotation? (See Glossary: *connotation and denotation*.)

3. Consider the connotative values of the words Johnson uses to name his categories. What does this add to what you've already learned about the whole phenomenon of faith healing?

4. Consult the dictionary to be sure you understand the meanings of the following words and phrases: *sacramental* (par. 3); *charismatic* (3); *psychic* (3); *encompasses* (4); *shaman* (4); *thrash doctors* (4); *blood stoppers* (4); *healing theology* (5); *Pentecostal* (6); *revivalist* (6); *volatile* (7); *proximity* (7); *charisma* (8); *deity* (8); *credibility* (9); *phenomenon* (9); *Spiritualism* (11); *augment* (10); *attribute* (10); *seance* (11); *telepathy* (11); *spirit guide* (11); *omniscient* (12); *penicillin* (13); *supranatural* (13); *aura* (14); *physiologically* (15); *malfunction* (16); *obstruction* (16); *tangible* (17); *solar plexus* (19); *components* (24); *rudimentary* (24); *auto-suggestion* (24); *crowd hysteria* (24); *thought transference* (24); *lurking* (24); *intrinsic* (24).

HANS SELYE

Personality Types

Hans Selye, M.D., is professor and director of the Institue of Experimental Medicine and Surgery in the University of Montreal and was born in 1907 in Vienna. Dr. Selye, who holds earned doctorates in science and philosophy as well as in medicine, is the author of some thirty books and 1,500 articles in technical journals. His work on the "stress" syndrome is well-known. This essay was adapted from *Dream to Discovery* (1964). It is an example of pure classification, done with the elaborate divisions and subdivisions in which a scientist is at home.

1 Sketches of personality types tend to become caricatures or idealized portraits if you have strong feelings about your subject. I cannot help being prejudiced toward certain types of scientists, I might as well admit it. Some types I love and admire, others I hate and despise, so let me start by bringing out through exaggeration the features that I dislike most in them. Then, I shall draw idealized portraits of the perfect chief and perfect disciple. None of these characters exist in a pure state, but it would take a Tolstoi or a Dostoevski to picture scientific personalities as they really are. These sketches of the repulsive and the divine in the scientists I knew, are the best I can offer to remind us of what to avoid and what to emulate. (Just between us, in myself I can discern at least traces of all these types.)

The Doers

2 *1. The fact collector.* He is interested only in the discovery of new facts. As long as they have not been previously published, all findings are equally interesting (and equally meaningless) to him, because he does not try to evaluate them; any attempt at evaluation strikes him as objectionable blabber.

3 This type is usually a good observer and very conscientious about his work, but he completely lacks imagination. He keeps regular hours, but rarely has any inducement to work overtime. His teachers or colleagues feel compelled to suggest that he should try a dynamic analysis of his findings, but their remarks invariably fall upon deaf ears. For example, he may spend years on a meticulous examination of the microscopic structure of the tiny pineal gland in all animal species to which he can gain access, without ever attempting to perform a pinealectomy or to

prepare a pineal extract in order to find out what this organ is good for. He may conscientiously determine the effect of every newly synthesized steroid hormone upon the preputial gland without ever examining any other effects of these compounds or showing any interest in the function of this gland.

Fact Collectors may find things that are subsequently useful to others —still, I am glad that this type rarely occurs in pure form. 4

2. *The gadgetter.* This kind is closely related to the preceding one. He 5 constantly tries to improve apparatus or techniques and becomes so interested in their perfection that he never gets to use them. Like the Fact Collector, he considers material for discovery as an end in itself. However, the Gadgetter is much more original, imaginative and emotionally involved in his work; he rarely limits his activity to regular hours.

The Thinkers

1. *The bookworm.* This is the purest form of theoretician. He reads 6 voraciously and may accumulate encyclopedic knowledge. The Bookworm is usually very intelligent and shows a great disposition for philosophy, mathematics or statistics; he is well informed about the most complex theoretic aspects of biochemistry and biophysics. Owing to the hours spent in the library, the Bookworn is awkward with his hands in the lab, so he rarely uses them, which makes them still more awkward. He must know everything about his field before starting an experiment and then he decides not to do it after all, because it has been done before or would not reveal anything.

"He who can does. He who cannot, teaches" [George Bernard Shaw]. 7 The Bookworm likes to teach and teaches well. His lessons are highly informative but impersonal. Like the superannuated ballet dancer, he can teach his art to others without being able to perform it any more—the difference being that the Bookworm never was able to perform. He is implacable at examinations, which he uses largely to show off his own knowledge. His superb memory and experience in the construction of indexes and files, often combined with a talent for the clear expression of his views, may become a formidable tool in committee work. The Bookworm agrees to sit on many committees and to do much teaching as welcome excuses for his failure in the laboratory.

2. *The classifier.* As a child, he used to collect stamps, matchbox covers, 8 butterflies or plants, which he arranged in albums. As a scientist, he may still collect butterflies or plants for Linnaean systematization, or he may classify scientific literature, steroid hormones, pharmacologic actions, anything that lends itself to the dispelling of confusion by bringing like items together. The Classifier is closely related to the Fast Collector, but likes only closely related facts that fit into a series. To a certain extent he is a theorist, since he assumes something inherently common in the

groups he creates; but he rarely goes on to analyze the nature of this commonness. Instead, he labels his groups, which satisfies his need in this respect. Among the medical specialities, dermatology has been most intensely subjected to the work of Classifiers. Following the example of zoologic, botanical, and microbiologic terminologies, innumerable minor variants of skin diseases have received scholarly Greco-Latin designations (often embodying the names of the baptizers).

9   Classifiers have had a great share in the creation of modern science. As we shall see, the identification of natural units and their classification into a system is the first step in theory formation. The Classifier has a true scientific soul; he derives pleasure from the contemplation of lawfulness in nature, although he rarely explores further after he has succeeded in putting similar things together. His greatest dangers are the arrangement of items according to irrelevant characteristics, and a plethora of neologisms, sometimes aggravated by egocentric eponymism.

10   *3. The analyst.* As a boy, he took his wrist watch apart (although he could not put it together again) because he just had to know what made it tick. Later, as a scientist, he continued to display the same type of curiosity. One of the purest variants of this personality is the analytical chemist, who spends all his time in the search for components, without giving much thought to the manufacture of new compounds by synthesis. In medicine, the Analyst likes anatomy, histology and analytical biochemistry. (As these Notes show, he may even become curious about what makes himself and his friends tick, and feel the urge to analyze the scientific mentality.)

11   Some analytical work is an indispensable prerequisite for all classification and synthesis; hence, no investigation can have a broad scope without it. The danger lies in forgetting that the only purpose in taking things apart is to find out how they are put together—perferably with improvements.

12   *4. The synthetist.* As a child, he liked to build cardhouses, or bridges and towers out of putty and matches. In science, his synthetic talent depends largely upon certain manual and intellectual skills. The gift for synthesis shows up well in the most varied fields: synthetic chemistry, instrumentation, theory construction, or plastic surgery. The Synthetist is the highest type of scientist, because analysis and classification are only preambles for synthesis. His greatest danger is that he may forget to ask himself whether the thing he tries to put together is really worth having. Synthesis, like all other skills, may become an aim in itself and never get past the card house stage.

The Emotionalists

13   *1. The big boss.* As a child, he was the captain of the team—the winning team. Later he went into science because it has "class." He knew he

could win at this game too, and he was right, for he is the born "Fuehrer."
His main aim is success, success in anything, success for its own sake.
His distorted mind is directed by a monumental inferiority complex,
which he despises, and he must hide behind a self-certain, iron façade.
His deep wounds were acquired early in childhood. They may have been
caused by abject poverty, the ugliness of his features, or social ostracism
of his family because of race, religion, alcohol or crime. In any case he
was determined to get out from down under; he would show them that,
in this big tavern of a world, he can lick anyone at his own game. He
might have made almost the same career in business, politics, or the army
—but circumstances got him into the "science racket" and, being an
opportunist, he wasn't going to miss his chance.

During his early days, as a research assistant, he published some quite 14
creditable work in association with others, but it never became very clear
how much of it was done by himself.

He had many love affairs which he always terminated quite brutally, 15
and finally he "married well," thereby improving his social and financial
position. Being an excellent politician, committee man, and organizer, it
did not take him long to become chief of a research department.

Even now, his greatest asset is string-pulling and making others do his 16
work. His shifty eyes never look straight at you, except to give an order
which he knows will be obeyed. Despite his egocentric cruelty, he is
hearty, in a condescendingly back-slapping way. He is easily on first-
name terms, even with his subordinates, and loves to use jargon. His expressions are hypererudite or vulgar, depending upon the occasion; he
uses them with equal ease to play the role of the remote Olympian or the
democratic "good guy," as required by the circumstances. He has a
prima-donna complex and is essentially a narcissist, very proud of his
"vision for what is important in science," although this extroverted, self-
centered, cast-iron mind refuses to understand the real values beneath
the surface. By skillful participation on the advisory boards of granting
agencies and at the dinner table of millionaires, he succeeds in attracting
a great deal of money to his university. Thereby, he manages to enlarge
his department and staff to a point where he can keep informed about
their work just sufficiently to report on it (though not always correctly)
at meetings with "important people." He no longer has time for the lab,
but after all, he did just as well as the best among the eggheads, the
ivory-tower dreamers, when it came to the tangible status symbols of
research. He is satisfied. But, during the rare moments of introspection—
when he is tired or slightly drunk—he wonders . . . he wishes he had . . .
but no, all he needs is a rest.

As you may gather, I don't like this type very much, but don't under- 17
rate him; one or the other variant of him will have power over you
throughout your life.

2. *The eager beaver.* He is so anxious to get there fast that he has no 18

time to think about where he really wants to go. Being an opportunist and a compulsive worker, he explores questions, not because they interest him particularly, but because he happens to have everything needed for a quick solution. When he is young, he hurries to get on the next rung of the career ladder, because there is still such a long stretch to the top— and when he is on top, he hurries because there is so little time left. Actually, he likes speed for its own sake, as the sportsman does.

19   These young men in a hurry do not love Nature, but merely rape her. They may possess her body as much as we do—but not her spirit.

20   *3. The cold fish.* He is the ostentatiously unemotional skeptic. With his blank face he murmurs the mottoes of his breed: "Take it easy"; "This is not likely to work"; "You didn't prove your point and there is really no way to prove it"; "You aren't the first to find this." His social life is guided by the code: "Ask no favors, do no favors." And at the end of his course we find the epitaph: "No hits, no runs, no errors."

21   *4. The desiccated-laboratory-female.* She is the bitter, hostile, bossy and unimaginative female counterpart of the Cold Fish. Usually a technician, she rarely gets past the B.Sc., or at most, the M.Sc. degree, but she may be a Ph.D., less commonly an M.D. In any event, she assumes a dominant position in her own group, has very little understanding of human frailties among her subordinates and almost invariably falls in love with her immediate boss. She may be very useful in performing exacting, dull jobs herself and in enforcing discipline upon others, but tends to create more tension and dissatisfaction than the results warrant. Some women make excellent scientists, but this type never does.

22   *5. The narcissist.* The embodiment of pure egocentricity, he stands in constant awe of his own talents and is ready for any sacrifice to promote their fulfillment. Each time he performs an operation he relates, to everyone within reach, the incredible complications that have arisen and how they were all successfully overcome. Each time he makes a new (or not so new), significant (or not so significant) observation, he enumerates all the far-reaching consequences this discovery may have upon the progress of science. Sometimes he takes pains to emphasize the great intricacy and originality of his train of thought and the almost insuperable technical difficulties that had to be mastered to make his observation possible. But, curiously, at other times he derives just as much pleasure from having done it all with the greatest of ease, or even by sheer accident. To the Narcissist, the conquest of obstacles and the stroke of luck are equally eloquent witnesses of his greatness. Since he is not unintelligent, he sometimes senses the danger of inviting derision, if not hostility, by what others may consider obnoxiously ostentatious vanity, but this does not faze him. He merely suggests, with a contented smile, that his apparent immodesty is only make-believe, or a charming exaggeration for fun—but of course, facts are facts, and we are allowed to read between the lines of his modest remarks.

The self-assured Narcissist goes no further, but there are two in- 23 secure variants of this type who constantly scan the horizon for possible threats to their prestige and honor:

(a) The *mimosa type* responds to most stimuli by freezing in his tracks and assuming the pouting countenance of complete indifference. He often feels boycotted or left out of things and complains, "Nobody ever tells ME anything."

(b) The cantankerous *toreador type* creates emergencies on purpose so that he may exhibit the manly courage with which he can meet them. "No one is going to tell ME what to do," he says, kicking up a terrible row whenever he thinks someone might question his authority.

6. *The aggressive-arguer.* In school he was the smart aleck who knew 24 it all, and in the research labortory he remains insufferably cocksure. In scientific arguments, he is interested mainly in being right and defends his point by special pleading, using misleading argument or even straight bluff. This is a dangerous variant of the Narcissist; he can singlehandedly create tensions which destory the harmony of even the most congenial group.

7. *The credit-shark.* His main preoccupation is with getting his name 25 on as many papers as possible. In the lab, he constantly irritates his colleagues by suggesting that whatever they are doing was actually stimulated by his own earlier remarks. He may be brutally blunt about this if he thinks he is right, or he will take great care to camouflage his assertions in an air of self-evidence, if he knows he is bluffing. For example, he may exclaim with enthusiasm: "As I was saying just the other day, this is exactly the kind of work you should be going," or "This is a beautiful confirmation of my thesis that. . . ." At the autopsy table, he hurries to a colleague's animals, so that he may be first to point out anatomic changes that anyone would have observed in due course. In papers, he writes long legalistic introductions to prove that, although what he is about to describe has been seen by many others, he is the first to describe and interpret it quite the right way, and his contribution is what really counts.

8. *The saint.* Truly chaste in thought, word and deed, he is the Knight 26 of the Holy Grail. As a boy scout, he vowed to do not one, but ten good deeds a day. Later, he went into medicine only because of its humanitarian goals. At first, the Saint studied tropical medicine, because he planned to practice in a leprosarium; but upon reading Sinclair Lewis' "Arrowsmith," he came to the conclusion that in the laboratory he could do even more for his fellow man. He does not play the role of the Saint, he really is one. And although his self-effacing altruism represents a terrible handicap to his efficiency in the lab, I lack the courage to draw the caricature of such a truly likeable and respectable person. The qualifications of the Saint would have suited him better for the leprosarium than for the laboratory. He should not have chosen the life of an

investigator, but the desecration of icons is in bad taste, even if they do not render special services. In any event, he is only one in a million, so let us keep his image untarnished as a symbol of purity, beyond the reach of our worldly critique.

27   *9. The saintly one.* He imitates the real Saint. With an ostentatiously modest, sanctimonious bearing, he strikes the attitude of the "knight in shining armor" when he speaks about his aims in medicine. His smile is benign and self-righteous; it suggests tolerance and compassion for his colleagues who just do not have a properly developed sense of right and wrong. This type is almost as rarely found in laboratories as the true Saint.

28   *10. The goody-goody.* In grade school he was the teacher's pet; in medical school, he asked the professor, "What are we responsible for at examinations?" After he got married, he became a conscientious bread-winner, but his work as a scientist suffers severely from his sincere desire to give his wife the attention she deserves. He lives mainly for her and for his children and is willing to do (or renounce) anything for their happiness. Despite the superficial resemblance, he is quite unlike the Saint who, on the contrary, sacrifices the family to his moral ideals. The Goody-Goody may be quite intelligent, but his insipid innocence, his complete lack of imagination and initiative disqualify him for meaningful scientific research, and he tends to use his self-imposed restrictions as an excuse for inefficiency. He is willing to sacrifice his career for that of his children, who must receive all the privileges that he never had; the Goody-Goody does not feel that in the succession of generations he is the one whose work should bear fruit. His desires are honorable, but he forgets that he could have fulfilled them better had he chosen another walk of life.

29   The basic defects of the preceding ten personality types are excessive self-effacement or egocentricity and exhibitionism which over-shadow all other forms of scientific motivation. These personality traits, whether morally good or bad, are sterilizing because they focus attention upon the investigator rather than the investigation. Both the Saint and the Narcissist, to take extreme opposites, are more preoccupied with the value of their own conduct than with the progress of knowledge. We may admire or despise them, but their place is not in the laboratory.

The Ideals

30   *1. Faust:*[1] *the ideal teacher and chief.* The pure philosopher-scientist has a religious reverence for Nature, but is humbly aware of man's limited

---

[1] *Faust.* A magician and alechemist, subject of dramatic works by Goethe and Marlowe, who sells his soul to the devil in exchange for power—in the form of knowledge, mainly—and worldly experience. Here Selye uses the name to symbolize knowledge.

power to explore its secrets. He has a profound and compassionate under-standing for human frailties, but his kindness does not mislead him into unwarranted tolerance for lack of discipline, superficiality of work, or any other form of behavior incompatible with his calling. His somewhat romantic attitude toward research exhibits sentiment, but no sentimen-tality. His main assets are: an enthusiasm for the possibilities of research rather than for his own possibilities; respect for the interests of others; a great capacity for singling out important facts; a keen power of observa-tion; lack of blinding prejudice toward man and scientific data; an iron-cast self-discipline, as well as great originality and imagination, combined with scrupulous attention to detail both in laboratory technique and in the logical evaluation of results.

He is neither broken by failure, nor corrupted by victory. Having de- 31 cided early in life what he considers to be worth living for, he follows a steady course uninhibited by remorse, temptation, fear or even success. Despite the infinite complications of his work, he remains a simple and real person; no amount of adulation can turn him into a "distinguished personage."

2. *Famulus:*[2] *the ideal pupil and assistant.* I left him to the last for, like 32 his master, he is the perfect blend of all other types, but in addition he represents the Future. Famulus combines some of the Saint's austere idealism with just enough of each kind of sinful lust to give him the worldliness and healthy appetite needed for an eager and efficient ex-ploration of the world in and around us. The ideal junior basic scientist differs from his teacher and chief only in that we meet him at an earlier point in his course—when he is still less mellowed by experience. His mind is not as mature as that of his spiritual father, still not necessarily richer in youthful vigor. Daring and perseverance in strenuous tasks are qualities we associate with the vigor and strength of youth. Yet, young Famulus may be more cautious and preoccupied with his own security than old Faust, and his less trained mind may not be as resistant to the stress of prolonged abstract thinking. But his body stands up much better to the exigencies of the lab; his eyesight is keener, his movements more certain; he can stand at the work bench for hours without fatigue, and, most important of all, he has so much more time ahead to make his dreams come true. That is why Famulus is really the most important of our personages. But I need not explain him to you, young man. You know him well already. For you want to be he as much as I want to be Faust, though neither of us can ever succeed. Ideals are not created to be attained, but to point the way. It is good to see clearly in whose image we should try, as best we can, to create ourselves.

---

[2] *Famulus.* From the Latin word *famulus* or servant, it refers to the attendant or servant of a medieval magician or scholar.

Epilogue

33 None of these prototypes exist in pure form; their characteristics overlap and many other personality traits may be so dominant in certain individuals as to justify the listing of innumerable additional types. Here, I have tried to sketch only the type of people whom I have met most often, or who left the most profound impressions upon me—good or bad.

34 If we now look back upon our list, we see that some scientists are predominantly doers, others thinkers, and yet others, the emotionalists, so intensely preoccupied with themselves that their interest in Nature takes second place.

35 The ideal scientist is not, and perhaps even should not be free of characteristics distasteful to the average citizen. Society sanctions the motives that are best for the majority, and scienists are a very small minority. Men are not created equal and should not try to be alike. The splendid musculature of the athlete is admired but not coveted by his wife; the scientist's passion for objectivity would be no asset to the nonobjective painter.

36 In my long career, I have met no outstanding scientist who was entirely free of egotism or vanity, and in the single-minded pursuit of their aims, few of them spent as much time with their families or gave as much attention to political problems as the average good citizen should. To my mind, the highest qualities of mankind are a warmhearted attitude toward our kin, and particularly compassion for all who suffer from disease, poverty or oppression. Yet, each of us needs different, additional motivations and skills to contribute his best in the service of his fellow man. My purpose here is not to sit in judgment over good and bad, but merely to identify the basic qualifications that characterize the scientists I know. Such an analysis can help each of us select and reject what does or does not fit his personality. All I can do is to dissect and characterize the parts that I have learned to see, but the reader of these Notes will have to do the selecting and rejecting himself, in consonance with his own needs and abilities.

Questions for the Critical Reader

1. What qualities in scientists does Selye admire most? How do his choices compare with your own?
2. From what Selye says about the work of the scientist and the personalities of those who work in science, does science seem an attractive profession to enter? Explain.
3. Would you say that his personality types are limited to scientists? In what way or ways do his types apply to nonscientists? Do you recognize yourself in any or some of these categories? How so?

4. Why does he warn us at the outset (par. 1) that "it would take a Tolstoi or a Dostoievski to picture scientific personalities as they really are"?
5. Why does Selye give us information about the romantic and family life of *The big boss* (pars. 13 ff.) in such detail?
6. Of this same type, Selye says (par. 17) that "one or the other variant of him will have power over you throughout your life." Do you agree? Explain precisely how and in what areas of your life the big boss will come to have this power.
7. There is a kind of subconclusion given in paragraph 29. What is its purpose?
8. If you have not already done so, read Morton Cronin's "The Tyranny of Democratic Manners" (chapter 1). Then compare Cronin's idea that the boss and the worker are not equal (par. 2 there) and Selye's idea on equality in his paragraph 35. Compare also Cronin's *nice guy* and Selye's *democratic good guy* (par. 16).

Rhetorical Technique

1. Describe the system of classification employed. Is it consistent? Be specific. (See introduction to this chapter.)
2. Are the *insecure variants* mentioned in paragraph 23 and described in the paragraphs following true subclasses? Explain.
3. Considering the information given in the introduction to this chapter, evaluate the Classifier by the information given about him in paragraph 8 and, especially, in the last sentence of paragraph 9.
4. Consider the parenthetical remarks in the last sentence of the first paragraph and in the third sentence of paragraph 22. Are these effective techniques? Explain.
5. Evaluate the technique of using elision marks (that is, spaced periods) at the end of paragraph 16.
6. What other methods of exposition are used here? Are they effective? (See introduction to the student.)
7. How does Selye achieve emphasis (see Glossary: *emphasis*)?
8. Give at least one example of parallel structure, and evaluate its effectiveness (see Glossary: *parallel structure*).
9. Which general types of introduction and conclusion are used here? Are they effective? Does it help or hinder your understanding that Selye has waited until the conclusion to state his purpose? (See Glossary: *introductions; conclusions*.)
10. What is Selye's point of view? What audience is he addressing? (See Glossary: *point of view*.)
11. How would you describe the tone of this essay? (See Glossary: *style and tone*.)

Diction and Vocabulary

1. The labels Selye gives to each type he describes are all analogies (see Glossary: *analogy*). How effective are these? Can you think of better ones?

2. Consider the following expressions: *fall upon deaf ears* (par. 3); *what made it tick* (10); *string-pulling* (16); *eager beaver* (18); *smart aleck* (24); *teacher's pet* (28). Find as many others as you can that resemble these and then, after consulting the Glossary entry for *colloquial language*, classify all of them into *cliché, slang, colloquial language*, or another category of your own devising. Could the essay have been improved if some of these had been eliminated? More added? How do they contribute to the tone of the essay? (See Glossary: *style and tone*.)

3. Consult the Glossary entry for *figures of speech*, and then analyze the whole of paragraph 19 for specific types.

4. Isolate at least one example of metaphor that is *not* in paragraph 19. (See Glossary: *figures of speech*.)

5. In paragraph 16, Selye uses the phrase *cast-iron mind* and in paragraph 30, *iron-cast discipline*. Why the reversal?

6. Consider the connotative values of *brutally* (par. 15) and *cruelty* (par. 16). Substitute more denotative terms for these and estimate what has been gained or lost in the process. (See Glossary: *connotation and denotation*.)

7. Consult the dictionary to be sure you understand the meanings of the following words and phrases: *caricatures, exaggeration, disciple, idealized, emulate* (par. 1); *inducement, meticulous, pineal gland, pinealectomy, synthesized, steroid hormone, preputial gland* (3); *voraciously, encyclopedic, disposition* (6); *superannuated, implacable, formidable* (7); *Linnaean systematization, pharmacologic, dispelling, inherently, dermotology, variants, designations* (8); *irrelevant, plethora, neologisms, aggravated, egocentric, eponymism* (9); *histology* (10); *indispensable, prerequisites* (11); *ostracism* (13); *jargon, hypererudite, prima-donna, narcissist, extroverted, tangible, introspection* (16); *opportunist, compulsive* (18); *ostentatiously, skeptic* (20); *enumerate, intricacy, insuperable, derision* (22); *mimosa, cantankerous, toreador* (23); *insufferably cocksure, congenial* (24); *camouflage* (25); *leprosarium, self-effacing altruism, desecration, icons, render* (26); *sanctimonious, benign* (27); *conscientious, insipid, initiative* (28); *self-effacement, exhibitionism* (29); *superficiality, scrupulous* (30); *uninhibited, adulation* (31); *exigencies* (32); *sanctions* (35); *in consonance* (36).

8. What does the preceding long list of fairly difficult words indicate about the tone of the essay? (See Glossary: *style and tone*.)

Writing Suggestions for Chapter 4: *Classification*

I.

Write an essay in classification/division. After selecting a subject that interests you, you should adopt a scheme of classification. In any case, you should make your classification into at least three categories. Listed below are a number of possible subjects. In parentheses after each are suggestions on how to classify/divide them.

1. American heroes (by what they risk; by what their exploits teach or inspire).
2. TV watchers (by their programming preferences; attitudes as they watch; and so on).
3. Money (by its uses; by how it corrupts).
4. Marriages (by what the relationship means to the respective parties).
5. Comedians (by style—what they make fun of and how).
6. Bores (by the things that make them boring).
7. Campus clotheshorses (by what they hope their clothes will say about them).
8. Roommates (by styles of relating to their roommates).
9. Inventions (by the kinds of impact they have had on mankind or on you personally).
10. Exercise freaks (by degree of fanaticism; by motives).

II. A. Writing Assignment Based on "Species of Students"

Write an essay using Runnion's as a model. But turn the tables, and classify teachers into types. Use your considerable experience with teachers at all levels of schooling. Keep your tongue in your cheek, but don't lose sight of your serious purposes, that is, your effort to make useful categories. Some suggested character types (by one of the characters): The General, The Joker, The Actor, The "Pal," The Cynic. You fill in the details.

B. Writing Assignment Based on "The Technology of Medicine"

Write an essay in classification after studying the things that contribute to your own health. Make a list of everything that either makes you sick or enhances your good health. See if these fit into categories. Write an essay describing these categories, and give us good concrete examples in each category.

5

Making a Clear *Definition*

Dictionaries offer two kinds of definitions. The first kind clarifies the meaning of words on which there is a fair amount of agreement. The second type makes a number of subtle distinctions between meanings and shades of meanings. The reason for these two types of dictionary entry is a characteristic of language known as *connotation* and *denotation*. The denotation of a word is the thing it explicitly names. A *table*, for example, is an object having a flat surface resting on legs or a pedestal. The word *table*, however, can suggest other shades of meaning, for example, eating, working, or any of the things we can associate with its uses. *Submarine* denotes an underwater boat; but it may also connote warfare, stealth, and a number of other things as well. Nevertheless, both *table* and *submarine* are essentially denotative terms. We can pretty much agree on what they mean.

We can also agree pretty much on the meanings of certain connotative words. For example, although the word *cancer* is highly connotative for most of us, it is essentially denotative. Other words in this class are words like *home* and *mother*.

But there is another, much larger, class of connotative words on whose meanings we cannot agree too easily. And it is this class of words that calls for the form of exposition known as *extended definition*. We need to spend time defining these words in public—by writing about them—because the shades of meaning attaching to them are more extensive than the things they explicitly name. Words like *democracy* and *communism, freedom* and *religion* are important in the social world because they are continually being redefined by a natural social process of thought, discussion, and action. We all know what those four words mean—denotatively—but the additional shades of meaning possessed by each are crucial to the question of how we live our lives. We cannot take a meaningful part in this process unless, as social beings, we are more or less constantly engaged in the reexamination and redefinition of crucial connotative words.

Thus a *group*, which we may once have thought to be a loose association of like-minded persons, becomes in Kaplan and Schwerner's definition a matter of deep seriousness, involving as it does the surrender of individual ideals to those of the group. By enriching language, extended definition enriches thought and extends human possibilities.

In writing an extended definition, we may use a number of techniques. Peculiar to definition are two of these. For example, we can simply recount the experiences that the word denotes, as George Orwell does in "Poverty." Or, we could, as Kaplan and Schwerner do in "Group," distinguish between numbers of animals ("herds and packs") and numbers of people ("groups," which are feasible between those who have "evolved a necessity to maintain ideals"). The latter technique is essentially *classification*. It follows the forms of the sentence, "A president is a head of state whose power derives from popular election," where *president* is the word to be defined, "heads of state" is a class, and "power derives from popular election" is one of its subclasses.

Similarly, the other techniques we have been using in this book are also useful in making definitions. To define *tyrant*, for example, a list of them and their behaviors would be an appropriate definition. In this way, we would be using *illustrative examples*—as Irving Kristol does in "What Is A 'Neo-Conservative'?" *Freedom* and *slavery* might each be defined by comparing and contrasting them. And the *process* by which *attitudes* are formed would be an adequate definition of that difficult word. But there are also others. By arguing "In Defense of Flirting," Anne Taylor Fleming gives a cutting edge to her definition.

Like the reader of a dictionary entry, the reader of an extended definition seeks accuracy in the definition. For definitions can be too broad or too narrow. For example, the definition of a closet as a small, enclosed space in the home where clothes are kept is too narrow a definition because it fails to account for the many other kinds of closets (linen, storage, sewing, and so on). Conversely, the statement that democracy is a form of government may be true, but it is not an accurate definition because "form of government," the definer, is much larger than "democracy," the word to be defined; therefore, such a definition is too broad.

The structure of an extended definition follows any number of patterns, depending on what is being defined. Planning and thought usually isolate the one most suitable to the writer's purposes.

GEORGE ORWELL

Poverty

> George Orwell is the pseudonym of Eric Arthur Blair (1903–1950),
> an English novelist and essayist whose passionate interest in politics
> and the oppressed made him into a figure who disturbed the con-
> science of the twentieth century. It was Orwell's novel of the
> future, *Nineteen Eighty-Four* (1949), that lent the phrase to the
> English language. Among his best-known works are *Burmese Days*
> (1935), *Homage To Catalonia* (1938), *Animal Farm* (1945), and
> *Shooting an Elephant* (1950). This essay, a definition arrived at
> through agonizing firsthand experience, was adapted from his
> *Down and Out in Paris and London* (1933).

It is altogether curious, your first contact with poverty. You have
thought so much about poverty—it is the thing you have feared all your
life, the thing you knew would happen to you sooner or later; and it is
all so utterly and prosaically different. You thought it would be quite
simple; it is extraordinarily complicated. You thought it would be
terrible; it is merely squalid and boring. It is the peculiar *lowness* of
poverty that you discover first; the shifts[1] that it puts you to, the complicated meanness, the crust-wiping.[2]

You discover, for instance, the secrecy attaching to poverty. At a
sudden stroke you have been reduced to an income of six francs[3] a day.
But of course you dare not admit it—you have got to pretend that you
are living quite as usual. From the start it tangles you in a net of lies,
and even with the lies you can hardly manage it. You stop sending
clothes to the laundry, and the laundress catches you in the street and
asks you why; you mumble something, and she, thinking you are sending the clothes elsewhere, is your enemy for life. The tobacconist keeps
asking why you have cut down your smoking. There are letters you
want to answer, and cannot, because stamps are too expensive. And
then there are your meals—meals are the worst difficulty of all. Every
day at meal-times you go out, ostensibly to a restaurant, and loaf an

[1] *shifts.* British usage. A shift is an expedient or device, a way of managing in
spite of difficulties.

[2] *crust-wiping.* British usage. Adopting a different posture or attitude.

[3] *francs.* The unit of French currency. The rate of exchange in 1976 was about
4½ francs to the dollar. At the time Orwell writes of, the franc was worth about
3 cents.

hour in the Luxembourg Gardens,[4] watching the pigeons. Afterwards you smuggle your food home in your pockets. Your food is bread and margarine, or bread and wine, and even the nature of the food is governed by lies. You have to buy rye bread instead of household bread, because the rye loaves, though dearer, are round and can be smuggled in your pockets. This wastes you a franc a day. Sometimes, to keep up appearances, you have to spend sixty centimes[5] on a drink, and go correspondingly short of food. Your linen gets filthy, and you run out of soap and razor-blades. Your hair wants cutting, and you try to cut it yourself, with such fearful results that you have to go the barber after all, and spend the equivalent of a day's food. All day you are telling lies, and expensive lies.

3   You discover the extreme precariousness of your six francs a day. Mean disasters happen and rob you of food. You have spent your last eighty centimes on half a litre[6] of milk, and are boiling it over the spirit lamp. While it boils a bug runs down your forearm; you give the bug a flick with your nail, and it falls, plop! straight into the milk. There is nothing for it but to throw the milk away and go foodless.

4   You go to the baker's to buy a pound of bread, and you wait while the girl cuts a pound for another customer. She is clumsy, and cuts more than a pound. *"Pardon, monsieur,"*[7] she says, "I suppose you don't mind paying two sous[8] extra?" Bread is a franc a pound, and you have exactly a franc. When you think that you too might be asked to pay two sous extra, and would have to confess that you could not, you bolt in panic. It is hours before you dare venture into a baker's shop again.

5   You go to the greengrocer's[9] to spend a franc on a kilogram[10] of potatoes. But one of the pieces that make up the franc is a Belgium piece, and the shopman refuses it. You slink out of the shop, and can never go there again.

6   You have strayed into a respectable quarter, and you see a prosperous friend coming. To avoid him you dodge into the nearest café. Once in the café you must buy something, so you spend your last fifty centimes on a glass of black coffee with a dead fly in it. One could multiply these disasters by the hundred. They are part of the process of being hard up.

7   You discover what it is like to be hungry. With bread and margarine in your belly, you go out and look into the shop windows. Everywhere there is food insulting you in huge, wasteful piles; whole dead pigs, baskets of hot loaves, great yellow blocks of butter, strings of sausages, mountains of potatoes, vast Gruyère cheeses like grindstones. A snivel-

---

[4] *Luxembourg Gardens.* A park on the Left Bank in Paris.
[5] *centimes.* One hundred centimes = one franc.
[6] *litre.* Also spelled *liter.* One litre = 1.057 quarts.
[7] *"Pardon, Monsieur."* Excuse me, sir.
[8] *sous.* A sou is a five-centime piece.
[9] *greengrocer's.* A store that retails fresh fruits and vegetables.
[10] *kilogram.* One kilogram = 1.1 pounds.

ling self-pity comes over you at the sight of so much food. You plan to grab a loaf and run, swallowing it before they catch you; and you refrain, from pure funk.[11]

You discover the *boredom* which is inseparable from poverty; the **8** times when you have nothing to do and, being underfed, can interest yourself in nothing. For half a day at a time you lie on your bed, feeling like the *jeune squelette* in Baudelaire's poem.[12] Only food could rouse you. You discover that a man who has gone even a week on bread and margarine is not a man any longer, only a belly with a few accessory organs.

This—one could describe it further, but it is all in the same style—is **9** life on six francs a day. Thousands of people in Paris live it—struggling artists and students, prostitutes when their luck is out, out-of-work people of all kinds. It is the suburbs, as it were, of poverty.

Questions for the Critical Reader

1. Consider carefully what the author says in the introductory first paragraph, and, on the basis of the information you gather there, build up a picture of him.
2. Where is "home" for Orwell? (See par. 2)
3. Comment on the examples of secrecy given in paragraph 2. Are they effective? Are these things generally true of persons living in poverty, or are they peculiar to Orwell's special situation? Is it necessary, in your view, to tell the lies that Orwell, at the end of this paragraph, says it is necessary to tell?
4. If you have experienced poverty, compare your experiences to Orwell's.
5. If you have ever been hungry—not just at mealtimes but in the sense that Orwell means hungry—compare your experiences to his.
6. What does paragraph 3 tell you about Orwell? Compare this with what you learn about him from paragraphs 4 and 5. Are these qualities special to Orwell? Or do they apply to all who live in poverty?
7. What does he mean by "respectable quarter"? What can you infer from this about poverty?
8. If what Orwell has been describing is something he calls at the end "the suburbs of poverty," describe what might be called the *inner city* of poverty.
9. How would you describe the tone of this essay? (See Glossary: *style and tone.*)
10. On what does this tone depend?

[11] *funk.* British usage. Lack of energy.
[12] *jeune squelette.* The poem is number 88 in the poet's *Spleen et Idéal,* and the French words mean "young skeleton."

Rhetorical Technique

1. Which method of extended definition is employed here?
2. If you haven't already done so, read "Group." Then compare the method Orwell uses with the method used there, and list the advantages and disadvantages of each.
3. Describe the point of view Orwell writes from. (See Glossary: *point of view.*) Comment on its effectiveness considering the subject matter.
4. Which other methods of exposition are employed here? (See Introduction to the Student.)
5. How does Orwell achieve emphasis? Cite at least two examples. (See Glossary: *emphasis.*)
6. How does he achieve coherence? (See Glossary: *coherence.*)
7. For what special purpose does Orwell use the word *discover*? Comment on the effectiveness of this usage. (See Glossary: *purpose.*)

Diction and Vocabulary

1. What are the connotations of the word *curious* as Orwell employs it in paragraph 1? What do these tell you about the author's state of mind? (See Glossary: *connotation and denotation.*)
2. How does Orwell define *lowness*? Does it differ from your own definition of the word?
3. Does Orwell use metaphor or simile? Comment on his use of figurative language in general. (See Glossary: *figures of speech.*)
4. In indicating weights, Orwell usese both *kilogram* and *pound.* Can you think of a reason why he might have chosen to do so, or was it just carelessness?
5. Consult the dictionary to be sure you understand the meanings of the following words and phrases: *prosaically* (par. 1); *squalid* (1); *dearer* (2); *ostensibly* (2); *spirit lamp* (3).

ANNE TAYLOR FLEMING

In Defense of Flirting

Anne Taylor Fleming lives in Los Angeles, where she was born and
went to school. A free-lance journalist, she has published widely in
national magazines and, with her husband Karl, is coauthor of
The First Time (1975), a report of the first sexual encounters of 28
prominent Americans. The essay printed here was first published
in *Newsweek* (April 26, 1976). It contains a good deal of biographical material, Ms. Fleming's firsthand experience; it also has an
argumentative edge, contrasting flirting favorably with more recent
sexual manners. In the course of the writing, however, there is a
first-rate definition of the thing itself.

There was, I think, only a brief period in my life when I actually turned   1
heads. It was the summer of my seventeenth year when, newly graduated
from a private girls' school, I was in that transition stage between being
an old child and a young woman, a state of half and half that men of all
ages apparently find disarmingly erotic. I guess each one looking at such
a wobbly almost-woman fancies that he shall be the first. It was that
summer that I learned to flirt with the opposite sex. I learned a whole
host of new smiles with which to invite, or fend off, the attentions of my
sudden suitors: the shy smile, the half-smile, the serious smile, the
come-on smile, the go-away smile. I learned when to use each one and
when not to. I understood for the first time that if I wore white against
my summer skin I was much more appealing than if I wore red or
green or any other color. So I wore white.

It was as if I had suddenly caught on to some very complicated and   2
subtle dance steps. From then on those steps were part of my act. From
then on flirting was just something I did when I bumped into someone
who was male; it seemed to soften the edges of our collision. It made
things easier, nicer, gentler, and certainly more fun.

Touchless Touching

Right from the beginning I understood that flirting had its own rules   3
and its own chivalry. I knew I should not flirt a serious favor out of
someone; a small favor was OK. I knew that I must not as a woman
abuse my privilege to flirt, that I should not flirt to inflame the jealousy
of a present love or to tease the passion of a prospective one. Then
flirting became a weapon and to my mind just wasn't flirting any more.
To me flirting was the delicate eye-play, talk-play, touchless touching

by which I could show affection or approval for someone else, tell him
he was pleasing to me, without promising anything or hurting anyone.

4   Those days of delicate flirtation are apparently over. Flirting is a
casualty of the two great revolutions of our times: the women's liberation movement and the so-called sexual revolution. Women seeking their
liberation cast a cold eye on flirting and found it to be sexist, divisive,
demeaning, role-playing and otherwise ugly and useless. With men they
would be straight, demanding, fair, nonfrivolous—no games, no lowered
lids, no blushing cheeks, no sleight of hand or eye. They would get their
jobs, and their sex, on merit.

5   A friend of mine once told me that before she finished college she
intended as a matter of course to sleep with all of her friends. She wasn't
talking about just the friends she loved or lusted for; she was talking
about all those chums one studied with past many midnights, those
steady, stolid friends with whom one debated through endless hours over
endless cups of weak cafeteria coffee the fate or state of the world. These,
one after the other, like taking required courses for her major, she would
sleep with.

Matter-of-fact Sex

6   I remember feeling slightly sick when she told me. It all sounded so cold-
blooded, so listless, so lustless, so totally without flirtation. I had a deep
fear of ending up in bed with someone for whom I felt no passion or
desire. That to me was really dirty. And flirting, it seemed, was a way of
protecting myself from that kind of nonpassionate sex, a way of trying
out my lust before bedding—like trying out a play in Boston before
opening on Broadway.

7   I understand that for my college girlfriend, as for many other women,
bedding with friends was a safe starting place, a way of stretching one's
limbs after a long winter. And, of course, by the time I was in college in
the late '60s, the sexual revolution was in full swing and bed-hopping
was *de rigueur*. If flirting was offensive to the fledgling feminists among
us, to the free lovers and flower children it was child's play. Bed was for
the asking anytime anywhere. I remember a typical college party where
there was a lot of drink and a lot of dope, then a lot of sex and a boy I
knew ended up in the arms of a woman with whom he had shared a
house for more than a year, a woman he said he regarded as a sister,
not as a sex partner. Why, I asked him the next day, had they finally
shared a bed? "Well," he said simply, "someone had to sleep with her."

8   Clearly this was a different world from the one into which I awakened
that summer when I was 17, when shy smiles and tentative touches were
the limits to sex. This new world was a world of matter-of-fact, purposeful sex where flirting was no more than frivolous and unnecessary fore-
play.

Goo-Goo Eyes

Perhaps flirting is only possible in a society of definite limits and thwarted lusts, the kind of society, for example, that nurtured the Southern belle. Obviously, I don't want to have all the limitations back. I'm as grateful as any woman for my freedoms. But now that my body is somewhat unbuckled and my consciousness reasonably raised I would very much like to be able to flirt with immunity again. Flirting is evocative of tenderer times in all of our lives and of tenderer times in the lives of our marriages. I miss those times. I still think making goo-goo eyes (there is no dignified way to say it) at someone and having them made back at me is nicely sexy—and safe. 9

I've discovered that I really don't want to talk to, let alone touch, most people, and flirting is a way of being affable, even affectionate, even slightly wicked without having to do either. It's a way of saying maybe, and I've always been a sucker for the romance of the near miss. 10

Questions for the Critical Reader

1. In paragraph 4, Fleming asserts, regarding her teen-age experience, that "those days of delicate flirtation are apparently over":
   a) Comment on the qualification "apparently."
   b) Do you agree with her on this point? Explain.
2. Is it possible that Fleming's sense that flirtation is gone is really a comment on her growing up, that flirting is really limited to the very young?
3. If the women's liberation movement is, as Fleming claims, against flirting, give reasons for their attitude.
4. Fleming suggests, especially in paragraph 5, that the attitude of those who are matter-of-fact about sex is "without flirtation." Do you agree? Justify your answer.
5. a) Are you flirtatious?
   b) If you are, what rules do you follow?
   c) If you aren't, what is your attitude?
6. What does Fleming mean by her reference to "the kind of society . . . that nurtured the Southern belle"?

Rhetorical Technique

1. Which methods of definition do you find used in this essay?
2. If definition is the principal method employed, what other methods are also used?
3. Which methods of emphasis are used here? Give at least three examples. (See Glossary: *emphasis*.)

4. Which general types of introduction and conclusion are employed here? (See Glossary: *introductions; conclusions.*)
5. Describe at least two methods by which Fleming achieves transitions between paragraphs. (See Glossary: *transition.*)
6. What is the central theme of this essay? (See Glossary: *subject; unity.*)

Diction and Vocabulary

1. Identify and estimate the effectiveness of at least two examples of metaphor and/or simile. (See Glossary: *metaphor; simile.*)
2. Can *you* think of a "dignified" substitute for "goo-goo eyes" (par. 9)?
3. Consult the dictionary to be sure you understand the meanings of the following words: *disarmingly* (par. 1); *chivalry* (3); *stolid* (5); *de rigueur* (7); *fledgling* (7); *evocative* (9); *affable* (10).

DONALD M. KAPLAN, LOUISE J. KAPLAN,
ARMAND SCHWERNER

Group

Louise J. Kaplan, Ph.D., is a professor of psychology in the
Graduate School of New York University and a member of the
Clinical Psychology Program faculty. She is a noted child psychologist and the author of many papers on the subject, as well as
editor of *The Domesday Dictionary* (1963), from which "Group"
is taken. Of the authors of that book, Donald M. Kaplan is a practicing psychoanalyst in New York and the president of the New
York Society of Freudian Psychologists. An associate professor in
the Post-Doctoral Psychology Program of New York University,
he, too, is the author of numerous papers on clinical and applied
psychoanalysis. Professor Armand Schwerner teaches English at
Staten Island Community College, CUNY, and is an American poet
of distinction. His *Tablets*, a poetic sequence in the American tradition, have been appearing since the middle 1960s. This brief entry
in their dictionary, "Group," is a succinct definition of an abstract
term that broadens our conception considerably.

Beasts form herds and packs. They do not form groups. Groups are 1
feasible only between creatures who, for better or for worse, have
evolved a necessity to maintain ideals through an inner struggle with
conscience and desire. Groups communalize ideals and thus provide
refuge from inner struggle. In groups there is good conscience: man
follows, leads, cavorts, studies, learns, pillages, murders, prays. There
is no ideal for which a group cannot be formed. Of the individual the
group demands obedience to the ideals. Of the group the individual
demands perpetuation of the ideals. Even when struggle arises over
these demands, it is never a struggle within the individual. It is outward
and is therefore waged in continuing good conscience.

For the validation which groups provide him, the individual forgoes 2
some commensurate portion of his privacy. This cannot be otherwise;
privacy is the saboteur of groups; it is an opportunity for personal, con-
templative adventure, out of which an individual may emerge with
misgivings about the group's ideals. The family, the political party, the
religious order, the military organization, the professional association
all have overt methods of invading, to a greater or lesser extent, the
privacy of members. In social groups and clubs, the methods are covert;
they are based on the latent possibility of withheld good-fellowship and

affection; in these groups, the individual is required to display conduct which affirms and reaffirms that what he does away from the group does not alter the ideals which have insured his standing.

3   There is ample evidence that man cannot do for very long away from groups; periodic relief from the burden of self-criticism seems to be vital; prolonged isolation from groups leads to various forms of madness. There is also evidence that prodigal affiliation with groups goes hand in hand with an impoverishment of moral stamina and a sense of alienation in the very midst of multitudes.

4   A group begins with three or more people. Two people cannot form a group. A group exists only when there is a chance for coalition.

Questions for the Critical Reader

1. How does the essay distinguish between "herds and packs" on the one hand and "groups" on the other?
2. How do these authors define *ideals*?
   a) Do you agree with this definition? Explain.
   b) If you do not agree, offer your own definition.
   c) In either case, give some examples of ideals you currently hold.
3. The word *conscience* is obviously heavily connotative. Do you agree with the authors' implied and stated definitions of this word? Explain. (See Glossary: *connotation and denotation*.)
4. Of what use is it for the individual to have "misgivings" (par. 2) about the ideals of
   a) The family?
   b) The political party?
   c) The religious order?
   d) The military organization?
5. These authors have a taste for pithy assertions that sound like they are true because of the way they are stated, for example, "There is no ideal for which a group cannot be formed" (par. 1); "privacy is the saboteur of groups" (2); "prolonged isolation from groups leads to various forms of madness" (3). Comment on the truth or falsity of each of these statements.
6. Explain the concluding paragraph by making a careful analysis of its sentences and their connections with each other. (See Glossary: *conclusions*.)
7. How would you describe the tone of this essay? (See Glossary: *style and tone*.)

Rhetorical Technique

1. Is this definition too broad or too narrow? (See the headnote to this chapter.)

2. Which primary method or methods of definition are employed here?
3. In paragraph 1, the authors state that "in groups there is good conscience: man follows, leads, cavorts, studies, learns, pillages, murders, prays." Are these to be taken as literal examples of "good conscience"? Or are the authors using irony? (See Glossary: *irony*.)
4. Identify four examples of parallel structure in this definition. Does parallelism have some special function here? (See Glossary: *parallel structure*.)
5. What is the authors' attitude toward groups? Which elements of the essay helped form your opinion?
6. What is the central theme of this piece? Do the authors make a thesis statement? (See Glossary: *subject; thesis statement; unity*.)

Diction and Vocabulary

1. Is the language of this essay primarily abstract or concrete? Could the definition of a "group" have been improved by a greater use of one or the other? Explain. (See Glossary: *abstract and concrete*.)
2. Consider the authors' use of the word *adventure*. How are its connotations being deployed here? (See Glossary: *connotation and denotation*.)
3. Do the same for *covert*.
4. *Multitudes* is a word with Biblical connections. Comment on its use here.
5. Consult the dictionary if you do not understand the meanings of the following words: *feasible* (par. 1); *cavorts* (1); *communalize* (1); *validation* (2); *commensurate* (2); *saboteur* (2); *overt* and *covert* (2); *latent* (2); *prodigal* (3); *coalition* (4).

IRVING KRISTOL

What Is a "Neo-Conservative"?

Irving Kristol, who was born in 1920, is a writer, editor, and Henry
Luce Professor of Urban Values at New York University. He is
currently coeditor of the magazine *Public Interest* and has been a
contributing editor of *Commentary*, *The Reporter*, and *Encounter*.
His book, *On the Democratic Ideal in America* (1972), had for its
central theme the breakdown of American democratic ideals. This
essay, which was first printed in *Newsweek* (January 19, 1976),
defines Professor Kristol's political position by referring it to themes
and ideas prominent in American social life for two decades.

1   There can no longer be any question about it. I am for better or worse, a
"neo-conservative" intellectual. NEWSWEEK, Time and The New York
Times have all identified me as such, and that settles the matter. As with
the original Adam, theirs is the power to give names to all the political
creatures in the land, who in turn can only be grateful for having been
rescued from anonymity.

2   So I have no complaint. On the other hand, I must report that some
of my friends who have been identified as fellow neo-conservatives are
less complaisant about this business. Daniel Patrick Moynihan, for instance, suggests that he is a modern version of a Wilsonian progressive.
Prof. Daniel Bell of Harvard asserts that he is, as he always has been, a
right-wing social democrat. I keep telling them (and others) that such
resistance to Higher Authority is not only useless—it positively verges
on sedition. But they retort that this is a free country, which the Garden
of Eden was not.

An Influential Tendency

3   Before this situation gets out of control and spreads great turmoil among
the citizenry, I should like to offer my services as a mediator. There can
be no doubt that the political tendency deemed neo-conservative does
exist, that it is represented in such journals as The Public Interest and
Commentary, that it has become quite influential of late in shaping
political attitudes in intellectual and academic circles, and that its views
have even infiltrated the world of media and government. But it is also
true that it is only a tendency, not a clearly defined "movement," that
there is much heterogeneity in it, and that to those who do not closely
follow intellectual controversy in America the term "conservative" can
be misleading.

Let me see, therefore, if I can briefly outline the substance beneath the   **4**
label, the vague consensus that seems to affiliate men and women who
are frequently not even aware that they are part of a tendency, much less
a neo-conservative one. It's a real enough thing we are talking about—I
am not disputing that. But, at the moment, it needs describing more than
it needs naming.

1. Neo-conservatism is not at all hostile to the idea of a welfare state,   **5**
but it is critical of the Great Society[1] version of this welfare state.[2] In
general, it approves of those social reforms that, while providing needed
security and comfort to the individual in our dynamic, urbanized society,
do so with a minimum of bureaucratic intrusion in the individual's affairs.
Such reforms would include, of course, social security, unemployment
insurance, some form of national health insurance, some kind of family-
assistance plan,[3] etc. In contrast, it is skeptical of those social programs
that create vast and energetic bureaucracies to "solve social problems."
In short, while being for the welfare state, it is opposed to the paternalistic state. It also believes that this welfare state will best promote the
common good if it is conceived in such a way as not to go bankrupt.

2. Neo-conservatism has great respect—it is fair to say it has learned   **6**
to have great respect—for the power of the market to respond efficiently
to economic realities while preserving the maximum degree of individual
freedom. Though willing to interfere with the market for overriding
social purposes, it prefers to do so by "rigging" the market, or even
creating new markets, rather than by direct bureaucratic controls. Thus
it is more likely to favor housing vouchers[4] for the poor than government-built low-income projects.

3. Neo-conservatism tends to be respectful of traditional values and   **7**
institutions: religion, the family, the "high culture" of Western civilization. If there is any one thing that neo-conservatives are unanimous
about, it is their dislike of the "counter-culture"[5] that has played so

---

[1] *Great Society.* A tag given to the legislative programs and social purposes of
the administration of President Lyndon Johnson (1963–1968).

[2] *welfare state.* The name given to the social style of the United States during
the presidency of Harry S. Truman (1945–1952). The gist of the style was the
government's assumption of responsibility, through specific legislative programs
generating jobs, unemployment benefits, and retirement plans for the welfare of its
citizens.

[3] *family-assistance plan.* A plan for the government to provide direct assistance
to poor families based on the size of the family and its total income.

[4] *housing vouchers.* Pieces of scrip that could be used as money only for the
purchase of housing by poor families or individuals.

[5] *"high culture" of Western civilization . . . "counter-culture."* Here Kristol in-
tends to contrast the first term—the culture that includes Homer, Greek philosophy,
the Bible, Dante, Shakespeare, the great painters of the Renaissance, Bach, Mozart,
and Beethoven, and so on—with the culture that sprang up in the sixties and that
ran deliberately "counter" to it, that is, the counter-culture of Eastern (Oriental)
mysticism and religion, gurus, meditation, psychedelics, rock music, found poetry,
pop art, and so on.

remarkable a role in American life over these past fifteen years. Neo-conservatives are well aware that traditional values and institutions do change in time, but they prefer that such change be gradual and organic. They believe that the individual who is abruptly "liberated" from the sovereignty of traditional values will soon find himself experiencing the vertigo and despair of nihilism. Nor do they put much credence in the notion that individuals can "create" their own values and then incorporate them into a satisfying "life-style." Values emerge out of the experience of generations and represent the accumulated wisdom of these generations; they simply cannot be got out of rap sessions about "identity" or "authenticity."

8   4. Neo-conservatism affirms the traditional American idea of equality, but rejects egalitarianism—the equality of condition for all citizens—as a proper goal for government to pursue. The equality proclaimed by the Declaration of Independence is an equality of natural rights—including the right to become unequal (within limits) in wealth, or public esteem, or influence. Without *that* right, equality becomes the enemy of liberty. To put it in more homely terms: the encouragement of equality of opportunity is always a proper concern of democratic government. But it is a dangerous sophistry to insist that there is no true equality of opportunity unless and until everyone ends up with equal shares of everything.

9   5. In foreign policy, neo-conservatism believes that American democracy is not likely to survive for long in a world that is overwhelmingly hostile to American values, if only because our transactions (economic and diplomatic) with foreign nations are bound eventually to have a profound impact on our own domestic economic and political system. So neo-conservatives are critical of the post-Vietnam isolationism[6] now so popular in Congress, and many are suspicious of "détente"[7] as well. On specific issues of foreign policy, however, the neo-conservative consensus is a weak one. In the case of Vietnam, neo-conservatives went every which way.

The Right Label?

10   So there it is—oversimplified but not, I think, distorted. Not all neo-conservatives will accept all of those tenets; but most will accept most of them. Is neo-conservatism the right label for this constellation of attitudes? I don't mind it—but then, if the political spectrum moved rightward, and we should become "neo-liberal" tomorrow, I could accept that too. As a matter of fact, I wouldn't be too surprised if just that happened.

---

[6] *isolationism*. An American foreign policy that aimed at removing the country, as far as possible, from all foreign involvements.

[7] *détente*. An American foreign policy that aimed at accommodation with Russian communism.

Questions for the Critical Reader

1. Is the distinction made in paragraph 5 (numbered 1 by Kristol) a clear one? Why? Why not? Use concrete examples in your explanation.
2. Consider the last sentence of paragraph 6: why is the provision of housing vouchers for the poor less bureaucratic than providing low-income, government-built projects?
3. In his discussion of culture in paragraph 7, Kristol opposes "high culture" and the counter-culture. Is this a fair distinction to make? Justify your answer.
4. Comment on sentences 3 and 4 in paragraph 7. What does Kristol mean by "organic" change? How quick is "abruptly"?
5. *Identity* and *authenticity* would appear to have had great currency in recent times. What is Kristol's attitude toward these words?
6. In paragraph 8, Kristol makes a distinction between egalitarianism and equality.
   a) What does he mean by each?
   b) Comment on his definitions and, especially, on what you think he bases these definitions on.
7. Comment on the neo-conservative's views on foreign policy. Are these views clear? Explain.
8. In his concluding paragraph, Kristol admits that his account is "over-simplified." What would you add to make a more complex picture?
9. Comment on the possibilities outlined in the last two sentences.

Rhetorical Technique

1. Which method of extended definition is used most prominently here?
2. Explain to what extent this is an essay in classification. (See introduction to Chapter 4.)
3. Comment on the effectiveness of the introduction. How much of the essay would you classify as introduction? (See Glossary: *introductions.*)
4. Cite the methods of emphasis Kristol uses, and explain their effects. (See Glossary: *emphasis.*)
5. Locate the one rhetorical question used in this essay, and comment on its effectiveness. (See Glossary: *rhetorical questions.*)

Diction and Vocabulary

1. Explain what the author is saying in the last sentence of paragraph 2.
2. Comment on this author's use of quotation marks.

3. Consult the dictionary to be sure you understand the meanings of the following words: *complaisant* (par. 2); *sedition* (2); *heterogeneity* (3); *consensus* (4, 9); *bureaucratic* (5); *skeptical* (5); *paternalistic* (5); *sovereignty* (7); *vertigo* (7); *nihilism* (7); *credence* (7); *egalitarianism* (8); *sophistry* (8); *tenets* (10).

G. K. CHESTERTON

Madness

G[ilbert]. K[eith]. Chesterton (1874–1936) was born in London. An industrious, ebullient, colorful, and provocative writer, Chesterton produced poetry, criticism, and fiction with equal ease. He became known to a wider public with the creation of the amiable detective-priest, Father Brown, whom Chesterton depicted in a series of novels beginning in 1911. This piece was taken from an essay collection, *Orthodoxy* (1908), and is a fine definition based on an analysis of the experience of both the mad and the sane.

The last thing that can be said of a lunatic is that his actions are cause- 1
less. If any human acts may loosely be called causeless, they are the minor acts of a healthy man; whistling as he walks; slashing the grass with a stick; kicking his heels or rubbing his hands. It is the happy man who does the useless things; the sick man is not strong enough to be idle. It is exactly such careless and causeless actions that the madman could never understand; for the madman (like the determinist) generally sees too much cause in everything. The madman would read a conspiratorial significance into these empty activities. He would think that the lopping of the grass was an attack on private property. He would think that the kicking of the heels was a signal to an accomplice. If the madman could for an instant become careless, he would become sane. Every one, who has had the misfortune to talk with people in the heart or on the edge of mental disorder, knows that their most sinister quality is a horrible clarity of detail; a connecting of one thing with another in a map more elaborate than a maze. If you argue with a madman, it is extremely probable that you will get the worst of it; for in many ways his mind moves all the quicker for not being delayed by the things that go with good judgment. He is not hampered by a sense of humor or by charity, or by the dumb certainties of experience. He is more logical for losing certain sane affections. Indeed, the common phrase for insanity is in this respect a misleading one. The madman is not the man who has lost his reason. The madman is the man who has lost everything except his reason.

The madman's explanation of a thing is always complete, and often in 2
a purely rational sense satisfactory. Or, to speak more strictly, the insane explanation, if not conclusive, is at least unanswerable; this may be observed specially in the two or three commonest kinds of madness. If a man says (for instance) that men have a conspiracy against him, you

From *Orthodoxy* by G. K. Chesterton. Reprinted by permission of Dodd, Mead & Company, publishers, and Miss D. E. Collins and the Bodley Head.

cannot dispute it except by saying that all the men deny that they are conspirators, which is exactly what conspirators would do. His explanation covers the facts as much as yours. Or if a man says that he is the rightful King of England, it is no complete answer to say that the existing authorities call him mad; for if he were King of England, that might be the wisest thing for the existing authorities to do. Or if a man says that he is Jesus Christ, it is no answer to tell him that the world denies his divinity; for the world denied Christ's.

Questions for the Critical Reader

1. Do you agree that a common definition of a madman is that he has lost his reason? Explain.
2. How would you define *reason*?
3. "Careless," "causeless," and "useless" are all terms that Chesterton applies to sane persons. Do you agree that they fit? Explain.
4. Chesterton says of the madman that "his mind moves quicker." Which sane activities would benefit from this quality of mind? Which would not?
5. Why is the madman more "logical for losing certain sane affections"? And what *are* these "sane affections"?
6. Do you think that Chesterton wrote this piece out of firsthand experience with insane people? Explain.
7. Compare your first hand experience of insanity with Chesterton's.
8. Are there people you regard as "crazy," though you realize they are not insane to the degree that they should be committed? Do they exhibit traits that Chesterton describes? Have you ever had a firsthand experience with insanity?
9. How would you describe the tone of this essay? (See Glossary: *style and tone.*)

Rhetorical Technique

1. Which method of definition is the primary one?
2. Which sentence offers an abstract definition of madness?
3. Comment on the effectiveness of the paragraph structure leading up to this sentence?
4. How effective are Chesterton's examples in this paragraph?
5. Which elements of this essay account for its coherence? (See Glossary: *coherence.*)
6. Because this is an excerpt from a longer essay, it seems unfair to discuss its introduction and conclusion. But does this piece seem to you to be complete? Explain.
7. Give two examples of parallel structure and comment on their effectiveness. (See Glossary: *parallel structure.*)

Diction and Vocabulary

1. What is the meaning of the part common to all three of the following words: *causeless, useless, careless*? What considerations motivated the writer to use the three to describe sane persons?
2. Why, in his first sentence, does Chesterton say *lunatic* instead of, say, *madman*, or *insane person*? Is there something in the connotative value of *lunatic* that is useful to his purposes? (See Glossary: *connotation and denotation*.)
3. What is Chesterton's purpose in qualifying the word *certainties* (1) with the word *dumb*?
4. Consult the dictionary to be sure you understand the meanings of the following words: *determinist* (1); *lopping* (1); *rational* (2); *conclusive* (2).

Writing Suggestions for Chapter 5: *Definition*

I.

Write an extended definition, using any of the standard approaches discussed at the beginning of this chapter, of one of the words listed below. Try for clarity and precision in saying exactly what you mean.

1. Pleasure.
2. Ecstasy.
3. Family.
4. Intelligence.
5. A positive attitude.
6. Conservative.
7. Radical.
8. Reactionary.
9. "Them."
10. "Us."
11. Friendship.
12. Personal freedom.
13. Charm.
14. A *typical* Western movie.
15. Genius.
16. An idealist/a realist.
17. The silent majority.
18. Success.
19. Trust.
20. Work/leisure.

II. A. Writing Assignment Based on "Poverty"

Using Orwell's point of view, that is, the point of view of someone who has lived through an experience and uses an essay to tell the reader what he has "discovered," write an extended definition of the "condition" in which you, like Orwell, unexpectedly found yourself. It could be a situation of affluence (that is, when you suddenly came into some money after being without it for a long time); it could be a condition of *prestige* (that is, suddenly, after performing well in some way or other, publicly or privately—you rescued someone who was over his head in a swimming pool; you won a basketball game single-handedly—you find that people are looking up to you in a new way); it could be a condition of *ostracism* (that is, you are being given the "silent" treatment for some real or imagined transgression on your part). The title of the essay then would be one of these words, that is, the word that describes the condition. Give the reader many concrete examples of what it is like to live in that condition—many conditions of what you "discover"—and reread Orwell to get more hints on what kind of example you can use.

B. Writing Assignment Based on "What Is a 'Neo-Conservative'?"

Write an extended definition of your own political position. Do so by giving your views with respect to a number of political issues—as Kristol does. You may use his categories, that is, traditional values, the welfare state, equality and individual rights, and so on, or develop categories of your own.

C. Writing Assignment Based on "Madness"

Write an extended definition of one of the states of mind listed below. Investigate the possibility that, like Chesterton, you can find some singular quality that will characterize your subject.

1. Fearfulness.
2. Anxiety.
3. Anger.
4. Calm.
5. Ambition.
6. Playfulness.
7. Exasperation.
8. Lethargy.
9. Despair.
10. Enthusiasm.

Explaining by *Process Analysis*

To analyze anything is to separate it into its component parts. We can analyze the *structure* of an automobile by describing the connections between its engine, gearbox, drive shaft, and so on. We can also analyze how something works—its *functioning*—the digestive process of animals, for example, or the legislative processes of the state assembly. Analyzing such functions would involve separating a complex whole into separate stages of action. Analyzing both structure and function is called *process analysis*.

Causal analysis, which considers the causes of human events (for example, why did the South secede from the Union, or what were the causes of Watergate, or what factors accounted for the Yankees' winning the pennant), differs from process analysis and will be dealt with in detail in Chapter 7. In making a causal analysis, we would try to analyze something more complex than either a mechanism like a car or a body part like the digestive tract. Causal analysis deals with human issues. Because people are involved there, so are motives, and the analysis of historical events, human actions, social movements—the possible subjects of causal analysis—are correspondingly more complicated than the subjects of process analysis. To put it simply, process analysis tries to answer the question "How?" and causal analysis tries to answer the question "Why?"

Under process analysis, we would list such kinds of writing as, on the simplest level, a cooking recipe, and, on a more complicated level, how to manufacture maple syrup from tree to bottle. Another kind of process analysis is advice to the lovelorn: "Dear Worried, You must first determine how much you love her. Then examine your behavior toward her. Try to be thoughtful in little ways . . ."

By now it should be evident that process analysis passes through a series of steps and is controlled by time. It should also be evident that writing an essay in this method depends on the writer's knowing a great deal about his or her subject.

In these respects, process analysis is one of the easier expository methods. Nobody writes about a process he or she doesn't know well, and the structure of an essay in process simply follows time and procedure. The difficulties of this kind of writing fall into two categories: (1) In explaining a complex functional process, the operation of a nuclear reactor, for example, certain simultaneous actions cannot be explained all at once. In such cases, the writer must find a way to organize his material so that the reader understands this fact. (2) The writer must be clear about the audience he or she is addressing, because it is important to be able to judge how much technical information to give. In a description of the functioning of the nuclear reactor, for example, it may be important to estimate whether the reader knows the meaning of the word *isotope*. (In this little process analysis, the writer judges that you, reader, *know* what an isotope is.) But here the difficulty is like a double-edged sword. If the writer assumes too much ignorance on the part of the reader and consequently supplies too much information, the essay can be tedious reading. If he or she assumes too little and, consequently, does not supply enough information, the essay can be confusing.

As is always the case in trying to write well, the writer must use restrained good judgment, and nothing develops this more than constant practice.

Finally, process analysis is sometimes called technical description. This kind of description, however, is not to be confused with the method called *description* and described in Chapter 8. In impressionistic description, described in the later chapter, the purpose is to make a reader *see* —an appeal to the sensory imagination. The purpose here is to convey information—an appeal to the intellect, to the capacity for understanding.

ERNEST HEMINGWAY

Camping Out

Ernest Hemingway (1898–1961), born in Oak Park, Illinois, can simply be called a great American writer. Starting as a newspaperman and war correspondent, he developed the terse and understated style that affected all those writing in English who came after him. Awarded the Nobel Prize in 1954, Hemingway published his first book *The Torrents of Spring* in 1926. But he is best known for the works that followed: *The Sun Also Rises* (1926), *A Farewell to Arms* (1929), *For Whom the Bell Tolls* (1940), *The Old Man and the Sea* (1952), and his brilliant short stories. The author was a notable sportsman and lover of the outdoors, and this piece, written for the *Toronto Star-World* in 1920, clearly demonstrates how much he knew about the subject even at the tender age of twenty-two.

1 Thousands of people will go into the bush this summer to cut the high cost of living. A man who gets his two weeks' salary while he is on vacation should be able to put those two weeks in fishing and camping and be able to save one week's salary clear. He ought to be able to sleep comfortably every night, to eat well every day and to return to the city rested and in good condition.

2 But if he goes into the woods with a frying pan, an ignorance of black flies and mosquitoes, and a great and abiding lack of knowledge about cookery the chances are that his return will be very different. He will come back with enough mosquito bites to make the back of his neck look like a relief map of the Caucasus. His digestion will be wrecked after a valiant battle to assimilate half-cooked or charred grub. And he won't have had a decent night's sleep while he has been gone.

3 He will solemnly raise his right hand and inform you that he has joined the grand army of never-agains. The call of the wild may be all right, but it's a dog's life. He's heard the call of the tame with both ears. Waiter, bring him an order of milk toast.

4 In the first place he overlooked the insects. Black flies, no-see-ums, deer flies, gnats and mosquitoes were instituted by the devil to force people to live in cities where he could get at them better. If it weren't for them everybody would live in the bush and he would be out of work. It was a rather successful invention.

5 But there are lots of dopes that will counteract the pests. The simplest

From "When You Camp Out, Do It Right" by Ernest Hemingway, originally published in the *Toronto Star-World*, June 26, 1920. Reprinted by permission of Alfred Rice on behalf of the Ernest Hemingway estate.

145

perhaps is oil of citronella. Two bits' worth of this purchased at any pharmacist's will be enough to last for two weeks in the worst fly and mosquito-ridden country.

6   Rub a little on the back of you neck, you forehead and your wrists before you start fishing, and the blacks and skeeters will shun you. The odor of citronella is not offensive to people. It smells like gun oil. But the bugs do hate it.

7   Oil of pennyroyal and eucalyptol are also much hated by mosquitoes, and with citronella they form the basis for many proprietary preparations. But it is cheaper and better to buy the straight citronella. Put a little on the mosquito netting that covers the front of your pup tent or canoe tent at night, and you won't be bothered.

8   To be really rested and get any benefit out of a vacation a man must get a good night's sleep every night. The first requisite for this is to have plenty of cover. It is twice as cold as you expect it will be in the bush four nights out of five, and a good plan is to take just double the bedding that you think you will need. An old quilt that you can wrap up in is as warm as two blankets.

9   Nearly all outdoor writers rhapsodize over the browse bed. It is all right for the man who knows how to make one and has plenty of time. But in a succession of one-night camps on a canoe trip all you need is level ground for your tent floor and you will sleep all right if you have plenty of covers under you. Take twice as much cover as you think that you will need, and then put two-thirds of it under you. You will sleep warm and get your rest.

10   When it is clear weather you don't need to pitch your tent if you are only stopping for the night. Drive four stakes at the head of your made-up bed and drape your mosquito bar over that, then you can sleep like a log and laugh at the mosquitoes.

11   Outside of insects and bum sleeping the rock that wrecks most camping trips is cooking. The average tyro's idea of cooking is to fry everything and fry it good and plenty. Now, a frying pan is a most necessary thing to any trip, but you also need the old stew kettle and the folding reflector baker.

12   A pan of fried trout can't be bettered and they don't cost any more than ever. But there is a good and bad way of frying them.

13   The beginner puts his trout and his bacon in and over a brightly burning fire the bacon curls up and dries into a dry tasteless cinder and the trout is burned outside while it is still raw inside. He eats them and it is all right if he is only out for the day and going home to a good meal at night. But if he is going to face more trout and bacon the next morning and other equally well-cooked dishes for the remainder of two weeks he is on the pathway to nervous dyspepsia.

14   The proper way is to cook over coals. Have several cans of Crisco or

Cotosuet or one of the vegetable shortenings along that are as good as lard and excellent for all kinds of shortening. Put the bacon in and when it is about half cooked lay the trout in the hot grease, dipping them in corn meal first. Then put the bacon on top of the trout and it will baste them as it slowly cooks.

The coffee can be boiling at the same time and in a smaller skillet 15 pancakes being made that are satisfying the other campers while they are waiting for the trout.

With the prepared pancake flours you take a cupful of pancake flour 16 and add a cup of water. Mix the water and flour and as soon as the lumps are out it is ready for cooking. Have the skillet hot and keep it well greased. Drop the batter in and as soon as it is done on one side loosen it in the skillet and flip it over. Apple butter, syrup or cinnamon and sugar go well with the cakes.

While the crowd have taken the edge from their appetites with flap- 17 jacks the trout have been cooked and they and the bacon are ready to serve. The trout are crisp outside and firm and pink inside and the bacon is well done—but not too done. If there is anything better than that combination the writer has yet to taste it in a lifetime devoted largely and studiously to eating.

The stew kettle will cook you dried apricots when they have resumed 18 their predried plumpness after a night of soaking, it will serve to concoct a mulligan in, and it will cook macaroni. When you are not using it, it should be boiling water for the dishes.

In the baker, mere man comes into his own, for he can make a pie 19 that to his bush appetite will have it all over the product that mother used to make, like a tent. Men have always believed that there was something mysterious and difficult about making a pie. Here is a great secret. There is nothing to it. We've been kidded for years. Any man of average office intelligence can make at least as good a pie as his wife.

All there is to a pie is a cup and a half of flour, one-half teaspoonful 20 of salt, one-half cup of lard and cold water. That will make pie crust that will bring tears of joy into your camping partner's eyes.

Mix the salt with the flour, work the lard into the flour, make it up 21 into a good workmanlike dough with cold water. Spread some flour on the back of a box or something flat, and pat the dough around a while. Then roll it out with whatever kind of round bottle you prefer. Put a little more lard on the surface of the sheet of dough and then slosh a little flour on and roll it up and then roll it out again with the bottle.

Cut out a piece of the rolled out dough big enough to line a pie tin. I 22 like the kind with holes in the bottom. Then put in your dried apples that have soaked all night and been sweetened, or your apricots, or your blueberries, and then take another sheet of the dough and drape it gracefully over the top, soldering it down at the edges with you fingers.

Cut a couple of slits in the top dough sheet and prick it a few times with a fork in an artistic manner.

23   Put it in the baker with a good slow fire for forty-five minutes and then take it out and if your pals are Frenchmen they will kiss you. The penalty for knowing how to cook is that the others will make you do all the cooking.

24   It is all right to talk about roughing it in the woods. But the real woodsman is the man who can be really comfortable in the bush.

Questions for the Critical Reader

1. Name the three aspects of camping out that Hemingway is most interested in.
2. On what basis do you suppose Hemingway concludes that one of two weeks' salary can be saved while camping out?
3. Try to describe as fully as you can the circumstances of one of Hemingway's camping out experiences on the basis of what he says in paragraphs 11–23.
4. Explain the reference to the kissing Frenchmen in paragraph 23.
5. Which specific features of the references and/or language can you point to that would verify the year in which this piece was written?

Rhetorical Technique

1. What main types of process analysis is this? (See the introduction to this chapter.)
2. In paragraph 14, Hemingway says that the proper way to cook is over coals. What exactly does he mean by this? Has he assumed too much knowledge on the part of the reader? Too little?
3. What assumption about fishing does he make in paragraph 6?
4. What form of exposition is used in the first two paragraphs? (See the introduction to the student.)
5. Which general type of introduction is used here? (See Glossary: *introductions*.)
6. What is Hemingway's central theme? Does the main body of the essay express this adequately? Explain. (See Glossary: *central theme; subject; unity*.)
7. Can you account for the fact that there are many short paragraphs here?
8. How would you describe the author's point of view? (See Glossary: *point of view*.)

Diction and Vocabulary

1. How would you describe the tone of this essay? (See Glossary: *style and tone*.)
   a) Cite two examples of figurative language (see Glossary: *figures of speech*), and estimate how these contribute to the tone.
   b) Cite two examples of unusual diction and do the same. (See Glossary: *diction*.)
2. Identify any expression you would call a cliché. (See Glossary: *cliché*.) Would it have been better to have avoided any of these? Or do they serve a specific purpose?
3. The third word in the essay is *people*, but in the second sentence Hemingway uses *man* and the mascline pronoun and continues to do this elsewhere. Comment on this apparent contradiction. See question 1 under "Diction and Vocabulary" following Norman Runnion's essay in Chapter 4.
4. Hemingway appears to have coined the phrase *no-see-ums* (par. 4). Is it an effective term for what he describes?
5. Consult the dictionary to be sure you understand the meanings of the following words and phrases: *bush* (par. 1); *skeeters* (6); *proprietary* (7); *tyro* (11); *browse bed* (9); *dyspepsia* (13); *mulligan* (18).

GORDON LISH

How to Brew the World's Greatest Cup of Coffee

Gordon Lish, who was born in 1934, is the fiction editor of *Esquire* magazine where this essay was first printed (March 1976). He has been a wrangler, a disc jockey, a school teacher, and a radio actor— all of which are activities conducive to acquiring knowledge about brewing coffee. Mr. Lish was formerly editor in chief of Behavioral Research Laboratories and is the author of *English Grammar* (1962) and the editor of *Why Work?* (1964), *A Man's Work* (1966), and *New Sounds in American Fiction* (1967). In addition to his duties at *Esquire*, he teaches fiction writing at Yale University. The point of view of this disarmingly simple piece of process analysis is, in part at least, that of a man who *knows*.

1   I know coffee. Trust me. I wasn't born this way, mind you. But some hefty time disc-jockeying and dude-wrangling settled a large habit on me made downright huge in recent years now that I'm dieting every whipstitch. Keep on trusting me, please—because you can't name me the coffee I haven't tried, the oddball brewing routine I haven't fussed over. I've even read *books* about how to do it while everybody else in the Free World was reading books about how to do things I wouldn't want to say. Anyhow, books got me nowhere. Nothing got me anywhere but plain old backyard horsing around. Here—save yourself the trouble. I'm giving— you can take.

2   French roast is okay, but why spend big? Better if you get Café Bustelo, which Tetley is now spreading all over the place. If you can't turn up Bustelo, Estrella is a close enough second. These are fine grinds we're talking about—*fino*, right? You've got some favorite bean thing you like to do, okay—but grind it fine. Now bring to boil six cups of cold water in a saucepan, and now let it cool so it's still throwing off steam, but just *some*—wisps. Dump in *one third* of a can of whatever you want. If you can't eyeball a third of a can, then measure out one and one-third cups. If it's not Bustelo, that's your lookout. Stir until all grind is delumped and saturated. (I use a wooden spoon: it gets good and stained, which is very impressive if you have an audience.) Cover. Let sit no less than six, no more than nine, minutes. In there somewhere. Now strain through flannel into whatever you want to keep your coffe in. You can buy these flannel sieves—like a little wind sock on a hoop with a handle. I make one when I can't buy one. But the French export them. The better ones—and a whole lot cheaper ones—come from South America. I pay a quarter to forty cents for the jobbies I pick up at this

or that culinary specialty shop or fancy supermarket here in New York. Generally, your flannel strainer is displayed where the coffee is or else where the assorted kitchen oddments are. Use the thing maybe one, two months and then discard when the fibers have gone skinny on you.

That's it. Nothing else. I don't care what you're hearing from other parties, I say you can reheat, leave on the stove all day, skip refrigeration, hit it with a hammer, you can't hurt the poem I just told you how to write. **3**

Questions for the Critical Reader

1. Why do so many Americans make such a big fuss over the proper way to make coffee?
2. Why would cowboys and disc jockeys know more about coffee than the rest of us?
3. Is Lish a snob? Why? Why not?
4. Why didn't Lish title his piece, "How to Brew an Excellent Cup of Coffee"?

Rhetorical Technique

1. A simpleminded question: what general type of process analysis is this? (See the introduction to this chapter.)
2. Yes, but in what way is it different from others of the same general type?
3. Despite its disarming brevity and simplicity, can you extract the central theme of this essay? (See Glossary: *central theme; subject; unity.*)

Diction and Vocabulary

1. How would you describe the tone of this piece? Which features of Lish's language contribute most to this tone? Why has he adopted it? (See Glossary: *style and tone.*)
2. "You can't hurt the poem I just told you how to write." What kind of *figurative language* is this? (See Glossary: *figures of speech.*)
3. Be sure you understand the meanings of *whipstitch* (1) and *culinary* (2).

FRANÇOIS LIERRES

How to Get Along with Americans

> François Lierres, a French journalist, writes for the newsmagazine
> *Le Point* of Paris, which first printed the essay. It was translated in
> *Atlas World Press Review* in March 1975. The essential purpose in
> Lierres's piece is to give advice on how to do something. Thus it
> is a good example of process analysis that answers the question
> "How?" Nevertheless, he cannot resist the impulse to classify his
> advice into do's and don'ts.

1   They are the Vikings of the world economy, descending upon it in their
jets as the Vikings once did in their *drakkars*.[1] They have money, technology, and nerve. And the energy crisis certainly won't prevent them
from remaining what they are: the champions of the system, the champions of commerce, industry, investment, and profitability. Even Moscow
has conceded the title to them. As for us French, we have for some time
been to a great extent "colonized" by them. American businesses, poised
and irresistible, directly or through intermediaries, have firmly established
themselves in our midst. And increasing numbers of us work for them.

2   These Romans of the marketing art, these Pharaohs of management,
have their habits. And we would be wise to get acquainted with them, if
we are to work with them and get along well. Of course, Americans are
basically subject to the same laws of nature that govern us. They are
neither Martians nor Papuans. They have two ears, two eyes, and two
hands, like everyone else. But Americans do not use these parts of their
bodies in exactly the same way as others. The following are some of the
traits and mannerisms peculiar—and important—to them:

Do's

3   *Leave your own eyeglasses in the foyer!* The first thing you must learn is
to adapt to their ways, to their manner of looking at the world. Because
in all the areas of life the ideas they profess and practice are different
from those of the Europeans: both on the personal level—in saying
"hello," for instance—and on a global scale—in conducting business.
Since they are the bosses, it would be idiotic for us to dispute their concept which they bring along with their luggage and which they consider
good because they have proved successful.

First published in *Le Point*, Paris newspaper, and translated in *Atlas World Press
Review*, March 1975 ©. Reprinted by permission.

[1] *drakkars.* The long ships of the Vikings.

Greet. But do not shake hands, except when you are first introduced. 4
After that merely make a small gesture of sorts, as you come forward,
and emite a brief cluck of joy: "Hi!"

Speak without emotion. Speak your piece in a simple and direct 5
fashion, without flourish, and—above all—with assurance and self-
assertion, conveying the impression that you have command of the subject, even if you haven't.

Forget your best French writing style. In a letter, note, or report, be 6
sure to underline the basic points and refrain from using courtesy phrases
or superfluous elucidations. On the other hand, they look favorably on
the ability to get straight to the point and convey the essential idea—no
more and no less—briefly and concisely.

Check the collar of your jacket. Nothing is uglier in their eyes than 7
dandruff, even on cashmere. Clothes without stains and shined shoes
are the minimum mark of respect that one person owes another. Unfortunate the man who is so attached to his shirt that he forgets to
change it! If he smells of perspiration, he will first be told so in the face,
then—if this continues—he will be dismissed.

Invite them to your home. Americans adore meeting the families of 8
their coworkers.

Radiate congeniality and show a good disposition. To be able to 9
socialize means to be on good terms with everybody. A big smile and a
warm expression are essential. Rid yourself of the bad habit—common
in France—of taking out your personal annoyances on your co-workers
or employees and allowing your state of mind to affect your work.
Briefly, avoid being a character.

Be a lowbrow, rather than a highbrow. This means that, while nobody 10
forbids you to be an intelligent, thinking person, it is futile and conducive
to misunderstandings to indulge in Machiavellian games, or remain aloof
and reserved. Be pedestrian.

Learn how to play golf. American men love to meet every week at the 11
"links."

Attend parties. These are small friendly gatherings, not regularly 12
organized but rather thrown on occasion for the purpose of having three
or more drinks, or to celebrate Christmas together. It would be most
discourteous to steal away from one of these parties and be noticed to
boot.

Don'ts

Don't expect to have sun or daylight in your office. In most cases, the 13
light of day does not penetrate the air conditioned buildings of the
Americans. Sometimes being assigned an office with a window is tan-
tamount to receiving a promotion.

Don't tamper with your accent. Maurice Chevalier's is perfectly accept- 14 able and well liked. You won't impress anybody by imitating nasal Yankee speech.

15   *Don't think that they love labor unions.* Quite the contrary is true. Unions inspire them with a holy terror, at least the European unions which they see as "too red." While in France the display of zealous unionism may be taken for political consciousness, in an American company it won't guarantee you a brilliant career.

16   *Don't forget the name,* the surname, and the given name of any American with whom you may have spoken. Incidentally, in most cases, he will almost immediately address you—and you will have to address him—by his first name: "Good morning, Claude!" "Hello, Walter!" And you would be wise to learn how to spell his family name correctly.

Questions for the Critical Reader

1. Consider Lierres's assertion about Americans in paragraph 3, that "they are the bosses." Is this true? Why? Could the statement gain in truthfulness or persuasiveness if it were qualified? How would you do this? Or is it enough to say that Lierres *does* qualify the statement by the title he gives to the paragraph, that is, *Leave your own eyeglasses in the foyer!*
2. Is Lierres giving accurate directions in paragraph 4?
    a) Or is he being ironic? (See Glossary: *irony.*)
    b) Is he making fun of us? Explain.
3. What is your opinion of the assumptions underlying paragraph 7, *Check the collar of your jacket?*
4. What does paragraph 8 tell you about the French? Why is it legitimate to make such an inference?
5. What would you add to or subtract from each of the main sections (do's and dont's) in order to improve this piece of advice?
6. What audience is Lierres addressing in this essay? (See Glossary: *point of view.*)

Rhetorical Technique

1. In what sense is this a process analysis? (See the introduction to this chapter.)
2. Under the general headings of "Do's" and "Don'ts," Lierres has used some system of classification. Consult the introduction to Chapter 4, and describe this system. Is it logical? Inconsistent? How? What is its basic scheme?
3. How much does this essay depend upon the author's having made a causal analysis of Americans? (See Chapter 7.)

4. Comment on the author's use of the word *some* in the last sentence of paragraph 2.
5. In a sentence or two, give Lierres's central theme.

Diction and Vocabulary

1. Identify three examples of *allusion* in this essay. (See Glossary: *allusion.*)
2. Which figure of speech is being employed in paragraph 2 where the author says "they are neither Martians nor Papuans?" (See Glossary: *figures of speech.*)
3. From where does a Papuan come?
4. Who is Maurice Chevalier?
5. Consult the dictionary to be sure you understand the meanings of the following words: *drakkars* (par. 1); *poised* (1); *intermediaries* (1); *foyer* (3); *superfluous* (6); *elucidation* (6); *Machiavellian* (10); *pedestrian* (10); *zealous* (15).

RACHEL CARSON

Birth of a Mackerel

Rachel Carson (1907–1964), a writer and scientist, was employed for sixteen years by the U.S. Fish and Wildlife Service. From this position she was able to acquire an extraordinary grasp of the delicate interdependence of all the living things that go to make up ecological systems. She was the author of *The Sea Around Us* (1951), and her *Silent Spring* (1962) touched off an international controversy over the effects of pesticides on the ecosystem. This piece is taken from *Under the Sea-Wind* (1941). It demonstrates mastery of the difficulty in process analysis of describing simultaneous processes.

1   So it came about that Scomber, the mackerel, was born in the surface waters of the open sea, seventy miles south by east from the western tip of Long Island. He came into being as a tiny globule no larger than a poppy seed, drifting in the surface layers of pale-green water. The globule carried an amber droplet of oil that served to keep it afloat and it carried also a gray particle of living matter so small that it could have been picked up on the point of a needle. In time this particle was to become Scomber, the mackerel, a powerful fish, streamlined after the manner of his kind, and a rover of the seas.

2   The parents of Scomber were fish of the last big wave of mackerel migration that came in from the edge of the continental shelf in May, heavy with spawn and driving rapidly shoreward. On the fourth evening of their jounrey, in a flooding current straining to landward, the eggs and milt had begun to flow from their bodies into the sea. Somewhere among the forty or fifty thousand eggs that were shed by one of the female fish was the egg that was to become Scomber.

3   There could be scarcely a stranger place in the world in which to begin life than this universe of sky and water, peopled by strange creatures and governed by wind and sun and ocean currents. It was a place of silence, except when the wind went whispering or blustering over the vast sheet of water, or when sea gulls came down the wind with their high, wild mewing, or when whales broke the surface, expelled the long-held breath, and rolled again into the sea.

4   The mackerel schools hurried on into the north and east, their journey scarcely interrupted by the act of spawning. As the sea birds were finding their resting places for the night on the dark water plains, swarms of

small and curiously formed animals stole into the surface waters from hills and valleys lying in darkness far below. The night sea belonged to the plankton, to the diminutive worms and the baby crabs, the glassy, big-eyed shrimp, the young barnacles and mussels, the throbbing bells of the jellyfish, and all the other small fry of the sea that shun the light.

It was indeed a strange world in which to set adrift anything so fragile   5
as a mackerel egg. It was filled with small hunters, each of which must live at the expense of its neighbors, plant and animal. The eggs of the mackerel were jostled by the newly hatched young of earlier spawning fishes and of shellfish, crustaceans, and worms. The larvae, some of them only a few hours old, were swimming alone in the sea, busily seeking their food. Some snatched out of the water with pincered claws anything small enough to be overpowered and swallowed; others seized any prey less swift and agile than themselves in biting jaws or sucked into cilium-studded mouths the drifting green or golden cells of the diatoms.

The sea was filled, too, with larger hunters than the microscopic larvae.   6
Within an hour after the parent mackerel had gone away, a horde of comb jellies rose to the surface of the sea. The comb jellies, or cteno-phores, looked like large gooseberries, and they swam by the beating of plates of fused hairs or cilia, set in eight bands down the sides of the transparent bodies. Their substance was scarcely more than that of sea water, yet each of them ate many times its own bulk of solid food in a day. Now they were rising slowly toward the surface, where the millions of new-spawned mackerel eggs drifted free in the upper layers of the sea. They twirled slowly back and forth on the long axes of their bodies as they came, flashing a cold, phosphorescent fire. Throughout the night the ctenophores flicked the waters with their deadly tentacles, each a slim, elastic thread twenty times the length of the body when extended. And as they turned and twirled and flashed frosty green lights in the black water, jostling one another in their greed, the drifting mackerel eggs were swept up in the silken meshes of the tentacles and carried by swift contraction to the waiting mouths.

Often during this first night of Scomber's existence the cold, smooth   7
body of a ctenophore collided with him or a searching tentacle missed by a fraction of an inch the floating sphere in which the speck of proto-plasm had already divided into eight parts, thus beginning the develop-ment by which a single fertile cell would swiftly be transformed into an embryo fish.

Of the millions of mackerel eggs drifting alongside the one that was   8
to produce Scomber, thousands went no farther than the first stages of the journey into life until they were seized and eaten by the comb jellies, to be speedily converted into the watery tissue of their foe and in this reincarnation to roam the sea, preying on their own kind.

Throughout the night, while the sea lay under a windless sky, the   9
decimation of the mackerel eggs continued. Shortly before dawn the

water began to stir to a breeze from the east and in an hour was rolling heavily under a wind that blew steadily to the south and west. At the first ruffling of the surface calm the comb jellies began to sink into deep water. Even in these simple creatures, which consist of little more than two layers of cells, one inside the other, there exists the counterpart of an instinct of self-preservation, causing them in some way to sense the threat of destruction which rough water holds for so fragile a body.

10   In the first night of their existence more than ten out of every hundred mackerel eggs either had been eaten by the comb jellies or, from some inherent weakness, had died after the first few divisions of the cell.

11   Now, the rising up of a strong wind blowing to southward brought fresh dangers to the mackerel eggs, left for the time being with few enemies in the surface waters about them. The upper layers of the sea streamed in the direction urged upon them by the wind. The drifting spheres moved south and west with the current, for the eggs of all sea creatures are carried helplessly wherever the sea takes them. It happened that the southwest drift of the water was carrying the mackerel eggs away from the normal nursery grounds of their kind into waters where food for young fish was scarce and hungry predators abundant. As a result of this mischance fewer than one egg in every thousand was to complete its development.

12   On the second day, as the cells within the golden globules of the eggs multiplied by countless divisions, and the shieldlike forms of embryo fish began to take shape above the yolk spheres, hordes of a new enemy came roving through the drifting plankton. The glassworms were transparent and slender creatures that cleaved the water like arrows, darting in all directions to seize fish eggs, copepods, and even others of their own kind. With their fierce heads and toothed jaws they were terrible as dragons to the smaller beings of the plankton, although as men measure they were less than a quarter of an inch long.

13   The floating mackerel eggs were scattered and buffeted by the dartings and rushes of the glassworms, and when the driftings of current and tide carried them away to other waters a heavy toll of the mackerel had been taken as food.

14   Again the egg that contained the embryonic Scomber had drifted unscathed while all about him other eggs had been seized and eaten. Under the warm May sun the new young cells of the egg were stirred to furious activity—growing, dividing, differentiating into cell layers and tissues and organs. After two nights and two days of life, the threadlike body of a fish was taking form within the egg, curled halfway around the globe of yolk that gave it food. Already a thin ridge down the midline showed where a stiffening rod of cartilage—forerunner of a backbone—was forming; a large bulge at the forward end showed the place of the head, and on it two smaller outpushings marked the future eyes of Scomber. On the third day a dozen V-shaped plates of muscle were

marked out on either side of the backbone; the lobes of the brain showed through the still-transparent tissues of the head; the ear sacs appeared; the eyes neared completion and showed dark through the egg wall, peering sightlessly into the surrounding world of the sea. As the sky lightened preparatory to the fifth rising of the sun a thin-walled sac beneath the head—crimson tinted from the fluid it contained—quivered, throbbed, and began the steady pulsation that would continue as long as there was life within the body of Scomber.

Throughout that day development proceeded at a furious pace, as 15 though in haste to make ready for the hatching that was soon to come. On the lengthening tail a thin flange of tissue appeared—the fin ridge from which a series of tail finlets, like a row of flags stiff in the wind, was later to be formed. The sides of an open groove that traversed the belly of the little fish, beneath and protected by the plate of more than seventy muscle segments, grew steadily downward and in midafternoon closed to form the alimentary canal. Above the pulsating heart the mouth cavity deepened, but it was still far short of reaching the canal.

Throughout all this time the surface currents of the sea were pouring 16 steadily to the southwest, driven by the wind and carrying with them the clouds of plankton. During the six days since the spawning of the mackerel the toll of the ocean's predators had continued without abatement, so that already more than half of the eggs had been eaten or had died in development.

It was the nights that had seen the greatest destruction. They had been 17 dark nights with the sea lying calm under a wide sky. On those nights the little stars of the plankton had rivaled in number and brilliance the constellations of the sky. From underlying depths the hordes of comb jellies and glassworms, copepods and shrimps, medusae of jellyfish, and translucent winged snails had risen into the upper layers to glitter in the dark water.

When the first dilution of blackness came in the east, warning of the 18 dawn into which the revolving earth was carrying them, strange processions began to hurry down through the water as the animals of the plankton fled from the sun that had not yet risen. Only a few of these small creatures could endure the surface waters by day except when clouds deflected the fierce lances of the sun.

In time Scomber and the other baby mackerel would join the hurrying 19 caravans that moved down into deep green water by day and pressed upward again as the earth swung once more into darkness. Now, while still confined within the egg, the embryonic marckerel had no power of independent motion, for the eggs remained in water of a density equal to their own and were carried horizontally in their own stratum of the sea.

On the sixth day the currents took the mackerel eggs over a large 20 shoal thickly populated with crabs. It was the spawning season of the crabs—the time when the eggs, that had been carried throughout the winter by the females, burst their shells and released the small, goblin-like lavae. Without delay the crab larvae set out for the upper waters, where through successive moltings of their infant shells and transformations of appearance they would take on the form of their race. Only after a period of life in the plankton would they be admitted to the colony of crabs that lived on that pleasant undersea plateau.

21   Now they hastened upward, each newborn crab swimming steadily with its wandlike appendages, each ready to discern with large black eyes and to seize with sharp-beaked mouth such food as the sea might offer. For the rest of that day the crab larvae were carried along with the mackerel eggs, on which they fed heavily. In the evening the struggle of two currents—the tidal current and the wind-driven current—carried many of the crab larvae to landward while the mackerel eggs continued to the south.

22   There were many signs in the sea of the approach to more southern latitudes. The night before the appearance of the crab larvae the sea had been set aglitter over an area of many miles with the intense green lights of the southern comb jelly Mnemiopsis, whose ciliated combs gleam with the colors of the rainbow by day and sparkle like emeralds in the night sea. And now for the first time there throbbed in the warm surface waters the pale southern form of the jellyfish Cyanea, trailing its several hundred tentacles through the water for fish or whatever else it might entangle. For hours at a time the ocean seethed with great shoals of salpae—thimble-sized, transparent barrels hooped in strands of muscle.

23   On the sixth night after the spawning of the mackerel the tough little skins of the eggs began to burst. One by one the tiny fishlets, so small that the combined length of twenty of them, head to tail, would have been scarcely an inch, slipped out of the confining spheres and knew for the first time the touch of the sea. Among these hatching fish was Scomber.

24   He was obviously an unfinished little fish. It seemed almost that he had burst prematurely from the egg, so unready was he to care for himself. The gill slits were marked out but were not cut through to the throat, so were useless for breathing. His mouth was only a blind sac. Fortunately for the newly hatched fishlet, a supply of food remained in the yolk sac still attached to him, and on this he would live until his mouth was open and functioning. Because of the bulky sac, however, the baby mackerel drifted upside down in the water, helpless to control his movements.

25   The next three days of life brought startling transformations. As the processes of development forged onward, the mouth and gill structures were completed and the finlets sprouting from back and sides and

underparts grew and found strength and certainty of movement. The eyes became deep blue with pigment, and now it may be that they sent to the tiny brain the first messages of things seen. Steadily the yolk mass shrank, and with its loss Scomber found it possible to right himself and by undulation of the still-rotund body and movement of the fins to swim through the water.

Of the steady drift, the southward pouring of the water day after day, he was unconscious, but the feeble strength of his fins was no match for the currents. He floated where the sea carried him, now a rightful member of the drifting community of the plankton. 26

Questions for the Critical Reader

1. In paragraph 3, Carson says that "there could be scarcely a stranger place in the world in which to begin life" than the place she describes. Exactly why does she seem to think so? Do you agree?
2. How would you describe the general atmosphere of the mackerel's environment?
3. How big a role does chance play in the life cycle of the mackerel? Explain.
4. What part does man play in all this?

Rhetorical Technique

1. Describe the range of the process being described here.
2. How much of this essay is impressionistic description? (See the introduction to Chapter 8.)
3. Why would a scientist choose that method of description? What effect does it have?
4. How much of this essay is narration? What is the effect of using it? (See the introduction to Chapter 9.)
5. How does Carson achieve emphasis? (See Glossary: *emphasis*.)
6. What is the author's point of view? (See Glossary: *point of view*.) Be specific in your answer.
7. How does this point of view affect her tone? (See Glossary: *style and tone*.)
8. From what other point of view might the same material be approached? Again, be specific in your answer.
9. Why does Carson choose to give the fish a name (that is, Scomber)?
10. Isolate two examples of parallel structure and comment on their effectiveness. (See Glossary: *parallel structure*.)
11. Consider the conclusion: what general type is it? How effective is it? (See Glossary: *conclusions*.)

Diction and Vocabulary

1. Considering the subject matter, do you find the language too scientific? Why? Why not? Be specific in your answers.
2. Which terms in paragraphs 2, 3, and 4 suggest personification of water, fish, and other sea creatures? What is the effect of using this figure of speech? (See Glossary: *personification*.)
3. Make a list of every word in the essay with which you are not familiar. Then go carefully over the context in which it appears to see if you can figure out the meaning from the way it is used in its place. Consult the dictionary if you are still stumped.

NENA AND GEORGE O'NEILL

Communicating with Yourself

George O'Neill received his Ph.D. from Columbia University and is a professor of anthropology at the City College, CUNY. Nena O'Neill received her B.A. from Barnard College and is currently earning her Ph.D. in anthropology. Dr. O'Neill and Nena O'Neill are a husband/wife anthropology team who have done field work in Mexico, Peru, the Caribbean, and the United States. Articles on their projects have been published in various anthropological and other professional journals. They have been researching modern marriage since 1967, have been married twenty-six years, and have two grown sons. This essay is adapted from *Open Marriage* (1972). The necessity for communicating with yourself, they say in the book, stems from the necessity for communicating openly with your mate. This cannot be done unless you are able to communicate with yourself. Their essay is thus the form of process analysis that gives directions on how to do something.

If you want your mate to stop guessing about your feelings and motives, 1 you have to be prepared to reveal yourself. And in order to reveal yourself you have to know yourself. You can't talk openly and honestly with your mate until you have tried being honest with yourself first. Take time off to be alone. Use that time not simply to engage in passive meditation, but to carry on an active inner dialogue with yourself, between the person you think you are and the inner you that operates at gut level. Communicating with yourself involves revelation, self-analysis and re-evaluation. Change is impossible otherwise. No architect of change, in any field, will attempt to make new plans without assessing the present situation. So, too, each of us can and must make an assessment of our own assets and liabilities.

Level with yourself. Remove your inner as well as your outer mask. 2 We all put on some sort of mask when we face others. But we have inner masks, too, behind which we hide from ourselves. Take a fresh look at yourself. What do you really feel, about yourself and others? Try to view yourself and your actions objectively, without praise or blame, simply trying to understand why you behave as you do, analyzing yourself as though you were an observer and not the doer. What would the judgment of an impartial observer be concerning a given action of yours?

If you are honest with yourself, you may come up with an unflattering 3 objective analysis of your behavior. And at that point you will probably start arguing with yourself, rationalizing your actions, seeking external causes that impelled you to act as you did. The boss yelled at you, you weren't in a position to yell back, and went home in a temper. At home you then yelled at your wife, who subsequently yelled at the children. And so on. But there's nothing wrong with attempting to rationalize your behavior so long as it's part of a debate with that other "objective" part of yourself. Which half of you "wins" the debate is beside the point. It is the debate itself that is important, because it gives you an opportunity to get to know yourself better. If you happen to be a person who is easily depressed, with a tendency to run yourself down and take too much blame on yourself, then you should try to reverse the procedure, using the "objective" part of yourself to praise your actions and point out the redeeming aspects of your behavior.

4   Some people are naturally given to analyzing themselves, having discovered long ago that doing so gave them added confidence—other people's criticism is far less likely to hurt you if you have already gone over the pros and cons in your own head. If the criticism is just, then you will be able to more easily admit your mistake and move on without wallowing in self-pity or guilt. On the other hand, if the criticism is unjust, then you will be able to better defend yourself, since both sides of the argument are clear in your own mind.

5   In devising other exercises for getting acquainted with yourself, you can provide your own best guidelines. Professional analysts' books on the subject may be a help, but they are generally made up of case histories of people whose situations may be very different from your own. More useful, because it is more personal, is the analysis of your own dreams. An interesting and effective method of analysis is presented by Dr. Fritz Perls in *Gestalt Psychology Verbatim.* The book is based on taped sessions in which Dr. Perls demonstrates how to use dreams as a vehicle for self-exploration. You need only a segment of a dream. From that segment you take each element and *become* it, personifying it and giving a voice to it. You assume the role of the train, the butterfly, the menacing stranger, whatever—each object or person in the dream. In this way you can learn to recognize your inner conflicts and translate your own private symbolism in terms that are more readily understandable.

6   The usefulness of such devices will depend upon the kind of person you are. But you should try to discover some way in which to communicate better with yourself. To understand why you acted as you did in one case is an important step toward the prevention of future overreaction or miscommunication in your relationship with your mate. Your insights become part of you, unconscious as well as conscious, and the more knowledgeable you are concerning yourself, the easier it will be for you to communicate that self to your mate.

Questions for the Critical Reader

1. In paragraph 1, the authors suggest that three elements are involved in communicating with oneself. Where in the subsequent paragraphs do they discuss each of these?
2. Give some examples of what it is we do when we wear an inner mask.
3. Estimate the difficulty or ease of looking at yourself "objectively, without praise or blame" (par. 2).
4. What does it mean to rationalize one's behavior?
5. In what sense is it "the debate itself that is important"? (Par. 3.)
6. Does your own self-analyzing tendency give you "added confidence" (par. 4)?
7. Do you have any "exercises" (par. 5) for getting better acquainted with yourself? Con you think of some?
8. Evaluate Dr. Perls's dream exploration technique in paragraph 5.
9. Would the kind of intimate and open communication advocated by the O'Neills also be suitable for other relationships? Justify your answer.

Rhetorical Technique

1. Is this like any of the other kinds of process analysis you have read in this chapter? Isolate the differences. (See the introduction to this chapter.)
2. What is the difficulty that the O'Neills faced in writing this? (See the introduction to this chapter.)
3. Is there one specific direction they give that is more important than all the rest?
4. How does time figure in this analysis?
5. What was the O'Neills' purpose in writing this? (See Glossary: *purpose.*)
6. How does that purpose relate to the central theme? (See Glossary: *central theme; subject; unity.*)
7. Which other methods of exposition are employed here? Isolate specific paragraphs. (See the introduction to the student.)
8. Which general type of introduction is this one? (See Glossary: *introductions.*)
9. Comment on the balance between abstract and concrete here. (See Glossary: *abstract and concrete.*)

Diction and Vocabulary

1. Consider the tone of this essay. (See Glossary: *style and tone*.)
    a) How much of a contribution to the tone is made by the relative absence of psychological terms?
    b) How much is contributed by such terms as "gut level" (par. 1), "level with" (par. 2), and "yelled" (par. 3)?
2. Consult the dictionary to be sure you understand the meanings of *impartial* (par. 2); *subsequently* (3); *rationalize* (3); *redeeming* (3).

Writing Suggestions for Chapter 6: *Process Analysis*

I.

Write an analysis of some process in which you describe either how something works or how to do something. Remember when you choose a subject that *it* will determine what approach you must take in order to reach a specific reader (audience). The same point of view or level of objectivity cannot always be used for different purposes and/or subjects. You may use one of the following suggestions, or you may select a subject of your own.

1. How to relax on vacation.
2. How to take good photographs.
3. How to get the most out of visiting a foreign city.
4. How to care for plants.
5. How maple syrup is made.
6. How to diet successfully.
7. How to improve an aspect of one's tennis game.
8. How to find out your rights in some specific area.
9. How to select a stereo rig.
10. How to reduce local pollution.

II. A. Writing Assignment Based on "How to Brew the World's Greatest Cup of Coffee"

Simple. Trust me. Just write a brief little essay in process analysis telling the reader exactly how to do something that *you really know about*. The way Lish claims *he* knows about coffee. In this, you're the best. Your favorite thing. The thing you are most certain of. For example, (1) how to test a speaker, (2) how to drive to the basket and get your own offensive rebound, (3) how to mow a lawn, (4) how to make friends with the opposite sex, or (5) how to repair something.

B. Writing Assignment Based on "How to Get Along with Americans"

(1) Do Lierres's piece all over again. Assume you are a foreigner who *really* knows Americans, and address your countrymen exactly as Lierres does—with dos and don'ts. Only use what you, an American, *really* know about how to get along with Americans.

(2) Or use Lierres's basic form as a model. Now write an essay in which you give advice (a list of dos and don'ts) to someone who is about to make contact for the first time with (and wants to make a good impression on) one of the following groups: (1) your family, (2) a group of your intimate friends, (3) your college community, (4) your townspeople, or (5) your neighborhood community.

7

Arriving at a *Causal Analysis*

As we saw in the preceding chapter, an analysis breaks down a whole into its component parts: a process analysis depicts *how* things work, but a causal analysis says why they do. The kind of analysis to be applied depends upon the writer's purpose and interest. The Battle of the Bulge in World War II, for example, can be analyzed both ways. A class in military tactics would be interested in a detailed study of *how*, an analysis of the process; on the other hand, a news reporter or a politician might want to know *why* it took place. On a simpler level, someone operating a typewriter must know how to do it but probably wouldn't be interested in why it works.

Causal analyses are usually written in order to examine complex human affairs; process analyses are usually written to explain complex mechanical affairs.

To begin to understand what is involved in a causal analysis, consider this hypothetical sequence of events:

A twenty-two-year-old farmer, dissatisfied with a series of personal defeats suffered on the small piece of land that he works, takes a bus to the city. Near the terminal he buys a rifle and some ammunition. That night, in a cheap hotel, he broods over his situation. He looks out the window. A couple is sitting together on a park bench. Moved perhaps by their apparent closeness, he suddenly and impulsively shoves the gun out the window and fires at them. The man on the bench is killed; the woman, seriously wounded.

Question: What is the cause of the man's death and the woman's wounds?

The legal responsibility in the case is very clear. Obviously, the farmer caused the death and the wounding. But suppose we had a broader interest in the case and wanted to look further into it. Then we could ask other questions. For example, could we assign some of the blame (cause) to the fact that the farmer could so easily buy a dangerous weapon? Certainly, we would not assign any of the causality to, say, the bus that brought him to the city (a cause we would label *remote*). Could we say that *a* farmer's living conditions together with *this* farmer's personal circumstances were enough to disturb him to the point where he committed his act?

Probing analyses of real criminal events, some of them much like our hypothetical case, can lead and have led to important and useful conclusions about crime control. And, as individuals and social beings, we are always in need of making causal analyses—not only of past events but also of future possibilities. Thus we would not only analyze the results of an election but also consider the effects to be caused by, say, a population increase in a residential district, the effects of a manufacturing process on air quality, or the effects of a new traffic control pattern.

Of course, nothing takes place in isolation, and there is an almost infinitely extended texture of interrelations between things in our world. If we could analyze all of them we would know everything. Because we cannot, we need to concentrate on a range of causes from the *incidental* to the most remote and find the most satisfying middle ground. In the case of the farmer, for example, we could say that the *incidental* cause of the tragedy was the gun. The *remote* causes were the bus that took him to the city and the random chance that took the couple to the park bench. Yet neither of these is satisfactory. Human action, purposeful or uncontrolled, is the usual wellspring of events or conditions, and we would have to say that the *immediate* cause of the tragedy was the complicated emotional state of the farmer. If we looked into that state, we would probably be satisfied that it was the causative agent.

A fair rule of thumb to apply when seeking immediate causes is to work with these formulas:

1. Without event A, event B cannot take place.
2. Where there is A, there will be B.

The reader will be able to see how these work if he will substitute for A each of the causes outlined above and for B the effect in the case (the shooting).

Key points to remember in making causal analyses are these:

1. Do not assume that because something happened (A) *before* something else (B), it must have been the cause of the *later* event. Falling in love on Monday may be wonderful, but it is not likely to be the cause of your receiving an acceptance to medical school on Tuesday. Similarly, an apple that falls from a tree is not necessarily ripe; the wind may have caused it to fall.

2. Try to be objective and broad-minded in your analysis. This means

that you must be prepared to acknowledge that we live in a complex world where numerous causes can contribute to a single event. Thus, in the case of the farmer, it might be more accurate to say that the immediate causes were his condition *and* the ease with which he bought a gun.

3. The structure of a causal analysis can proceed from the effect to the immediate cause by way of the most remote, or the writer can begin with the incidental and proceed from there. Usually, the best structural plan evolves from the writer's careful thought about his particular subject.

4. Finally, the writer should understand that a causal analysis has the purpose of arriving at the truth but that it is a form very similar to argument (whose purpose it is to persuade or convince). Thus the writer should rely not on statements or guesses but on evidence. For this purpose, go back to Chapter 1, and review what is said there about the nature of evidence.

SHANA ALEXANDER

Kids' Country

Shana Alexander was born in 1925. Journalist, editor, commentator, and social critic, Ms. Alexander writes a regular column for *Newsweek* and appears regularly on the CBS-TV news magazine, *Sixty Minutes*. She has won many awards for her work and has recently (1975) published *Shana Alexander's State-by-State Guide to Women's Legal Rights*. "Kids' Country," one of her *Newsweek* columns, appeared there just before Christmas in 1972. Her analysis of certain prominent features of American culture leads her back to a single cause.

1   Children are a relatively modern invention. Until a few hundred years ago they did not exist. In medieval and Renaissance painting you see pint-size men and women, wearing grown-up clothes and grown-up expressions, performing grown-up tasks. Children did not exist because the family as we know it had not evolved. In the old days most people lived on the land, and life was a communal affair.

2   Children today not only exist; they have taken over. God's Country has to an astonishing degree become Kids' Country—in no place more than in America, and at no time more than now. Once more 'tis the season, holiday time has begun, the frantic family skedaddle from pumpkin to holly when Kids' Country runs in its jumpingest high gear.

3   But it is always Kids' Country here. Our civilization is child-centered, child-obsessed. A kid's body is our physical ideal. Weightwatchers grunt and pant. Sages jog from sea to shining sea. Plastic surgeons scissor and tuck up. New hair sprouts, transplanted, on wisdom's brow. One way or another we are determined to "keep in shape," and invariably this means keeping a kid's shape—which we then outfit in baby-doll ruffles, sneakers and blue jeans.

4   The food we live on is kids' food: pizza, hot dogs, fried chicken, ice cream, hamburgers. This bizarre diet is the reason we have such trouble maintaining our kids' bodies.

Soft Switch

5   The stuff we now drink has thrown the beverage industry into turmoil. Our consumption of soft drinks has risen 80 per cent in a decade. Americans not only are switching *en masse* from hot coffee to iced tea, and bitter drinks to sweet. The popularity of alcoholic soda pop—the

so-called "fun" wines like Thunderbird and apple wine has jumped 168 per cent in five years!

Children hate spinach, vitamins and *haute cuisine*. They like their food kooked, not cooked: you pop, thaw, dissolve or explode it into eatability. To buy it you push around a wire perambulator, and at the end of the supermarket line you get prizes of colored stamps. 6

In Kids' Country, every day must be prize day. Miss America, Miss Teen-Age America, Miss Junior Miss America and probably Miss Little Miss America trample each other down star-spangled runways. Volume mail-order giveaways will shortly silt up our postal system entirely. All day long TV shows like "Concentration," "Dating Game," Hollywood Squares" and "Jackpot" hand out more toys: wrist watches, washing machines, trips to Hawaii. 7

The rest of the world may be in fee to the Old Boy Network,[1] carried on to the point of senility, but here there are no elder statesmen left. Seniority in an American politician no longer denotes wisdom, only power or tenure. The old age of the present Congress is a major hindrance. No one considers the Héberts and Eastlands[2] as Athenian men.[3] 8

Golden Boys

Our contemporary heroes are a series of golden boys. A direct line links Charles Lindbergh to Billy Graham[4] to the astronauts to John F. Kennedy—and to his kid brothers. 9

The philosopher-kings of Kids' Country are professors like Erich Segal and Charles Reich,[5] who saw in Woodstock and the flower children a new golden age of innocence he called Consciousness III. The totem animal in Kids' Country just now is a talking, philosophizing seagull who soars on vast updrafts of hot air, and the beloved bogeyman is a wicked movie *mafioso* with a heart of gold. 10

The ideal of American parenthood is to be a kid with your kid. Take him to Disneyland; take him fishing, take him out to the ball game. Our national pastimes are kids' games, and we are all hooked. When the Redskins are blacked out in Washington, the President holes up in 11

---

[1] *Old Boy Network.* Loosely, a system of seniority in which power resides in a group of older men and is passed down through them to the younger ones.

[2] *the Héberts and the Eastlands.* Rep. Edward Hébert and Sen. James O. Eastland were both powerful congressional committee chairmen.

[3] *Athenian men.* That is, wise men—philosopher-kings, such as were commonly believed to have been the best rulers in ancient Athens.

[4] *Charles Lindbergh to Billy Graham.* Lindbergh (1902–1974), became an American folk hero when he made the first solo flight across the Atlantic in 1927. The Rev. Billy Graham (b. 1918) is an evangelist, a charismatic religious leader.

[5] *Erich Segal and Charles Reich.* Segal, a professor of classics, wrote the best seller *Love Story*, from which the movie starring Ryan O'Neal and Ali McGraw was made. Reich, a professor of law, wrote *The Greening of America*, in which he discusses Consciousness III.

New York so as not to miss the big game. Bobby Fischer,[6] the quintessential smart boy of every school, turns the whole country on to chess. "The Boys of Summer"[7] becomes a best seller. In nostalgia's golden haze, we forget the poet's full line, "I see the boys of summer in their ruin."

12   In Kids' Country we do not permit middle age. Thirty is promoted over 50, but 30 knows that soon his time to be overtaken will come. Middle-aged man must appear to run, even if it is only running in place. Often the big kid outruns his heart. In our over-60 population there are ten widows for every man.

13   Like a child's room, Kids' Country is a ness. New York City seems about to disappear under its load of litter, graffiti and dog droppings. How is it that China can eliminate the house fly, and we can't even clean up Central Park?

14   In Kids' Country, not so ironically, Mommy and Daddy are household gods, and so we have two immense national holidays, elsewhere virtually unknown, called "Mother's Day" and "Father's Day."

15   We are the first society in which parents expect to learn from their children. Such a topsy-turvy situation has come about at least in part because, unlike the rest of the world, ours is an immigrant society, and for immigrants the *only* hope is in the kids. In the Old Country, hope was in the father, and how much family wealth he could accumulate and pass along to his children. In the growth pattern of America and its ever-expanding frontier, the young man was ever advised to Go West; the father was ever inheriting from his son: the topsy-turviness was built-in from the beginning. In short, a melting pot needs a spoon. Kids' Country may be the inevitable result.

16   Kids' Country is not all bad. America is the greatest country in the world to grow up in *because* it's Kids' Country. We not only wear kids' clothes and eat kids' food; we dream kids' dreams, and make them come true. It was, after all, a boys' game to go to the moon.

Youth Eternal

17   Certainly as a people we thrive. By the time they are 16, most American kids today are bigger, stronger—and smarter—than Mommy and Daddy ever were. And if they are not precisely "happier," they may well be more "grown up." But being a civilization with no genuine rites of passage, what we are experiencing now seems in many ways the exact opposite of medieval and Renaissance life. If in the old days children did not exist, it seems equally true today that adults, as a class, have begun to disappear, condemning all of us to remain boys and girls forever, jogging and doing push-ups against eternity.

[6] *Bobby Fischer.* Chess prodigy. Former U.S. and world champion.
[7] *"The Boys of Summer."* A book by Roger Kahn about the accomplishments of the old Brooklyn Dodgers.

Questions for the Critical Reader

1. The opening paragraph starts with the assertion that "children are a relatively modern invention" and then goes on to analyze why children have not been prominent in family life until modern times. Is this a convincing analysis? Could it be improved?
2. *Is* a kid's body "**our** physical ideal"? Consider the type of body implied by that phrase. Could it be an ideal of ours for reasons other than that it's a kid's body? Explain.
3. In paragraph 4, Alexander suggests that fast food is kids' food. Are these foods produced to meet the kids' wishes? Do kids like them because they are available? Or is there another reason for the proliferation of fast food chains?
4. Still on the food question: what foods is the author talking about in paragraph 6? How does this relate to the preceding questions?
5. Paragraph 12 begins with the assertion that "in Kids' country we do not permit middle age." Comment on the meaning of this statement. Can you give examples?
6. What is the author's attitude toward kids' country—up to but not including paragraph 16?
7. Does she successfully qualify this attitude in or after paragraph 16? Justify your answer. How would you have improved such a qualification?
8. What features can you imagine for something called "Old Folks' country"?

Rhetorical Technique

1. Locate the statement of the author's central theme. (See Glossary: *central theme; subject; unity.*)
2. What exactly is being analyzed here?
3. Of the many effects or types of effects cited here, which do you think most effectively "prove" the central theme? Explain.
4. Which are least effective?
5. Considering the relationship between argument and causal analysis, estimate the extent to which this essay is argumentative. (See Chapter 1.)
6. Analyze the content of each paragraph, and then describe the structural pattern employed here.
7. Describe the means of transition between paragraphs 3 and 4 and 6 and 7. Then comment on their effectiveness. (See Glossary: *transition.*)
8. Of what general type is the conclusion to this piece? (See Glossary: *conclusions.*)

Diction and Vocabulary

1. Why is the word *Kids'* capitalized throughout?
2. In paragraph 6, why does the author choose the word *perambulator* instead of *shopping cart*? What other verbal tactics does the author use to illustrate her theme?
3. Consult the dictionary to be sure you understand the meanings of the following words and phrases: *bizarre* (par. 4); *en masse* (5); *haute cuisine* (6); *perambulator* (6); *silt up* (7); *in fee* (8); *senility* (8); *quintessential* (10); *rites of passage* (17).
4. Take the figure of speech in paragraph 15, "a melting pot needs a spoon," and carefully work out the comparison being made. Then answer the question, How effective is it? (See Glossary: *figures of speech*.)

WALTER LAQUEUR

Terrorist Myths

Walter Laqueur, journalist, foreign correspondent, author, and
university professor, was born in Germany in 1921. Since 1966, he
has been coeditor of the *Journal of Contemporary History* and
from 1967–1972 was professor of the history of ideas and politics
at Brandeis University. The author of numerous books and articles
on foreign policy and international affairs, he is currently chairman
of the Research Council of the Center for Strategic and International Studies in Washington, D.C. This essay, adapted from "The
Futility of Terrorism," a somewhat longer essay that first appeared in *Harper's* in 1976, uses the technique of analyzing previous analyses (which he calls myths) and demolishing them with
deeper explanations.

The current terrorist epidemic has mystified a great many people, and 1
various explanations have been offered—most of them quite wrong. Only
a few will be mentioned here:

Political terror is a new and unprecedented phenomenon. It is as old as 2
the hills, only the manifestations of terror have changed. The present
epidemic is mild compared with previous outbreaks. There were more
assassinations of leading statesmen in the 1890s in both America and
Europe, when terrorism had more supporters, than at the present time.
Nor is terrorist doctrine a novelty. In 1884 Johannes Most, a German
Social Democrat turned anarchist, published in New York a manual,
Revolutionary (Urban) Warfare, with the subtitle "A Handbook of
Instruction Regarding the Use and Manufacture of Nytroglycerine,
Dynamite, Guncotton, Fulminating Mercury, Bombs, Arson, Poisons,
etc." Most pioneered the idea of the letter bomb and argued that the
liquidation of "pigs" was not murder because murder was the willful
killing of a human being, whereas policemen did not belong in this
category.

It is sometimes argued that guerrilla and terrorist movements in past 3
ages were sporadic and essentially apolitical. But this is not so; the
Russian anarchists of the last century were as well organized as any
contemporary movement, and their ideological and political sophistication was, if anything, higher. The same goes for the guerrilla wars of
the nineteenth century. The guerrilla literature published in Europe in
the 1830s and 1840s is truly modern in almost every respect. It refers
to "bases," "liberated areas," "protracted war" as well as the gradual

transformation of guerrilla units into a regular army. The basic ideas of Mao and Castro all appeared at least a hundred years ago.

4   **Terrorism is left-wing and revolutionary in character.** Terrorists do not believe in liberty or egality or fraternity. Historically, they are elitists, contemptuous of the masses, believing in the historical mission of a tiny minority. It was said about the Tupamaros[1] that one had to be a Ph.D. to be a member. This was an exaggeration but not by very much. Their manifestos may be phrased in left-wing language, but previous generations of terrorists proclaimed Fascist ideas. Nineteenth-century European partisans and guerrillas fighting Napoleon were certainly right-wing. The Spanish guerrilleros wanted to reintroduce the Inquisition, the Italian burned the houses of all citizens suspected of left-wing ideas. Closer to our own period, the IRA[2] and the Macedonian IMRO[3] at various times in their history had connections with Fascism and Communism. The ideology of terrorist movements such as the Stern gang[4] and the popular Front for the Liberation of Palestine encompasses elements of the extreme Left and Right. Slogans change with intellecual fashions and should not be taken too seriously. The real inspiration underlying terrorism is a free-floating activism that can with equal ease turn right or left. It is the action that counts.

5   **Terrorism appears whenever people have genuine, legitimate grievances. Remove the grievance and terror will cease.** The prescription seems plausible enough, but experience does not bear it out. On the level of abstract reasoning it is, of course, true that there would be no violence if no one had a grievance or felt frustration. But in practice there will always be disaffected, alienated, and highly aggressive people claiming that the present state of affairs is intolerable and that only violence will bring a change. Some of their causes may even be real and legitimate— but unfulfillable. This applies to the separatist demands of minorities, which, if acceded to, would result in the emergence of nonviable states and the crippling of society. It is always the fashion to blame the state or the "system" for every existing injustice. But some of the problems may simply be insoluble, at least in the short run. No state or social system can be better than the individuals constituting it.

6   It is ultimately the perception of grievance that matters, not the grievance itself. At one time a major grievance may be fatalistically accepted, whereas at another time (or elsewhere) a minor grievance may produce the most violent reaction. A comparison of terrorist activities over the last century shows, beyond any shadow of doubt, that violent

[1] *Tupamaros.* Uruguayan revolutionaries.

[2] *IRA.* The Irish Republican Army, a revolutionary group.

[3] *Macedonian IMRO.* A nationalist group that functioned between 1890 and 1935 in Bulgaria and Yugoslavia.

[4] *the Stern gang.* An extremist group of Zionists, active during the Israeli war for independence (ca. 1947–1948).

protest movements do not appear where despotism is worst but, on the contrary, in permissive democratic societies or ineffective authoritarian regimes. There were no terrorist movements in Nazi Germany, nor in Fascist Italy, nor in any of the Communist countries. The Kurdish[5] insurgents were defeated by the Iraqi government in early 1975 with the greatest of ease, whereas terrorism in Ulster continues for many years now and the end it not in sight. The Iraqis succeeded not because they satisfied the grievances of the Kurds but simply because they could not care less about public opinion abroad.

Terror is highly effective. Terror is noisy, it catches the headlines. Its 7 melodrama inspires horror and fascination. But seen in historical perspective, it has hardly ever had a lasting effect. Guerrilla wars have been successful only against colonial rule, and the age of colonialism is over. Terrorism did have a limited effect at a time of general war, but only in one instance (Cuba) has a guerrilla movement prevailed in peacetime. But the constellation in Cuba was unique and, contrary to Castro's expectations, there were no repeat performances elsewhere in Latin America. The Vietnam war in its decisive phase was no longer guerrilla in character. There is no known case in modern history of a terrorist movement seizing political power, although terror has been used on the tactical level by radical political parties. Society will tolerate terrorism as long as it is no more than a nuisance. Once insecurity spreads and terror becomes a real danger, the authorities are no longer blamed for disregarding human rights in their struggle against it. On the contrary, the cry goes up for more repressive measures, irrespective of the price that has to be paid in human rights. The state is always so much stronger than the terrorists, whose only hope for success is to prevent the authorities from using their full powers. If the terrorist is the fish following Mao Tse-tung's parable[6] the permissiveness and the inefficiency of liberal society is the water. As Regis Debray, apostle of the Latin-American guerrillas, wrote about the Tupamaros: "By digging the grave of liberal Uruguay, they dug their own grave."

The importance of terrorism will grow enormously in the years to 8 **come as the destructive power of its weapons increases.** This danger does indeed exist, with the increasing availability of missiles, nuclear material, and highly effective poisons. But it is part of a wider problem, that of individuals blackmailing society. To engage in nuclear ransom, a "terrorist movement" is not needed; a small group of madmen or

---

[5] *Kurdish.* Kurds are a pastoral and agricultural people occupying a plateau region that cuts across several mid-Eastern countries, notably Iran, Iraq, Turkey, and Syria; they also reside in parts of the Soviet Union.

[6] *Mao Tse-tung's parable.* According to Mao, the guerrilla fighter is the fish, and the water, which nurtures and supports him, is the people, the peasantry. Laqueur's comparison is therefore ironic.

criminals, or just one person, could be equally effective—perhaps even more so. The smaller the group, the more difficult it would be to identify and combat.

9 **Political terrorists are more intelligent and less cruel than "ordinary" criminals.** Most political terrorists in modern times have been of middle- or upper-class origin, and many of them have had a higher education. Nevertheless, they have rarely shown intelligence, let alone political sophistication. Larger issues and future perspectives are of little interest to them, and they are quite easily manipulated by foreign intelligence services. As for cruelty, the "ordinary" criminal, unlike the terrorist, does not believe in indiscriminate killing. He may torture a victim, but this will be the exception, not the rule, for he is motivated by material gain and not by fanaticism. The motivation of the political terrorist is altogether different. Since, in his eyes, everyone but himself is guilty, restraints do not exist.

10 Political terror therefore tends to be less humane than the variety practiced by "ordinary" criminals. The Palestinian terrorists have specialized in killing children, while the Provisional IRA[7] has concentrated its attacks against Protestant workers, and this despite their professions of "proletarian internationalism." It is the terrorists' aim not just to kill their opponents but to spread confusion and fear. It is part of the terrorist indoctrination to kill the humanity of the terrorist—all this, of course, for a more humane and just world order.

11 **Terrorists are poor, hungry, and desperate human beings.** Terrorist groups without powerful protectors are indeed poor. But modern transnational terrorism is, more often than not, big business. According to a spokesman of the Palestine "Rejection Front"[8] in an interview with the Madrid newspaper *Platforma*, the income of the PLO is as great as that of certain Arab countries, such as Jordan, with payments by the oil countries on the order of $150 million to $200 million. Officials of the organizations are paid $5,000 a month and more, and everyone gets a car as a matter of course; they have acquired chalets and bank accounts in Switzerland. But the "Rejection Front," financed by Iraq, Libya, and Algeria is not kept on a starvation diet either. The Argentine ERP[9] and the Montoneros[10] have amassed many millions of dollars through bank robberies and extortion. Various Middle Eastern and East European governments give millions to terrorist movements from Ulster to the Philippines. This abundance of funds makes it possible to engage in all

---

[7] *Provisional IRA.* A branch of the IRA noted for its violent tactics.

[8] *Palestine "Rejection Front."* A splinter group of Palestinian terrorists who reject all possibilities of a peaceful settlement of the Palestinian question.

[9] *Argentine ERP.* Another nationalist group. Originally Trotskyite Socialists, they have become associated with Castroite tendencies.

[10] *Montoneros.* A group of guerrillas active in Argentina. They can be characterized as leftist Peronistas.

kinds of costly operations, to bribe officials, and to purchase sophisticated weapons. At the same time, the surfeit of money breeds corruption. The terrorists are no longer lean and hungry after prolonged exposure to life in Hilton hotels. They are still capable of carrying out gangster-style operations of short duration, but they become useless for long campaigns involving hardship and privation.

All this is not to say that political terror is always reprehensible or 12 could never be effective. The assassination of Hitler or Stalin in the 1920s or 1930s would not only have changed the course of history, it would have saved the lives of millions of people. Terrorism is morally justified whenever there is no other remedy for an intolerable situation. Yet it seldom occurs, and virtually never succeeds, where tyranny is harshest.

Questions for the Critical Reader

1. What is the author's attitude toward terrorism?
2. How would you describe the difference between terrorism and violent protest?
3. Comment on the myth being dealt with in paragraph 4. From what you know about the subject, would you say that Laqueur's explanation is a satisfying one? Justify your answer.
4. In paragraph 5, "the separatist demands of minorities" are referred to. Is this reference clear? Why? Why not? What is your opinion of the author's stand with respect to these demands?
5. Comment on the assertion made to begin paragraph 6?
6. Does Laqueur really address the myth in paragraph 7, "Terror is highly effective?" Explain.
7. Is it true, as he says in paragraph 7, that "society will tolerate terrorism as long as it is no more than a nuisance"? Suppose it were to go beyond being a nuisance, what ways might society take to end it?
8. Do you believe that "the age of colonialism is over"? Give evidence for your opinion.

Rhetorical Technique

1. In what way is this essay an example of causal analysis?
2. Laqueur's unusual technique is to take *previous* explanations (myths) and show how his explanation of these is superior. In his opening paragraph, he says that he is mentioning only a few of these myths. Does this invalidate his explanations? Can you name others that he neglects?

3. Which methods does he use to explode each myth?
4. To what extent does Laqueur use the method we have called illustrative example?
5. How much of this analysis is an argument? Be specific in citing paragraphs and/or ideas. (See Chapter 1.)
6. In two sentences or less, state the author's central theme. Can you point to a thesis statement? (See Glossary: *central theme; subject; thesis statement; unity.*)
7. What principle of order governs the numbering of the myths he discusses?
8. Cite an example of paradox. (See Glossary: *paradox.*)
9. Locate an example of this author's irony. (See Glossary: *irony.*)
10. What is the author's point of view? (See Glossary: *point of view.*)

Diction and Vocabulary

1. Consider the connotative values of the words *guerrilla, terrorist,* and *partisan.* Then comment on the effectivess of their use by this author. (See Glossary: *connotation and denotation.*)
2. Cite one example of a metaphor. (See Glossary, *figures of speech.*)
3. Consider the following expressions: *old as the hills* (par 1); *shadow of a doubt* (6); *greatest of ease* (6); *end is not in sight* (6); *could not care less* (6); *catches the headlines* (7):
   a) Which of these is colloquial and which cliché? (See Glossary: *colloquial language; cliché.*)
   b) What is the effect of the use of each?
4. Consult the dictionary to be sure you understand the meanings of the following words and phrases: *unprecedented, manifestation, anarchist* (par. 2); *sporadic, apolitical, ideological, protracted* (3); *egality, Ph.D., manifestos, partisans, free-floating activism* (4); *separatist, acceded, nonviable* (5); *fatalistically, despotism, insurgents* (6); *melodrama, constellation, tactical, irrespective* (7); *indiscriminate, fanaticism* (9); *proletarian internationalism, indoctrination* (10); *chalets, surfeit* (11).

ANDRA MEDEA AND KATHLEEN THOMPSON

Why Do Men Rape Women?

> Kathleen Thompson was born in Oklahoma City, Oklahoma, was
> graduated from Northwestern University, and works as a com-
> mercial artist in Chicago. She was one of the founders of Chicago
> Women Against Rape and has traveled and lectured widely in the
> Midwest on the subject of women and rape. Andra Medea was
> born in Chicago and attended the University of Illinois and
> Columbia College in Chicago. She is a commercial artist and
> photographer and teaches self-defense. Ms. Medea has been a
> speaker for Chicago Women Against Rape in many areas in the
> Midwest. This essay is the second chapter of their book, *Against
> Rape* (1974). It is a careful causal analysis of rape that depends on
> an analysis of certain types of men and the experience of rape
> victims.

In researching this book, we relied heavily on descriptions by rape   1
victims. From these women's experiences and from our own experiences,
we were able to gain some insight into the way a rape situation works.
It appears that there are two dynamics operating: hostility (including
such emotions as rage, hatred, contempt, and the desire to humiliate)
and gratification. A rape may be motivated entirely by one or the other,
but it is much more often a combination of the two.

The rape in which hostility is the main factor is a very dangerous and   2
frightening situation. Here sexual release is a secondary, perhaps even
negligible, factor. This sort of rape is not necessarily characterized by
brutality, but includes it more frequently than the other; in any case,
whether actual brutality is involved or not, the act is essentially one of
violence. The subjugation of the victim is basic to the rapist's satisfaction.

The second sort of rape, in which sexual gratification is the primary   3
motivation, is more ambiguous, more confusing to the woman and to
the people she turns to for help afterward. It is not likely that the rapist
will go so far as to brutalize the woman to gain what he wants: the
brutality itself is not particularly appealing to him. He will threaten,
overpower, and blackmail, but not kill or beat her to get what he wants.

One must begin to wonder about a society that produces so many men   4
capable of either sort of rape.

The first sort of rapist is the man who buys the John Wayne brand of   5
masculinity. Ideally, the qualities we call masculine and the qualities we

call feminine should be balanced in an individual. When they are out of balance, the result is a monster. The personality traits which have been labeled masculine include strength, independence, aggressiveness, self-control, rationality. The feminine ideal is soft, sensitive, accepting, intuitive, loving. These are all positive terms. But to see what horrors can result from an imbalance in either direction, let us use the negative terms, the words which would be used to describe the same characteristics in a member of the "wrong" sex. A woman would be hard, bullheaded, pushy, cold, and calculating if she took on "masculine" traits. A man would be weak, spineless, stupid, and a sissy if he took on "feminine" traits.

6   To take this one step further, we would suggest that the very masculine *man* is hard, bullheaded, pushy, cold, and calculating. He is also a potential rapist. Aggressiveness—unchecked by sensitivity, gentleness, and concern for others—is a basic trait of the rapist. Similarly, the woman who lives up, or down, to the feminine ideal *is* weak. She is unprotected against her "natural" opposite, the "aggressive male." Both are in bad shape, but it doesn't take much to figure out which one is going to be hurt. It may be restrictive to be reared to beat up other people, but there is no doubt that to be trained to be beaten up is more painful.

7   The result of this conditioning is that it incapacitates women for an independent existence, making them dependent on men for protection. And it makes men who buy what is essentially the code of chivalry likely *either* to protect women or to victimize them. The two impulses come from the same source, and the same men will probably do both, at different times and to different women. If this sort of man wants to vent his hostility, even a general, nonspecific hostility, he sees women as the victims authorized by society. The code of chivalry decrees that only a coward would hit a woman, but millions of men beat their wives, hit their girl friends, and, sometimes, rape strangers on the street: clearly, it is only certain women, under certain circumstances, who are protected by that code. It makes the rest of womankind more, not less, likely to be attacked. As Susan Griffin pointed out, Sir Thomas Malory, whose *Morte d'Arthur* is the most nearly perfect statement of chivalry and its glories, was repeatedly arrested for rape.

8   This ultramasculine male or, more usually, the man who needs to see himself that way, is trying to play a role that is not natural to any human being. In his extreme form, he must constantly be on guard against any evidence of "femininity" in himself, and so he becomes frightened of that femininity. He fears and hates women. In order to bolster his own masculinity, he expresses contempt for women. The more insecure he is, the more he exaggerates the qualities he sees as masculine—aggressiveness, brutality, violence. And when he comes closest to being what he sees as the ideal, he becomes a rapist.

The second sort of rapist differs from this pattern. He is like the first 9 (like most men in our society) in his basic inability to see women as human beings. To the first type they are contemptible and threatening. To the second they are simply objects. Life the first sort of rape, the rape for gratification is a product of sexual conditioning in our society, but in a slightly different way. It derives directly from the patterns of sexual behavior, the courtship ritual in which a woman possesses and guards a prize which the man attempts to win from her.

This kind of rapist is the man who thinks of sex as something he has 10 to pay for, manipulate for, work for, perhaps marry and support a family for. He has always been taught that no woman really wants to have sex and that he will have to bargain for it. The most successful man, to him and to most of our society, is the man who makes the best bargain, who pays the least for his sex.

When this man rapes, he is simply taking sex without paying for it. 11 In his own mind he is not degrading the woman or humiliating her, he is simply getting the best of her. He does not hate her, or even especially lust after her: almost any vaguely attractive woman would suit his purpose. If he knows the woman and she lets herself be put into the situation that allows him to rape her, he will almost certainly not think that he has raped her. She has made a false move in the game and it only makes sense for him to take advantage of it. If he doesn't know her, as in the case of the man who picks up a hitchhiker, he may realize that he has raped her, but it will not register with him as RAPE. He knows as well as everyone else what a rapist is, and he knows he isn't like that.

Perhaps the most common reason for rape is that a man sees the 12 opportunity to have intercourse with a woman, under circumstances where she is unlikely to tell anyone about it or she is unlikely to be believed. One woman reported to us that she was raped while trying to arrange an illegal abortion. The rapist knew that she would not report him for fear that information about her abortion would come out. So he took advantage of the situation.

That is one obvious example of this sort of rape. There are many 13 which are not so obvious. Any time a woman is in a "compromising" situation, rape is a possibility. On our questionnaires the *majority* of the women who responded that they did not know the men who raped them had been hitchhiking at the time of the rape. The fact that she is hitchhiking makes any woman fair game for this kind of man. She will probably not report him, and if she does, he will almost certainly not be prosecuted. One woman reported to us that she was able to relate her story to a captain in the police department of the city where she was raped only because a friend knew him. He listened sympathetically to her and then said that there simply was no possibility that the rapist would be prosecuted, even though he had held a knife to her throat, because she had been hitchhiking at the time and not wearing a bra.

14   It is outrageous, of course, that a man can rape a woman without being punished, but what is worse is that the freedom from the consequences of his action seems to be a motivation for the rapist's attack, sometimes the sole motivation. The man rapes the woman *because* he will not have to pay for his actions. That same man would be no danger to the woman who lives next door, the woman who is a friend of his wife's, the woman he works with—unless he found himself in a situation with one of them that he knew would prevent her from telling anyone.

15   · As we said, this seems to be the most common kind of rape, and the one for which there is the least sympathy. It is marked by a lack of any feeling of guilt on the part of the rapist and an extraordinary amount of guilt on the part of the victim. And, since it arises directly from the ordinary patterns of sexual behavior in our society, that reaction is understandable. The male is the aggressor, the soldier laying siege to the castle; the woman is the guardian of the gate, the defender of the sacred treasure. If the male forces his way in with a battering ram and captures the treasure, he has succeeded in his purpose. There is no cause for guilt or remorse. The woman, on the other hand, has failed in her purpose. She has allowed the treasure to be taken and feels herself to be at fault. She suffers from feelings of guilt, besides the feelings of violation, humiliation, and defeat. And society, her family, the police, and the courts see her the same way. She has lacked the proper vigilance in guarding the treasure. Why was she hitchhiking? Why was she out so late at night? Why did she let him into her apartment? they will ask, as they would ask a sentinel why he fell asleep on guard duty. Seeing man and woman in these terms makes it impossible to deal with rape rationally. No woman who sees herself that way can be free from guilt. To be raped is to be guilty, in one's own eyes as well as in everyone else's.

16   Assume for the moment that both men and women have sexual desires and that both are capable either of acting on them or ignoring them (and not that men must act on their sexual desires and women must ignore theirs, if indeed they have them). Assume that a man may ask a woman if she would like to have sex with him and that a woman may do the same (and not that he will have to trick her or talk her into it, or that she will have to make coy suggestions and flirtatious gestures). Assume that the one who is asked will respond truthfully. What happens then to our perception of this common form of rape? Under these circumstances, the man who forced the woman would have to face the consequences. The woman would be outraged at the violation of her sexual self-determination instead of feeling humiliated at the loss of her treasure. Society would respond as it now responds to murder or a brutal assault, with compassion for the victim and rage at the attacker.

17   All of the above assumptions are at least talked about in our present sexual revolution. Some women believe that they are already true.

These women act on that belief and often they find themselves caught in a trap that ends in rape. Moreover, women who believe in sexual self-determination are further shocked when they hear other people's reactions to their predicament. Again and again women told us, "The reaction of the police was, if possible, worse than the rape," or "I couldn't understand my boy friend's response when I told him. He was angry with me for being stupid enough to get raped." These reactions often seem worse than the rape because they are so unexpected and what they imply is so terrible.

The rape victim's first reaction is usually to see the rape as a freakish accident or an isolated event and to see the rapist as a lunatic. But when the authorities and her family treat her with the same horror and contempt that should be directed at the rapist, she is forced either to question society's attitude toward rape or to begin to doubt herself. Unfortunately, the latter is what most often happens. 18

Perhaps the most horrible thing to deal with in these cases is the attitude of the rapist himself. However profound one's feelings of rage against him, they are unlikely to pierce his armor of indifference. He does not feel guilty for what he has done and is likely to see his victim as a raving idiot. One woman reported that her attacker called her and asked her for a date the next weekend—and was taken completely by surprise when she screamed with anger. He shrugged it off and called someone else. 19

In the end, the victim is likely to bury the attack in the back of her mind as a horrible, bewildering incident that she cannot cope with. And when she is asked, as we asked at rape conferences and on our questionnaires, "Have you ever been raped?" she will answer, as so many women did, "I don't know." 20

Questions for the Critical Reader

1. What is your response to paragraph 4?
2. Comment on the analysis contained in paragraphs 5, 6, and 7.
3. Would it be helpful if, in paragraph 8, we were given some reason why men must "constantly be on guard against any evidence of 'femininity' "? Justify your answer.
4. What do these authors think should be the ideal sex relations between men and women? On what do you base your opinion?
5. Evaluate the analysis in paragraph 12.
6. Do the same for paragraphs 14 and 15.
7. What *are* the "terrible" implications cited at the end of paragraph 17?
8. Compare the attitude of these authors toward "flirtatious gestures" (par. 16) with that of Fleming in "In Defense of Flirting" in Chapter 5.

Rhetorical Technique

1. What two kinds of rape do the authors distinguish?
2. Which paragraphs elucidate the causal patterns behind each? (See Glossary: *cause.*)
3. Which causes do the authors assign to each kind of rape?
4. Are there common causes for both kinds?
5. A fair part of this essay concerns the effects rather than the causes of rape. Cite the kinds of effects the authors establish, and comment on their attitude toward these.
6. Which other forms of exposition are employed here? Cite the paragraphs and the methods. (See Glossary: *exposition.*)
7. To what degree is the essay argumentative? Are there propositions of action or of fact? (See Chapter 1 for a review of *argument.*)
8. Which methods are employed to achieve emphasis? (See Glossary: *emphasis.*)
9. Comment on the type and effectiveness of the conclusion. (See Glossary: *conclusions.*)
10. Discuss the function of the parenthetical statement in the second sentence of paragraph 9.

Diction and Vocabulary

1. In paragraph 15, the authors refer to the male as a "soldier" and the woman as "the guardian" of the castle "gate." What name would you give to this use of language?
2. Consult the dictionary to be sure you understand the meanings of the following words: *dynamics* (par. 1); *negligible* (2); *subjugation* (2); *ambiguous* (3); *incapacitates* (7); *chivalry* (7).

MARYA MANNES

The Thin Grey Line

Ms. Mannes is an American journalist, poet, novelist, dramatist, and social critic. From 1925 onward she has published widely in such national magazines as *Vogue, Esquire, The New Republic,* and *The Reporter.* Her first novel, *Message from a Stranger,* appeared in 1948. She is the coauthor of *Uncoupling* (1972), described as a "guide to sane divorce." "The Thin Grey Line" first appeared in somewhat longer form in *McCall's* in January 1964. The analysis attempted here is of a problem that has not ceased to be of concern.

"Aw, they all do it," growled the cabdriver. He was talking about cops   1
who took payoffs for winking at double parking, but his cynicism could
as well have been directed at any of a dozen other instances of corruption, big-time and small-time. Moreover, the disgust in his voice was
overlaid by an unspoken "So what?": the implication that since this
was the way things were, there was nothing anybody could do.

Like millions of his fellow Americans, the cabdriver was probably a   2
decent human being who had never stolen anything, broken any law or
willfully injured another; somewhere, a knowledge of what was probably right had kept him from committing what was clearly wrong. But
that knowledge had not kept a thin grey line that separates the two
conditions from being daily greyer and thinner—to the point that it was
hardly noticeable.

On one side of this line are They: the bribers, the cheaters, the   3
chiselers, the swindlers, the extortioners. On the other side are We—
both partners and victims. They and We are now so perilously close
that the only mark distinguishing us is that They get caught and We
don't.

The same citizen who voices his outrage at police corruption will slip   4
the traffic cop on his block a handsome Christmas present in the belief
that his car, nestled under a "No Parking" sign, will not be ticketed.
The son of that nice woman next door has a habit of stealing cash from
her purse because his allowance is smaller than his buddies'. Your
son's friend admitted cheating at exams because "everybody does it."

Bit by bit, the resistance to and immunity against wrong that a   5
healthy social body builds up by law and ethics and the dictation of
conscience have broken down. And instead of the fighting indignation
of a people outraged by those who prey on them, we have the admission of impotence: "They all do it."

6   ' Now, failure to uphold the law is no less corrupt than violation of the law. And the continuing shame of this country now is the growing number of Americans who fail to uphold and assist enforcement of the law, simply—and ignominiously—out of fear. Fear of "involvement," fear of reprisal, fear of "trouble." A man is beaten by hoodlums in plain daylight and in view of bystanders. These people not only fail to help the victim, but, like the hoodlums, flee before the police can question them. A city official knows of a colleague's bribe but does not report it. A pedestrian watches a car hit a woman but leaves the scene, to avoid giving testimony. It happens every day. And if the police get cynical at this irresponsibility, they are hardly to blame. Morale is a matter of giving support and having faith in one another; where both are lacking, "law" has become a worthless word.

7   How did we get this way? What started this blurring of what was once a thick black line between the lawful and the lawless? What makes a "regular guy," a decent fellow, accept a bribe? What makes a nice kid from a middle-class family take money for doing something he must know is not only illegal but wrong?

8   When you look into the background of an erring "kid" you will often find a comfortable home and a mother who will tell you, with tears in her eyes, that she "gave him everything." She probably did, to his everlasting damage. Fearing her son's disapproval, the indulgent mother denies him nothing except responsibility. Instead of growing up, he grows to believe that the world owes him everything.

9   The nice kid's father crosses the thin grey line himself in a dozen ways, day in and day out. He pads his expenses on his income-tax returns as a matter of course. As a landlord, he pays the local inspectors of the city housing authority to overlook violations in the houses he rents. When his son flunked his driving test, he gave him ten dollars to slip to the inspector on his second test. "They all do it," he said.

10   The nice kid is brought up with boys and girls who have no heroes except people not much older than themselves who have made the Big Time, usually in show business or in sports. Publicity and money are the halos of their stars, who range from pop singers who can't sing to ballplayers who can't read: from teen-age starlets who can't act to television performers who can't think. They may be excited by the exploits of spacemen, but the work's too tough and dangerous.

11   The nice kids have no heroes because they don't believe in heroes. Heroes are suckers and squares. To be a hero you have to stand out, to excel, to take risks, and above all, not only choose between right and wrong, but defend the right and fight the wrong. This means responsibility—and who needs it?

12   Today, no one has to take any responsibility. The psychiatrists, the sociologists, the novelists, the playwrights have gone a long way to help promote irresponsibility. Nobody really is to blame for what he

does. It's Society. It's Environment. It's a Broken Home. It's an Under-privileged Area. But it's hardly ever You.

Now we find a truckload of excuses to absolve the individual from   13
responsibility for his actions. A fellow commits a crime because he's basically insecure, because he hated his stepmother at nine, or because his sister needs an operation. A policeman loots a store because his salary is too low. A city official accepts a payoff because it's offered to him. Members of minority groups, racial or otherwise, commit crimes because they can't get a job, or are unacceptable to the people living around them. The words "right" and "wrong" are foreign to these people.

But honesty is the best policy. Says who? Anyone willing to get   14
laughed at. But the laugh is no laughing matter. It concerns the health and future of a nation. It involves the two-dollar illegal bettor as well as the corporation price-fixer, the college-examination cheater and the payroll-padding Congressman, the expense-account chiseler, the seller of pornography and his schoolboy reader, the bribed judge and the stealing delinquent. All these people may represent a minority. But when, as it appears now, the majority excuse themselves from responsibility by accepting corruption as natural to society ("They all do it"), this society is bordering on total confusion. If the line between right and wrong is finally erased, there is no defense against the power of evil.

Before this happens—and it is by no means far away—it might be   15
well for the schools of the nation to substitute for the much-argued issue of prayer a daily lesson in ethics, law, and responsibility to society that would strengthen the conscience as exercise strengthens muscles. And it would be even better if parents were forced to attend it. For corruption is not something you read about in the papers and leave to courts. We are all involved.

Questions for the Critical Reader

1. Is the picture painted by Mannes in the first six paragraphs an accurate one? Explain.
2. Why is Mannes so sure that the cabdriver was "probably a decent human being who had never stolen anything, broken any law or willfully injured another"?
3. What precisely does the "dictation of conscience" (par. 5) have to do with law and/or ethics?
4. Do you agree with the statement made in the first sentence of paragraph 6? Explain.
5. Paragraph 8 looks into the causes behind the actions of an "erring 'kid'." Paragraph 9 describes the corrupt character of a father.
   a) Comment on the validity of the analysis of the child's actions.

b) Why doesn't Mannes offer a parallel analysis of the father's actions?

c) Offer your own analysis of the father's behavior.

6. Comment on the analysis presented in paragraphs 10 and 11.
7. Do the same for paragraphs 12 and 13.
8. Compare the last sentences of paragraphs 7 and 13. Is there a contradiction here? Justify your answer.
9. The concluding paragraph offers a plan to combat corruption. What is your opinion of it?

Rhetorical Technique

1. What exactly is being analyzed in this essay? Write a one-paragraph definition of this effect.
2. The symbol of the "grey line" is central to the essay. Isolate the instances where the author uses the phrase or some variation on it, and then estimate the effectiveness of the symbol. (See Glossary: *symbols.*)
3. What other methods of exposition are used here? (See the introduction to the student.)
4. How much of the essay is argumentative? (See Chapter 1.)
5. Comment on the characterization of "They" and "We" in paragraph 3.
6. Describe the chief methods of emphasis employed here. (See Glossary: *emphasis.*)
7. Identify two examples of parallel structure, and comment on their effectiveness. (See Glossary: *parallel structure.*)
8. On a number of occasions, Mannes makes use of questions. Are they rhetorical (see Glossary: *rhetorical questions*)? Explain.

Diction and Vocabulary

1. In "*cops* who took payoffs" (par. 1) and "a *policeman* loots a store" (par. 13), Mannes uses different words for a police officer. Why? Is this a matter of connotation (see Glossary: *connotation and denotation*)? Analyze her purposes in using each.
2. Mannes employs two colloquial words, *winking* (par. 1) and *slip* (9) for their clear connotative values. Substitute more denotative terms for these, and then estimate what is lost or gained thereby. (See Glossary: *colloquial language; connotation and denotation.*)
3. Characterize the following list of expressions (see Glossary: *colloquial language*). and then evaluate the effectiveness with which they are used: "So what?" (par. 1); "regular guy" (7); nice kid (7); "gave

him everything" (8); day in and day out (9); suckers and squares (11); who needs it (11); Says who? (14).

4. Give reasons for the capitalization of words and phrases in paragraphs 3, 10, and especially 12.
5. How would you characterize the use of language in "Publicity and money are halos of their stars" (par. 10)?
6. Consult the dictionary to be sure you understand the meanings of the following words: *ignominiously* (par. 6); *reprisal* (6); *colleague* (6); *indulgent* (8); *absolve* (13).

ELIZABETH JANEWAY

The Question Is, What Is a Family, Anyway?

Novelist, essayist, and short story writer, Elizabeth Janeway published her first book, *The Walsh Girls*, in 1943. Since then she has produced a number of works, including *Daisy Kenyon* (1945) and, more recently, *Man's World, Woman's Place* (1971) and *Between Myth and Meaning* (1974). This essay, which first appeared on the Op-Ed page of *The New York Times* (April 1, 1972), was inspired by pieces appearing on the same page by two women (Frances Kaufman and Shelley List, whom Ms. Janeway refers to in her first sentence). In the course of their remarks, they had indicated that they were all the family their children had. Elizabeth Janeway's reply supplies an analysis that widens the context considerably and places the family in a larger perspective.

1   Laments by Frances Kaufman and Shelley List—two women who struggle to cope alone with the social demands of the wife-mother role—call for some reality principles.

2   I want to suggest that we widen the context in which we look at these problems. The family, (as Talcott Parson[1] says), is a subsystem of society, not a complete-in-itself operating unit. It can't, therefore, resolve dilemmas that surrounding circumstances create. It's too small. And today, it's smaller than ever. Sociologists still talk about "the nuclear family," but Mrs. List's family includes only one adult, not two. There are 20 million other people living in families with one, female head. Those are less-than-nuclear families. Most families today can be described as less than nuclear—if you count how many working hours fathers and children are at home together, sharing each other's thoughts and company.

3   If a family runs into trouble, the reason may lie outside the family, in the surrounding circumstances. Trying to solve it inside the family won't work, and may make things worse because of the emotional strains that will result from effort and failure.

4   What is a family anyway? What is it supposed to do? Its economic functions have changed over the centuries, the emotional satisfaction provided there is always a personal thing, but the one task it's always undertaken has been the rearing of children. Believe me, working women know this just as well as mothers who can afford the choice to stay home.

[1] Talcott Parsons is a functionalist sociologist and has written important works dealing with the theoretical analysis of social systems.

194

Now, to raise the children well, a family has to be clued in to the operations of the community in which it exists. Adults have to understand the goals of a society (that doesn't mean they have to approve of them), and show the children how to operate within the guidelines these goals set. Processes of living ought to be understandable and open to exploration and participation.

Families have become isolated from the world of action. In his book on the alienated young, "The Uncommitted," Prof. Kenneth Keniston of Yale dubbed them "home havens," retreats from the rat race. No doubt that's a bitter and deserved comment on the rat race; but it raises a grave question. Can one really raise children successfully in a residential ghetto, cut off from the life of the world?

This is what women—mothers—are charged with doing. They have very little help. Cross-cultural studies show American women have less support today from family and community than mothers in other contemporary cultures and much less than did their mothers and grandmothers. And when they fail, they blame themselves. To bear a load of guilt on top of the task of doing alone one of society's major jobs is a shocking, a crippling burden which demands a conscious effort to set it right.

What the family needs is a re-creation, artificially, of the old community connections, the old extended family. Communal living is one way to do this and I expect it will spread in various forms. Another approach that can easily be undertaken and could have stunning effect is the establishment of childhood enrichment centers, or youth environments, or assemblies for educational opportunities. We call these places day-care centers now, and denigrate them in our own minds by doing so; for we appear to mean no more than places to dump children.

Giving them a new name won't ennoble them by itself, but adjusting our thinking and expectations to match the name can do so. I would like to see every plant, business, commercial establishment or gathering place above a minimum size establish such a center. Mothers (or fathers) could bring little children with them to the places where they work, could check on them during the day and be with them for meals. Older children could gather there after school. In so doing they would re-create something of the atmosphere of the old-fashioned big family which our attention to the population explosion has got to make less frequent. Retired men and women could come to talk and play with the children, and act as the grandparent generation, bringing a sense of the continuity of life to the everyday experience of growing up.

Government might well share the cost of these centers by granting a tax credit for establishing them, just as it does for other capital investment, and some government officials I've talked with agree. In fact, I would guess that industry, faced with government orders to cease discrimination against women, would find it profitable to have unworried mothers in the work force and to know that training given to young women would not be lost in the years when they might otherwise be dropouts.

11   Utopian? Nonsense. We're living with the alternative, and we know what it costs. Mothers of the World, Unite! What our children need from us isn't guilt, tears and frustration, but positive action to bring the community back home and open the home to the community.

Questions for the Critical Reader

1. Compare the idea of "communal living" expressed here (in par. 8) with the same idea as it is expressed in Shana Alexander's "Kids' Country."
2. What *are* the economic functions of the family (par. 4)? What *were* they? Is this matter explained to your satisfaction, or could it have been better handled? Explain.
3. Comment on the ideas expressed in paragraph 5. Do you agree with this analysis?
4. From your own experience as a family member, what *is* a family, anyway?
5. If your experience as a family member included contact with a number of cousins, aunts, and uncles, can you testify to the roles played by these people in your development?
6. Compare the ways in which you were helped to develop (a) by your immediate family and (b) by your extended family.
7. Consider the first sentence of paragraph 7. Is it true that this is what mothers are charged with doing? Does Janeway's proposed solution seem to you one that could succeed? Explain.
8. What are the functions of existing day-care centers? Are they equipped to handle the problems alluded to?

Rhetorical Technique

1. Is this essay an example of "pure" causal analysis? Explain.
2. How much of this piece is a definition?
3. How much relies on the testimony of authority?
4. The purpose of a causal analysis is to explain a complex event, idea, or state of affairs. Does this essay succeed in doing so? To what degree?
5. What is the central theme of this essay? (See Glossary: *central theme; subject; unity.*) Where is it expressed?
6. Which part of this essay could be improved by more concrete language and example? (See Glossary: *abstract and concrete.*)

7. Locate two examples of the use of rhetorical question, and comment on their effectiveness. (See Glossary: *rhetorical questions.*)
8. How would you describe the tone of this essay? (See Glossary: *style and tone.*)

Diction and Vocabulary

1. Consider formations like *complete-in-itself* (1) and *less-than-nuclear* (2). Are they awkward? Useful? Can you think of substitutes?
2. What is the purpose and effectiveness of "Believe me" (par. 4)? (See Glossary: *purpose.*)
3. Consider the expressions *clued in* (par. 5), *rat race* (6), and *dump* (8). Estimate their contribution to the tone of the essay. (See Glossary: *style and tone.*)
4. How effective is the use of the slogan in paragraph 11?
5. Consider the connotative values of the words *ghetto* (par. 6) and *charged* (7). What was Janeway's purpose in using each? (See Glossary: *connotation and denotation.*)
6. Consult the dictionary to be sure you understand the meanings of the words *denigrate* (par. 8), *ennoble* (9), and *utopian* (11).

Writing Suggestions for Chapter 7: *Causal Analysis*

I.

Bearing in mind that a list of reasons is not a causal analysis, write a rigorous causal analysis analyzing the incidental and immediate causes and/or effects of one of the subjects listed below. The structure of Mannes's essay—in which she first describes the subject and then analyzes it—is a useful model.

1. The deterioration of a neighborhood.
2. The demise of farming as a family way of life.
3. The high cost of living.
4. The low level of television fare.
5. The big-time nature of professional sports.
6. The escalating divorce rate in the United States.
7. The current style of dress of some subgroup.
8. College students' orientation toward job-related studies.
9. The popularity of camping out/tennis/CB radios, and so on.
10. The widespread fascination with trivia, antiques, and other items of nostalgic interest.
11. The anxiety of students to achieve high grades.
12. The widespread distrust of big government.

II. Writing Assignment Based on "Terrorist Myths"

Write a causal analysis in the form of Laqueur's; that is, first divide your subject into its principal and most pervasive myths, and then analyze the truth or falsity of each.

The following subjects are suitable for division into myths:

1. The youth culture.
2. American materialism.
3. The American dream.
4. Health foods.
5. A college education.
6. Sex or sexual health.
7. Life in a big city.

8

The *Description* That Makes Us See

Suppose two people were to report to you on a local rainstorm. Suppose further that Report No. 1 declared that "2.6 inches of rain fell over the metropolitan area during the last forty-eight hours," while Report No. 2 noted that "rain fell stolid, a wall of lines/So that you could see where the air stopped open/and where the rain fell beside it." Same rain, two different reports. The first can be called a *technical description* because it offers exact technical information; the second we would call—if it were not also a piece of poetry (by Ezra Pound), chosen to make the point being made—an *impressionistic description*. Another kind of technical description might go like this: "3rms. hi flr. riv.vu. See supt." It would be accurate—within limits—but it would hardly convey the warmth, beauty, and lived-in comfort of your apartment. Both kinds of description are useful, depending on the kind of experience and information to be conveyed. In this chapter, we shall be concerned with impressionistic description. And this kind of prose has its own special purposes and techniques and a unique area in which to best serve the reader.

That unique area is the realm of human feeling. The writer of the first report (above) is a weather forecaster and analyst and has no special interest in conveying states of feeling. The poet (who wrote Report No. 2) *has*. The purpose of someone interested in writing an impressionistic description is thus to make us *see* and thereby share an experience (rain as a "wall of lines"). To achieve this purpose, the writer must use concrete details ("a *wall*"). No amount of technical accuracy will assist the writer working in this vein. Colette's feeling, impression of those two rooms could hardly have been improved if she had used a slide rule to measure the size of each to within a tenth of an inch. For what is beautiful and

199

enriching in an impressionistic description is precisely the fact that we get to see the room as the writer experienced (or felt) it. For this purpose, only telling, concrete detail will do.

All forms of writing make some use of impressionistic description. But here we are concerned with description in its purer form, as a sensitive medium for the transmission of personal experience.

The writer preparing to write a description should proceed by first amassing as many details about the person, place, or scene to be described. At this stage of the job it is essential to let your imagination loose in an effort to gather a great deal, because the more you are able to loosen the bonds of selection the more likely it is that you will gather usable materials. Nor, at this point, should you limit yourself to visual details; how a place or a scene smells, sounds, feels—even tastes; some writers get vivid effects by suggesting that the very air has discernible flavor—can contribute greatly to a verbal portrait.

The next step is to sift through this uncataloged list and arrive at a *dominant impression.* That is, when you sift, you might try sorting them into groups—and one of these groups might be more impressive and, you realize, truer to the real "feel" of the subject than the others. Such a group of details might have in common, for example, the fact that each detail in the group emphasizes the nightmarish quality of the subject. The nightmarish quality of the place would then be your dominant impression. Like the thesis statement (see Glossary: *thesis statement; subject; unity*), it would control and organize your writing. The final selection of details should be made from the group that gave you the dominant impression. They will illustrate and support the statement of your dominant impression. (You need *not* use all the details on your uncataloged list.)

The structure of a description is fairly easy to arrive at. We can describe people from their shoes to their hats (and in movement and conversation too, of course) or vice versa; or we could describe them from the outside to the inside, describing things on the surface first and then proceeding to deeper layers. We can approach scenes by letting the writer's eye act as the structural guide to the reader's experience. That is, the writer can describe in a pattern going from near to far, far to near, or from one side to the other. The far-to-near pattern is like the rhythm of movie technique: from the long shot (or overall, faraway view) to the medium shot (or closer look) to the close-up, a final concentration on a small, sharp, central detail.

COLETTE

A Third Floor . . .

Sidonie Gabrielle Colette (1873–1954), who wrote under her last name alone, was a French novelist and short story writer. Perhaps best known in America for her *Cheri* series, she wrote her first books in collaboration with her first husband (who used the pen name Willy and who is the "M. Willy" in this essay). After their divorce, however, she wrote entirely alone and achieved considerable distinction. Her work is characterized by an intense preoccupation with immediate sense experience caught in a poetic prose. This piece is taken from *Earthly Paradise* (1966), a collection of fragments of autobiography, and it exhibits all her characteristic gifts—those that enable the reader to see so well.

A third floor in the rue[1] Jacob, between two courtyards. One of the court- 1
yards faced the north and the rue Visconti, so that I had, at least, a
glimpse of old tiled roofs to remind me of the tiles of Burgundy.

No sun. Three living rooms; a small, dark study; a kitchen on the other 2
side of the landing—all this for fourteen hundred francs a year. In the
square drawing room was a salamander stove, and in the recess where I
had set out my tub, my basins, and my ewers, a gas fire. It was almost a
poor man's flat, yet its white doors were early nineteenth century and
still had their little carved wreaths and garlands, now half clogged with
paint. I had not chosen it. On the day I saw it first it was empty, and I
felt that I was only half awake. The last tenant had lived there for fifty
years, long enough to complete a most singular form of decoration. The
doors, the ornaments on the doors, the cornices, the skirtings, the niche
for the porcelain stove in the dining room, the sham wood panels, the
shelves of the cupboards, the window frames, and a large surface of the
walls themselves, were covered with tiny diamond-shaped confetti of
many colors, cut out and glued on by hand, one by one.

"I understood from the gentleman himself," the concierge confided to 3
me in a low, reverent voice, "that there were more than 275,000 pieces. I
call that work."

Work such as you do in nightmares. The thought of living in these 4
rooms, in the presence of walls that had witnessed so secret a madness,
so evil a joy, appalled me. And then I forgot about it. I was only a young
bride.

[1] *rue.* The French word for "street."

5 No light, no air, the dark enchantment that sometimes lingers in places that have crushed and stifled many souls. The little flat must, I think, have been profoundly melancholy. And yet, to me, it seemed agreeable. What it is to have known worse! I had gone to it from another lodging, M.[2] Willy's bachelor establishment, a quaking, echoing garret, at the top of one of the houses on the quays, that shivered at every passing bus and truck. I have never been able to forget that attic and its murky, rattling double windows. Painted in bottle green and chocolate brown, filled with unspeakably sordid cardboard files, soaked in a sort of horrible office gloom, it looked uninhabited, utterly forsaken. The drafts crept over the creaking boards; their slightest breath brought forth out of the black shadows, from under the sagging springs of the bed, a gray snow, a drift of flakes born, as some frail nests are born, of a thread, a hair, woven with dust as light and soft as down. Heaps of yellowing newspapers occupied the chairs; German postcards were strewn more or less everywhere, celebrating the attractions of underclothes, socks, ribboned drawers and buttocks. The master of the house would have strongly objected to any attempt on my part to remedy the disorder.

6 It was a relief to get away, every morning, from these indecent surroundings. The place had been adapted solely to the use, the careless convenience of a dissolute bachelor, and I welcomed the daylight that took me from it. I welcomed the daylight also for its own sake, because it drew me out of bed and into the open air. And because I was hungry. By half past eight or thereabouts, M. Willy and I were crossing the bridge. Ten minutes' walk took us to the humble milkshop where the blue-smocked packers from La Belle Jardinière[3] kept up their strength, as we did, on rolls dipped in pale mauve chocolate.

Questions for the Critical Reader

1. What do you *see* in Colette's tub, basins, ewers (par. 2)?
2. Why does the decorative work of the man who used to occupy the rue Jacob flat seem to Colette "work such as you do in nightmares?"
3. How do you explain the contradiction that seems to exist in par. 4?
4. Describe the author's attitude toward living space. Reread Tuan's "American Space, Chinese Place," and then see where Colette stands on the space-place issue.
5. Consider your own attitude toward where you live. Which factors make it a good or a bad experience for you?
6. Compare Colette's attitude toward the married state—as it affects room decor—and her attitude toward bachelorhood.

[2] M. Abbreviation for the French word *Monsieur* (Mister).
[3] *La Belle Jardinière.* "The beautiful gardener."

Rhetorical Technique

1. This piece has been abridged from a biographical memoir of this great French writer. Bearing that in mind, why would you classify this piece as impressionistic description? (See the introduction to this chapter.)
2. What is the dominant impression Colette gives of each of the rooms she describes? Try to use her own technique in writing two sentences to describe each.
3. Which details contribute best to the dominant impression in each?
4. What kinds of details about these two rooms might interest you that Colette has omitted? Would adding these details have enhanced or weakened her description?
5. Consider the author's point of view (see Glossary: *point of view*). Considering that Burgundy (par. 1) is a province of France far from Paris (where these rooms are located), what other details give you a handle on this point of view?
6. How does the dialogue relate to the following and the preceding paragraphs? Would the description have been better or worse without it? Explain.
7. Consider the style and tone here, especially with regard to Colette's distinctive syntax (see Glossary: *style and tone; syntax*). How do the numerous sentence fragments contribute to style and tone? (See par. 1, sentence 1; par, 2, sent, 1; par. 4, sent. 1, and so on.)
8. How does the concluding paragraph comment on her descriptions? (See Glossary: *conclusions*.)

Diction and Vocabulary

1. Identify examples of personification, metaphor, and simile; and comment on the effectiveness of these. (See Glossary: *figures of speech*.)
2. Comment on the significance of color throughout, but especially in the last sentence.
3. Consider the connotative work done by the following words and phrases by substituting others of the same denotative value and then seeing what has been gained or lost (see Glossary: *connotation and denotation*):
   a) so secret a madness (par. 4)
   b) so evil a joy (4)
   c) unspeakably sordid (5)
   d) horrible office gloom (5)

4. Why *German* postcards (par. 5)?
5. Consult the dictionary to be sure you understand the meanings of the following words and phrases: *salamander stove* (par. 2); *ewers* (2); *cornices* (2); *skirtings* (2); *niche* (2); *confetti* (2); *concierge* (3); *appalled* (4); *garret* (5); *quays* (5); *sordid* (5); *dissolute* (6).

RICHARD HOGGART

A Working Class Mother

Richard Hoggart, who was born in Leeds, Yorkshire, in 1918, is an
English scholar and critic. He has been, since 1962, a professor of
English at the University of Birmingham, where he is also the
director of the Centre for Contemporary Cultural Studies—an institution he founded. From *Auden* (1951) to *The Uses of Literacy*
(1957), from which this description is taken, and beyond, he has
published books and articles on literary, cultural, and social subjects. He has been a visiting professor in the United States and has
acted as a governor of the Royal Shakespeare Company and the
Birmingham Repertory Theatre. The picture of a working class
mother that he gives us here is one informed by personal judgment
of a moral nature—which adds an important dimension to what
we see in his subject.

1   . . . Her clothes looked as though they had been picked up individually
from second-hand-clothing shops, and she wasn't very clean. Over a
torn, old and grubby blouse and skirt she had for the street an ex-army
gas-cape; from that there stuck what might have been the head of one
of the witches in *Macbeth*. She must have been in her middle forties,
so that her face could not be called young; but it was not yet old or
"past everything." It was well-lined but not haggard; it was scored with
hard work, insufficient attention and the lines which "making shift,"
doggedness, fighting for your own and an overriding bravado bring. Her
left eye had a violent cast and her lower lip a drop to the right, so that
on the whole the bravado won. But it was a *farouche* bravado, even
when she was in the easiest of spirits. Her hair was a dirty mouse color,
hanging in straggly locks from either side of an old felt hat which she
wore rammed hard and unshapenly to the head, held in place by a large
pin with a piccaninny's head carved on the blunt end—a relic of a day
at the sea, I suppose. Her shoes were split, sloppy and entirely uncleaned;
her lisle stockings hung in circles from the knees. Her voice was raucous
and had been developed over the years by area and backyard "callings"
(the "a" is pronounced as in "shall") and "bawlings-out." She was not,
as those who knew her only slightly thought, a widow: her husband had
been in a mental home for about a dozen years, during which time she
had looked after the family single-handed. Her effective married life had
begun with three days' holiday at home, and had ended five or six years
later, when "They took 'im away." So there she was at forty-odd with

From *The Uses of Literacy* by Richard Hoggart. Oxford University Press, 1957,
1970. Reprinted by permission.

five of them to look after, or more accurately four, since the eldest son of eighteen was in the army. Then there was a fourteen-year-old girl who was "bright" and had won a scholarship to the local grammar-school, a boy of ten who looked like resembling her, a girl of seven who had inherited several kinds of ill-health, and a girl of four, already pasty and with a continual cold.

2   They were all solidly ranged behind the mother and very cheerful, as she was. She had the spirits, and I say this with no intention of disparaging her, of a mongrel bitch. She fought hard and constantly for her children, but it never "got 'er down," though she often exploded with temper among them. She was without subservience or deference, or a desire to win pity; she was careless of many things affecting her children and refused to worry or to take life earnestly. She asked those she worked for "not to mention it to the Guardians,"[1] but did not cadge or respond to a gift in a way which might have suggested that further gifts would be gratefully received. If someone gave her a dress or an item of food she took it with a short word of thanks, and that was all. No doubt she often felt she could have done with some of the surplus money her employers seemed to have, but she obviously had no envy of their manner of life. The young middle-class housewives for whom she did the heavy work in a vigorous if careless-at-the-edges and knockabout fashion soon learned that any social pretensions or attempts at patronage would have been out of place. The truth was that she had a fuller life than some of those for whom she worked. Thus, if she had a day off, she thought nothing of moving with all available members of the family to the nearest seaside resort, which wasn't far, for a noisily enjoyable day, ending with fish-and-chips for all.

Questions for the Critical Reader

1. From the quality of the author's sympathy for his subject, try to estimate what his own background might have been like?
2. How well do you suppose he knew the mother he describes? Try to imagine what concrete relationship existed between them.
3. Why does he describe her as in her "middle forties" or "forty-odd" instead of giving a more precise estimate of her age? He *does* seem to know some very precise things about her.
4. Why is the youngest child described as "already" pasty?
5. An important aspect of description is the fact that it frequently registers internal judgments on the part of the author. For example, here Hoggart (in par. 2) comments that his subject "often felt she could have done with some of the surplus money her employers

---

[1] *the Guardians.* A British welfare organization.

seemed to have." What do you suppose is the source of this and other judgments like it?

6. Try to describe the complex attitude the author has toward his subject; that is, what does he like about her and what doesn't he like?

Rhetorical Technique

1. What dominant impression is given?
2. Which details contribute most toward expressing it?
3. Would it be possible to take some of these details and actually reverse the impression? How?
4. What structural pattern is employed?
5. Which details help you *see* best? Why?
6. How much is contributed to this description by the many background details the author gives us?
7. The author uses rather unpleasant, even grotesque, details about the mother in the first part of the first paragraph. Identify these, and then suggest how he plays these off later on against her character.
8. Identify two examples of parallel structure and comment on their effectiveness. How does the author avoid monotony in using this technique? (See Glossary: *parallel structure.*)

Diction and Vocabulary

1. Hoggart quotes his subject three times, seeming to get the ring of her special colloquial diction ['past everything, par. 1; 'They took 'im away,' par. 1; 'got her down,' par. 2]. How do these quotations contribute to the total picture of her? (See Glossary: *connotation and denotation.*)
2. Identify at least two examples of figurative language (see Glossary: *figures of speech*). How effective are they?
3. Identify what you believe to be examples of British usage. Then, if the context in which they are used does not make them clear, ask your instructor for help.
4. Consult the dictionary to be sure you understand the meanings of the following words: *farouche* (par. 1); *raucous* (1); *disparagingly* (2); *subservience* (2); *deference* (2); *cadge* (2).

JAMES AGEE

Knoxville: Summer, 1915

James Agee (1909–1955), who was born in Knoxville, was an American poet, novelist, critic, and screenwriter. His book of poems *Permit Me Voyage* (1934) preceded his employment by *Fortune* magazine, out of which experience he produced (with the photographs of Walker Evans) his classic study of a poor sharecropper family, *Let Us Now Praise Famous Men* (1941). Agee also wrote the screenplays for *The African Queen* and *The Quiet One* and wrote film criticism for *The Nation* from 1943–1948. This description is the beginning section of his Pulitzer Prize novel (of 1957), *A Death in the Family*, which was published posthumously. It embodies Agee's distinctive verbal gifts, his capacity to render an ordinary scene with a great richness of language and linguistic effects.

1   *We are talking now of summer evenings in Knoxville, Tennessee, in the time that I lived there so successfully disguised to myself as a child. It was a little bit mixed sort of block, fairly solidly lower middle class, with one or two juts apiece on either side of that. The houses corresponded: middle-sized gracefully fretted wood houses built in the late nineties and early nineteen hundreds, with small front and side and more spacious back yards, and trees in the yards, and porches. These were softwooded trees, poplars, tulip trees, cottonwoods. There were fences around one or two of the houses, but mainly the yards ran into each other with only now and then a low hedge that wasn't doing very well. There were few good friends among the grown people, and they were not poor enough for the other sort of intimate acquaintance, but everyone nodded and spoke, and even might talk short times, trivially, and at the two extremes of the general or the particular, and ordinarily nextdoor neighbors talked quite a bit when they happened to run into each other, and never paid calls. The men were mostly small businessmen, one or two very modestly executives, one or two worked with their hands, most of them clerical, and most of them between thirty and forty-five.*

2   *But it is of these evenings, I speak.*

3   *Supper was at six and was over by half past. There was still daylight, shining softly and with a tarnish, like the lining of a shell; and the carbon lamps lifted at the corners were on in the light, and the locusts were started, and the fire flies were out, and a few frogs were flopping in the dewy grass, by the time the fathers and the children came out. The*

children ran out first hell bent and yelling those names by which they were known; then the fathers sank out leisurely in crossed suspenders, their collars removed and their necks looking tall and shy. The mothers stayed back in the kitchen washing and drying, putting things away, recrossing their traceless footsteps like the lifetime journeys of bees, measuring out the dry cocoa for breakfast. When they came out they had taken off their aprons and their skirts were dampened and they sat in rockers on their porches quietly.

It is not of the games children play in the evening that I want to speak now, it is of a contemporaneous atmosphere that has little to do with them: that of the fathers of families, each in his space of lawn, his shirt fishlike pale in the unnatural light and his face nearly anonymous, hosing their lawns. The hoses were attached at spiggots that stood out of the brick foundations of the houses. The nozzles were variously set but usually so there was a long sweet stream of spray, the nozzle wet in the hand, the water trickling the right forearm and the peeled-back cuff, and the water whishing out a long loose and low-curved cone, and so gentle a sound. First an insane noise of violence in the nozzle, then the still irregular sound of adjustment, then the smoothing into steadiness and a pitch as accurately tuned to the size and style of stream as any violin. So many qualities of sound out of one hose: so many choral differences out of those several hoses that were in earshot. Out of any one hose, the almost dead silence of the release, and the short still arch of the separate big drops, silent as a held breath, and the only noise the flattering noise on leaves and the slapped grass at the fall of each big drop. That, and the intense hiss with the intense stream; that, and that same intensity not growing less but growing more quiet and delicate with the turn of the nozzle, up to that extreme tender whisper when the water was just a wide bell of film. Chiefly, though, the hoses were set much alike, in a compromise between distance and tenderness of spray (and quite surely a sense of art behind this compromise, and a quiet deep joy, too real to recognize itself), and the sounds therefore were pitched much alike; pointed by the snorting start of a new hose; decorated by some man playful with the nozzle; left empty, like God by the sparrow's fall, when any single one of them desists: and all, though near alike, of various pitch; and in this unison. These sweet pale streamings in the light lift out their pallors and their voices all together, mothers hushing their children, the hushing unnaturally prolonged, the men gentle and silent and each snail-like withdrawn into the quietude of what he singly is doing, the urination of huge children stood loosely military against an invisible wall, and gentle happy and peaceful, tasting the mean goodness of their living like the last of their suppers in their mouths; while the locusts carry on this noise of hoses on their much higher and sharper key. The noise of the locust is dry, and it seems not to be rasped or vibrated but urged from him as if through a small orifice by a breath that can never

4

give out. Also there is never one locust but an illusion of at least a thousand. The noise of each locust is pitched in some classic locust range out of which none of them varies more than two full tones: and yet you seem to hear each locust discrete from all the rest, and there is a long, slow, pulse in their noise, like the scarcely defined arch of a long and high set bridge. They are all around in every tree, so that the noise seems to come from nowhere and everywhere at once, from the whole shell heaven, shivering in your flesh and teasing your eardrums, the boldest of all the sounds of night. And yet it is habitual to summer nights, and is of the great order of noises, like the noises of the sea and of the blood her precocious grandchild, which you realize you are hearing only when you catch yourself listening. Meantime from low in the dark, just outside the swaying horizons of the hoses, conveying always grass in the damp of dew and its strong green-black smear of smell, the regular yet spaced noises of the crickets, each a sweet cold silver noise three-noted, like the slipping each time of three matched links of a small chain.

5   But the men by now, one by one, have silenced their hoses and drained and coiled them. Now only two, and now only one, it left, and you see only ghostlike shirt with the sleeve garters, and sober mystery of his mild face like the lifted face of large cattle enquiring of your presence in a pitchdark pool of meadow; and now he too is gone; and it has become that time of evening when people sit on their porches, rocking gently and talking gently and watching the street and the standing up into their sphere of possession of the trees, of birds hung havens, hangars. People go by; things go by. A horse, drawing a buggy, breaking his hollow iron music on the asphalt; a loud auto; a quiet auto; people in pairs, not in a hurry, scuffling, switching their weight of aestival body, talking casually, the taste hovering over them of vanilla, strawberry, pasteboard and starched milk, the image upon them of lovers and horsemen, squared with clowns in hueless amber. A street car raising its iron moan; stopping, belling and starting; stertorous; rousing and raising again its iron increasing moan and swimming its gold windows and straw seats on past and past and past, the bleak spark crackling and cursing above it like a small malignant spirit set to dog its tracks; the iron whine rises on rising speed; still risen, faints; halts; the faint stinging bell; rises again, still fainting, lifting, lifts, faints forgone: forgotten. Now is the night one blue dew.

6   Now is the night one blue dew, my father has drained, he has coiled the
    hose.
    Low on the length of lawns, a frailing of fire who breathes.
    Content, silver, like peeps of light, each cricket makes his comment over
    and over in the drowned grass.
    A cold toad thumpily flounders.

Within the edges of damp shadows of side yards are hovering children
   nearly sick with joy of fear, who watch the unguarding of a tele-
   phone pole.
Around white carbon corner lamps bugs of all sizes are lifted elliptic,
   solar systems. Big hardshalls bruise themselves, assailant: he is
   fallen on his back, legs squiggling.
Parents on porches: rock and rock: From damp strings morning glories
   hang their ancient faces.
The dry and exalted noise of the locusts from all the air at once enchants
   my eardrums.

   On the rough wet grass of the back yard my father and mother have   7
spread quilts. We all lie there, my mother, my father, my uncle, my aunt,
and I too am lying there. First we were sitting up, then one of us lay
down, and then we all lay down, on our stomachs, or on our sides, or
on our backs, and they have kept on talking. They are not talking much,
and the talk is quiet, of nothing in particular, of nothing at all in par-
ticular, of nothing at all. The stars are wide and alive, they seem each
like a smile of great sweetness, and they seem very near. All my people
are larger bodies than mine, quiet, with voices gentle and meaning-
less like the voices of sleeping birds. One is an artist, he is living at home.
One is a musician, she is living at home. One is my mother who is good
to me. One is my father who is good to me. By some chance, here they
are, all on this earth; and who shall ever tell the sorrow of being on this
earth, lying, on quilts, on the grass, in a summer evening, among the
sounds of night. May God bless my people, my uncle, my aunt, my
mother, my father, oh, remember them kindly in their time of trouble;
and in the hour of their taking away.
   After a little I am taken in and put to bed. Sleep, soft smiling, draws   8
me unto her: and those receive me, who quietly treat me, as one familiar
and well-beloved in that home: but will not, oh, will not, not now, not
ever; but will not ever tell me who I am.

Questions for the Critical Reader

1. What inferences about the people in the neighborhood can you draw
   from the sentence in paragraph 1 that begins "There were few good
   friends . . . ?"
2. How does Agee qualify what he says in paragraph 1?
3. Why do you suppose the author chooses to describe the evenings—
   especially supper time—rather than some other part of the day, if
   he's speaking of his childhood?

4. In addition to the vivid pictures Agree gives us, his piece is filled with other kinds of information about the "I" who is speaking:
   a) Describe his attitude toward fathers.
   b) Can you tell exactly what roles were assigned to men and women in that Knoxville neighborhood in 1915?
5. Taken together, hose, nozzle, and spray of water seem to constitute a symbol—of what? Authority, control, creativity? What do you think?
6. The sense of place is powerfully felt here, but no single person seems to come into sharp focus. Why do you suppose the author has chosen to have it that way?
7. Compare and contrast this scene with the scene in your own neighborhood at supper time in the summer. What do the differences or similarities tell you about time, place, and culture?

Rhetorical Technique

1. Why should this piece be classified as description instead of narration? Cite specific passages to support your view.
2. How much of this is objective and how much impressionistic description? (See the introduction to this chapter.)
3. What is the dominant impression? Which details contribute to it most strongly?
4. Read aloud paragraph 4, and analyze the role played by rhythm in Agree's description.
5. In describing, it is possible to focus on large details or small ones or some combination of these. Analyze which angle of focus Agee uses most, and comment on its contribution to this piece.
6. What relation is there between the first and the last sentences?
7. Originally, the whole of this piece was printed in italics, as if to give emphasis to the whole of it in relation to the rest of the book. What other methods of emphasis are used here? (See Glossary: *emphasis*.)
8. Analyze the transition from prose to poetry between paragraphs 5 and 6. What is the purpose of this technique? (See Glossary: *transition*.)
9. The point of view here is a complex one. How would you describe it? (See Glossary: *point of view*.)

Diction and Vocabulary

1. Consider the second sentence of paragraph 3. What is the effect of the repetitive use of *and*? Locate two other examples of verbal repetition, and analyze their effects.

2. Identify five examples of figurative language. Analyze their effects. (See Glossary: *figures of speech*.)
3. *Onomatopoeia* is the formation of names or words from sounds that resemble those associated with the object or action being named or that seem naturally suggestive of its qualities. Can you locate examples of onomatopoeia here?
4. There is here a special abundance of concrete language of great vividness. Can you locate two especially effective examples? (See Glossary: *abstract and concrete*.)
5. Give two examples of compound words and analyze their effects.
6. How does original syntax contribute to the effect of this piece? (See Glossary: *syntax*.)
7. Consult the dictionary to be sure you understand the meanings of the following words: *fretted* (par. 1); *contemporaneous* (4); *pallors* (4); *aestival* (5); *stertorous* (5).

NORMAN MAILER

The Ali-Foreman Fight: Rounds 6 and 7

Norman Mailer, who was born in 1923, is a distinguished American writer whose province is both fiction and nonfiction. His novels, beginning with *The Naked and the Dead* (1948) and continuing through *Barbary Shore* (1951), *The Deer Park* (1955), and *An American Dream* (1965), have a place on the shelf of our literature along with his books of his nonfiction, *Advertisements for Myself* (1959), *The Armies of the Night* (1968), *Of a Fire on the Moon* (1971), *The Prisoner of Sex* (1971), and *Existential Errands* (1972). Mailer's hallmark is the startling originality of an original mind.

This selection is taken from *The Fight* (1975), Mailer's account of the heavyweight championship boxing bout between Muhammad Ali and George Foreman that took place in Zaire, Africa, on October 30, 1974. Ali won, but Mailer's interest is in conveying action, first, but also in describing the subtle interplay between opponents. In doing this, he deploys a formidable set of comparisons. (*Note*: The title of this piece is supplied by the editor. Mailer's chapter title was "The Executioner's Song.")

1   So began the third act of the fight. Not often was there a better end to a second act than Foreman's failure to destroy Ali on the ropes. But the last scenes would present another problem. How was the final curtain to be found? For if Foreman was exhausted, Ali was weary. He had hit Foreman harder than he had ever hit anyone. He had hit him often. Foreman's head must by now be equal to a piece of vulcanized rubber. Conceivably you could beat on him all night and nothing more would happen. There is a threshold to the knockout. When it comes close but is not crossed, then a man can stagger around the ring forever. He has received his terrible message and he is still standing. No more of the same woe can destroy him. He is like the victim in a dreadful marriage which no one knows how to end. So Ali was obliged to produce still one more surprise. If not, the unhappiest threat would present itself as he and Foreman stumbled through the remaining rounds. There is agony to elucidate even a small sense of the aesthetic out of boxing. Wanton waste for an artist like Ali to lose then the perfection of this fight by wandering down a monotonous half hour to a dreary unanimous decision.

2   A fine ending to the fight would live in legend, but a dull victory, anticlimactic by the end, could leave him in half a legend—overblown in reputation by his friends and contested by his enemies—precisely that

state which afflicted most heroes. Ali was fighting to prove other points. So he said. So Ali had to dispose of Foreman in the next few rounds and do it well, a formidable problem. He was like a torero after a great faena who must still face the drear potential of a protracted inept and disappointing kill. Since no pleasure is greater among athletes than to overtake the style of their opponent, Ali would look to steal Foreman's last pride. George was an executioner. Ali would do it better. But how do you execute the executioner?

The problem was revealed in all its sluggish intricacies over the next three rounds. Foreman came out for the sixth looking like an alley cat with chewed-up brows. Lumps and swellings were all over his face, his skin equal to tar that has baked in the sun. When the bell rang, however, he looked dangerous again, no longer a cat, but a bull. He lowered his head and charged across the ring. He was a total demonstration of the power of one idea even when the idea no longer works. And was immediately seized and strangled around the neck by Ali for a few valuable and pacifying seconds until Zack Clayton broke them. Afterward, Foreman moved in to throw more punches. His power, however, seemed gone. The punches were slow and tentative. They did not reach Ali. Foreman was growing glove-shy. His fastest moves were now in a nervous defense that kept knocking Ali's punches away from his own face.

At this point Ali proceeded to bring out the classic left jab everyone had been expecting for the first round. In the next half-minute, he struck Foreman's head with ten head-ringing jabs thrown with all the speed of a good fencer's thrust, and Foreman took them in apathy to compound the existing near-apathy of his hopes. Each time his head snapped back, some communication between his mind and his nerves must have been reduced. A surgical attack.

Yet something in Foreman's response decided Ali to give it up. Perhaps no more than his own sense of moderation. It might look absurd if he kept jabbing Foreman forever. Besides, Ali needed rest. The next two minutes turned into the slowest two minutes of the fight. Foreman kept pushing Ali to the ropes out of habit, a dogged forward motion that enabled George to rest in his fashion, the only way he still knew, which was to lean on the opponent. Ali was by now so delighted with the advantages of the ropes that he fell back on them like a man returning home in quiet triumph, yes, settled in with the weary pleasure of a working man getting back into bed after a long day to be treated to a little of God's joy by his hardworking wife. He was almost tender with Foreman's laboring advance, holding him softly and kindly by the neck. Then he stung him with right and left karate shots from the shoulder. Foreman was now so arm-weary he could begin a punch only by lurching forward until his momentum encouraged a movement of the arm. He looked like a drunk, or rather a somnambulist, in a dance marathon. It would be wise to get him through the kill without ever waking him up. While it ought to be a simple matter to knock him down, there might not be enough violence left in the spirit of this ring to knock him out. So the shock of finding himself on the floor could prove a stimulant. His ego might reappear: once on the floor, he was a champion in dramatic danger of losing his title—that is an unmeasurable source of energy. Ali was now taking in the reactions of Foreman's head the way a bull-fighter lines up a bull before going in over the horns for the kill. He bent to his left and, still crouched, passed his body to the right under Foreman's fists, all the while studying George's head and neck and shoulders. Since Foreman charged the move, a fair conclusion was that the bull still had an access of strength too great for the kill.

6   Nonetheless, Foreman's punches were hardly more than pats. They were sufficiently weak for any man in reasonable shape to absorb them. Still, Foreman came on. Sobbing for breath, leaning, almost limping, in a pat-a-pat of feeble cuffs, he was all but lying over Ali on the ropes. Yet what a problem in the strength of his stubbornness itself. Endless powers of determination had been built out of one season of silence passing into another. The bell rang the end of the sixth. Both men gave an involuntary smile of relief.

7   Foreman looked ready to float as he came to his corner. Sandy Saddler could not bring himself to look at him. The sorrow in Foreman's corner was now heavier than in Ali's dressing room before the fight.

8   In his corner Ali looked thoughtful, and stood up abstractedly before the bell and abstractedly led a cheer in the stadium, his arm to the sky.

9   The cheer stirred Foreman to action. He was out of his corner and in the middle of the ring before the bell rang. Ali opened his eyes wide and stared at him in mock wonder, then in disdain as if to say, "Now you've done it. Now you're asking for it." He came out of his corner too, and the referee was pushing both men apart as the bell rang.

10   Still it was a slow round, almost as slow as the sixth. Foreman had no speed, and in return Ali boxed no faster than he had to, but kept shift-ing more rapidly than before from one set of ropes to another. Foreman was proving too sluggish to work with. Once, in the middle of the round, Foreman staggered past Ali, and for the first time in the fight was literally nearer the ropes. It was a startling realization. Not since the first five seconds of the fight had Ali crossed the center of the ring while moving forward. For seven rounds his retreating body had been between Foreman and the ropes except for the intervals when he traveled back-ward from one set of ropes to another. This time, seeing Foreman on the ropes instead, Ali backed up immediately and Foreman slogged after him like an infantryman looking at the ground. Foreman's best move by now might be to stand in the center of the ring and invite Ali to come to him. If Ali refused, he would lose the luster of his performance, and

if he did come forward it would be George's turn to look for weaknesses. While Foreman waited for Ali, he could rest. Yet George must have had some unspoken fear of disaster if he shifted methods. So he would drive, thank you very much, into the grave he would determine for himself. Of course, he was not wholly without hope. He still worked with the idea that one punch could catch Ali. And with less than a minute left, he managed to drive a left hook into Ali's belly, a blow that indeed made Ali gasp. Then Foreman racked him with a right uppercut strong enough for Ali to hold on in a clinch, no, Foreman was not going to give up. Now he leaned on Ali with one extended arm and tried to whale him with the other. He looked like he was beating a rug. Foreman had begun to show the clumsiness of a street fighter at the end of a long rumble. He was reverting. It happened to all but the most cultivated fighters toward the exhausted end of a long and terrible fight. Slowly they descended from the elegance of their best style down to the knee in the groin and the overhead punch (with a rock in the fist) of forgotten street fights.

Ali, half as tired at least, was not wasting himself. He was still grace- 11
ful in every move. By the end of the round he was holding Foreman's head tenderly once more in his glove. Foreman was becoming reminiscent of the computer Hal in 2001[1] as his units were removed one by one, malfunctions were showing and spastic lapses. All the while something of the old panache of Sadler, Saddler, and Moore[2] inserted over those thousands of hours of training still showed in occasional moves and gestures. The weakest slaps of his gloves, however, had begun to look like entreaties. Still his arms threw punches. By the end of the seventh he could hardly stand: yet he must have thrown seventy more punches. So few were able to land. Ali had restricted himself to twenty-five—half at least must have gone to target. Foreman was fighting as slowly as a worn-out fighter in the Golden Gloves,[3] slow as a man walking up a hill of pillows, slow as he would have looked if their first round had been rerun in slow motion, that was no slower than Foreman was fighting now, and thus exposed as in a film, he was reminiscent of the slow and curving motions of a linebacker coiling around a runner with his hands and arms in the slow-motion replay—the boxing had shifted from speed and impact to an intimacy of movement. Delicately Ali would cradle Foreman's head with his left before he smashed it with his right. Fore-man looked ready to fall over from exhaustion. His face had the soft

---

[1] *Hal in 2001.* The talking computer in the Stanley Kubrick movie.

[2] *Sadler, Saddler and Moore.* Dick *Sadler* was Foreman's manager. Sandy Saddler, himself a former champion (lightweight), was one of Foreman's trainers. Archie Moore was also a former champion, in the light heavyweight division, whose career had been ended when he fought Ali years before. At this time, he was also one of Foreman's trainers.

[3] *Golden Gloves.* An amateur boxing tournament.

scrubbed look of a child who has just had a dirty face washed, but then they both had that gentle look boxers get when they are very tired and have fought each other very hard.

Questions for the Critical Reader

1. Mailer seems to think that there is something aesthetic about box-ing? Do you agree? Justify your answer.
2. How much of his absorption in this spectacle depends upon his knowledge of the fine points of boxing? Can you conceive of some-one who knows nothing of boxing becoming interested in this fight to the same degree?
3. Mailer asks two questions about the fight in paragraphs 1 and 2. Are these questions in the minds of the fighters or in Mailer's and to what degree? You should remember that description frequently registers internal judgments on the part of the author.
4. Comment on Mailer's psychological acuteness by evaluating the ex-pression in his sentence in paragraph 5 that begins, "His ego might reappear."
5. Are there confrontations in life that you yourself think of as aesthe-tic spectacles though the rest of us would not be likely to agree? What are they, and what is it about them that makes them seem to you to be artistic?
6. If you are not a boxing fan, what is the effect of this piece for you? Does it enable you to see boxing in a new and different light? Is it an interesting piece of reading nevertheless, or not?
7. Whether or not you are a boxing fan, you might agree that Mailer is interested in human values. What relationship between the two fighters does he depict?

Rhetorical Technique

1. How much of this is objective and how much impressionistic de-scription? Cite specific paragraphs. (See the introduction to this chapter.)
2. Is there a dominant impression? If so, what is it?
3. Which details contribute to it most strongly?
4. Comment on the brevity of paragraphs 7, 8, and 9. Why are these considerably shorter than the average length of the others?
5. A description of people engaged in some process, in this case boxing, must report changes in the condition of the participants. How does Mailer do this most effectively?

6. How much is contributed to this description by Mailer's attention to what is going on in each fighter's corner?
7. How would you describe Mailer's point of view (see Glossary: *point of view*).
8. From what other point or points of view could this piece have been written? Be specific.
9. What accounts most for the style and tone of this piece? (See Glossary: *style and tone.*)

Diction and Vocabulary

1. The theater, marriage, bullfighting, and an act of execution—all these comparisons are made in the first two paragraphs. Identify the figure of speech appropriate to each use (see Glossary: *figures of speech*) and evaluate their effectiveness. Which seems most useful to the description? Which least?
2. Do the same for the cat/bull references in paragraphs 3 and 5. Is either one a cliché? (See Glossary: *cliché.*)
3. What use does Mailer make of the phrase *equal to* in paragraphs 1 and 3? Is it effective? Explain.
4. Identify five examples of simile, and evaluate their effectiveness. (See Glossary: *simile.*)
5. Identify two examples of unusual syntax, and evaluate their effectiveness. (See Glossary: *syntax.*)
6. Comment on the absence or presence of colloquial language in this piece. (See Glossary: *colloquial language.*) Is there enough? Too much? If you think there is not enough, what would you have added to achieve a more striking descriptive effect?
7. Consult the dictionary to be sure you understand the meanings of the following words and phrases: *vulcanized* (par. 1); *elucidate* (1); *aesthetic* (1); *anticlimactic* (2); *afflicted* (2); *torero* (2); *faena* (2); *momentous* (5); *somnambulistic* (5); *cuffs* (6); *reverting* (10); *reminiscent* (11); *malfunctions* (11); *panache* (11); *entreaties* (11).

VIRGINIA WOOLF

Dawn

Virginia Woolf (1882–1941), an English novelist and essayist, was the daughter of Sir Leslie Stephen, a prominent Victorian man of letters. Mrs. Woolf was a pioneer of modern fiction, evolving an impressionistic stream-of-consciousness technique in such novels as *Mrs. Dalloway, To the Lighthouse, Orlando,* and *The Waves.* She also wrote on feminist subjects with force and subtlety (especially perhaps in *A Room of One's Own*) and was an essayist on literary and cultural subjects of uncommon distinction. The piece printed here, under a title supplied by the editor, is an adaptation of her essay "The Sun and the Fish," which appears in her *The Captain's Death Bed and Other Essays* (1950). In her description, Mrs. Woolf imparts a sense of mystery and awe to the natural event that is her subject. In doing so, she reveals her underlying feelings about nature.

1   Never was there a stranger purpose than that which brought us together that June night in Euston Railway Station. We were come to see the dawn. Trains like ours were starting all over England at that very moment to see the dawn. All noses were pointing north. When for a moment we halted in the depths of the country, there were the pale yellow lights of motor cars also pointing north. There was no sleep, no fixity in England that night. All were on the roads; all were travelling north. All were thinking of the dawn. As the night wore on, the sky, which was the object of so many million thoughts, assumed greater substance and prominence than usual. The consciousness of the whitish soft canopy above us increased in weight as the hours passed. When in chill early morning we were turned out on a Yorkshire roadside, our senses had orientated themselves differently from usual. We were no longer in the same relation to people, houses, and trees; we were related to the whole world. We had come, not to lodge in the bedroom of an inn; we were come for a few hours of disembodied intercourse with the sky.

2   Everything was very pale. The river was pale and the fields, brimming with grasses and tasselled flowers which should have been red, had no colour in them, but lay there whispering and waving round colourless farmhouses. Now the farmhouse door would open, and out would step to join the procession the farmer and his family in their Sunday clothes, neat, dark and silent as if they were going uphill to church; or sometimes

women merely leant on the window-sills of the upper rooms watching the procession pass with amused contempt, it appeared—they have come such hundreds of miles, and for what? they seemed to say—in complete silence. We had an odd sense of keeping an appointment with an actor of such vast proportions that he would come silently and be everywhere.

By the time we were at the meeting-place, on a high fell where the **3** hills stretched their limbs out over the flowing brown moorland below, we had put on too—though we were cold and with our feet stood in red bog water were likely to be still colder, though some of us were squatted on mackintoshes among cups and plates, eating, and others were fantastically accoutred and none were at their best—still we had put on a certain dignity. Rather, perhaps, we had put off the little badges and signs of individuality. We were strung out against the sky in outline and had the look of statues standing prominent on the ridge of the world. We were very, very old; we were men and women of the primeval world come to salute the dawn. So the worshippers at Stonehenge must have looked among tussocks of grass and boulders of rock. Suddenly, from the motor car of some Yorkshire squire, there bounded four large, lean, red dogs, hounds of the ancient world, hunting dogs, they seemed, leaping with their noses close to the ground on the track of boar or deer. Meanwhile, the sun was rising. A cloud glowed as a white shade glows when the light is slowly turned up behind it. Golden wedge-shaped streamers fell from it and marked the trees in the valley green and the villages blue-brown. In the sky behind us there swam white islands in pale blue lakes. The sky was open and free there, but in front of us a soft snowbank had massed itself. Yet, as we looked, we saw it proving worn and thin in patches. The gold momentarily increased, melting the whiteness to a fiery gauze, and this grew frailer and frailer till, for one instant, we saw the sun in full splendour. Then there was a pause, a moment of suspense, like that which precedes a race. The starter held his watch in his hand, counting the seconds. Now they were off.

The sun had to race through the clouds and to reach the goal, which **4** was a thin transparency to the right, before the sacred seconds were up. He started. The clouds flung every obstacle in his way. They clung, they impeded. He dashed through them. He could be felt, flashing and flying when he was invisible. His speed was tremendous. Here he was out and bright; now he was under and lost. But always one felt him flying and thrusting through the murk to his goal. For one second he emerged and showed himself to us through our glasses, a hollowed sun, a crescent sun. Finally, he went under for his last effort. Now he was completely blotted out. The moments passed. Watches were held in hand after hand. The sacred twenty-four seconds were begun. Unless he could win through before the last one was over, he was lost. Still one felt him tearing and racing behind the clouds to win free; but the clouds held him.

They spread; they thickened; they slackened; they muffled his speed. Of the twenty-four seconds only five remained, and still he was obscured. And, as the fatal seconds passed, and we realized that the sun was being defeated, had now, indeed lost the race, all the colour began to go from the moor. The blue turned to purple; the white became livid as at the approach of a violent but windless storm. Pink faces went green, and it became colder than ever. This was the defeat of the sun, then, and this was all, so we thought, turning in disappointment from the dull cloud blanket in front of us to the moors behind. They were livid, they were purple; but suddenly one became aware that something more was about to happen; something unexpected, awful, unavoidable. The shadow growing darker and darker over the moor was like the heeling over of a boat, which, instead of righting itself at the critical moment, turns a little further and then a little further on its side; and suddenly capsizes. So the light turned and heeled over and went out. This was the end. The flesh and blood of the world was dead; only the skeleton was left. It hung beneath us, a frail shell; brown; dead; withered. Then, with some trifling movement, this profound obeisance of the light, this stooping down and abasement of all splendour was over. Lightly, on the other side of the world, up it rose; it sprang up as if the one movement, after a second's tremendous pause, completed the other, and the light which had died here rose again elsewhere. Never was there such a sense of rejuvenescence and recovery. All the convalescences and respites of life seemed rolled into one. Yet, at first, so light and frail and strange the colour was, sprinkled rainbow-like in a hoop of colour, that it seemed as if the earth could never live decked out in such frail tints. It hung beneath us, like a cage, like a hoop, like a globe of glass. It might be blown out; it might be stove in. But steadily and surely our relief broadened and our confidence established itself as the great paint-brush washed in woods dark on the valley, and massed hills blue above them. The world became more and more solid; it became populous; it became a place where an infinite number of farmhouses, of villages, of railway lines have lodgement; until the whole fabric of civilization was modelled and moulded. But still the memory endured that the earth we stand on is made of colour; colour can be blown out; and then we stand on a dead leaf; and we who tread the earth securely now have seen it dead.

Questions for the Critical Reader

1. Identify the "us" referred to in the first sentence.
2. What were they really coming to see?
3. Woolf says about this, "Never was there a stranger purpose." Should this be taken literally? Justify your answer.

4. Can you think of any natural phenomenon that would attract your attention with the same intensity as this attract's Woolf's? Explain.
5. What is the significance of the last two sentences?

Rhetorical Technique

1. To what extent is this a narrative?
2. What is the dominant impression? Which details contribute most strongly to it?
3. Which of the senses is most strongly appealed to by Woolf's details?
4. How much of the effect of this piece depends on Woolf's attention to the details of light and color?
5. How are the details in paragraph 4 organized? Why did the author choose this pattern over another?
6. Identify two examples of parallel structure, and comment on their effectiveness. (See Glossary: *parallel structure.*)
7. How does Woolf achieve emphasis here? (See Glossary: *emphasis.*)
8. The tone of this essay is partly determined by Woolf's attitude toward the event she is watching. How would you describe this attitude? What specific features of the text lead you to your conclusions? (See Glossary: *style and tone.*)

Diction and Vocabulary

1. *Synecdoche* is a figure of speech by which a more inclusive term is used for a less inclusive term or vice versa. For example, instead of asking a rancher how many cattle he has, one might ask how many *head* of cattle, or, in speaking of a police officer, one might call him *the law.* Identify an example of *synecdoche* (pronounced sin-*ek*-duh-key) in Woolf's essay.
2. Give two examples each of metaphor and simile, and comment on their effectiveness. (See Glossary: *figures of speech.*)
3. Where does Woolf use personification? (See Glossary: *figures of speech.*) Is it effective?
4. What effect does Woolf achieve with her reference to Stonehenge? (Par. 3).
5. Consult the dictionary to be sure you understand the meanings of the following words: *orientated* (par. 1); *fell* (3); *bog* (3); *mackintoshes* (3); *accoutred* (3); *primeval* (3); *obeisance* (4); *abasement* (4); *rejuvenescence* (4); *convalescence* (4); *impeded* (4).

Writing Suggestions for Chapter 8: *Description*

I.

Write an impressionistic description of a place. Begin by jotting down *all* your impressions, making no attempt at organization until your list is complete. After that, examine the list carefully to select a dominant impression, and then organize your essay in such a way that you use only those jotted down impressions that contribute to the dominant impression. In jotting down impressions of place, employ the whole range of the senses—the reader wants to know how the place looks, smells, sounds, feels. Reread Colette, Woolf, and Agee to see what else contributes to a sense of place. Here is a list of possible subjects:

1. A ski lift.
2. A favorite beach.
3. Your room after a night of cramming.
4. A rooftop.
5. A gloomy classroom.
6. The view from the top of a mountain or a high building.
7. An official office—someplace where you were forced to wait for a long and perhaps tedious time.
8. A dentist's or a doctor's office.
9. A hospital room.
10. A stadium.
11. A museum.
12. A movie theater.

II. Writing Assignment Based on "A Working Class Mother"

Write an impressionistic description of a person that shows your underlying judgment of that person either as positive or negative. Follow the same basic procedure outlined above under Roman numeral I. Reread Hoggart to see what elements contribute to the delineation of a person. These will include details of clothing, speech, posture, attitude, movement, and so on. Here are a few possible subjects:

1. A teacher.
2. A neighbor.
3. Somebody you saw on a bus.
4. The campus joker.
5. Your kid sister or brother.
6. Your grandfather or grandmother.
7. A musician you saw at a concert.
8. Someone you've just met.
9. Someone you saw on television news.
10. A character in a film.

III. Writing Assignment Based on "Knoxville: Summer, 1915" and "The Ali-Foreman Fight: Rounds 6 and 7"

Write an impressionistic description of a scene that includes details of place and the actions of people. Follow the basic procedure outlined above under Roman numeral I. Reread Agee and Mailer for help with the kinds of details that contribute to a scene full of movement. Here are a few possible subjects:

1. People waiting in line for a big event (a hit movie, a rock concert) find out they can't get in after all.
2. A demolition derby.
3. The student union cafeteria at the height of the lunch hour.
4. Jimmy Carter's visit to the campus.
5. Spring plowing.
6. The first day of a new term on campus.
7. A discotheque.
8. Somebody's surprise party.
9. A meeting of an encounter group.
10. An auction.
11. Main Street at high noon.
12. Christmas eve.

The Telling *Narration*

A narration is a story and a story is—well, everybody knows what a story is. There are newspaper stories, life stories (biographies), histories, personal stories, tall stories, fairy tales, short stories, novels. The stories with which this chapter is concerned are those that, like the first four kinds in the preceding list, can be called *factual stories*. The others on the list are all *fiction*.

Fictional narrative appeals to our imagination by making us part of the imagined world: we can actually undergo the experience of the characters. In *Catch 22* by Joseph Heller, we are made to feel what it is like to be an American Air Corps flier in World War II and be a party to the convoluted insanity taking place in that fictional world—partly by being immersed in a timeless world. We *feel*, with Yossarian, that it is crazy to try to kill somebody because Heller has enlisted our capacity to imagine. Furthermore, Heller's (and other fictionists') additional purpose is to help us experience the events he describes. Thus we can participate in the strafing of the airfield by Milo Minderbinder and the antics of Major Major.

On the other hand, factual narration, the kind we are most interested in here, has no such purposes. The reporting of an airplane hijacking, for example, does not—although it may without intending to—appeal to our imaginations but rather to our *understanding*. What we get out of such a story is not necessarily the imaginative feel of the events but a grasp of what happened and its significance. We do not "understand" the events in *Catch 22*, and we do not "imagine" the jet hijack. Just the opposite.

(A special case is Woody Allen's story. It appeals, somehow, to *both* understanding and imagination because although it is pure fiction, it is based on an actual event.)

But in any kind of story, three things are most important (in this order): the characters (what kind of people took part in the story), the action (the things that happen), and the setting, or physical locale, in which the events take place. It is the relation of these three aspects of storytelling that permits us to grasp the significance of the story and *understand*. (Who tells the story and the degree of his or her involvement in it are also factors that help a reader to understand. Four of the stories in this chapter were written by participants in the action; the other, "Siege of the Pearls," was written by someone who was close by when the events took place. But in your own writing, you need not limit yourself to writing stories told as these are.

Your stories can be written from the point of view of someone not so closely involved.)

Therefore, the writer's concentration should be focused on these three aspects of storytelling.

Characters should be described clearly. The way to report a character—some actual person, since we're dealing with factual narrative—is to give appropriate details of what he or she does, feels, and says, and what he or she looks like, too. People's styles of dress are valuable clues to who they are. In this connection, we might mention dialogue. Writers should make every effort to keep dialogue as close to human speech as they can and to use it for effect by using it sparingly. (See Friedrich's use of dialogue for a good example.)

You might think that since the stories you write are true ones, you must include *everything* that was said. In the first place, no writer could possibly report with such completeness, and in the second place, *emphasis* (see Glossary entry) requires that you choose, use proportion. Similarly, about the action: you need not record in your story everything that *happened*. The main events will do because these are the ones that will help us understand. With respect to the locale, you need only describe as much of it as figures importantly in the story. For a hypothetical example of how lack of restraint in these matters can ruin a story, consider the very short sketch by Eldridge Cleaver. Imagine what would happen to the spare excellence of that little story if the author had inserted a scene *after* the one with the priest, this one describing how he went to the prison cafeteria for lunch and including the dialogue (what he said to his friends, what they said to him), the setting (a description of the cafeteria), and a description of the other inmates (more characterization)—*just because things actually had happened that way!*

Finally, you should also pay close attention to the order in which the events of a story are presented. Real-life stories happen without interruption, usually, one event following after another in succession. But you should notice that the writers of the stories in this chapter frequently interrupt the strict time order of their stories (both Allen and Cleaver, for example, use the flashback technique, beginning their stories by explaining that they are writing about the distant past and then taking you back to the beginning of what happened). The purpose here is to create variety and interest in the patterns of events: it's not very interesting to read a succession of paragraphs that start with some variant of "The next thing that happened..."

But the purpose of interrupting is also to offer necessary comments and background material so that the reader can better understand the events that follow the interruption. The writer who was sufficiently impressed with the story he or she saw, heard, or was involved in will help the reader greatly by the controlled writing he or she does. For the storyteller who *understands* the story will go a long way to help the reader understand.

OTTO FRIEDRICH

The History Lesson

Otto Friedrich was born in Boston in 1929 and is a writer, editor, and novelist. A former senior editor of *Time*, he describes in *Going Crazy* (1975) the varieties of experience of insanity among the great and the near great, the ordinary and not-so-ordinary in American life. This essay, taken from the Op-Ed page of *The New York Times* (January 23, 1974), is a particularly poignant example of factual narrative, made more telling perhaps by the perspective of many years.

The new boy did his best to avoid attention, as new boys generally do. 1
He arrived one day at my sixth-grade classroom in the Green Street School in Brattleboro, Vt., and silently took a seat in the back row, in a corner next to the window.

Almost thirty-five years have passed since that day, but I see him still, 2
a thin, pale boy, with steel-rimmed spectacles and sandy hair parted in the middle. His mother had evidently dressed him in what she hoped would be the most respectable of outfits. He wore a brown tweed suit, with a brown cardigan underneath, neatly buttoned. His name was George Grass.

Nowadays, I suppose, George Grass would probably be tested and 3
classified as retarded, or disturbed, or some such thing, and then put into one of those special classes where children who cannot compete are consigned to limbo. Even then, in 1940, there were euphemisms like "a little slow" or "not quite right," but the Vermont public schools made no allowance for intellectual weaknesses. The farm boys who could not master third grade arithmetic remained in the third grade as long as necessary, sometimes up to the age of sixteen, when they were permitted to drop out of school and fulfill their destiny of hoeing corn-fields and milking cows.

In the sixth grade of the Green Street School, the bright children sat 4
in the front rows, where Mrs. Forbes made an earnest attempt to teach them long division. The older and dumber children sat toward the rear, and their only duty was to keep quiet and not interfere with the learning process. Back among all these sat George Grass, stiffly smiling. None of us ever really knew him; there was no way to know him. During the lunch period, when we all clattered into the home-ec room to eat, he sat by himself, carefully opening his green metal lunchbox, unfolding the waxed paper and eating his jelly sandwiches.

230 *Otto Friedrich*

5   Mrs. Forbes, a handsome, dark-haired woman of about forty, was, according to the Vermont traditions, a good teacher. She drove her pupils to the limits of their abilities, exhorted them to work harder, scolded them for every mistake. Those who could be shamed or scared into learning how to spell learned how to spell. My brother, who was left-handed, was made to stand at the blackboard and do sums with his right hand. I, who repeatedly said "uh" while reciting a composition, was made to stay after school until I could recite without pauses. The farm boys who failed to meet Mrs. Forbes's standards simply flunked. They returned to her class the next year, to the seats at the back of the room.

6   About a week after George Grass arrived in our class, Mrs. Forbes gave a history test, and the next day she handed back the papers, all numerically graded, with every error marked by a large X. But George Grass's paper puzzled her. "I just don't understand George," she said. "I don't understand George's paper. He seems to have answered every question by writing 'vegetables.'" There was a ripple of nervous laughter, and we all turned to stare at George Grass, sitting wide-eyed in his corner by the window.

7   There is some instinct, I guess, that makes a teacher sense applause, and respond to it, that makes her sense the class as an audience.

8   "Listen to this," Mrs. Forbes said, holding up George Grass's paper and beginning to read aloud from it. "When did the Pilgrims land at Plymouth Rock? 'Vegetables.'"

9   There is some instinct, too, that makes a roomful of sixth-graders turn on a victim. We laughed at George Grass's answer, and as we laughed, Mrs. Forbes read on.

10   "Who was Miles Standish? 'Vegetables.' Who was Pocahontas? 'Vegetables'."

11   I realized that an awful ritual was taking place, and I wanted it to stop, but I knew there was nothing I could do that would make Mrs. Forbes stop. Or the rest of us. I laughed. We all laughed.

12   "What happened to the witches of Salem? 'Vegetables'."

13   I looked furtively back at George Grass, in his spectacles and his brown tweed suit. He sat there, helpless, with a grin frozen on his pale face. Then he too began giggling.

14   "Well, George," Mrs. Forbes said, "we'll have to do better next time."

15   George Grass didn't come back to school the next day, or ever again.

Questions for the Critical Reader

1. From what you know of Friedrich's interests, can you guess why he is telling a story that happened thirty-five years in the past?

2. Is there a specific place where the author contrasts the past and the present?
3. Does he think things have changed?
4. Consider the fact that George Grass takes a seat in the "very back row." Does your experience of seat selection in your classes suggest anything about George? Why is the point about George's seat made in the very first paragraph?
5. In paragraph 4 we are told that none of the pupils "ever really knew" George Grass because "there was no way to know him." Why was there no way?
6. In paragraphs 7 and 9, Friedrich refers to two "instincts." Can you expand on the nature of each of these? Do you agree that they exist? Have you had experiences that would tend to confirm or deny what he says?
7. Who is responsible, in your opinion, for the "awful ritual" involving George's test paper?
8. Is this ritual different in effect from those described in paragraph 5?
9. Friedrich says that as a little boy he "realized" something about an "awful ritual." Do you think a little boy would have had such a thought, or is it just that he is *now* elaborating on what he thought *then*? Explain.

Rhetorical Technique

1. One of the purposes of description is to make us *see*. Note that the author uses that verb in the first sentence of paragraph 2 and that the description of George's clothing helps us to see him. But how would the description be without the reference to George's mother? What does that reference add?
2. If a story is defined as a *sequence* of events, we might have expected paragraph 6 to follow right after paragraph 2. What would be lost if things were rearranged that way?
3. Starting with the third sentence of paragraph 6, the author could have eliminated all the dialogue and just given us a summary of what Mrs. Forbes did. Instead he has quoted her extensively. What is the effect of using the dialogue instead of a summary?
4. Which details contribute best to his characterization of Mrs. Forbes?
5. Describe how this piece begins. Is it an effective introduction? (See Glossary: *introductions*.)
6. What is the effect of the short, final paragraph?
7. What is the central theme of this essay? Can you locate a thesis statement? (See Glossary: *subject; thesis statement; unity*.)
8. How would you describe the tone of this essay? (See Glossary: *style and tone*.)

Diction and Vocabulary

1. Friedrich uses concrete language in spelling out the name of his school and the town and state in which it was located. He even gives us the names of the boy and the teacher and the kind of sandwiches he ate. What difference do these concrete details make to your understanding the central theme of this story (see question 7 under "Rhetorical Technique")? (See Glossary: *abstract and concrete*.)
2. Read paragraph 3 carefully, and offer a definition of the word *euphemisms*. Now check yours against a dictionary definition. How do they compare?
3. Why does Friedrich use the verb *clattered* in paragraph 4?
4. What does it mean to be *consigned to limbo*?
5. Be sure you are clear about the meanings of these words: *cardigan* (par. 2); *home-ec* (4); *exhorted* (5); *furtively* (13).

TOM WALKER

Siege of the Pearls

"Siege of the Pearls" is taken from the book *Fort Apache*, by Tom
Walker, a veteran police officer. The book offers a horrifyingly
objective account of conditions in the area of the 41st Police
Precinct in the South Bronx, New York City. Because of these
conditions, the precinct has been nicknamed Fort Apache. "Siege
of the Pearls" was first printed in the magazine *New York* of
February 23, 1976, as "The Siege of Fort Apache."

Sometimes, though, residents of the Four-one prove more resilient than 1
one might expect. A family named the Pearls, black, close-knit, moved
to the city from North Carolina, where the father had been killed in a
hunting accident. There were nine children, ranging in age from four to
nineteen. After several frustrating months in search of decent housing
and jobs, the family went on welfare, and was eventually placed in a
deteriorating house on Longfellow Avenue. Their drop into welfare and
poverty distressed them. The boys found the violence of the street and
the politics of the gangs in their neighborhood disturbing; the daughters
were repelled by the tough, promiscuous girls.

In turn, the Pearls' aloofness piqued the gangs' pride. So they beat up 2
a couple of the younger boys. They were in turn warned by the older
brothers. The warning only accelerated the beatings. Then, one day,
Simon, nineteen, and Butch, seventeen, caught five of the gang torturing
nine-year-old Sammy Pearl. They unmercifully beat three of the tor-
turers.

Two of the attackers belonged to the Royal Jades; the third was a 3
visiting member of the Black Devils. We had lists of their activities on
the wall. Unfortunately, we didn't know of the fight or of the meeting
that followed in which the beating was reported to the gang leaders.
That night a rock was thrown through the front-door window of the
Pearls' home. They made a complaint, and a radio car took the report.
Rather than seek our protection, the two oldest boys decided to buy guns.

Before they could find guns to buy, however, Mrs. Pearl heard noises 4
at the front door one evening. Four youngsters were trying to jimmy the
lock of the front door. Her sudden screams drove them away and brought
Butch and Simon racing downstairs. They had kept the harassment and
the beatings from their mother. Now they knew the situation would only

From *Fort Apache* by Tom Walker, reprinted in *New York* Magazine as "The
Siege of Fort Apache," copyright © 1976 by Thomas J. Walker. Reprinted with
permission of Thomas Y. Crowell Co., Inc., Publisher.

get worse. Although we assigned a patrol car to watch the house, the boys still felt threatened.

5   Early the next morning, they went outside, and from the empty lots and tenement cellars they collected bricks, rocks, and bottles, their first-strike capability. These they stored on the porch roof facing the street. Throughout the night, the boys kept their own vigil, staggering sleep periods. Nothing happened.

6   The next day, Simon finally bought guns from a candy-store owner, a sawed-off shotgun and a .45-caliber automatic. That night, the family spent the evening eating dinner and watching TV. (Neither boy said anything. The danger, they felt, was too enormous for their mother to comprehend.) At 10:30, as the summer heat slowly subsided, Eloise, the ten-year-old, excitedly claimed she saw someone in the backyard. Simon and Butch checked but found no one.

7   About this time, a thirteen-year-old, wearing the Royal Jade colors, strolled into a cellar a short distance away and calmly announced, "It's done. I cut the phone lines." Two others reported that the Molotov cocktails and other weapons were in position. Both gangs now worked in concert. They numbered 40. At 10:45, the assault groups moved out.

8   Twelve Jades and Devils charged the front porch and started to knock out all the windows with pipes and bats. Down came the front door. The door in the rear gave way to a strong assault. Two squads in the street peppered the house with bricks and rocks which had been neatly concealed in the Pearls' own garbage cans.

9   As the family realized the phone was dead, a squad from the gang broke through to the vestibule. Simon and Butch gathered the children together and then Simon raced upstairs for the weapons. One firebomb landed on the porch. A second set fire to the front of the house. Simon returned downstairs as the main attack hit the front door. He fired two blasts from his shotgun. Several of the attackers, wounded, retreated. That gave the two boys time to hustle the mother, the grandmother, and the kids upstairs. Thick, oily flames lapped at the living room. As Simon tried to beat them back, the cellar door slowly opened; he grabbed the shotgun and let go with two blasts. Then he retreated upstairs.

10   By this time, the rest of the family was terrified and screaming un-restrainedly. Looking out the window, both Simon and Butch realized they were surrounded, with no immediate help in sight. Time, they knew, favored the attackers. The flames slowly spread.

11   Simon had not lost his sense of command. He gave Butch the shotgun and ordered him to the front-bedroom windows. With the .45 he guarded the stairs. They waited. Simon admitted later that his legs shook so much he had to kneel and prop his body against the wall.

12   Several shotgun blasts came from the front room. Butch had spotted firebombers on the roof across the street. The pellets from his gun hit a young boy who had been at his window watching the action. Irate, the

mother called us. It was our first report of the siege, and it took the injury of a child, whose mother would otherwise have been unconcerned, to alert us.

By that time, eleven attackers were in the living room, fanning the 13 fire. Several gang members crouched at the foot of the darkened stairs. They held .25-caliber pistols and exchanged shots with Simon. They were still blasting away when we reached the scene. I sent one unit around to the back of the building, and we breached the front door. We managed to nab seven of the gang. As we brought the children and their guardians out of the house, the Fire Department arrived.

After the fire was out, the family returned to their home. They refused 14 to go to a welfare hotel. When they first arrived in the city, they had spent a couple of months in one. Their fourteen-year-old girl was raped during that stay. I stationed a radio car in front of the house until the family could be relocated. Nobody went to jail.

Questions for the Critical Reader

1. What is your main response to the story? Which detail or details were most important in forming that response?
2. How do you feel about the information contained in the last sentence?
3. After reading Walker's story, one might get the impression that all the violence in it was directed *at* the Pearls.
   a) Is there some place in the story, before the assault on their home, where the Pearls directed some violence at others?
   b) What justification was there for the action they took? Was there an alternative?
4. Comment on the conflict between the Pearls on the one hand and the neighborhood on the other and their respective responses to one another.
   a) How does Walker contrast and compare the Pearls and the gang members?
   b) Read or reread "Group" in Chapter 5. Does that definition help you to understand the actions of the family on the one hand or the gangs on the other?
5. Consider the last two sentences in paragraph 3. Is there a contradiction here? Justify your answer.
6. What can you say about conditions in Fort Apache's area from the fact that the Pearls are on welfare and that Simon Pearl was able to buy a sawed-off shotgun and a .45-caliber automatic from a candy-store owner?

Rhetorical Technique

1. For what purpose does the author give us, in par. 1, the background information about the Pearls?
2. Why are we told that the father was killed in a hunting accident?
3. At only one point in the action does the author offer us a piece of dialogue. Locate it and comment on its effectiveness.
4. Are there other places in the story where you think dialogue might have added to its effectiveness? Where? Why?
5. Are any members of the Pearl family characterized so that you feel you have knowledge of his or her distinctive personality? Point out where and how this was done. If you can't, why has the author made such a choice?
6. As we noted in the introduction to this chapter, expository narrative depends upon a time sequence.
   a) The only place in the story where chronology is interrupted is in paragraph 11. Comment on the effectiveness of this.
   b) Note the transition between paragraphs 6 and 7. For what purpose is it made? (See Glossary: *transition*.)
7. Are the author's descriptions mainly objective or impressionistic? Why do you suppose he has made such a choice? What does it have to do with his point of view? (See Glossary: *point of view*; see also the introduction to Chapter 8.)
8. What is the author's attitude toward the Pearl family? How does he indicate or reveal this attitude? How much does it contribute to the tone of this story? (See Glossary: *style and tone*.)
9. Which form of irony is suggested by the last sentence? (See Glossary: *irony*.)
10. Consider the contribution to the story of the unusual syntax you find in paragraphs 8 and 10. (See Glossary: *syntax*.)

Diction and Vocabulary

1. In paragraph 4, the author uses the word *youngsters* for the four gang members who are trying to jimmy the lock on the door of the Pearls' house. From the connotative value of this word, estimate the contribution of its use in revealing his attitude. (See Glossary: *connotation and denotation*.)
2. Locate at least five examples of military language, and comment on the effectiveness of this usage.
3. What can you tell about the attitudes of the gangs from the names they chose, that is, the *Royal Jades* and the *Black Devils*?
4. Consider such colloquial language as *hustle* (par. 9), *kids* (9), *blasting away* (13) and *nab* (13). How much do these expressions con-

tribute to the story? Could there be more or less of it? (See Glossary: *colloquial language.*)

5. *Flames lapped* (par. 9): what figure of speech is this? (See Glossary: *figures of speech.*)

6. Consult the dictionary to be sure you understand the meanings of the following words and phrases: *resilient* (par. 1); *promiscuous* (1); *aloofness* (2); *piqued* (2); *accelerated* (2); *harassment* (4); *vigil* (5); *subsided* (6); *in concert* (7); *unrestrainedly* (10); *irate* (12); *breached* (13).

WOODY ALLEN

Nefarious Times We Live In

Woody Allen was born in 1935. We know his comic genius chiefly
through his films, among which are *Play It Again, Sam; Everything
You Always Wanted to Know About Sex (but Were Afraid to Ask);
Sleeper;* and *Love and Death.* But Allen is also a Broadway playwright, a nightclub performer, and a frequent contributor of satiric
pieces to *The New Yorker* and other magazines. These pieces have
been collected in *Getting Even* (1971) and *Without Feathers* (1975).

"Nefarious Times We Live In" first appeared in *The New Republic* on November 22, 1975. It is included here as an example
of a funny narrative, and, though it is clearly fictional, its aim is to
explain by satire some outlandish facets of American life. The
immediate impetus for the piece was the fact that in the fall of
1975, President Gerald Ford twice came under the threat of
assassination. This is Allen's comment on American life at that
time.

1   Yes. I confess. It was I, Willard Pogrebin, mild mannered and promising
at one time in life, who fired a shot at the President of the United States.
Fortunately for all concerned, a member of the on-looking crowd
jostled the Luger in my hand causing the bullet to ricochet off a Mc-
Donald's sign and lodge in some bratwurst at Himmelstein's Sausage
Emporium. After a light scuffle in which several G-men laced my
trachea into a reef knot, I was subdued and carted off for observation.

2   How did it happen that I had come to this, you ask? Me, a character
with no pronounced political convictions; whose childhood ambition was
to play Mendelssohn on the cello or perhaps dance on point in the great
capitals of the world? Well, it all began two years ago. I had just been
medically discharged from the army, the results of certain scientific
experiments performed on me without my knowledge. More precisely,
a group of us had been fed roast chicken stuffed with lysurgic acid, in
a research program designed to determine the quantity of LSD a man
can ingest before he attempts to fly over the World Trade Center.
Developing secret weapons is of great importance to the Pentagon and
the previous week I had been shot with a dart whose drugged tip
caused me to look and talk exactly like Salvador Dali. Cumulative side
effects took their toll on my perception and when I could no longer tell
the difference between my brother Morris and two soft-boiled eggs, I
was discharged.

Electroshock therapy at the Veterans Hospital helped although wires   3
got crossed with a behavioral psychology lab and I along with several
chimpanzees all performed *The Cherry Orchard* together in perfect
English. Broke and alone upon my release, I recall hitchhiking west and
being picked up by two native Californians: a charismatic young man
with a beard like Rasputin's and a charismatic young woman with a
beard like Svengali's. I was exactly what they were looking for, they
explained, as they were in the process of transcribing the Kaballah on
parchment and had run out of blood. I tried to explain that I was en
route to Hollywood seeking honest employment but the combination of
their hypnotic eyes and a knife the size of a sculling oar convinced me
of their sincerity. I recall being driven to a deserted ranch where several
mesmerized young women force fed me organic health foods and then
tried to emboss the sign of the pentagram on my forehead with a soldering iron. I then witnessed a black mass in which hooded adolescent
acolytes chanted the words, "Oh wow," in Latin. I also recall being made
to take peyote and cocaine and eat a white substance that came from
boiled cactus, which caused my head to revolve completely around like
a radar dish. Further details escape me although my mind was clearly
affected as two months later I was arrested in Beverly Hills for trying to
marry an oyster.

Upon my release from police custody I longed for some inner peace   4
in an attempt to preserve what remained of my precarious sanity. More
than once I had been solicited by ardent proselytizers on the street to
seek religious salvation with the Reverend Chow Bok Ding, a moon-faced
charismatic, who combined the teachings of Lao-Tze with the wisdom of
Robert Vesco. An esthetic man who renounced all worldly possessions
in excess of those owned by Charles Foster Kane, the Reverend Ding
explained his two modest goals. One was to instill in all his followers the
values of prayer, fasting and brotherhood and the other was to lead them
in a religious war against the NATO countries. After attending several
sermons, I noticed that Reverend Ding thrived on robot-like fealty and
any diminution of divine fervor met with raised eyebrows. When I
mentioned that it seemed to me the Reverend's followers were being
systematically turned into mindless zombies by a fraudulent megalo-
maniac, it was taken as criticism. Moments later I was led swiftly by
my lower lip into a devotional shrine, where certain minions of the
Reverend who resembled Sumo wrestlers suggested I rethink my position for a few weeks with no petty distractions like food or water. To
further underscore the general sense of disappointment with my attitude,
a fist full of quarters was applied to my gums with pneumatic regularity.
Ironically, the only thing that kept me from going insane was the constant repeating of my private mantra, which was, "Yoicks." Finally, I
succumbed to the terror and began to hallucinate. I recall seeing Frank-
enstein stroll through Covent Gardens with a hamburger on skis.

5   Four weeks later I awoke in a hospital reasonably OK except for a few bruises and the firm conviction that I was Igor Stravinsky. I learned the Reverend Ding had been sued by a 15-year-old Maharishi over the question of which of them was actually God and therefore entitled to free passes to Loew's Orpheum. The issue was finally resolved with the help of the Bunco Squad and both gurus were apprehended as they tried to beat it across the border to Nirvana, Mexico.

6   By this time, although physically intact, I had developed the emotional stability of Caligula and hoping to rebuild my shattered psyche, I volunteered for a program called PET—Perlemutter's Ego Therapy, named after its charismatic founder, Gustave Perlemutter. Perlemutter had been a former bop saxophonist and had come to psychotherapy late in life but his method had attracted many famous film stars who swore that it changed them much more rapidly and in a deeper way than even the astrology column in *Cosmopolitan*.

7   A group of neurotics, most of whom had struck out with more conventional treatment, were driven to a pleasant rural spa. I suppose I should have suspected something from the barbed wire and the Dobermans but Perlemutter's underlings assured us that the screaming we heard was purely primal. Forced to sit upright in hard-backed chairs with no relief for 72 straight hours, our resistance gradually crumpled and it was not long before Perlemutter was reading us passages from *Mein Kampf*. As time passed it was clear that he was a total psychotic whose therapy consisted of sporadic admonitions to "cheer up."

8   Several of the more disillusioned ones tried to leave but to their chagrin found the surrounding fences electrified. Although Perlemutter insisted he was a doctor of the mind, I noticed he kept receiving phone calls from Yassir Arafat and were it not for a last minute raid on the premises by agents of Simon Weisenthal there is no telling what might have happened.

9   Tense and understandably cynical by the turn of events, I took up residence in San Francisco, earning money in the only way I now could, by agitating at Berkeley and informing for the FBI. For several months I sold and resold bits of information to federal agents, mostly concerning a CIA plan to test the resiliency of New York City residents by dropping potassium cyanide in the reservoir. Between this and an offer to be dialogue coach on a snuff porn movie, I could just make ends meet. Then one evening, as I opened my door to put out the garbage, two men leaped stealthily from the shadows and draping a furniture pad over my head, hustled me off in the trunk of a car. I remember being jabbed with a needle and before I blacked out hearing voices comment that I seemed heavier than Patty but lighter than Hoffa. I awakened to find myself in a dark closet where I was forced to undergo total sensory deprivation for three weeks. Following that I was tickled by experts and two men sang country and western music to me until I

agreed to do anything they wanted. I cannot vouch for what ensued as it is possible it was all a result of my brainwashing but I was then brought into a room where President Gerald Ford shook my hand and asked me if I would follow him around the country and take a shot at him now and then, being careful to miss. He said it would give him a chance to act bravely and could serve as a distraction from genuine issues, which he felt unequipped to deal with. In my weakened condition I agreed to anything. Two days later the incident at Himmelstein's Sausage Emporium occurred.

Questions for the Critical Reader

1. Many aspects of American life are being satirized here. Name as many as you can.
2. What is Allen's attitude toward the following objects of his satire:
   a) Authority, in general?
   b) Organized religion?
   c) The army?
   d) The FBI?
3. What is the significance of the fact that the hero is continually being kidnapped or otherwise victimized?
4. What is the significance of the fact that Pogrebin, the narrator, continually refers to transformations of his personality?
5. This piece was originally published in *The New Republic*, which is a journal of liberal politics; why do you suppose Allen chose to publish it there?

Rhetorical Technique

1. Describe the time order of this narrative.
2. What do you think is gained or lost by the fact that there is no dialogue?
3. What is the dominant impression in the description of Willard Pogrebin? (See Chapter 8.)
4. a) Name as many of the sources of the humor in this essay as you can.
   b) There are a great number of references to various people and places in this story: Mendelssohn (par. 2); the World Trade Center (2); Salvador Dali (2); *The Cherry Orchard* (3); Rasputin (3); Svengali (3); Kaballah (3); Lao-Tze (4); Robert Vesco (4); Charles Foster Kane (4); Sumo wrestlers (4); Covent Gardens (4); Igor Stravinsky (5); Maharishi (5); Bunco Squad (5); Nirvana (5); Caligula (6); *Mein Kampf* (7); Yassir Arafat (8); Simon

Weisenthal (8); Patty (9); Hoffa (9). Can you enjoy the story without knowing all these? Discuss these with your classmates, and see how many you can identify with your collective pool of information. Are these effective as humorous devices?

5. How would you describe the narrator's point of view? (See Glossary: *point of view*.)

6. Are there other methods of exposition employed here? What are they? Be specific in locating passages. (See the introduction to the student.)

Diction and Vocabulary

1. How is the tone of this story affected by such words and phrases as the following: mild mannered and promising (par. 1); lodge (1); I was subdued (1); the first sentence of par. 2; took their toll (2); en route (3); further details (3); upon my release (4); moments later (4); I should have suspected something (7); as time passed (7); I took up residence (9)?

2. Describe the purpose and effect of Allen's repetitive use of the word *charismatic*.

3. Consult the dictionary to be sure you understand the meanings of the following words and phrases: *trachea* (par. 1); *reef knot* (1); *cumulative* (2); *charismatic* (3); *sculling oar* (3); *emboss* (3); *acolytes* (3); *esthetic* (4); *minions* (4); *proselytizers* (4); *fealty* (4); *diminution* (4); *pneumatic* (4); *mantra* (4); *hallucinate* (4); *sporadic* (7); *chagrin* (8); *sensory deprivation* (9). How do these words contribute to the tone of the story?

DICK GREGORY

Shame

Dick Gregory, who was born in St. Louis in 1932, was the candidate of the Peace and Freedom Party in 1968 for president of the United States. A popular comedian and entertainer, Mr. Gregory is also a thoughtful commentator on the American scene and a sought-after speaker on the lecture circuit. He is the author of a number of books, among which are *What's Happening* (1965), *The Shadow That Scares Me* (1971), *Dick Gregory's Political Primer* (1971), *Cookin' With Mother Nature* (1973), and *Dick Gregory's Bible Tales with Commentary* (1974). This story is taken from *Nigger: An Autobiography* (written with Robert Lipsyte, 1964). It is a poignant piece of personal revelation and explains powerfully the powerful feelings of a sensitive child.

I never learned hate at home, or shame. I had to go to school for that. I 1
was about seven years old when I got my first big lesson. I was in love
with a little girl named Helene Tucker, a light-complected little girl with
pigtails and nice manners. She was always clean and she was smart in
school. I think I went to school mostly to look at her. I brushed my hair
and even got me a little old handkerchief. It was a lady's handkerchief,
but I didn't want Helene to see me wipe my nose on my hand. The
pipes were frozen again, there was no water in the house, but I washed
my socks and shirt every night. I'd get a pot, and go over to Mr. Ben's
grocery store, and stick my pot down into his soda machine. Scoop out
some chopped ice. By evening the ice melted to water for washing. I
got sick a lot that winter because the fire would go out at night before
the clothes were dry. In the morning I'd put them on, wet or dry, because they were the only clothes I had.

Everybody's got a Helene Tucker, a symbol of everything you want. 2
I loved her for her goodness, her cleanliness, her popularity. She'd walk
down my street and my brothers and sisters would yell, "Here comes
Helene," and I'd rub my tennis sneakers on the back of my pants and
wish my hair wasn't so nappy and the white folks' shirt fit me better.
I'd run out on the street. If I knew my place and didn't come too close,
she'd wink at me and say hello. That was a good feeling. Sometimes I'd
follow her all the way home, and shovel the snow off her walk and try
to make friends with her Momma and her aunts. I'd drop money on

her stoop late at night on my way back from shining shoes in the taverns. And she had a Daddy, and he had a good job. He was a paper hanger.

3   I guess I would have gotten over Helene by summertime, but something happened in that classroom that made her face hang in front of me for the next twenty-two years. When I played the drums in high school it was for Helene and when I broke track records in college it was for Helene and when I started standing behind microphones and heard applause I wished Helene could hear it, too. It wasn't until I was twenty-nine years old and married and making money that I really got her out of my system. Helene was sitting in that classroom when I learned to be ashamed of myself.

4   It was on a Thursday. I was sitting in the back of the room, in a seat with a chalk circle drawn around it. The idiot's seat, the troublemaker's seat.

5   The teacher thought I was stupid. Couldn't spell, couldn't read, couldn't do arithmetic. Just stupid. Teachers were never interested in finding out that you couldn't concentrate because you were so hungry, because you hadn't had any breakfast. All you could think about was noontime, would it ever come? Maybe you could sneak into the cloakroom and steal a bite of some kid's lunch out of a coat pocket. A bite of something. Paste. You can't really make a meal out of paste, or put it on bread for a sandwich, but sometimes I'd scoop a few spoonfuls out of the paste jar in the back of the room. Pregnant people get strange tastes. I was pregnant with poverty. Pregnant with dirt and pregnant with smells that made people turn away, pregnant with cold and pregnant with shoes that were never bought for me, pregnant with five other people in my bed and no Daddy in the next room, and pregnant with hunger. Paste doesn't taste too bad when you're hungry.

6   The teacher thought I was a troublemaker. All she saw from the front of the room was a little black boy who squirmed in his idiot's seat and made noises and poked the kids around him. I guess she couldn't see a kid who made noises because he wanted someone to know he was there.

7   It was on a Thursday, the day before the Negro payday. The eagle always flew on Friday. The teacher was asking each student how much his father would give to the Community Chest. On Friday night, each kid would get the money from his father, and on Monday he would bring it to the school. I decided I was going to buy me a Daddy right then. I had money in my pocket from shining shoes and selling papers, and whatever Helene Tucker pledged for her Daddy I was going to top it. And I'd hand the money right in. I wasn't going to wait until Monday to buy me a Daddy.

8   I was shaking, scared to death. The teacher opened her book and started calling out names alphabetically.

"Helene Tucker?" 9

"My Daddy said he'd give two dollars and fifty cents." 10

"That's very nice, Helene. Very, very nice indeed." 11

That made me feel pretty good. It wouldn't take too much to top that. 12
I had almost three dollars in dimes and quarters in my pocket. I stuck
my hand in my pocket and held onto the money, waiting for her to call
my name. But the teacher closed her book after she called everybody
else in the class.

I stood up and raised my hand. 13

"What is it now?" 14

"You forgot me." 15

She turned toward the blackboard. "I don't have time to be playing 16
with you, Richard."

"My Daddy said he'd . . ." 17

"Sit down, Richard, you're disturbing the class." 18

"My Daddy said he'd give . . . fifteen dollars." 19

She turned around and looked mad. "We are collecting this money 20
for you and your kind, Richard Gregory. If your Daddy can give fifteen
dollars you have no business being on relief."

"I got it right now, I got right now, my Daddy gave it to me to turn 21
in today, my Daddy said . . ."

"And furthermore," she said, looking right at me, her nostrils getting 22
big and her lips getting thin and her eyes opening wide, "we know you
don't have a Daddy."

Helene Tucker turned around, her eyes full of tears. She felt sorry for 23
me. Then I couldn't see her too well because I was crying, too.

"Sit down, Richard." 24

And I always thought the teacher kind of liked me. She always picked 25
me to wash the blackboard on Friday, after school. That was a big thrill,
it made me feel important. If I didn't wash it, come Monday the school
might not function right.

"Where are you going, Richard?" 26

I walked out of school that day, and for a long time I didn't go back 27
very often. There was shame there.

Now there was shame everywhere. It seemed like the whole world 28
had been inside that classroom, everyone had heard what the teacher had
said, everyone had turned around and felt sorry for me. There was
shame in going to the Worthy Boys Annual Christmas Dinner for you
and your kind, because everybody knew what a worthy boy was. Why
couldn't they just call it the Boys Annual Dinner, why'd they have to
give it a name? There was shame in wearing the brown and orange and
white plaid mackinaw the welfare gave to 3,000 boys. Why'd it have to
be the same for everybody so when you walked down the street the
people could see you were on relief? It was a nice warm mackinaw and

it had a hood, and my Momma beat me and called me a little rat when she found out I stuffed it in the bottom of a pail full of garbage way over on Cottage street. There was shame in running over to Mister Ben's at the end of the day and asking for his rotten peaches, there was shame in asking Mrs. Simmons for a spoonful of sugar, there was shame in running out to meet the relief truck. I hated that truck, full of food for you and your kind. I ran into the house and hid when it came. And then I started to sneak through alleys, to take the long way home so the people going into White's Eat Shop wouldn't see me. Yeah, the whole world heard the teacher that day, we all know you don't have a Daddy.

Questions for the Critical Reader

1. What do we know about childhood and human development that makes clear why this incident should have initiated Gregory's sense of shame?
2. Why would the author think he would have "gotten over Helene by summertime" par. 3)—except for the incident he describes?
3. At what point does Gregory say "really got her out" of his system? And why then?
4. Is there a relation between the answers to questions 2 and 3?
5. What was Helene's attitude toward him originally? How does it change?
6. Compare the first sentence of paragraph 25 and the first sentences of paragraphs 5 and 6. Is there a contradiction? Justify your answer.
7. Consider the first sentence of paragraph 2; is it true? Who was *your* Helene Tucker? Or did you have another, nonhuman symbol?

Rhetorical Technique

1. Describe the time order of this narrative. Is it consistent? Where does it deviate and why?
2. Consider the introduction and the time order used there. Comment on the purposes of this particular scheme. (See Glossary: *introductions; purpose.*)
3. Is there any real characterization in this narrative? Which characters are most fully realized? Specify details of description, character, and action that contribute best to these realizations. If you think there is very little characterization here, suggest a reason why the author chose to have it that way.
4. Comment on the effectiveness of the dialogue.
5. Which types of transition are crucial to holding together paragraphs 4, 5, 6, and 7? (See Glossary: *transition.*)

6. Which general type of conclusion does Gregory employ? Comment on its effectiveness. (See Glossary: *conclusions.*)
7. Identify two instances of parallel structure, and comment on their effectiveness. (See Glossary: *parallel structure.*)

Diction and Vocabulary

1. Does Gregory use slang or colloquial language? Select at least three examples of usages that seem to you to be one or the other, and classify them. Then comment on the effectiveness of the use of all three. (See Glossary: *colloquial language.*)
2. There seem to be few—if any—difficult words in this selection. Why?
3. Comment on the use of the word *pregnant* in paragraph 5. Is this an effective use of metaphor? Does it go on too long? (See Glossary: *figures of speech.*)

ELDRIDGE CLEAVER

A Religious Conversion, More or Less

[Leroy] Eldridge Cleaver was born in 1935 in a small town not far from Little Rock, Arkansas. His *Soul on Ice* (1968) was written while he served a prison term in California. Mr. Cleaver, who was also an assistant editor of *Ramparts* magazine, became a leading spokesman for the Black Panther party and afterwards produced a volume of *Post-Prison Writings and Speeches* (1969). In exile in Europe and Africa for some years, Mr. Cleaver returned to America in 1976 to face an old indictment in California. His story of a religious conversion is taken from *Soul on Ice*, a book dealing with an intensely personal and painful set of educational experiences, and neatly dramatizes the loss of innocence and the acquisition of ironic experience.

1   Once I was a Catholic. I was baptized, made my first Communion, my Confirmation, and I wore a Cross with Jesus on it around my neck. I prayer at night, said my Rosary, went to Confession, and said all the Hail Marys and Our Fathers to which I was sentenced by the priest. Hopelessly enamored of sin myself, yet appalled by the sins of others, I longed for Judgment Day and a trial before a jury of my peers—this was my only chance to escape the flames which I could feel already licking at my feet. I was in a California Youth Authority institution at the time, having transgressed the laws of man—God did not indict me that time; if He did, it was a secret indictment, for I was never informed of any charges brought against me. The reason I became a Catholic was that the rule of the institution held that every Sunday each inmate had to attend the church of his choice. I chose the Catholic Church because all the Negroes and Mexicans went there. The whites went to the Protestant chapel. Had I been a fool enough to go to the Protestant chapel, one black face in a sea of white, and with guerrilla warfare going on between us, I might have ended up a Christian martyr—St. Eldridge the Stupe.

2   It all ended one day when, at a catechism class, the priest asked if anyone present understood the mystery of the Holy Trinity. I had been studying my lessons diligently and knew by heart what I'd been taught. Up shot my hand, my heart throbbing with piety (pride) for this chance to demonstrate my knowledge of the Word. To my great shock and embarrassment, the Father announced, and it sounded like a thunderclap, that I was lying, that no one, not even the Pope, understood the Godhead, and why else did I think they called it the *mystery* of the Holy

Trinity? I saw in a flash, stung to the quick by the jeers of my fellow catechumens, that I had been used, that the Father had been lying in wait for the chance to drop that thunderbolt, in order to drive home the point that the Holy Trinity was not to be taken lightly.

I had intended to explain the Trinity with an analogy to 3-in-1 oil, so it was probably just as well.

3

Questions for the Critical Reader

1. What is the significance of the title of this piece?
2. What was the author's purpose in relating this incident?
3. What attitude or attitudes toward religion are reflected here?
4. What is there to be said about the fact that blacks and Mexicans went to the Catholic chapel whereas whites went to the Protestant chapel?
5. Compare your own religious experiences—with respect to organized religion—with Cleaver's.
6. Do Cleaver's motivations seem consistent?

Rhetorical Technique

1. Would you call this a piece of expository narration in the sense that Walker's, Friedrich's, and Gregory's are? Consider the words *incident, episode, sketch,* and *story.* Which is most applicable? Why? Can you think of a more applicable term?
2. Whatever you call this piece, describe its time order.
3. How does Cleaver achieve emphasis? (See Glossary: *emphasis.*)
4. Identify two examples of parallel structure (see Glossary: *parallel structure*), and comment on their effectiveness.
5. Which general type of conclusion is used here? (See Glossary: *conclusions.*)
6. More specifically, what is 3-in-one oil? And what does Cleaver mean when he says it was "probably just as well" that he didn't have the chance to answer?
7. How would you describe Cleaver's point of view? (See Glossary: *point of view.*)

Diction and Vocabulary

1. Comment on the effectiveness of the word *sentenced* in the second sentence of paragraph 1. Identify other legal language used with reference to God or religion, and do the same for this whole strain of language.

2. Identify any expression you consider colloquial (see Glossary: *colloquial language*). What effect does it have on the style of this story? (See Glossary: *style and tone*.)
3. Consult the dictionary to be sure you understand the meanings of the following words: *indict* (par. 1); *catechism* (2); *catechumens* (3).

Writing Suggestions for Chapter 9: *Narration*

I.

Write a narrative of one of your own significant personal experiences, using Friedrich's story as a model; that is, use your present objectivity in order to gain a mature perspective on events that took place a long time ago. Use description, narrative, and dialogue—give details of setting and atmosphere as they are necessary to produce the desired effects. Here are some suggestions to set you thinking:

1. A party you didn't want to attend. You went anyway. What did you learn there?
2. An occasion when, according to your parents, you were too young to attend some event or go on some trip that you desperately wanted. Were they right? Were you? What mark did the incident leave on you? On them? On your relations?
3. An early love affair: its beginning, its middle, its end. What do you think of it now?
4. The story of some person or persons in your life whom you did not understand at the time you knew them but who, you subsequently realized, were crucial in your development.
5. A personal crisis at school. Use Gregory for ideas.

II.

Write a narrative of some incident in which you were not directly involved but to which you were a close enough observer to be able to narrate it. Here are some possible subjects:

1 A conflict between two families or two groups in your neighborhood or town.
2. How two people fell in love.
3. A significant encounter between friends, enemies, lovers, partners, and so on.
4. A school experience.
5. A job experience.

10

On *Language*

Each essay in this section uses one or another form of exposition. After you have had some experience in reading and writing, using other parts of the book, you might want to try reading and analyzing these to see if you can place them in their proper categories. The subject is the same in all cases, but the methods of exposition are different.

Language is like the food we eat. We become aware of it only when it is not what we expected. We notice it only when it is either very good or very bad or quite foreign, when it is over- or undercooked, when it is especially fresh or obviously stale, when it is too expensive or too cheap, or when, having swallowed it, we feel in its effects a certain amount of gaseous distress. Yet although we are likely to be careful about what we eat, we are not so likely to be careful about what we say, hear, read, write, or think.

And, of course, all these things have an intimate connection with language. But if we haven't thought much about language, we are likely to be astonished that language has *two* functions: to communicate *and* to conceal. Our own language influences our thoughts. It can clarify and enrich them or mask from us their real import. Our own language influences how we see the world and how others see us. The language of others, similarly, can help us to know them and the world—or it can classify, control, alienate, dehumanize, or just plain deceive us, things *we* can also do to *them*.

In fact, it may be that the real reason we are trying so hard to teach language to animals—other than for the *stated* scientific purposes—is to bring animals into the extraordinary world of possibilities called language, as if we cannot bear the thought that only we, of all God's creatures, should have the burden and the promise of language.

For, make no mistake, language is also a promise. Far more than being its victims, in fact, we are the beneficiaries of language. There is no greater resource than the capacity for language and no greater possibility than the development of the verbal imagination. Language is a human endowment, but each individual—no two of whom are alike— is free to develop his personal linguistic capability to the degree that he can. And it is in the exchange of developed, individual language habits that our greatest bounty lies. For in that exchange lie endless possibilities of thought, action, and creative human intimacy.

Because language is an endowment and because we rarely pause to think about our use of it, we tend to think that none of us can do anything about it. But the essays in this chapter all discuss *choices* in the use of words. It may be very difficult to change linguistic habits and patterns, but these essays all testify to a process of change going on continually—a process documented by all the sciences of language.

Thus the purpose of this chapter is to provide you with a fascinating field for study—in and of itself—and to help you to become aware of the possibilities for further study in a field of great vitality and consuming interest. But perhaps even more important, the chapter—like the whole of this book—aims to encourage you to use language more effectively and with a greater sense of what is at stake whenever language is employed. To achieve this aim, the chapter presents essays on our general need for linguistic accuracy and on the ways in which we use and misuse language in love, politics, journalism, art, and other fields of endeavor. And you who read carefully will doubtless find that these essays *speak* even more.

JANE OTTEN

Living in Syntax

Jane Otten, a free-lance writer presently living in Washington, D.C., was born in 1920 and has her B.A. from Barnard and her M.A. in journalism from Columbia. She is the coauthor of *When Your Parents Grow Old* (1976). This essay, which was first printed in *Newsweek* in 1974, suggests the intimate relations between things—in this case, an intimate relation—and the words that are used to describe them. Ms. Otten's dilemma makes clear how hard it is to talk about what cannot be given a proper name.

We like to think of ours as a living language—and it is. Successive   1
editions of Webster's Unabridged Dictionary testify to this, as do our
own ears—and our own vocabulary—in daily conversation.

We have constructed and adapted words to fit new technologies, situa-   2
tions and events, new kinds of people and attitudes. Hippie was not in
our vocabulary fifteen years ago, nor was ombudsman. Nobody had
ever heard of glitch or astronaut, ripoff or teach-in. Rap, cat and grass
had other connotions then, and a jock was an article of male apparel.
Today, when you hear these words, you know exactly what they mean.

But no new word has come into our vocabulary to describe precisely   3
the parties to a new kind of relationship, one that is becoming more and
more common. What do you call the person of the opposite sex who is
living with your son or daughter?

I have been struggling with this for some time now, in conversations   4
with friends and acquaintances. My daughter's er, I would start out, or
my daughter's um. But the listener would pin me down, and because
my daughter objected to boyfriend, I began to refer to my daughter's
boy. This went over all right for a time, until one startled neighbor
wanted to know when my daughter had had the baby.

Wanted: A Bon Mot

I realized I was not alone with this nomenclature problem when I had a   5
conversation with a friend whom I hadn't seen in a long time. We had a
lot to catch up on, and she began telling me about her son who was
living in Cambridge and publishing a little newspaper with his—er—
girlfriend. My ears leaped into that "er" and I told her why I had found
her pause the most interesting part of her narrative. She admitted that
she shared my problem.

6   This spurred me to conduct a small survey. I found many of my peers in the same predicament, but none close to a solution. Our vocabulary cries out now for a precise word to describe two young people of different sex who are living together. None of the old words works. They are fuzzy, beg the question and often have traditional connotations which misrepresent the current situation.

7   *Friend*, for example, could be of either sex and doesn't necessarily inply an intimate relationship. *Boyfriend* or *girlfriend* does suggest a close relationship, but these terms are really too old-hat and don't describe the living arrangement. *Roommate*, another possibility specifies joint living conditions but omits gender identification, and *apartment-mate* is much the same. *Companion* may connote certain kinds of sharing, but it hardly represents the full range that the relationship embraces.

Cohabitor?

8   Most consistently slighted in all of these terms is the undoubted sexual nature of the partnership. Here are some which do convey this aspect, but they, too, are flawed:

Swain—that's all right for him, but what do you call her?

Suitor—this is most often a totally inaccurate description.

Fiancé (or *fiancée*)—are you out of your mind?

Lover—too romantic and old-world to be applied to many contemporary relationships. The word also implies that one of the persons involved is married and is conducting an adulterous relationship.

Mistress—forget it.

Paramour—this could hardly be applied to couples who do their shopping at the Safeway on Saturday nights.

Consort—far too regal in its overtones and, besides, implies an existing marriage.

Partner—this suggests a close, sharing relationship, all right, but even though Masters and Johnson, David Reuben and others have given it a new sexual cachet, the word's principal connotation is still commercial.

Mate—this seems to be the official designation adopted by a New York-based group plugging non-parenthood, but the word mostly calls to mind the jungle and "me Tarzan, you Jane."

9   My research has brought out several designations by other desperate parents. None is acceptable to me, but here they are anyway.

10   The first is *lover-in-law*. Just try that in some simple sentences. If you say, "My lover-in-law is coming for dinner tonight," the interpretation is that you are having an affair with your spouse's parent or sibling. You must therefore attach the phrase specifically to your son or daughter, but that result is equally misleading. "My daughter's lover-in-law," you

say, "is having a play produced off-Broadway." That means that it's your daughter who is having a meaningful relationship with one of her in-laws.

Son-in-Common-Law?

Another freshly coined term is *outlaw*. "We are meeting our son-outlaw   11
at the airport," you say, and your listener concludes that he is a Vietnam defector returning from Canada or that you daughter is married to him and you detest him. Still another diverting term comes from some friends who are a bit bitter over the somewhat larger monthly allowance they must now send to their daughter. They refer to her male living companion as her *checkmate*.

In conversations with my spouse (there's no problem about that) I   12
sometimes refer to our child's *spose*, which contains the implicit question, "Do you 'spose they'll ever get married?" But I prefer to use this only in private conversations.

I hope somebody soon will come up with the precise handle to de-   13
scribe persons involved in this situation because the lack of it is severely limiting my conversation. I do love to talk about my children and I would like to do so in accurate terms. In the meantime, I can only make sparing references to my daughter's er and my son's um.

WILLIAM SAFIRE

Vogue Words Are Trific, Right?

William Safire, who was born in 1929, was a journalist, foreign
correspondent, and a radio-TV public relations executive before
joining the staff of the White House as a speech writer for then
President Nixon in 1969. Since 1973, he has been a regular
columnist for *The New York Times*. He is the author of (with
Marshal Loeb) *The Relations Explosion* (1963), *Plunging into
Politics* (1964), and The *New Language of Politics* (1968; rev. ed.,
1972). This essay, which first appeared in *The New York Times* in
1976, makes cogent observations about the currency of language
and takes a special interest in the fact that words gain momentum
within specific areas of our culture.

1   Vogue words are bits of language that slip into American speech, are
disseminated far and wide by television talk shows, and make a person
appear with-it. Many of the words run a flulike course and disappear,
leaving memories of semantic headaches and fevered articulation. Others,
like "détente," are formally banished by Presidential fiat. Here is my first
annual vogue-word watch, compiled with the help of a few lexicograph-
ical colleagues around the country.

Vogues from All Over

2   Is a word merely for the nonce, or worth including in a dictionary? Some
stalwart vogues seem to be establishing themselves as permanent features
of the language. Among businessmen, "net net" has already faded, but
bottom line (the "final accounting" or "essence") is spreading. Among
youthful linguists, "way to go" has faded, "no way" is borderline, but
the familiar *into*—as "he's into slang"—is putting down roots, and
lexicographer David Guralnik thinks it may get into non-nonce status.

3   "Getting it together," picked up by lemminglike copywriters for commercials, has been dropped by the coiners who originate these phrases;
"mellow," which went the opposite route, is also on the wane, as is
"laid back," which might originally have had a sexual connotation but
more likely springs from reclining seats on motorcycles. "Heavy," a
40's word for "villain," became a 60's, word for "depressing" but is
sinking. *Off the wall*, on the other hand—which comes from the squash
court and means "unexpected" or "veering crazily"—shows signs of life.

4   "That bums me out" has already given way to "that cracks me up,"
and the jazzman's "suss it out" (figure it out) doesn't seem to figure. The

disgusted "yecchy," with its comic-strip origins, fades, but the equally disgusted *gross* (ugly, objectionable, and sometimes used admiringly) shows staying power. (To many, a "gross national product" is a derogation of the country's goods.)

Televisionese

The use of the phrase *has learned* to mean "found out" has been grow- 5 ing. "CBS has learned" does three things: (1) removes the need for *sourcing* (a journalism vogue word for identifying the person responsible for a story), (2) gives the impression of being the first to know and to tell the viewer and (3) plugs the network. The report is given as a certainty—much more solid than "reliable sources say"—but conceals, or covers up, the fact that nobobdy is willing to stand behind the message except the medium.

Private person is the *sine qua non* of soap operas and daytime talk 6 shows. Nobody is an introvert any more; hermits no longer exist; damnable publicity-shunners have drifted from the scene—today, anybody who will not grant an interview is a "very private person."

Bleep has become a usable word-substitute, from the sound made when 7 a word is excised from a tape. Columnist Herb Caen has popularized this as a euphemism, lexicographer Peter Tamony reports—as in: "That's no bullbleep."

Testimony Talk

From the land of "to the best of my knowledge," comes the verb of 8 perjury-avoiding fuzziness; *indicate.* Under cross-examination, nobody ever "said" or "told me" or even "suggested"—rather, they "indicated." *To indicate,* which used to mean "to point to," as "he indicated they went thataway," has now become a cover-up word for "he may have told me this, but if he says no, then maybe I was mistaken." The use of "indicate" indicates guilt.

Cover-up was originally used to describe a specific obstruction of 9 justice. Now this compound word is used to describe a compounded felony. Of the recent vogue words, "cover-up," still too young to lose its hyphen, also stands a good chance of making it into the dictionary, just after the entry for *cover story,* a C.I.A.-ism whose cover appears to have been blown.

Adjectival Jive

Long ago, it was "hep," then it changed to "hip," then, in the 60's, "cool" 10 took hold; now, perhaps from a sanguine view of cool, comes *cold-blooded,* to convey in-group approval.

If a woman is "sexy" she is over 30 and not to be trusted. The re- 11 placement is *foxy*, a "counter word" with plenty of connotation but no denotation. (While *lady* has been replaced by "woman" or "person" in liberated discourse, it has taken over the place formerly held by "girl friend." "She's my lady," claims the former "fella," now the *dude*.)

12   Turning a noun into an adjective is the vogue among fun couples, but the vogue word fades fast: "dynamite" (sometimes pronounced "dyn-o-*mite*," as on the "Good Times" television show), was last year's favorite modifier, as in "Those are dynamite boots," which is being replaced by *killer*, as in "That's a killer whip."

Camp Following

13   "Camp" means "so banal as to be perversely sophisticated." It began as "establishing a camp," which was what the veterans of the Civil War called their reunions, then became a word to define any meeting of an insiders' group, and was taken up by homosexuals to mean the daring use in public of previously private ways.

14   The fashionable-by-being-unfashionable idea has several modern off-shoots, not synonymous but related: *kinky*, *funky*, and *glitzy*.

15   "Kinky," from the Scandinavian "kink," or curl, bend, or twist, be-came popularized in the United States as "kinky hair," and was applied in the past decade to young fashion, as "offbeat, deliberately bizarre." The word has moved to the sexy, or foxy, world, and now tumbles out of its pornucopia: "Kinky" means perverse or twisted, usually cruel, sex, and the word has held on long enough to merit serious lexicographic-attention.

16   "Funky" has traveled a happier road. Originally a jazz term referring to the smell of cigar smoke, the word bottomed out in meaning as "old cigars, old and decrepit surroundings, just plain old." (Louis Armstrong often referred to "Funky Butt Hall, where I first heard Buddy Bolden play.") Later, as "old" became desirable, "funky" gained its current meaning of "nostalgic," or sweetly memorable, if cornball. (Some of those old cigars were Havanas.)

17   "Glitzy," often used to describe *"kitsch"* (which is unconscious in its tastelessness) comes directly from the German *"glitzen,"* and means "sparkling," or dazzlingly meretricious.

18   In sum, "kinky" has curled away from "funky" in meaning, leaving funkiness next to glitziness, though that may be a glitzening generality.

Right?

19   Where funkiness is next to glitziness, trendiness is surely next to godli-ness, and nowhere is that better illustrated than in the interrogative reassurance.

20   In the early 70's, the grunted "y'know?" studded the speech of every teen-ager. Put it this way: "I was walking—y'know?—down the street

—y'know?—and I ran into this splivvy dude, y'know?" Youth responds quickly to ridicule (adults move slowly, which is why "viable" and "meaningful" linger on) and when others began saying "No, I don't know," "y'know?" began its disappearance.

However, the need for constant verbal reassurance remained. Many 21 people believe they are not being listened to, or believe their listeners do not believe in them as a source of communication. Thus, *right* has emerged, not as something that makes might, but as a word that makes a speaker feel secure, and usually as part of a historical present tense: "Now I'm taking this walk—right?—down the street—right?—minding my own business—right?"

Trific

Finally, the adjective-as-encouragement-to-continue. In some discourses, 22 encouragement is direct: "keep talking" became "I dig" which became "lay it on me" and now crosses its transcendental *t*'s with *keep it flowing.*

In most current speech, however, a single adjective is preferred. In 23 the 30's, this was "fine-'n-dandy." In the 50's, "super" made the grade; in the 60's "fantastic" became a word used not to express amazement, but understanding; and in the early 70's, "beautiful"—usually murmured, head nodding as if in mutual meditation—became the most frequently used word of approval and reassurance. "I found a fish, y'know?" "Beautiful."

Today, the adjective-as-encouragement has become *terrific*, sometimes 24 pronounced with two syllables, "trific." The root meaning—as that which causes one to "wriggle in fear"—changed to "tremble with enthusiasm": after a brief vogue in the early 60's, "terrific" has returned with a rush. "I found a fish—right?" "Trific." Often, the word is repeated, just as "beautiful" used to be: "Now we're sitting around here at The Times—right? and we get this idea—right? for a piece on the way people talk today—right?" "Trific, trific . . ."

ROBERT PATTISON

Being a Disquisition wherein were told whats happening to english including examples written by a man who no's;

Robert Pattison is a former copy editor for a university press, editor of pornography, and literary agent. He now teaches English at Queensborough Community College, CUNY, in Bayside, Queens, New York. This piece, which was first printed in *The New York Times* in 1974, uses a humorous tone to explore the possibilities that ignorance of standard English may not be so ignorant after all. The dramatic presentation—in the style of the ignorant—may cause a reader to have other ideas.

1   This sentence demonstrates alot of the to frequent errors that occur in my freshman composition classes, its not just there willingness to gleefully split an infinitive or end a sentence with a preposition which are the problems kindly boarding school masters used to be concerned with. Its true my students arent the good mannered middle class bunch who I went to school with, there more often cops or shoesalesmens or garbagemens (pardon me, sanitationmens) sons and daughters, and yet there a sharp group, wary, skeptical, bright.

2   So when I knock myself out day after day class after class explaining the genitive case in english, the proper position of commas, the runon sentence, the distinction between the three theres and still these mistakes appear even in the work of the best of them I wonder.

3   I wonder if just maybe they know something I dont about the english language. Something intuitive about its history and something instinctive about its future. After all, its been the movement of the language to progress toward simplicity. The case structure, with its confusing endings, was an early victim. Why say "On his dagum hierde Gregorius goda lara" when with a little reliance on word order and common sense you can more simply say "In his time Gregorys heard good lectures"?

4   Besides the nagging whom the last vestige of the case structure in english is the genitives use of the apostrophe. But surely common sense and word order indicate the genetive usage and my students perception is correct in eliminating the troublesome superscript.

5   Theres wisdom in doing away with punctuation that doesnt contribute to clarity and when my classes monolithically dispose of pointless spelling distinctions where the sense is obvious there judgment may be sound.

Then again, alot of my colleagues lose sleep over the way some stu- 6
dents slam two words or letters into one but metathesis or the changing
of the position of sounds or letters is a venerable tradition, or else a
newt might still be an ewt.

Words in english usually explain themselves by position and context, 7
though of course there exceptions to this rule which my students in
there foresight have not anticipated but give them awhile and they will.

I cant go into detail about every grammatical innovation made by my 8
students, theres alot to recommend them though and if you are an editor,
the author of an english grammar or the perpetrator of a work or foot-
note logic and you can read this you should pay attention to my class
because one day they might take over and one day you might wake up.
And discover your fired.

Robert pattison uses humor to
show how kids of today.
think of and use English.

Demonstration to the fact that
their has to be some rules
in english

Demonstrates that faulty usage
make it difficult to communicate
ideas.

Robert pattisons ~~effective~~
usage ~~diction~~ grammer shows the
reader that ~~██ ██ ████~~ faulty
usage makes it difficult
to communicate ideas.

GEORGE ORWELL

Politics and the English Language

Politics was a profound and abiding concern in the life of George Orwell. (For a biographical sketch, see the headnote to his "Poverty" in Chapter 5.) It became apparent to him, at an early stage in the development of that interest, that language was a crucial instrument in the possibility of political corruption. His noved *1984* details with great ingenuity and precision how a totalitarian regime accomplishes the enslavement of its citizens by enslaving their language, and words like *newspeak* and *double-think*—taken from the novel—are now important, if sinister, parts of our language. This essay, which appeared first in his *Critical Essays* (1946), has become an acknowledged classic. It discusses how and why the language has deteriorated—with special emphasis on the political causes and effects—and suggests ways in which purposeful action can be taken to arrest this linguistic decline.

1   Most people who bother with the matter at all would admit that the English language is in a bad way, but it is generally assumed that we cannot by conscious action do anything about it. Our civilization is decadent and our language—so the argument runs—must inevitably share in the general collapse. It follows that my struggle against the abuse of language is a sentimental archaism, like preferring candles to electric light or hansom cabs to aeroplanes. Underneath this lies the half-conscious belief that language is a natural growth and not an instrument which we shape for our own purposes.

2   Now, it is clear that the decline of a language must ultimately have political and economic causes: it is not due simply to the bad influence of this or that individual writer. But an effect can become a cause, reinforcing the original cause and producing the same effect in an intensified form, and so on indefinitely. A man may take to drink because he feels himself to be a failure, and then fail all the more completely because he drinks. It is rather the same thing that is happening to the English language. It becomes ugly and inaccurate because our thoughts are foolish, but the slovenliness of our language makes it easier for us to have foolish thoughts. The point is that the process is reversible. Modern English, especially written English, is full of bad habits which spread by imitation and which can be avoided if one is willing to take the necessary

trouble. If one gets rid of these habits one can think more clearly, and to think clearly is a necessary first step towards political regeneration: so that the fight against bad English is not frivolous and is not the exclusive concern of professional writers. I will come back to this presently, and I hope that by that time the meaning of what I have said here will have become clearer. Meanwhile here are five specimens of the English language as it is now habitually written.

These five passages have not been picked out because they are especially bad—I could have quoted far worse if I had chosen—but because they illustrate various of the mental vices from which we now suffer. They are a little below the average, but are fairly representative samples. I number them so that I can refer back to them when necessary: 3

(1) I am not, indeed, sure whether it is not true to say that the Milton who once seemed not unlike a seventeenth-century Shelley had not become, out of an experience ever more bitter in each year, more alien [*sic*] to the founder of that Jesuit sect which nothing could induce him to tolerate.

Professor Harold Laski (Essay in *Freedom of Expression*).

(2) Above all, we cannot play ducks and drakes with a native battery of idioms which prescribes such egregious collocations of vocables as the Basic *put up with* for *tolerate* or *put at a loss* for *bewilder*.

Professor Lancelot Hogben (*Interglossa*).

(3) On the one side we have the free personality: by definition it is not neurotic, for it has neither conflict nor dream. Its desires, such as they are, are transparent, for they are just what institutional approval keeps in the forefront of consciousness; another institutional pattern would alter their number and intensity; there is little in them that is natural, irreducible, or culturally dangerous. But *on the other side*, the social bond itself is nothing but the mutual reflection of these self-secure integrities. Recall the definition of love. Is not this the very picture of a small academic? Where is there a place in this hall of mirrors for either personality or fraternity?

Essay on psychology in *Politics* (New York).

(4) All the "best people" from the gentlemen's clubs, and all the frantic fascist captains, united in common hatred of Socialism and bestial horror of the rising tide of the mass revolutionary movement, have turned to acts of provocation, to foul incendiarism, to medieval legends of poisoned wells, to legalize their own destruction of proletarian organizations, and rouse the agitated petty-bourgeoisie to chauvinistic fervor on behalf of the fight against the revolutionary way out of the crisis.

Communist pamphlet.

(5) If a new spirit *is* to be infused into this old country, there is one thorny and contentious reform which must be tackled, and that is the humanization and galvanization of the B.B.C. Timidity here will bespeak canker and atrophy of the soul. The heart of Britain may be sound and

of strong beat, for instance, but the British lion's roar at present is like that of Bottom in Shakespeare's *Midsummer Night's Dream*—as gentle as any sucking dove. A virile new Britain cannot continue indefinitely to be traduced in the eyes or rather ears, of the world by the effete languors of Langham Place, brazenly masquerading as "standard English." When the voice of Britain is heard at nine o'clock, better far and infinitely less ludicrous to hear aitches honestly dropped than the present priggish, inflated, inhibited, school-ma'amish arch braying of blameless bashful mewing maidens!

Letter in Tribune.

4   Each of these passages has faults of its own, but, quite apart from avoidable ugliness, two qualities are common to all of them. The first is staleness of imagery; the other is lack of precision. The writer either has a meaning and cannot express it, or he inadvertently says something else, or he is almost indifferent as to whether his words mean anything or not. This mixture of vagueness and sheer incompetence is the most marked characteristic of modern English prose, and especially of any kind of political writing. As soon as certain topics are raised, the concrete melts into the abstract and no one seems able to think of turns of speech that are not hackneyed: prose consists less and less of *words* chosen for the sake of their meaning, and more and more of *phrases* tacked together like the sections of a prefabricated hen-house. I list below, with notes and examples, various of the tricks by means of which the work of prose-construction is habitually dodged:

Dying Metaphors

5   A newly invented metaphor assists thought by evoking a visual image, while on the other hand a metaphor which is technically "dead" (e.g., *iron resolution*) has in effect reverted to being an ordinary word and can generally be used without loss of vividness. But in between these two classes there is a huge dump of worn-out metaphors which have lost all evocative power and are merely used because they save people the trouble of inventing phrases for themselves. Examples are: *Ring the changes on, take up the cudgels for, toe the line, ride roughshod over, stand shoulder to shoulder with, play into the hands of, no axe to grind, grist to the mill, fishing in troubled waters, on the order of the day, Achilles' heel, swan song, hotbed.* Many of these are used without knowledge of their meaning (what is a "rift," for instance?), and incompatible metaphors are frequently mixed, a sure sign that the writer is not interested in what he is saying. Some metaphors now current have been twisted out of their original meaning without those who use them even being aware of the fact. For example, *toe the line* is sometimes written *tow the line.* Another example is the *hammer and the anvil*, now always used with the implication that the anvil gets the worst of it. In

real life it is always the anvil that breaks the hammer, never the other way about: a writer who stopped to think what he was saying would be aware of this, and would avoid perverting the original phrase.

Operators or Verbal False Limbs

These save the trouble of picking out appropriate verbs and nouns, and at the same time pad each sentence with extra syllables which give it an appearance of symmetry. Characteristic phrases are *render inoperative, militate against, make contact with, be subjected to, give rise to, give grounds for, have the effect of, play a leading part (role) in, make itself felt, take effect, exhibit a tendency to, serve the purpose of, etc., etc.* The keynote is the elimination of simple verbs. Instead of being a single word, such as *break, stop, spoil, mend, kill,* a verb becomes a *phrase,* made up of a noun or adjective tacked on to some general-purposes verb such as *prove, serve, form, play, render.* In addition, the passive voice is wherever possible used in preference to the active, and noun constructions are used instead of gerunds (*by examination of* instead of *by examining*). The range of verbs is further cut down by means of the *-ize* and *de-* formations, and the banal statements are given an appearance of profundity by means of the *not un-* formation. Simple conjunctions and prepositions are replaced by such phrases as *with respect to, having regard to, the fact that, by dint of, in view of, in the interests of, on the hypothesis that;* and the ends of sentences are saved from anticlimax by such resounding common-places as *greatly to be desired, cannot be left out of account, a development to be expected in the near future, deserving of serious consideration, brought to a satisfactory conclusion,* and so on and so forth.

Pretentious Diction

Words like *phenomenon, element, individual* (as noun), *objective, categorical, effective, virtual, basic, primary, promote, constitute, exhibit, exploit, utilize, eliminate, liquidate,* are used to dress up simple statements and give an air of scientific impartiality to biased judgments. Adjectives like *epoch-making, epic, historic, unforgettable, triumphant, age-old, inevitable, inexorable, veritable,* are used to dignify the sordid processes of international politics, while writing that aims at glorifying war usually takes on an archaic color, its characteristic words being: *realm, throne, chariot, mailed fist, trident, sword, shield, buckler, banner, jackboot, clarion.* Foreign words and expressions such as *cul de sac, ancien régime, deus ex machina, mutatis mutandis, status quo, gleichschaltung, weltanschauung,* are used to give an air of culture and elegance. Except for the useful abbreviations *i.e., e.g.,* and *etc.,* there is no real need for any of the hundreds of foreign phrases now current in English. Bad writers, and especially scientific, political and sociological writers, are nearly always haunted by the notion that Latin or Greek words are grander than Saxon ones, and unnecessary words like *expedite, ameliorate, predict, extraneous, deracinated, clandestine, subaqueous* and hundreds of others constantly gain ground from their Anglo-Saxon opposite numbers.[1] The jargon peculiar to Marxist writing (*hyena, hangman, cannibal, petty bourgeois, these gentry, lacquey, flunkey, mad dog, White Guard,* etc.) consists largely of words and phrases translated from Russian, German or French; but the normal way of coining a new word is to use a Latin or Greek root with the appropriate affix and, where necessary, the *-ize* formation. It is often easier to make up words of this kind (*deregionalize, impermissible, extramarital, non-fragmentary* and so forth) than to think up the English words that will cover one's meaning. The result, in general, is an increase in slovenliness and vagueness.

Meaningless Words

8 In certain kinds of writing, particularly in art criticism and literary criticism, it is normal to come across long passages which are almost completely lacking in meaning.[2] Words like *romantic, plastic, values, human, dead, sentimental, natural, vitality,* as used in art criticism, are strictly meaningless, in the sense that they not only do not point to any discoverable object, but are hardly ever expected to do so by the reader. When one critic writes, "The outstanding feature of Mr. X's work is its living quality," while another writes, "The immediately striking thing about Mr. X's work is its peculiar deadness," the reader accepts this as a simple difference of opinion. If words like *black* and *white* were involved, instead of the jargon words *dead* and *living,* he would see at once that language was being used in an improper way. Many political words are similarly abused. The word *Fascism* has now no meaning except in so far as it signifies "something not desirable." The words *democracy, freedom, patriotic, realistic, justice,* have each of them several different meanings which cannot be reconciled with one another. In the case of a word like *democracy,* not only is there no agreed definition, but the attempt to make one is resisted from all sides. It is almost

---

[1] An interesting illustration of this is the way in which the English flower names which were in use till very recently are being ousted by Greek ones, *snapdragon* becoming *antirrhinum, forget-me-not* becoming *myosotis,* etc. It is hard to see any practical reason for this change of fashion: it is probably due to an instinctive turning-away from the more homely word and a vague feeling that the Greek word is scientific.

[2] Example: "Comfort's catholicity of perception and image, strangely Whitmanesque in range, almost the exact opposite in aesthetic compulsion, continues to evoke that trembling atmospheric accumulative hinting at a cruel, an inexorably serene timelessness. . . . Wrey Gardiner scores by aiming at simple bull's-eyes with precision. Only they are not so simple, and through this contented sadness runs more than the surface bittersweet of resignation." (*Poetry Quarterly.*)

universally felt that when we call a country democratic we are praising it: consequently the defenders of every kind of régime claim that it is a democracy, and fear that they might have to stop using the word if it were tied down to any one meaning. Words of this kind are often used in a consciously dishonest way. That is, the person who uses them has his own private definition, but allows his hearer to thing he means something quite different. Statements like *Marshal Pétain was a true patriot, The Soviet Press is the freest in the world, The Catholic Church is opposed to persecution,* are almost always made with intent to deceive. Other words used in variable meanings, in most cases more or less dishonestly, are: *class, totalitarian, science, progressive, reactionary, bourgeois, equality.*

Now that I have made this catalogue of swindles and perversions, let me give another example of the kind of writing that they lead to. This time it must of its nature be an imaginary one. I am going to translate a passage of good English into modern English of the worst sort. Here is a well-known verse from *Ecclesiastes:* 9

"I returned and saw under the sun, that the race is not to the swift, nor the battle to the strong, neither yet bread to the wise, nor yet riches to men of understanding, nor yet favour to men of skill; but time and chance happeneth to them all." 10

Here it is in modern English: 11

"Objective consideration of contemporary phenomena compels the conclusion that success or failure in competitive activities exhibits no tendency to be commensurate with innate capacity, but that a considerable element of the unpredictable must invariably be taken into account." 12

This is a parody, but not a very gross one. Exhibit (3), above, for instance, contains several patches of the same kind of English. It will be seen that I have not made a full translation. The beginning and ending of the sentence follow the original meaning fairly closely, but in the middle the concrete illustrations—race, battle, bread—dissolve into the vague phrase "success or failure in competitive activities." This had to be so, because no modern writer of the kind I am discussing—no one capable of using phrases like "objective consideration of contemporary phenomena"—would ever tabulate his thoughts in that precise and detailed way. The whole tendency of modern prose is away from concreteness. Now analyse these two sentences a little more closely. The first contains forty-nine words but only sixty syllables, and all its words are those of everyday life. The second contains thirty-eight words of ninety syllables: eighteen of its words are from Latin roots, and one from Greek. The first sentence contains six vivid images, and only one phrase ("time and chance") that could be called vague. The second contains not a single fresh, arresting phrase, and in spite of its ninety syllables it gives only a shortened version of the meaning contained in the first. Yet without a doubt it is the second kind of sentence that is 13 gaining ground in modern English. I do not want to exaggerate. This kind of writing is not yet universal, and outcrops of simplicity will occur here and there in the worst-written page. Still, if you or I were told to write a few lines on the uncertainty of human fortunes, we should probably come much nearer to my imaginary sentence than to the one from *Ecclesiastes.*

14   As I have tried to show, modern writing at its worst does not consist in picking out words for the sake of their meaning and inventing images in order to make the meaning clearer. It consists in gumming together long strips of words which have already been set in order by someone else, and making the results presentable by sheer humbug. The attraction of this way of writing is that it is easy. It is earier—even quicker, once you have the habit—to say *In my opinion it is not an unjustifiable assumption that* than to say *I think.* If you use ready-made phrases, you not only don't have to hunt about for words; you also don't have to bother with the rhythms of your sentences, since these phrases are generally so arranged as to be more or less euphonious. When you are composing in a hurry—when you are dictating to a stenographer, for instance, or making a public speech—it is natural to fall into a pretentious, Latinized style. Tags like *a consideration which we should do well to bear in mind* or *a conclusion to which all of us would readily assent* will save many a sentence from coming down with a bump. By using stale metaphors, similes and idioms, you save much mental effort, at the cost of leaving your meaning vague, not only for your reader but for yourself. This is the significance of mixed metaphors. The sole aim of a metaphor is to call up a visual image. When these images clash—as in *The Fascist octopus has sung its swan song, the jackboot is thrown into the melting pot*—it can be taken as certain that the writer is not seeing a mental image of the objects he is naming; in other words he is not really thinking. Look again at the examples I gave at the beginning of this essay. Professor Laski (1) uses five negatives in fifty-three words. One of these is superfluous, making nonsense of the whole passage, and in addition there is the slip *alien* for akin, making further nonsense, and several avoidable pieces of clumsiness which increase the general vagueness. Professor Hogben (2) plays ducks and drakes with a battery which is able to write prescriptions, and, while disapproving of the everyday phrase *put up with,* is unwilling to look *egregious* up in the dictionary and see what it means; (3), if one takes an uncharitable attitude toward it, is simply meaningless: probably one could work out its intended meaning by reading the whole of the article in which it occurs. In (4), the writer knows more or less what he wants to say, but an accumulation of stale phrases chokes him like tea leaves blocking a sink. In (5), words and meaning have almost parted company. People who write in this manner usually have a general emotional meaning—they dislike one thing and want to express solidarity with another—but they are not inter-

ested in the detail of what they are saying. A scrupulous writer, in every sentence that he writes, will ask himself at least four questions, thus: What am I trying to say? What words will express it? What image or idiom will make it clearer? Is this image fresh enough to have an effect? And he will probably ask himself two more: Could I put it more shortly? Have I said anything that is avoidably ugly? But you are not obliged to go to all this trouble. You can shirk it by simply throwing your mind open and letting the ready-made phrases come crowding in. They will construct your sentences for you—even think your thoughts for you, to a certain extent—and at need they will perform the important service of partially concealing your meaning even from yourself. It is at this point that the special connection between politics and the debasement of language becomes clear.

In our time it is broadly true that political writing is bad writing. **15** Where it is not true, it will generally be found that the writer is some kind of rebel, expressing his private opinions and not a "party line." Orthodoxy, of whatever color, seems to demand a lifeless, imitative style. The political dialects to be found in pamphlets, leading articles, manifestos, White Papers and the speeches of under-secretaries do, of course, vary from party to party, but they are all alike in that one almost never finds in them a fresh, vivid, home-made turn of speech. When one watches some tired hack on the platform mechanically repeating the familiar phrases—*bestial atrocities, iron heel, bloodstained tyranny, free peoples of the world, stand shoulder to shoulder*—one often has a curious feeling that one is not watching a live human being but some kind of dummy: a feeling which suddenly becomes stronger at moments when the light catches the speaker's spectacles and turns them into blank discs which seem to have no eyes behind them. And this is not altogether fanciful. A speaker who uses that kind of phraseology has gone some distance towards turning himself into a machine. The appropriate noises are coming out of his larynx, but his brain is not involved as it would be if he were choosing his words for himself. If the speech he is making is one that he is accustomed to make over and over again, he may be almost unconscious of what he is saying, as one is when one utters the responses in church. And this reduced state of consciousness, if not indispensable, is at any rate favorable to political conformity.

In our time, political speech and writing are largely the defence of the **16** indefensible. Things like the continuance of British rule in India, the Russian purges and deportations, the dropping of the atom bombs on Japan, can indeed be defended, but only by arguments which are too brutal for most people to face, and which do not square with the professed aims of political parties. Thus political language has to consist largely of euphemism, question-begging and sheer cloudy vagueness. Defenceless villages are bombarded from the air, the inhabitants driven out into the countryside, the cattle machine-gunned, the huts set on fire with incendiary bullets: this is called *pacification*. Millions of peasants are robbed of their farms and sent trudging along the roads with no more than they can carry: this is called *transfer of population* or *rectification of frontiers*. People are imprisoned for years without trial, or shot in the back of the neck or sent to die of scurvy in Arctic lumber camps: this is called *elimination of unreliable elements*. Such phraseology is needed if one wants to name things without calling up mental pictures of them. Consider for instance some comfortable English professor defending Russian totalitarianism. He cannot say outright, "I believe in killing off your opponents when you can get good results by doing so." Probably, therefore, he will say something like this:

17   "While freely conceding that the Soviet régime exhibits certain features which the humanitarian may be inclined to deplore, we must, I think, agree that a certain curtailment of the right to political opposition is an unavoidable concomitant of transitional periods, and that the rigors which the Russian people have been called upon to undergo have been amply justified in the sphere of concrete achievement."

18   The inflated style is itself a kind of euphemism. A mass of Latin words falls upon the facts like soft snow, blurring the outlines and covering up all the details. The great enemy of clear language is insincerity. When there is a gap between one's real and one's declared aims, one turns as it were instinctively to long words and exhausted idioms, like a cuttlefish squirting out ink. In our age there is no such thing as "keeping out of politics." All issues are political issues, and politics itself is a mass of lies, evasions, folly, hatred and schizophrenia. When the general atmosphere is bad, language must suffer. I should expect to find—this is a guess which I have not sufficient knowledge to verify—that the German, Russian and Italian languages have all deteriorated in the last ten or fifteen years, as a result of dictatorship.

19   But if thought corrupts language, language can also corrupt thought. A bad usage can spread by tradition and imitation, even among people who should and do know better. The debased language that I have been discussing is in some ways very convenient. Phrases like *a not unjustifiable assumption, leaves much to be desired, would serve no good purpose, a consideration which we should do well to bear in mind*, are a continuous temptation, a packet of aspirins always at one's elbow. Look back through this essay, and for certain you will find that I have again and again committed the very faults I am protesting against. By this morning's post I have received a pamphlet dealing with conditions in Germany. The author tells me that he "felt impelled" to write it. I open it at random, and here is almost the first sentence that I see: "[The Allies] have an opportunity not only of achieving a radical transformation of Germany's social and political structure in such a way as to avoid

a nationalistic reaction in Germany itself, but at the same time of laying the foundations of a cooperative and unified Europe." You see, he "feels impelled" to write—feels, presumably, that he has something new to say—and yet his words, like cavalry horses answering the bugle, group themselves automatically into the familiar dreary pattern. The invasion of one's mind by ready-made phrases (*lay the foundations, achieve a radical transformation*) can only be prevented if one is constantly on guard against them, and every such phrase anaesthetizes a portion of one's brain.

I said earlier that the decadence of our language is probably curable. 20 Those who deny this would argue, if they produced an argument at all, that language merely reflects existing social conditions, and that we cannot influence its development by any direct tinkering with words and constructions. So far as the general tone or spirit of a language goes, this may be true, but it is not true in detail. Silly words and expressions have often disappeared, not through any evolutionary process but owing to the conscious action of a minority. Two recent examples were *explore every avenue* and *leave no stone unturned*, which were killed by the jeers of a few journalists. There is a long list of flyblown metaphors which could similarly be got rid of it enough people would interest themselves in the job; and it should also be possible to laugh the *not un-*formation out of existence,[3] to reduce the amount of Latin and Greek in the average sentence, to drive out foreign phrases and strayed scientific words, and, in general, to make pretentiousness unfashionable. But all these are minor points. The defence of the English language implies more than this, and perhaps it is best to start by saying what it does *not* imply.

To begin with, it has nothing to do with archaism, with the salvaging 21 of obsolete words and turns of speech, or with the setting up of a "standard English" which must never be departed from. On the contrary, it is especially concerned with the scrapping of every word or idiom which has outworn its usefulness. It has nothing to do with correct grammar and syntax, which are of no importance so long as one makes one's meaning clear, or with the avoidance of Americanisms, or with having what is called a "good prose style." On the other hand it is not concerned with fake simplicity and the attempt to make written English colloquial. Nor does it even imply in every case perferring the Saxon word to the Latin one, though it does imply using the fewest and shortest words that will cover one's meaning. What is above all needed is to let the meaning choose the word, and not the other way about. In prose, the worst thing one can do with words is to surrender to them. When you think of a concrete object, you think wordlessly, and then, if you

[3] One can cure oneself of the *not un-* formation by memorizing this sentence: *A not unblack dog was chasing a not unsmall rabbit across a not ungreen field.*

want to describe the thing you have been visualizing you probably hunt about till you find the exact words that seem to fit it. When you think of something abstract you are more inclined to use words from the start, and unless you make a conscious effort to prevent it, the existing dialect will come rushing in and do the job for you, at the expense of blurring or even changing your meaning. Probably it is better to put off using words as long as possible and get one's meaning as clear as one can through pictures or sensations. Afterwards one can choose— not simply *accept*—the phrases that will best cover the meaning, and then switch round and decide what impression one's words are likely to make on another person. This last effort of the mind cuts out all stale or mixed images, all prefabricated phrases, needless reptitions, and humbug and vagueness generally. But one can often be in doubt about the effect of a word or a phrase, and one needs rules that one can rely on when instinct fails. I think the following rules will cover most cases:

(i) Never use a metaphor, simile, or other figure of speech which you are used to seeing in print.
(ii) Never use a long word where a short one will do.
(iii) If it is possible to cut a word out, always cut it out.
(iv) Never use the passive where you can use the active.
(v) Never use a foreign phrase, a scientific word or a jargon word if you can think of an everyday English equivalent.
(vi) Break any of these rules sooner than say anything outright barbarous.

These rules sound elementary, and so they are, but they demand a deep change of attitude in anyone who has grown used to writing in the style now fashionable. One could keep all of them and still write bad English, but one could not write the kind of stuff that I quoted in those five specimens at the beginning of this article.

22   I have not here been considering the literary use of language, but merely language as an instrument for expressing and not for concealing or preventing thought. Stuart Chase and others have come near to claiming that all abstract words are meaningless, and have used this as a pretext for advocating a kind of political quietism. Since you don't know what Fascism is, how can you struggle against Fascism? One need not swallow such absurdities as this, but one ought to recognize that the present political chaos is connected with the decay of language, and that one can probably bring about some improvement by starting at the verbal end. If you simplify your English, you are freed from the worst follies of orthodoxy. You cannot speak any of the necessary dialects, and when you make a stupid remark its stupidity will be obvious, even to yourself. Political language—and with variations this is true of all political parties, from Conservatives to Anarchists—is designed to make lies sound truthful and murder respectable, and to give an ap-

pearance of solidity to pure wind. One cannot change this all in a moment, but one can at least change one's own habits, and from time to time one can even, if one jeers loudly enough, send some worn-out and useless phrase—some *jackboot, Achilles' heel, hotbed, melting pot, acid test, veritable inferno* or other lump of verbal refuse—into the dustbin where it belongs.

Purpose?

entertain   NON MESSAGE   what is it?

escape Reality   How?

(Mystery)

Message (serious)) exposition

INFORM   writes

How to achieve purpose?

technique

diction

connotation

1. thesis—

2. examples

3.

ALFRED F. ROSA AND PAUL A. ESCHHOLZ

Bunkerisms: Archie's Suppository Remarks in "All in the Family"

Alfred F. Rosa and Paul A. Eschholz are both associate professors
of English at the University of Vermont. Both share a major interest in language, popular culture, and English literature. They
both serve on the Committee on Public Doublespeak of the National Council of Teachers of English. They are coauthors of two
books: *Language Awareness* and *Language: Introductory Readings*.
The present article was first published in the *Journal of Popular
Culture* in 1972. It is an expert discussion of the sources of the
humor in "All in the Family." Professors Rosa and Eschholz find
that much of the humor depends on the variety of linguistic devices employed by Archie. These are named and many examples
given of each.

1   On January 12, 1971, American television viewers were first introduced
to "All in the Family." Now, at the end of its second highly successful
year, the Bunker family is an American institution. This award-winning
show reaches an estimated fifty to one hundred million viewers weekly.
It has spawned a huge commercial enterprise offering such items as
sweatshirts, T-shirts, posters, ashtrays, beer mugs, and "Bunker
Stickers"; many of these items have a "Bunker for President" motif.
The latest addition to this commercial bonanza is *The Wit & Wisdom of
Archie Bunker*, a book containing the most humorous lines and sequences
from the show. Indeed, the book indicates that the humor of the show
derives not only from the fact that it is a situational comedy but also
from Archie's use of language. Archie's command of the language is
legendary; viewers have witnessed him criticize Mike for reacting "on
the sperm of the moment," castigate Edith for taking things "out of
contest," and tell his family that his prejudice is a "pigment of their
imaginations." Archie's use of malapropisms, spoonerisms, and "Bunkerisms" is one aspect of the show that deserves to be examined. These
word formations are a major element in distinguishing "All in the
Family" from other television situational comedies.

2   The manipulation of language for comic purposes is not a recent
development. Shakespeare's Mistress Quickly in *Henry IV Parts I and II*
and *Henry V* and Dogberry in *Much Ado About Nothing* are notorious
for their comic misuse of the language. Mistress Quickly in *Henry V*
claims that she is sure that Falstaff's is "in Arthur's bosom" and Dog-

Reprinted from the *Journal of Popular Culture*, Vol. 6, No. 2 (Fall 1972), by permission of the editor.

berry states his belief that "comparisons are odorous." It is, however, Richard Sheridan's infamous Mrs. Malaprop who lends her name to this type of inappropriate usage. One recalls that in *The Rivals* she implores Lydia to "promise to forget this fellow—to illiterate him quite from [her] memory." The malapropism, in short, is the misapplication of a word; malapropisms indicate not only the ignorance but also the vanity and affectation of their speakers and in "All in the Family" Archie uses many of these malapropisms:[1]

> What is this, the United Nations? We gotta have a whole addenda?
> I come home and tell you one o' the great antidotes of all times, an item of real human interest, and you sit there like you're in a comma.
> You sound like a regular Billie Sol Graham!
> "Sorry" ain't gonna clench my thirst.
> . . . as one of your faithful constitutionals.
> You're taking it out of contest.
> . . . you gotta grab the bull by the corns and heave-ho.
> . . . this nation under God shall not diminish from the earth.
> I don't need their whole Dun and Broadstreet.
> We got a regular Edna St. Louis Millet here.
> If he don't yell "pig" or none of them other epaulets, . . .
> Ain't he took the exercise tax offa cars?
> No, Edith. I was out expectin' the street lights.
> How'd I know you had extensions to bein' an egghead.
> . . . we don't want people thinking we live in no pig's eye.
> Let's take a look here and see what new subversion you got fermentin' here.
> . . . he's comin' over to claim his pound of fish.
> It's the survivor of the fitness!
> Them eggs are starting to foment.
> I received your leaflet at my home residence and the words "substantial profit" fought my eye.
> It ain't German to this conversation.
> It's like looking for a needle in a hayride!
> Call it a father's intermission . . . but I smell a rat.
> You're invading the issue.
> No doubt about it there's somethin' broken off in there and it's ledged between the nervous system and the brain. . . .
> Looking like it's straight outta Missile Impossible, . . .
> Cold enough to freeze a witch's mitt.
> It's some of that Morgan David wine.
> You been standing on that phone like a pillow of salt.
> . . . 'cause Cousin Oscar is leavin' here, in post and haste.
> Rudy and me was as close as two peas in a pot.
> I give ya the biggest build-up since Grant took Richard.

[1] Examples used in this paper have been taken from *The Wit & Wisdom of Archie Bunker* (Popular Library), the record "All in the Family" (Atlantic), and the television show itself.

... right outta Science Friction.
For better or for worse, in secrets and in health till death do us part?
... on the sperm of the moment.
It's like trying to make a sow's purse outta silk!
We can suspense with the hellos, Edith.
Whoever sent 'em obviously wanted to remain unanimous.
I'll believe that when hell freezes under.

3   Several of the mistakes that Archie makes such as confusing *antidote*
and *anecdote* and *ferment* and *foment* excite nervous laughter because
we have all fallen into the trap at one time or another. Archie's pendant
for name dropping betrays his ignorance and his inner desire to be more
than the average American breadwinner. Although he is very funny,
much of his humor is the product of dramatic irony; his use of clichés,
humorous because of their inaccuracies, displays his lack of true wit and
imagination.

Some of Archie's slips produce made-up or nonsense words which are
akin to the spoonerism, an unintentional transposition of sounds, especially prefixes and suffixes, in spoken language. These bloopers are
spontaneous and are not the product of ignorance or vanity. Some that
Archie has used are:

What am I, a clairavoyage or somethin'?
... what you call, connubible difficulties ...
It's gonna take a lotta thinkin' and it's gonna take all my consecretion.
One of these days I will probably de-head myself.
It was said under dupress.
... making you an excessity after the fact!
It's a regular facsamile of the Apollo 14.
Like the Presidential, the Senatorial, the Governororial, the Mayororor-
ial ...
These things ain't exactly hairlooms, you know.
'Cause *that* evening is indeniably etched in my heart along with other
strong memories of the past—. . .
It's inedibly etched in my mind.
He had the infrontery to imply that . . .
... what you might call a certain lack of drive—you know, personal
inititianative.
Make this meathead take the literaracy test.
I remember some of the beauties you hung around with, and they wasn't
exactly no "Madonises."
Now lay off the social menuneties.
He's a morphidite.
... nothin' but out in out *pornagraphy.*
... some ground rules and some priorororities.
And then write yourself a little note—you know, like a reminderandum.
... you'd be layin' on that floor waitin' for Rigor Morris to set in.
I ain't sayin' it's largesse, smallesse or no' kinda esse.

Redeeming socialness is where they do the same old pornagraphs but they
give yau some four-dollar words while they're doin' it.
. . . a kind of special stanima . . .
You didn't go and do something unlegal, you big dumb Polack?
You've got a warfed sense of humor.

Two techniques that the show's writers use in the creation of these 4
nonsense words are the use of mnemonic devices and analogies. Archie
remembers *accessory* because it is "something extra," *facsimile* because
it is the "same as," and *memorandum* because it "reminds." The analogy
process, *dehead*, *Governororial*, *smallesse*, *socialness*, and *unlegal*, is
commonly found among children who are trying to cope with the com-
plexities of the English language. These usages are laughable since
Archie is trying to apply logic where tradition holds sway.

As humorous as Archie's malapropisms and made-up words are, the 5
comedy of "All in the Family" relies heavily on a special variety of
these two—the Bunkerism. Expressions such as "distinguished incrum-
bent," "Englebum Hunkerdunk," "dem bamboons," "like the immacu-
late connection," "pushy imported ricans," "Welfare incipients," and "A
regular Marco Polish" and Bunkerisms. In addition to showing Archie's
ignorance and pretentiousness, they illustrate his prejudicial nature. It is
Archie's narrow-mindedness that is the essence of the Bunkerism. In
The Wit & Wisdom of Archie Bunker, Archie's comic usages of the
language are referred to as "Archieisms." While this label recognizes the
unique quality of Archie's speech, it does not effectively label his
coinages. After all, Archie is the arch-conservative and arch-debunker,
and all his remarks are in one way or another "suppository." In a conversation with Edith, Archie says:

> You think he's a nice boy after he did what he did? Comin' in here,
> makin' suppository remarks about our country. And calling me preju-
> diced, while I was singin' "God Bless America," a song written by a well-
> known and respected Jewish guy. Milton Berlin.

Although Archie objects to someone else's derogatory remarks, the
comment in this context says more about Archie's bigoted attitude.

Certain types of situations within the show give rise to the Bunkerism. 6
When Archie is trapped by logic, usually by Mike, has an audience
and wishes to appear as a "know-it-all," is embarrassed by or impatient
with Edith, is nervous when confronted by a member of a minority
group, or is forced to talk about taboo subjects, he loses control of the
language and produces Bunkerisms, either proper words in the wrong
context or made-up words, both of which have pejorative connotations.
Some of the Bunkerisms of the first category include:

> Why don't you write a letter to dear Abie?
> And who are you supposed to be—Blackberry Finn?
> Yeah, well, we can't help bunkin' into each other now and then. . . .

I personally don't agree with all the conflagration on the college campuses. . . .

Just who in hell are we entertaining here tonight? The Count of Monte Crisco?

Throwin' debriss at officers of the law . . . Desecrating on the American flag.

It's a proven fact that Capital Punishment is a known detergent for crime.

And you don't need to draw me any diaphragms neither!

. . . who weren't fortunate enough to be born with the same natural endorsements.

If tampering with the United States mail is a federal offense, so is excitement to riot.

It's for when you get one of them hot flushes.

We've got the world's grossest national product.

You coming here, a priest, hiding behind your hassock—. . .

I'll let you know when I—in my intimate wisdom—decide that the time has ripened.

You and that Reverend Bleedin' Heart Felcher up there in his ivory shower.

Don't take everything so liberally.

Look I know you'se kids go by what you call this new mortality—. . .

This political percussion is over as of here and now.

In them days Notre Dame was playing hardknocks football! No fat scholarships, none of them pet parties—. . .

Until then *I'm* king, the princess is upstairs, and you're the pheasant that has to keep her here!

It's just a pigment of your imagination.

And position is nine-tenths of the law, right?

Smells like a house of ill refute if ya ask me.

I call Chinese food chinks 'cause that what it is . . . chinks.

There was no slurp intended against the Chinese.

Lady, you wanna stoop this conversation down to the gutter level, that's your derogative.

The sexual submissiveness? It don't matter whatever time of day or night—well, that's your dimissive society.

He takes that for granted. It's a tactic understanding.

Bunkerisms akin to spoonerisms are:

She's hangin' around my neck like an Albacross.

Comin' in here full of ascusations . . .

. . . and wouldn't be related to me for complexionary reasons.

One religion. Until they started splitting 'em up 'til all them other denumerations.

'Cause if I hadda face that bum on a full stomach, I'd detergerate . . .

It ain't a very fancy theory, but it's all mine. Lionel—Familyarity breeds content!

Your mother-in-law and me don't make no fatish over birthdays.

What you see here is a frigment of your imagination.

He comes from the gretto.

Back to the groinocologist!

... the worst hypochondrijerk in the neighborhood ...

... infilterating into our own house, Edith.

Which is just an excuse for Commie infliteration!

What do you mean by that insinuendo?

... insurruption of the campuses.

If you two malinjerers want anything ...

Your mother ain't got no preconscrewed ideas.

... and confirm the Bunkers is goin' to Florida as prederanged.

You ain't gonna sell me none of your pregressive pinko welfare ideas ...

The man don't have one regleaming feature.

He's got some big move up his sleeve that he can't revulge yet!

Well, goodbye and good ribbons.

People like your mother gotta be unpartial 'cause they got no subconceived notions.

The statements I made were supposed to be sub-rosy.

In my day we used to keep things in their proper suspective.

Don't you never read the papers about all them unflocked priests running around?

Laura Hobson in an article for the *New York Times* entitled "As I [7] Listened to Archie Say 'Hebe' . . ." criticizes the show for its implicit claims of complete and honest bigotry and what to her appears to be a very subtle manipulation of language. She claims that the show's producers have managed to make a distinction between "acceptable" terms of ethnic abuse and those which would be truly offensive. This, she contends, falsely permits Archie to be a lovable bigot and bigotry itself to be not so bad after all. Although Miss Hobson recognizes the subtlety of the ethnic terms used on the show, she fails to see the full import of the self-debunking Bunkerism. There is a general impression that Archie is only "done out" in the waning moments of the show; however, the unintentional self-deprecating nature of the Bunkerism serves to undermine Archie's bigotry throughout the whole show. The writers have successfully employed an age-old comic device in a contemporary setting to fulfill their satiric intentions.

VALERIE CARNES

The Language of Nowspeak

> Valerie Carnes is an associate professor of English at Roosevelt
> College in Chicago and has taught there since 1969. Professor
> Carnes has published articles on the poetry of George Herbert and
> John Milton. She and her husband are active in the Popular Culture
> Association, and with him she has done articles for the association
> on such subjects as fashion, body-building, and the Star Trek cult.
> The present article first appeared in a book that she edited with her
> husband (Ralph L. Carnes): *The New Humanities: Culture, Crisis,
> Change* (1972). In it she describes the language of a subculture—
> the youth culture so prominent in America at a time just before
> the article was written—and argues for its primacy in separating
> that subculture from the mainstream.

1   Now that much of the sound and fury over hippies, yippies, flower
power, student power, Berkeley, Chicago, and Columbia has begun to
die away, and pot, acid, and speed have become as much household words
as the name of Spiro T. Agnew it is time at last for a long look at the
language of the current youth movement. For at least one thing becomes increasingly clear as the underground begins to surface: the much-
celebrated generation gap of the sixties was—and still *is*—largely a
linguistic gap existing between standard English and Nowspeak, the
language of the movement, the youth under thirty and their over-thirty
sympathizers.

2   To accept even the mildest form of the linguistic relativity thesis en-
tails the admission that one's world view is to some extent relative to
his language system. Clearly the world view of a twenty-one-year-old
radical whose universe is built around large categories labeled "pigs,"
"heads," "the System," and "the Revolution" will manifest itself quite
differently from that of his Establishment counterpart who still operates
in terms of more conventional classes: "liberals," "conservatives," "Commie rats," "anarchists," "Democrats," "Republicans." The very existence of the language that I have christened Nowspeak affirms the existence of a large and active youth Underground. It also institutionalizes the
subculture of Beatles and Stones and Fugs and Ché Guevara-ism, of
"Hair" and Tarot cards, witches and warlocks, acid and grass, and gives
it in the public eye a local habitation and a name. Hippies, hipsters, beats,
pushers, and heads have been part of the Scene for a very long time—

since the 1920s, in fact; it is their group names that remind Peter Schrag's Forgotten Americans of these embarrassing Presences in a stolidly sentimental and conformist culture.

Thus for Movement and Establishment alike the language becomes 3 symbolic. It does not only "stand for" or "point to" the subculture: it *is* the subculture. This fact should remind us of Paul Tillich's useful distinction between a sign and a symbol: the sign, he says, points the way to the thing, but the symbol participates in it. Nowspeak is a symbol of the life-style of the emerging subculture and also serves as the System's plumber's-manual guide to that life-style. It is symbolic in this sense both for those who use it and those who do not. Users align themselves against non-users. Nowspeaking youth draw a sense of solidarity and community from the language that represents their chosen style while the Establishment feels itself to be the nation's anointed people in part because it still speaks standard English. Non-users, presenting their case in conventional pig-Americanese, argue that Movement lingo is mindless, non-expressive, illiterate, obscene, and meaningless, while the other side argues with equal fervor that all the assertions and experiences of youth are incapable of verbal expression. As one girl recently put it, "If you've been there, you'll know it, and you don't need to talk about it." In the opening bars of *Their Satanic Majesties* the Stones urge their listeners to "open your heads, let the pictures come." Indeed, one of the hidden premises of Nowspeak is the assumption that there are many classes of experience which cannot and should not be verbalized. The act of verbalization is itself a dodge, a corruption of the experience, a "sell-out" or "cop-out" from the pure moment of sensation. I am well aware of the irony implicit in this study. This is not an essay on the language of the youth culture but instead on abstractions from that language as it is spoken, transposed onto the printed page. The most important characteristic of the language is that it is spoken, not written, and is therefore in a constant state of flux. Yet paradoxically the very nonverbal nature of the language is symbolic of the world view it both influences and reflects—antirational, action-oriented, visual, tactile, highly sensuous, primitive, ritualistic, colorful, emotive, solipsistic, and so always the language of the present moment, the immediate Scene, the place where the action is, or was—in short, the language of Now.

The primary source of Nowspeak is of course the language of other 4 American bohemian movements. Nineteen-twenties bohemianism—Parisian expatriates, winos, Braque, Picasso, Hemingway, Stein and her beloved Alice B. Toklas, the rash of "little" magazines, and Zelda and Scott, those lovely lost children of Prohibition playing in the fountains at the Plaza—established the standard bohemian style and attitude: a sadly romantic, fatalistic, cosmopolitan, nonconforming, and lost generation of street-cafe and attic subcultures, writing poetry out of a golden alcoholic haze. Came the 1930s, and hipsters, jazz musicians, and an authentic hard-core drug underground began unwittingly to build the language that the young rebels of today's suburbia still speak. Jazz usages yielded such important terms as *action* (a general term for whatever is happening at the time), *bad* (for something very good, especially a woman), *blast* (get high), *bomb* (a failure), *bread* (money), *bug* (to annoy or disturb), *bust* (arrest), *cat* (any human being, especially a swinger), *chick* (a girl), *come down* (from a high), *cool* (ignore, snub, become less intense about a person or thing), *cut out* (leave), *dig* (understand or comprehend, in an emotional sense), *fag* (homosexual), *far out* (very advanced, ahead of its time), *funky* (basic, earthy, downhome), *groove* (a predilection or enjoyable thing), *head* (drug user), *lay* or *lay on* (to give or say), *make it* (have success), *put on* (to make fun of or ridicule without letting the victim know), *scene* (particular place or atmosphere), *stoned* (high or drunk), *turn on* (to get someone high on pot or to interest someone in a specific thing) and *wild* (remarkable). A high percentage of these terms still are in Nowspeak usage today.

5   Underworld language, which has found its way into Nowspeak, dates back to the time when the entire drug scene was largely confined to the fringes of society—the ghetto, the bohemian settlements, the underworld—and drug users were more or less forced by economic and social exigencies to live a life of petty crime. From this indigenous subculture come the standard slang terms referring to drug use: *cap* (drug capsule), *head* (user of drugs), *H, horse, shit, smack, duji* (heroin); *Mary Jane, MJ, pot, tea, grass, boo* (marijuana); *coke, snow, snowbird* (cocaine and its users). Most of these words are prepsychedelia and therefore refer to the more conventional drugs that were standard bohemian and ghetto fare from the twenties and thirties into the fifties and sixties—hashish, marijuana, heroin, cocaine, opium, benzedrine. Also from that nebulous area where underworld jargon coalesces with black ghetto talk come words dealing with the relations of the drug user and petty criminal with the police: *hit* (to be arrested), *bust* (to make an arrest, often for illegal drug use, as in "He got busted for possession last night"), *heat, fuzz*, or *the Man* (police), *uptight* and *strung out* (in desperate financial straits, usually as the result of intensive or prolonged drug use). One interesting term with underworld connotations is *straight*. A common word in homosexual and criminal society, it was first used to mean not with the particular "in" crowd in question (hence, heterosexual in one case, non-criminal in the other). Later the meaning became generalized so that the word now can refer to anyone who is not "with" a particular scene; hence, conventional, ordinary, not in the know, not "hip," generally "out of it." A more recent variant is more specific and less derogatory; it means "temporarily off drugs, clean for the moment," as in "Once I was straight for three days."

"Soultalk," the language of urban ghetto blacks, has become an 6
increasingly important element in the vocabulary of the Nowspeaker,
probably because of the heightened social consciousness of the Movement and its intense identification with minority groups of all kinds.
Black "hip" and "soul" talk has added to Nowspeak such important
words as *man* (generalized term of address, as in "Man, you're blowing
my mind"), *ball* (to have sexual intercourse), *the Man* (the police; more
generally, any Establishment figure, preferably white, in a position of
power), *mother* (short for motherfucker, a term of derision and often
hatred), *cat* (any male human being, especially a hip one), *hip* (with it,
cool, in the know, under control), *hipster* (hip cat), *shit* (drugs in general), *tell it* or *tell it, man, lis'en at him, nigger* (in a soulful affectionate
sense, not a condescending or derogatory one, as is "He's the baddest
nigger I ever saw"), *something else* (pronounced *sum'pn else*), *police*
(pronounced *po-lice*), *stuff* (heroin or the vagina), *bag* (originally, in the
thirties, graft paid to the po-lice; now, a person's vocation, hobby,
fancy, whimsy, or caprice, as in "that's your bag, man"), *strung out,
uptight, cop* (originally an abbreviation for copulation, but by 1955 a
synonym for the verb "to get," especially in relation to pot, hard drugs,
hot goods, pistols), *boss* (something extraordinarily good or great, later
replaced by *groovy, tough, beautiful,* and *out of sight*), *kill 'em* (for
"give 'em hell," not as an expression of malice or violence). Other classics
that often overlap into underworld and "beat" diction of the fifties and
that have by now wandered into Nowspeak include *solid, cool, jive* (as
noun), *jive-ass, thing, swing,* and *swinging* (the sixties added *swinger*),
pimp, dirt, freak, heat, right on (term of approbation), *piece, sheet* (a
jail record), *squat, square, stash, lay, gone, smooth, joint, blow, play,
shot, hassle, chick, junkie, bitch* (girl), *tight* (friendly), *O. D.* (overdose),
soul, soulfood, gig.

Perhaps the single most important contribution of the black hipster is 7
the word *baby* (pronounced "bay-buh," *a la* Janis Joplin), used in address
to another, highly masculine, black male. Claude Brown offers this
explanation of the elusive term in *Manchild in the Promised Land:*

> The first time I heard the expression "baby" used by one cat to address
> another was up at Warwick in 1951. Gus Jackson used it. The term had a
> hip ring to it, a real colored ring. The first time I heard it I knew right
> away I had to start using it. It was like saying, "Man, look at me, I've got
> masculinity to spare." It was saying at the same time to the world, "I'm
> one of the hippest cats, one of the most uninhibited cats on the scene. I
> can say 'baby' to another cat, and he can say 'baby' to me, and we can
> say it with strength in our voices." If you could say it, this meant that you
> really had to be sure of yourself, sure of your masculinity. . . . The real
> hip thing about the "baby" term was it was something that only colored
> cats could say the way it was supposed to be said. . . .

8   Haight-Ashbury summer of 1967, with the subsequent growth of the youth Underground and the more amorphous Movement, popularized and brought to the surface dozens of terms like these that had once been indigenous black soultalk in the thirties, forties, fifties, and early sixties, then found their way into the vocabularies of the children of affluent upper-middle-class WASP society. That the drug culture itself followed precisely the same pattern, out of the ghetto and into suburbia, is significant, for it suggests that the daily life-style of the Harlemite hipster and pusher was transformed into a middle-class elitist cult tinged with mystical overtones largely by the use of a bona fide drug-and-underworld language.

9   The hipster who came into prominence in the thirties and forties and finally sprang full-blown from the media in the fifties and sixties was a young male, often black, who was "hip" (originally, "hep" to the beat), extraordinarily aware, in the know, especially about jazz, drugs, and the street scene. The word "hippie," which came into national prominence in 1967, was being used in Harlem in the early 1950s to describe the up-town white who played at being a black hipster. Robert George Reisner's *The Jazz Titans* (1960) defines a "hippie" as a young person who is trying to put on hip airs but doesn't quite make it—thus, one who may be overly hip. Malcolm X's *Autobiography* recalls a similar incident: "A few of the white men around Harlem, younger ones whom we called 'hippies,' acted more Negro than Negroes. This particular one talked more 'hip' talk than we did" (p. 94).

10   Beat language of the fifties drew on all these sources—soultalk, jazz, drug, underworld and homosexual slang, hipster and hippie language. It incorporated all of these and yet, paradoxically, was unlike any of them. Norman Podhoretz in an early essay, "The Know-Nothing Bohemians" (reprinted as the first reading in this volume), comments on the "urban, cosmopolitan bias" of twenties' bohemianism, whose ideals were "intelligence, cultivation, spiritual refinement." By contrast bohemianism in the thirties, with its abundance of card-carrying Communists and Marxists, was colored by political radicalism, intellectual seriousness, and social reform. Podhoretz succinctly sums up the difference between earlier and later bohemianisms. The 1950s "beat" ethos, he comments, was hostile to civilization, worshipped primitivism, instinct, energy, "blood," was "cool" but mystical, irrational, spontaneous, anti-language, anti-analytical, and fascinated perennially, like Ginsberg's "angel-headed hipsters" and Kerouac's Dharma bums, with violence, drugs, Dada, surrealism, wine, and madness. Interestingly enough, the word "beatnik" was media-created: its genesis coincided with the furor over the Russian satellite Sputnik, and thus were the beats subtly and erroneously identified with Communist tendencies. The word "beat" itself referred at least in part to the ubiquitous jazz beat that was so much a part of the fifties Scene; it also meant, according to Kerouac, "beatified" or "beatific,"

suggesting a kind of frantic hip holiness in the beat stance. For the uninitiated it also meant disgust with middle-class philistinism and provinciality, utter disgust and exhaustion with the straight scene.

Beat language, like the Nowspeak of the sixties, was relatively simple. 11 Adjectives were pared down to an eloquent few: *great* (greatest), *tremendous, crazy, mad, wild, groovy*. Nouns and verbs were simple and expressive: *bread* (money), *crash* (to sleep, from an old Hell's Angels' term that means "to die"; may also be used to refer to a temporary residence or sleeping space, as in "He's running a cresh pad for pot heads"), *joint* (a marijuana cigarette), *roach* (the butt end of a joint), *pad* (place of residence, as in "Duke, they blowin' pot like mad up at Mildred's pad," from the R. Crumb cartoon, "The Adventures of Fritz"). Slang terms for drugs also were common beat usage, perhaps as a means of avoiding the fuzz: *MJ, pot, tea, grass, H, horse, shit, O, smack* and so on.

A merger between the beat culture and the folk song and the various 12 war–civil rights–free-speech protests of the early sixties brought the Movement as it then existed out of Greenwich Village and the Haight onto the college campuses and coffee shops and into the media. The Berkeley Free Speech Movement (FSM) institutionalized and sanctioned the use of four-letter words as an authentic gesture of protest; civil rights demonstrations publicized words like *sit-in, demonstration, nonviolence, passive resistance*, SNCC, CORE, NAACP, *civil disobedience* and *God is on our side* (both phrases from Thoreau's famous tract), *happening, love-in*, and *riot*. The folk-singing phase of the movement, centering around sad-eyed lady of the lowlands Joan Baez and early pre-electronic Dylan, was the aesthetic equivalent of social and political nonviolence. In it was the ageless lure of wild cold woods and wind and salty sea, snow-white doves and long black veils, cruel ladies and lovesick knights, and forlorn maidens haunted by restless ghosts. It was poignant, sad, archaic, funny, and full of a simple moral outrage at war and racism; yet it was also cruel with a kind of barbarous innocence, the savage tenderness of the most ruthless of the Scottish Child ballads. And of course since beauty hurts Mr. Vinyl it could not and did not last. Although folk singing added few new words as such to the growing lexicon of Nowspeak, it introduced a down-home earthy lowdown shackdown niggerbaby blues plainness of style that set the cultural stage for the earliest of hippie life-styles.

In the mid-sixties the long-standing feud of British Mods and Rockers 13 culminated in the cultural victory of Mod and so introduced a newly self-conscious element into the indigenous American youth cult. Magically the Scene shifted from Newport to Carnaby Street and Baez and Dylan were replaced overnight by Justin and Twiggy. Boutiques mushroomed in the most Establishment of department stores and funky sleazy minifashions, bell-bottoms, elephant pants, wide belts, boots, vinyl skirts, picture matches, fans, Tiffany paper lanterns, op, pop, the Liverpool sound. Victoriana, discothèques, light shows, go-go girls, vinyl hamburgers, and burgeoning Campbell soup cans spelled out the new message in dayglo colors: COME ALIVE, YOU'RE IN THE PEPSI GENERATION. Limp-haired and limpid-eyed Lolitas, chock full of vitamin pills and orange juice, put on granny glasses, French *yé-yé* knits, and little white vinyl boots. Boys adopted the Teddy Boy look and tried vainly to resemble John Lennon. The style of the hour was J. C. Penney transcendentalized by Quant and Courreges, and the media responded fittingly with a shiny new slickspeak: "where it's at," "the action generation," "the Now people," "the Pepsi generation," "the Beautiful People," "camp art," "happenings" (which included such questionable activities as smashing grand pianos with hammers while, in the background, thirteen radios blared *forte fortissimo* and painted go-go girls did action paintings on the side). Some of this jargonese was simulated British slang (girls were "birds" or "model girls," thanks to Twiggy and Mary Quant), and if they wore *minis* or *micro-minis*, they were *kooky, kinky,* and had "the knack" (after a British art film of that name). It was the heyday of the microcosm, the diminutive, a mod mod mod Lilliputian world for all the Little People. Everything from the poor-boy skinny-rib sweater to Vesuvius erupting was "fun," "crazy," "super," "marvellous," "fantastic" or "groovy." Clothes were fun things. Shoes were to fall in love with. Makeup was super stuff. Discothèques were fun places. Arnel was when. Yé-yé. Yeah. Yeah. Yeah.

14   Hippie summer of 1967, heralded by the Human Be-Iin in San Francisco and by the haunting imperative issuing from every jukebox across the nation, instructing the new generation to wear a flower in its collective hair, saw the first full-scale surfacing of the new-style Underground of the sixties. By August of 1967 every major magazine from *Playboy* to the *Saturday Evening Post* was preparing its own lead article on the hippie phenomenon, complete with full-color photographs of lush paradisal landscapes where lank golden girls ran barefoot forever through the Kodachrome grass, their long manes tumbling in the wind, light shows and artlessly painted bodies gyrating in time to invisible acid rock bands, gaunt gurus wordlessly holy on acid, celluloid flowers, newspaper posters, head shops, Diggers, Hell's Angels, Leary and Ginsberg leading mantras, and bespectacled bearded boys with beads and bells and Digger hats and bloodshot eyes that seemed to see beyond the world they never made to some better secret cloud—cuckoo-land green with the sweet aroma of burning grass. The ceremony of innocence had begun, and from everywhere the summer hippies converged on the Haight. When they arrived they found a prefabricated culture waiting for them: buttons, a ready-made dress style, head shops full of groovy merchandise, records, drugs, crash pads, free stores, free food, free love, free rock and an instant name, "hippies." To go along with all this there

was, not surprisingly, a language. With very minor variations it was 1920s bohemian, thirties hipster-drug-soultalk out of fifties beat by way of folk-protest-rock-yeah-yeah-mod-yé-yé, and all systematized and solidified by the ever-present media. The hippies' chief contribution to Nowspeak was in the area of drug euphemisms. Many of these were the old reliables of the twenties and thirties resurrected for the occasion: *pot, tea, boo, horse, O, joint, roach, grass, fix, connection, stash.* Others were relatively new, having sprung up like the holy mushrooms of Mexico in response to the new and popular psychedelics or "head" drugs: *hallucino-genic, buzz, flash, crash, LSD, acid, STP, speed, crystals, downer, bum-mer, freak-out, freaked out, freak* (as noun: acid freak, print freak, speed freak, motorcycle freak), *head, breakthrough* (also a military and sci-entific term), *trip, trip out, doing one's own thing, bag, groove.* Many words used to describe the effects of the psychedelics were phrases taken over from descriptions of the state of alcoholic inebriation: *high* (in a state of euphoria achieved by drugs or alcohol; as a noun, the state itself, or more generally, an overall sense of joy or well-being, as in "When I was on a high I thought I would found this groovy scene, see, 'Teen-age Evangelism' "), *stoned* (excessively high on drugs, "I want to save that for later when we're stoned") and so on.

Significantly, many "In" phrases at the time were implicit mechanical **15** metaphors like Timonthy Leary's famous injunction to "tune in, turn on, drop out"—figures of speech that are all drawn, implicitly or explicitly, from radio or television. "Turned on," used as an adjective, meaning high or under the influence of drugs or, more generally, receptive to drugs or to experience of any kind, especially that of an unconventional nature, illustrates the tendency of such words to broaden their range of possible meanings. (We already have noted that early jazz usage limited the "turn-on" to drugs and Charlie Parker's horn.) Another electronic-mechanical metaphor is the word *vibe,* short for *vibrations.* Like *turned on* it also has a more generalized meaning than merely the implicit mechanical metaphor: it may refer to the atmosphere or spirit of a scene or person, or to the cosmic forces present in a particular setting. Thus a person, scene, event, or general situation is said to send out *good vides* or *bad vibes,* depending on the speaker's reaction. Witches and warlocks were much prized on the Haight-Ashbury scene in 1967 for their ability to psych out good vibes. The term thus suggests a coalescence of elec-tronic and cosmic-mystic metaphors of popular occultism. Mysticism and the occult also added *guru, yoga, meditation* (one was said to be "on meditation"—an obvious transfer of the drug metaphor to a nondrug experience), *sadhana* (Hindu equivalent of one's own thing), *karma* (destiny), *horoscope, zodiac, warlock, witch, sitar, mantra, hare krishna, maharishi, swami, mandala, veda, Gita, om,* and the elusive *vibe.*

It is difficult to overestimate the importance of the hippie subculture **16** that began in 1967. It gave disaffected American youth, disillusioned by an ugly and senseless war and by a growing credibility gap, a rallying point and a locus of their new self-image. It also gave rise to a whole horde of movements that were and still are only tangentially related to hippiedom, but somehow still acquire guilt or innocence by association: SDS, student power, antiwar protest groups, YIPPIE (Youth International Party), the Chicago demonstrations of 1968, disturbances at Columbia, Harvard, Cornell, and San Francisco State, the Woodstock music festival, and the People's Park episode in Berkeley, 1969. Out of each of these small movements has arisen a set of chants, slogans, words, and phrases that for one reason or another caught on and became part of the language system: "all power to the people," "up against the wall, mofo," "into the streets," "down with pigs," "student power," "zap the world with love," "chicks up front," "give a flower to a cop," "Ho, Ho, Ho Chi Minh," "Hey, hey, LBJ," "Right on!" Specific events have also added to this new idiom. Thus Abbie Hoffman in a passage from *Rights in Conflict* describes the origin of the two terms *pig* (cop) and *Yippie* (Youth International Party member), which became the semantic poles of the Chicago riots in the summer of 1968: "There we were, all stoned, rolling around the floor . . . yippie! . . . Somebody says oink and that's it, pig, it's a natural, man, we gotta win" (p. 29).

17   As the passage above illustrates, much of the language was an authentic response to an immediate situation; some of it, however, was media-created or was given national prominence by the media: *name of the game, the generation gap, the credibility gap, where the action is, never trust anyone over thirty, the In Crowd, the Now Generation, the new morality, where it's at, the flower children, flower power* (this one attached to a photograph of a pig-hippie confrontation in San Francisco where the hippies zapped the barrels of the cops' guns with flowers), *charisma, tell it like it is* (possibly a corruption of the black "tell it" or "tell it, man"), *the Beautiful People* (originally a *Vogue-Bazaar* jet-set term transferred to the under-thirty crowd sometime during that eventful summer of 1967). Buttons contributed their share of slogans, too: "Save water, shower with a friend," "War is harmful to children and other living things," "Draft beer, not students," "Reality is a crutch," and "Frodo lives" and "Welcome to the Middle Earth," an in-signal for Tolkien lovers everywhere. Pop psychiatry and sociology contributed *confrontation, meaningful relationship* (*Newsweek*, 3 February 1969, calls this one a substitute for "campus sex"), *hang-up* (any psychological problem; also, any intense of consuming interest in anything), *strung out, relate, relevant, irrelevant* (said to be true of all academic pursuits), *therapy, shrink* (a psychiatrist, as in Arlo Guthrie's "Shrink, I wanna kill"), "group" (for group therapy), *group dynamics, T-group* (sensitivity-training session), *communicate, communication, nude therapy, body language, life-style, crisis, dialogue* (or *meaningful dialogue*) and *commitment.*

Like any language system, Nowspeak has its own value system built 18
into it. The language serves several purposes at once: it is a code to freak
out the ever-present Establishment, it solidifies the feeling of community
among this tenuously-bound subculture and assures its members that the
Underground, the Movement—even the Revolution—really do exist,
even if it's only in your head, and finally, it polarizes present-day society
into linguistic camps and thence into social and political camps that
follow from these linguistic sets. It is not great revelation to anyone that
the world looks quite different to a young man who thinks of everything from cutting his hair to negotiating with the college administration
in terms of "selling out to the System" than it looks to his father, who
is scarcely aware that there is a System, much less that he is himself a
part of it. A common geographical space and roughly coincident chronology is practically all that the two share: their politics, morality, aims,
ideology, aesthetics—in short, their culture—are quite different, and the
difference often starts and ends with the variance in languages. Ludwig
Wittgenstein has hypothesized that the words that are used to describe
aesthetic judgments play a very complicated but very definite role in
the culture of a period. To describe their use or to describe what you
mean by a cultured taste, you have to describe a whole culture. Since
an entirely different cultural game with different rules is played in
different ages, fully to describe a set of aesthetic rules means to describe
the culture of a period. The fact that the Nowspeaker's highest accolades
are "groovy," "wild," "beautiful!" "out of sight," and "naturally spaced"
as opposed to his father's or professor's "very intelligent," "cultivated,"
"sensible," "successful" or "well-rounded" means something far more
significant than merely the choice of one word over another: it means
a totally new aesthetics and hence a whole new value system for the
subculture.

Part of the point of the new aesthetic, of course, is that it is moving 19
toward a non-verbal orientation. Contentless courses, meditation, yoga,
chanting, drugs, T-groups, nude therapy, action painting, onstage
nudity, touch therapy, group gropes, guerilla theatre in the streets,
seances, satanism, be-ins, body language, dancing, rock festivals, procla-
mations of the Age of Aquarius and everywhere action, action, action—
all these signs of the times are indications that McLuhan's retribalized
youth are trying desperately to develop ways of communicating with
something other than words. It is not only the old politics, the old
imperialism, the old morality, the old society that is under attack; it is
rationality and language itself. To present the Now people with care-
fuly-worded logical arguments against their world view is only to compound the irony. Words are a large part of what their revolt is about.
If language is a tool of the Establishment, then to present a linguistic
argument to the Now people is already to have sold out to the System.

But the wheel of civilization has not yet turned full circle, and we are 20 living literally in a transitional age between the old culture when intelligence was verbal almost by definition and the new nonverbal total-experience aesthetic. It is possible, then, to make one further step beyond our examination of the language and say that from an analysis of Nowspeak we can drew a number of valid inferences about the culture that it describes: its latent but intense romanticism, its folkishness and tribal qualities, its highly emotive nature, its solipsism, its "this-here-nowness" and orientation toward the present existential moment, its connotative and reductive aspects. Let us see how this is so.

21   Perhaps the most striking quality of Nowspeak is that it is a highly romantic language, designed to mirror what all romanticisms ultimately mirror: the revolutionary transvaluation of all values. Thus the verbs of Nowspeak express action in onomatopoeic, slangy, quick and brittle phrases exploding like small balloons over the heads of some giant Superman or Phantom: *cop out, zap, zonk, sell out, bust, tune in, hit, flip, crash, groove.* They are comic-book and cartoon-time verbs for a TV generation. Among the most-quoted quotes of the Movement is the saying of Mao Tse-Tung, "Act first, then think, then act, then think, then act." Nowspeak is an action language for an action generation naturally "spaced" on the power of the moment. Print is irrelevant, hopelessly linear and static; it doesn't move, doesn't swing, groove, jiggle, gyrate, rock, or roll. Worst of all, it can't keep up with the Scene, can't go where it's at or where it's just been. Only with pure spontaneous action can things not fall apart and the center hold just a little longer.

22   Nowspeak nouns express a world view that is divided, like the world of the ancient Manicheans, into the powers of light and the powers of darkness, the Beautiful People and the System. The powers of darkness are identified with authority, uptightness, non-grooving, stodginess, and age: *the Man, the Establishment, pigs, sell-outs, game-players, uncools, hung-ups, fascists.* The powers of light in Nowspeak become *the New Left, the Movement,* the "good people," the In Crowd, the Underground, the Scene, the Age of Aquarius. Adjectives express superlative approval ("Beautiful!" "Wild!" "Freaky!") or describe emotional excesses of disapproval ("fascist pigs!" "You're uptight, man, you're blowing my mind, don't hassle me," "That's a heavy scene, man," "Oh no, you don't want grim, man; you want grim, you go to Chicago"). The vast and amorphous movement that gave birth to Nowspeak shows the same characteristics as nineteenth-century English, French, and German romanticisms: energy, boldness of thought, emphasis on creativity, the adulation of the new, the cult of personalities and the hero of the surface, stress on spontaneity and freedom of expression, anti-mechanistic and anti-scientific tendencies, supernaturalism, strangeness, a glorification of all sensory experience, the exaltation of wild freaky individualism, nonconformity, social responsibility, and the cult of sensibility. Nowspeak

reflects to a greater or lesser degree all these romantic tendencies. The words as we have seen are highly emotive, intensional rather than extensional, connotative rather than denotative, expressive rather than emotionally neutral; and their impact is fully realized only by the "cool head" community of participants in this new cult of sensibility. Words furnish a kind of verbal shorthand to communicate to others who are also hip to the Scene: they know, for example, that *happening* refers to an event that's a trip of some kind for its participants and implies the excitement of something meaningful going on with a possibility of wonder and surprise; that you can get a *contact high*, or vicarious buzz, from interacting with someone who's up on drugs; that to *turn on* means to come alive and carries with it the implication that ordinary straight society creates people who are not alive and must be switched on to exist in any real sense. They also realize that *where it's at* refers to the whole physical or psychological locus of real and significant activity going on at some place and time, as opposed to the ritual and sham of the Establishment scene, and are hip to the implicit theatrical overtones of *Scene* itself: it suggests the whole of a setting and the action occurring with it—the physical setting plus mood (vibes) plus people (the theatrical analogue is set plus props plus staging plus actors plus script plus promoters *ad infinitum*). But there is no way that the straight world can know all these things unless it too switches on, psychs out the vibes, and goes.

All Western romanticisms are Edenic in impulse and origin, for all **23** presuppose the fact of the Fall, symbolically if not literally, and all affirm the necessity of returning to the primordial Garden before the intrusion of the serpent machine. There are accurate and often chilling parallels to be drawn between the present youth cult in the United States and similar nineteenth- and early twentieth-century European cults with their fierce Rousseauism, their revolutionary cries for liberty, fraternity, equality, their *Sturm und Drang*, Pantisocracies, lyrical ballads, Satanism, Gothicism, *Volkgeists* and *Wanderlust*. The life-style of the young in twentieth-century America is also romantic, tribalized, and folkish, comprised of one part beat-academic-plain-style-Susan-Sontag-bricks-and-boards-white-washed-walls-authentic-products of cottage-industry-Chianti-drinking-yogurt-growing ethos; one part light-show-Quant-by-quant-psychotic-acid-freak-rock-stoned media-bag; and two parts idealized peasant and tribal ethos—hence the long hair, the fierce tribal loyalties, the barefoot hippie girls drifting artlessly through endless meadows of the mind, beards, mustaches, sideburns, dashikis, tatty raccoon coats, caftans, beads, bells, buttons, sandals (always the sign of the bohemian in Weejun'd America), Afros, Digger hats, minis, maxis, boots, and Indian headbands. Marshall McLuhan in a recent *Playboy* interview (March 1969) comments perceptively on what he calls the retribalization of American youth: "Our teenage generation is already becoming part of a jungle clan. . . . Sexual freedom is as natural to newly tribalized youth as drugs. . . . LSD and related hallucinogenic drugs . . . breed a highly tribal and communally oriented subculture, so it's understandable why the retribalized young take to drugs like a duck to water." The natural-man, tribal, folkish, Edenic aspect of the youth cult figures heavily in its language. There is a freer use of sexual, anal and other "taboo" terms and four-letter words: the language is simpler, the vocabulary is cut to a bare minimum, and there are many coined words, themselves authentic products of the Movement. Adjectives and nouns that denote approval are terms that express the ability to lose one's inhibitions, to move in a natural, uninhibited un-hung-up manner, to go where the action is and move with it, to put oneself in touch with cosmic rhythms—in short, to psych out the scene, feel its vibes, and then groove with it.

24   As we have seen, Nowspeak relies heavily on connotative power rather than denotative meaning for its impact. . . . Nowspeak at its worst can be a slick, vague, repetitive, and frustrating Hipspeak that smacks of the hard sell and fast deal quite as much as of the new morality and aesthetic. At its best, however, it is gutsy, emotive, colorful, and highly expressive of a whole range of thought and action that conventional English simply cannot express. Webster's offers us no exact equivalent for "pig" or "uptight" or "sell-out" or for the depth of ridicule and contempt that the terms convey, nor for the wildly enthusiastic approbation that lies behind "out of sight!" "spaced!" "freaky!" or "beautiful!" A friend of mine, recently turned twenty, spent a frustrating half-hour trying to describe to a gathering of cool heads the experiences of a recent acid trip and finally lapsed into "Oh, wow! If you only knew . . . like wild! freaky scene, man, just this freaky scene. . . . Oh, wow . . . spaced out . . . like you know, stoned . . . if you just knew, I mean, if you only knew." More intimate acquaintance with the dictionary would not have helped him communicate the incommunicable, for the experiences he was describing lie, for the moment at least, far beyond the pale of ordinary Sally-Dick-and-Jane reality. No wonder, then, that Nowspeak is against reason, against interpretation, against language itself: how else could it survive? Similarly for the use of taboo words, for it is a means of expressing utter disdain for ticky-tacky Establishment values to use obscenity in describing some of its more hallowed members and institutions.

25   If we think of the movement as McLuhan does in terms of a return to a romanticized primitive tribal ethos, we must also recognize that this language serves as an in-group sign, the verbal equivalent of a secret handclasp, a password that simultaneously gives solidarity to the inner circle and freaks out and excludes non-users, the ubiquitous Establishment. This use of language reminds us of Kenneth Burke's theory of language as gesture, for Nowspeak is indeed a sort of symbolic nose-thumbing at the Establishment—a complex and fun way of saying

"Screw you" in a linguistic set that only the initiates know. Nowspeak is the code that the System must break, and as such it unites the various branches of the nebulous movement with an often specious sense of community. Nowspeak appears deceptively simple; actually, it is quite complex and involves many subtleties of syntax and style. Since it is spoken, not written, it is transmitted and its conventions established by word-of-mouth communication. The only sure way to establish current usage is to be in constant contact with speakers, for the language changes daily and today's In phrase is liable to be tomorrow's tired-out cliché. A written version of the language is at best only an approximation of its spoken form. Youth-oriented magazines such as *Cavalier, Ramparts,* and *Evergreen* realize this and effect in their writing style a skillful synthesis between ordinary English and authentic Nowspeak by repeating key words in contexts that indicate the cultural sympathies of the editors. Dust jackets, theatre marquees, and record jackets also let the young audience know by verbal sleight-of-mouth that the designer or producer was "where it was at" when the artifact in question was produced. By succumbing to the hip sell and buying the product the young consumer is invited to join the cool community where he, too, can be Norman Mailer-ed, Maxwell Taylor-ed *ad nauseum.*

By nature Nowspeak is sensation-oriented rather than experience-oriented, solipsistic rather than chronological or historical. While typical standard English sentence structure is chronological ("It was raining," "They left with us on Tuesday," "He used to drop by for drinks on Wednesday nights"), Nowspeak is non-chronological, non-temporal, a language of, for, and about the present moment. It is a process language designed to express the shifts, the swift reversals, the kaleidoscopic flux, the insecurities and ephemera of an electric kool-aid acid world. Like the Hopi Indian's tongue, Nowspeak is designed to tell us only that "it is summering," not that "it is summer": witness the number of words that describe ongoing or continuing action (*happening, Scene, where it's at, swinging*). Thus the language is geared toward making what the American philosopher Charles Hartshorne has called "this-here-now" statements about immediate actions and present states of being. To listen to the Now people rapping or to read an underground newspaper is to live briefly in the historical present. Few if any of the verbs are in the past tense, and most of the sentences are short, simple declarative statements directed less toward imparting information than toward creating a mood or emotion. Most of the statements are action-directed imperatives ("screw in the streets," "kill the pigs," "stop the trial") or exclamatory-declarative statements with a pithy, down-home epigrammatic brevity about them ("All power to the people," "This is a racist culture," "The streets belong to the people"). Daniel J. Boorstin, writing for the October 1968 *Esquire,* calls the Movement "the social expression of a movement from Experience to Sensation"—the shift from cumulative and communicable observation of or acquaintance with facts and events to simple awareness of perception which by definition is personal, private, highly confined, and essentially incommunicable. "What history is to the person in quest of experience," he writes, "a 'happening' is to the person in quest of sensation. For a 'happening' is something totally discrete. It adds to our sensations without increasing our experience." Perhaps we can see in the sensation-orientation, the "this-here-now"-ness of Nowspeak and its speakers a popularization of pseudo-Whiteheadian process metaphysics. This new pop philosophy mirrors the shift in contemporary world view from traditional substance-attribute metaphysics to a *weltanschauung* where things fall apart, the center cannot hold, movies-within-films-within-metaflicks are cinematic commonplaces, and today's pop idol is tomorrow's Nowhere Man. Once-credible reality was shattered with the dreamy lyricism of early grass and acid rock ("Strawberry fields forever") and now like Humpty-Dumpty's egg, the pieces of this cosmic Chinese puzzle cannot be put back together. Nowspeak reflects all these things: for a fragmented and incoherent time it offers us a pastiche-lingo whose silences and ellipses are more eloquent than its words.

27   Nowspeak, like most subculture languages, is more incantation than analysis or definition and thus relies heavily on word connotation rather than denotation. We already have noted the proper names that have charisma and evocative power. Certain other words and phrases also have it: "The Revolution," "power (supply: black, student, flower)," "the System," "the Movement," "kill pigs," "do your own thing." Men have died for less clearly defined terms than these. Nat Hentoff in the April 1969 *Evergreen* tells the story of a recent meeting of young liberal teachers in New York that quickly degenerated into a name-Calling contest on the word "racist." The fact that the word was left undefined during the meeting was irrelevant. The evocative power of the word was enough. The important thing about words like the Movement and the Establishment is not that anyone can point to referents for them, but that they are sufficient in emotional force to generate their own new myths as they gather the tribes about them. For the Nowspeaker, as for Lewis Carroll's Humpty Dumpty, the word can mean anything that pleases the speaker at the time: for example, the word *uptight*, which seems to change meanings with the seasons. Claude Brown in "The Language of Soul" (*Esquire*, April 1968) remarks that the word came into use about 1953 in Harlem and meant being in financial straits. In time, it came to be popular with junkies to describe their perpetual condition of needing money for the next fix. In the early sixties when "uptight" was first making its way into under-thirty jargon, a younger generation of people in black urban communities of the East revived the word with new meaning: "everything is cool, under control, going my way." For the Nowspeaker "uptight" may be either a term of approbation ("everything is proceeding according to plan," "I have it all psyched

out," "I'm cool, I'm hip") or of derision (as an equivalent to "square," "uncool," "not with it"). Once again, it is not the denotative power of the word that counts (*uptight* may denote two completely antithetical states, depending on its usage); it is the connotation of the word, the manner of uttering it, the occasion, the context, and the emotive force that determine the word's meaning in a given situation.

Stanley Kripner's paper before the International Society of General **28** Semantics in August 1968 suggested that what the youthful user of "head drugs" learns from his earliest drug experiences is no very specific knowledge of information: instead he learns a new semantic set proper to the occasion ("spaced out," "groovy," "freak out," "high," "crash," "turned on"). To put the matter in good linguistic terminology, we might say that the Nowspeaker often mistakes the map for the territory; he speaks intensionally rather than extensionally, evocatively and incantatorially instead of analytically and rationally. Both in popular and a McLuhanesque sense of the word, Nowspeak is a "cool" language —indefinable, vague, often imprecise, requiring rigorous audience participation to fill in the holes in the content. Thus for the Nowspeaker the medium is quite literally the message.

Like George Orwell's famous Newspeak, Nowspeak is essentially a **29** reductive language intended to facilitate rather than stimulate thought by limiting the possible alternatives that can be articulated within the language set. Designed for instant speech, minimum thought, and instant replay, it is built around an implicit two-value logic that denies or disregards the possibility of compromise or alternative systems. It is easy for America's retribalized youth to think in terms of these neat polar opposites—pig and Yippie (the poles of the 1968 Chicago confrontation), New Left and Establishment, System and Revolution—for it provides a comfortable means of instantly categorizing all the possible experiences that one might have. For the Nowspeaker the world is all black or white with no redeeming shade of grey in between. Black is beautiful and white is a sell-out. The student is a nigger. All power to the people, death to pigs. Down with the System; up, up, and away with the Beautiful People. Reason is bad, feeling is good. Act, think, act, think, then act, act, act. Nietzsche's prophetic transvaluation of all values has at last come to pass. The lack of a middle ground, a middle term somewhere between the extremes of total conformity and total assault on the culture, makes it impossible for Nowspeak to reflect with accuracy any world other than one drawn in the starkest of blacks and whites. There is, for example, no such animal as "pig-hippie" for that would be an animal as anomalous and absurd as Suzanne Langer's "rabbit-dog." One must be one or the other, never both at once. Thus, for all its dayglo colors, its newspaper taxis and marshmallow people, plasticene ponies and insanity's horse adorning the skies, the world of Nowspeak is a strangely sinister, almost medieval world, a battlefield where the children of light and the sons of darkness, the Now Generation and the Old-thinkers, play out the psychedelic *psychomachia* to the finish. The lines were drawn long ago with deadly clarity, and it may be too late to turn back the clock. As Gore Vidal reminds us in the final essay of *Sex, Death and Money*, the wheel of civilization is once more beginning to turn and most of us can only watch in morbid fascination as the flower kids in this strangest of all Children's Crusades are pied-piped away by the idol of the hour.

30   Yet the case for language may not be totally lost. It may well be this polarizing tendency of Nowspeak that will spell its end as the ruling subculture jargon. All philosophical systems have built into them certain basic assumptions that substantially limit the types of statements possible within each system. The same can be said of languages, for the verbal set of any culture (or subculture) determines to a great extent the limits of its possible assertions, its knowledge, its ideology, its perceptions, and hence its achievements. Like the heroine of Vilgot Sjöman's *I Am Curious (Yellow)* we all are feeling the need to smash our tidy op art cardboard archives with all the groovy letters and slogans and In words pasted all over the slick surface, and to find a new box with new labels for our collective files. Already hip young journalists, politicans, students, teachers, playwrights, poets, and critics are beginning to chafe at the restrictions of a language designed for incantation and slogans rather than for thoughtful analysis and action. Nat Hentoff's *Evergreen* article speaks of the New Left's "prison of words," and, after analysis of such phrases as Herbert Marcuse's "discriminative tolerance," Hentoff concludes that it is a polite euphemism for "elitist authoritarianism"; that "all power to all people" means not what it seems to say, but rather implies the implicitly snobbish view, "all power to me and everyone else who believes exactly as I do." For the first time perhaps in this decade we are beginning to look behind the words to the things and ideas, to search out hidden paradoxes ("All power to all people," and "America is a nation of fascist pigs," for example, are slogans as compatible as "Buddha is and is not"—and about equally meaningful).

31   Nowspeak has served its function and served it well and faithfully. Despite obvious limitations of its own, it has freed standard Americanese from the impoverishment of Webster's, Madison Avenue, pop psychiatry, military-industrial jargon, academese, and koffee-klatch-and-pizza-late-late-show TV. It has introduced a colorful, freaky, rhythmic, whimsical, gutsy, outrageous, "sexy, childish, irreligious and mad" element into a language that was giving signs of languishing in its prime. It has elevated the jargon of the hipster, the black, the drug pusher, bohemian, beat, hippie, and general rebel with or without a cause to the status of legitimate usage and has infused instant glamour and expressiveness into the speech of millions (both the *New York Times* and David Brinkley have noted a special affinity for *uptight*). In a very real

sense, Nowspeak is itself the pop poetry of the new age just as rock is its lyric voice. Yet in an equally real sense the greatest strength of Nowspeak lies in its power and need to be superseded. C. D. Burns put it this way in an essay called "The Sense of the Horizon" (1933):

> The experience of any moment has its horizons. Today's experience, which is not tomorrow's, has in it some hints and implications which are tomorrow on the horizon of today. . . . However wide it may be, that common world also has its horizon; and on that horizon new experiences are always appearing.

That Nowspeak's horizon is Now is significant: that is at once its lifeblood and its death knell. Already the neon lights have burnt out on Carnaby Street, the Beatles have gone their separate ways, the Haight stands emptied of its brilliant frisking flower children, the orchard gone to ashes, and the dry leaves swirl like fallen Lucifer's host in the People's Park. Sergeant Pepper's buried; he will not come out of his grave. The summer people have taken to the streets, and the old hippies have fled into the mountains, feeling some new wind brewing in them as they breathe. And which of us knows what rough beast of a newer Nowspeak, its hour come 'round at last, slouches toward San Francisco to be born? 32

S. I. HAYAKAWA

Contexts

S[amuel]. I[chiye]. Hayakawa, who was born in 1906 in Vancouver, B.C., is a pioneer in the field of semantics. A former college president and author of numerous books in his field, he has been on the editorial board of Funk & Wagnalls Standard Dictionaries and edited *ETC: A Review of General Semantics*. He is presently professor of language arts at San Francisco State College. Adapted from his influential book, *Language in Thought and Action* (rev. ed., 1963), this essay takes up the whole question of the interdependency of words—the relationship of meaning to context—by examining how dictionaries are made.

> *[On being asked to define New Orleans jazz]: Man, when you got to ask what it is, you'll never get to know. . . .*
> —Louis Armstrong

> Dictionary definitions frequently offer verbal substitutes for an unknown term which only conceal a lack of real understanding. Thus a person might look up a foreign word and be quite satisfied with the meaning "bullfinch" without the slightest ability to identify or describe this bird. Understanding does not come through dealings with words alone, but rather with the things for which they stand. Dictionary definitions permit us to hide from ourselves and others the extent of our ignorance.
> —H. R. Huse[1]

How Dictionaries Are Made

1   It is widely believed that every word has a correct meaning, that we learn these meanings principally from teachers and grammarians (except that most of the time we don't bother to, so that we ordinarily speak "sloppy English"), and that dictionaries and grammars are the supreme authority in matters of meaning and usage. Few people ask by what authority the writers of dictionaries and grammars say what they say. The writer once got into a dispute with an Englishwoman over the pronunciation of a word and offered to look it up in the dictionary. The Englishwoman said firmly, "What for? I am English. I was born and brought up in England.

From *Language in Thought and Action*, Second Edition, by S. I. Hayakawa, copyright 1941, 1949, © 1963, 1964, by Harcourt Brace Jovanovich, Inc., and reprinted with their permission.

[1] From *The Illiteracy of the Literate* by H. R. Huse, copyright 1933, by D. Appleton-Century Company, Inc.

The way I speak *is* English." Such self-assurance about one's own language is not uncommon among the English. In the United States, however, anyone who is willing to quarrel with the dictionary is regarded as either eccentric or mad.

Let us see how dictionaries are made and how the editors arrive at 2 definitions. What follows applies, incidentally, only to those dictionary offices where first-hand, original research goes on—not those in which editors simply copy existing dictionaries. The task of writing a dictionary begins with reading vast amounts of the literature of the period or subject that the dictionary is to cover. As the editors read, they copy on cards every interesting or rare word, every unusual or peculiar occurrence of a common word, a large number of common words in their ordinary uses, and also the sentences in which each of these words appears, thus:

```
pail
The dairy pails bring home increase of milk
                Keats, Endymion
                    I, 44–45
```

That is to say, the context of each word is collected, along with the 3 word itself. For a really big job of dictionary writing, such as the *Oxford English Dictionary* (usually bound in about twenty-five volumes), millions of such cards are collected, and the task of editing occupies decades. As the cards are collected, they are alphabetized and sorted. When the sorting is completed, there will be for each word anywhere from two or three to several hundred illustrative quotations, each on its card.

To define a word, then, the dictionary editor places before him the 4 stack of cards illustrating that word; each of the cards represents an actual use of the word by a writer of some literary or historical importance. He reads the cards carefully, discards some, rereads the rest, and divides up the stack according to what he thinks are the several senses of the word. Finally, he writes his definitions, following the hard-and-fast rule that each definition *must* be based on what the quotations in front of him reveal about the meaning of the word. The editor cannot be influenced by what *he* thinks a given word *ought* to mean. He must work according to the cards or not at all.

The writing of a dictionary, therefore, is not a task of setting up 5 authoritative statements about the "true meanings" of words, but a task of *recording*, to the best of one's ability, what various words *have meant* to authors in the distant or immediate past. *The writer of a dictionary is a historian, not a lawgiver.* If, for example, we had been writing a dictionary in 1890, or even as late as 1919, we could have said that the word "broadcast" means "to scatter" (seed and so on) but we could not have decreed that from 1921 on, the commonest meaning of the word

should become "to disseminate audible messages, etc., by radio transmission." To regard the dictionary as an "authority," therefore, is to
credit the dictionary writer with gifts of prophecy which neither he nor
anyone else possesses. In choosing our words when we speak or write,
we can be *guided* by the historical record afforded us by the dictionary,
but we cannot be *bound* by it, because new situations, new experiences,
new inventions, new feelings, are always compelling us to give new uses
to old words. Looking under a "hood," we should ordinarily have found,
five hundred years ago, a monk; today, we find a motorcar engine.[2]

Verbal and Physical Contexts

6   The way in which the dictionary writer arrives at his definitions merely
systematizes the way in which we all learn the meanings of words, beginning at infancy, and continuing for the rest of our lives. Let us say
that we have never heard the word "oboe" before, and we overhear a
conversation in which the following sentences occur:

> He used to be the best *oboe* player in town. . . . Whenever they came to
> that *oboe* part in the third movement, he used to get very excited. . . . I
> saw him one day at the music shop, buying a new reed for his *oboe*. . . .
> He never liked to play the clarinet after he started playing the *oboe*. . . .
> He said it wasn't much fun, because it was too easy.

7   Although the word may be unfamiliar, its meaning becomes clear to
us as we listen. After hearing the first sentence, we know that an "oboe"
is "played," so that it must be either a game or a musical instrument.
With the second sentence the possibility of its being a game is eliminated.
With each succeeding sentence the possibilities as to what an "oboe" may
be are narrowed down until we get a fairly clear idea of what is meant.
This is how we learn by *verbal context.*

8   But even independently of this, we learn by physical and social context. Let us say that we are playing golf and that we have hit the ball
in a certain way with certain unfortunate results, so that our companion
says to us, "That's a bad *slice.*" He repeats this remark every time our
ball fails to go straight. If we are reasonably bright, we learn in a very
short time to say, when it happens again, "That's a bad slice." On one
occasion, however, our friend says to us, "That's not a *slice* this time;
that's a *hook.*" In this case we consider what has happened, and we
wonder what is different about the last stroke from those previous. As
soon as we make the distinction, we have added still another word to our

[2] *Webster's Third New International Dictionary* lists the word "hood" also as a
shortened form of "hoodlum."

The time that elapsed between *Webster's Second Edition* (1934) and the *Third*
(1961) indicates the enormous amount of reading and labor entailed in the preparation of a really thorough dictionary of a language as rapidly changing and as rich
in vocabulary as English.

vocabulary. The result is that after nine holes of golf, we can use both these words accurately—and perhaps several others as well, such as "divot," "number-five iron," "approach shot," *without ever having been told what they mean.* Indeed, we may play golf for years without ever being able to give a dictionary definition of "to slice": "To strike (the ball) so that the face of the club draws inward across the face of the ball, causing it to curve toward the right in flight (with a right-handed player)" (*Webster's New International Dictionary, Second Edition*). But even without being able to give such a definition, we should still be able to use the word accurately whenever the occasion demanded.

We learn the meanings of practically all our words (which are, it will   9
be remembered, merely complicated noises), not from dictionaries, not from definitions, but from hearing these noises as they accompany actual situations in life and then learning to associate certain noises with certain situations. Even as dogs learn to recognize "words," as for example by hearing "biscuit" at the same time as an actual biscuit is held before their noses, so do we all learn to interpret language by being aware of the happenings that accompany the noises people make at us—by being aware, in short, of contexts.

The definitions given by little children in school show clearly how they   10
associate words with situations; they almost always define in terms of physical and social contexts: "Punishment is when you have been bad and they put you in a closet and don't let you have any supper." "Newspapers are what the paper boy brings and you wrap up the garbage with it." These are good definitions. They cannot be used in dictionaries mainly because they are too specific; it would be impossible to list the myriads of situations in which every word has been used. For this reason, dictionaries give definitions on a high level of abstraction; that is, with particular references left out for the sake of conciseness. This is another reason why it is a great mistake to regard a dictionary definition as telling us all about a word.

Extensional and Intensional Meaning

Dictionaries deal with the world of intensional meanings, but there is   11
another world which a dictionary by its very nature ignores: the world of extensional meanings. *The extensional meaning of an utterance is that which it points to in the extensional (physical) world.* That is to say, the extensional meaning cannot be expressed in words, because it is that which words stand for. An easy way to remember this is *to put your hand over your mouth and point* whenever you are asked to give an extensional meaning.

Of course, we cannot always point to the extensional meanings of the   12
words we use. Therefore, so long as we are *discussing* meanings, we shall refer to that which is being talked about as the *denotation* of an

utterance. For example, the denotation of the word "Winnipeg" is the prairie city of that name in southern Manitoba; the denotation of the word "dog" is a class of animals which includes dog_1 (Fido), dog_2 (Rex), dog_3 (Rover) . . . dog_m.

13   The *intensional meaning* of a word or expression, on the other hand, is that which is *suggested* (connoted) inside one's head. Roughly speaking, whenever we express the meaning of words by uttering more words, we are giving intensional meaning, or connotations. To remember this, put your hand over your eyes and let the words spin around in your head.

14   Utterances may have, of course, both extensional and intensional meaning. If they have no intensional meaning at all—that is, if they start no notions whatever spinning about in our heads—they are meaningless noises, like foreign languages that we do not understand. On the other hand, it is possible for utterances to have no extensional meaning at all, in spite of the fact that they may start many notions spinning about in our heads. The statement, "Angels watch over my bed at night," is one that has intensional but no extensional meaning. This does not mean that there are no angels watching over my bed at night. When we say that the statement has no extensional meaning, we are merely saying that we cannot see, touch, photograph, or in any scientific manner detect the presence of angels. The result is that, if an argument begins on the subject whether or not angels watch over my bed, *there is no way of ending the argument to the satisfaction of all disputants*, the Christians and the non-Christians, the pious and the agnostic, the mystical and the scientific. Therefore, whether we believe in angels or not, knowing in advance that any argument on the subject will be both endless and futile, we can avoid getting into fights about it.

15   When, on the other hand, statements have extensional content, as when we say, "This room is fifteen feet long," arguments can come to a close. No matter how many guesses there are about the length of the room, all discussion ceases when someone produces a tape measure. This, then, is the important difference between extensional and intensional meanings: namely, when utterances have extensional meanings, discussion can be ended and agreement reached; when utterances have intensional meanings only and no extensional meanings, arguments may, and often do, go on indefinitely. Such arguments can result only in conflict. Among individuals, they may result in the breaking up of friendships; in society, they often split organizations into bitterly opposed groups; among nations, they may aggravate existing tensions so seriously as to become real obstacles to the peaceful settling of disputes.

16   Arguments of this kind may be termed "non-sense arguments," because they are based on utterances about which no sense data can be collected. Needless to say, there are occasions when the hyphen may be omitted—that depends on one's feelings toward the particular argument

under consideration. The reader is requested to provide his own examples of "non-sense arguments." Even the foregoing example of the angels may give offense to some people, despite the fact that no attempt is made to deny or affirm the existence of angels. Imagine, then, the uproar that might result from giving a number of examples from theology, politics, law, economics, literary criticism, and other fields in which it is not customary to distinguish clearly sense from non-sense.

The "One Word, One Meaning" Fallacy

Everyone, of course, who has ever given any thought to the meanings of 17 words has noticed that they are always shifting and changing in meaning. Usually, people regard this as a misfortune, because it "leads to sloppy thinking" and "mental confusion." To remedy this condition, they are likely to suggest that we should all agree on "one meaning" for each word and use it only with that meaning. Thereupon it will occur to them that we simply cannot make people agree in this way, even if we could set up an ironclad dictatorship under a committee of lexicographers who would place censors in every newspaper office and microphones in every home. The situation, therefore, appears hopeless.

Such an impasse is avoided when we start with a new premise altogether—one of the premises upon which modern linguistic thought is 18 based: namely, that *no word ever has exactly the same meaning twice.* The extent to which this premise fits the facts can be demonstrated in a number of ways. First, if we accept the proposition that the contexts of an utterance determine its meaning, it becomes apparent that since no two contexts are ever *exactly* the same, no two meanings can ever be exactly the same. How can we "fix the meaning" even for so common an expression as "to believe in" when it can be used in such sentences as the following:

> I believe in you (I have confidence in you).
> I believe in democracy (I accept the principles implied by the term democracy).
> I believe in Santa Claus (It is my opinion that Santa Claus exists).

Second, we can take, for example, a word of "simple" meaning, like 19 "kettle." But when John says "kettle," its intensional meanings to him are the common characteristics of all the kettles John remembers. When Peter says "kettle," however, its intensional meanings to him are the common characteristics of all the kettles he remembers. *No matter how small or how negligible the differences may be between John's "kettle" and Peter's "kettle," there is some difference.*

Finally, let us examine utterances in terms of extensional meanings. If 20 John, Peter, Harold, and George each say "my typewriter," we would have to point to four different typewriters to get the extensional meaning in each case: John's new Olivetti, Peter's old Remington, Harold's

Smith-Corona portable, and the undenotable intended "typewriter" that George plans some day to buy: "My typewriter, when I buy it, will be an electric." Also, if John says "my typewriter" today, and again "my typewriter" tomorrow, the extensional meaning is different in the two cases, because the typewriter is not exactly the same from one day to the next (nor from one minute to the next): slow processes of wear, change, and decay are going on constantly. Although we can say, then, that the differences in the meanings of a word on one occasion, on another occasion a minute later, and on still another occasion another minute later, are negligible, we cannot say that the meanings are *exactly* the same.

21   To insist dogmatically that we know what a word means *in advance of its utterance* is nonsense. All we can know in advance is *approximately* what it will mean. After the utterance, we interpret what has been said in the light of both verbal and physical contexts, and act according to our interpretation. An examination of the verbal context of an utterance, as well as the examination of the utterance itself, directs us to the intensional meanings; an examination of the physical context directs us to the extensional meanings. When John says to James, "Bring me that book, will you?" James looks in the direction of John's pointed finger (physical context) and sees a desk with several books on it (physical context); he thinks back over their previous conversation (verbal context) and knows which of those books is being referred to.

22   Interpretation *must* be based, therefore, on the totality of contexts. If it were otherwise, we should not be able to account for the fact that even if we fail to use the right (customary) words in some situations, people can very frequently understand us. For example:

> A: Gosh, look at that second baseman go!
> B (looking): You mean the shortstop?
> A: Yes, that's what I mean.

> A: There must be something wrong with the oil line; the engine has started to balk.
> B: Don't you mean "gas line"?
> A: Yes—didn't I say "gas line"?

Contexts often indicate our meaning so clearly that we do not even have to say what we mean in order to be understood.

Ignoring Contexts

23   It is clear, then, that the ignoring of contexts in any act of interpretation is at best a stupid practice. At its worst, it can be a vicious practice. A common example is the sensational newspaper story in which a few words by a public personage are torn out of their context and made the basis of a completely misleading account. There is the incident of a Veterans

Day speaker, a university teacher, who declared before a high-shool assembly that the Gettysburg Address was "a powerful piece of propaganda." The context clearly revealed that "propaganda" was being used, not according to its popular meaning, but rather, as the speaker himself stated, to mean "explaining the moral purposes of a war." The context also revealed that the speaker was a very great admirer of Lincoln. However, the local newspaper, ignoring the context, presented the account in such a way as to suggest that the speaker had called Lincoln a liar. On this basis, the newspaper began a campaign against the instructor. The speaker remonstrated with the editor of the newspaper, who replied, in effect, "I don't care what else you said. You said the Gettysburg Address was propaganda, didn't you?" This appeared to the editor complete proof that Lincoln had been maligned and that the speaker deserved to be discharged from his position at the university. Similar practices may be found in advertisements. A reviewer may be quoted on the jacket of a book as having said, "A brilliant work," while reading of the context may reveal that what he really said was, "It just falls short of being a brilliant work." There are some people who will always be able to find a defense for such a practice in saying, "But he did use the words, 'a brilliant work,' didn't he?"

People in the course of argument very frequently complain about **24** words meaning different things to different people. Instead of complaining, they should accept such differences as a matter of course. It would be startling indeed if the word "justice," for example, were to have the same meaning to each of the nine justices of the United States Supreme Court; we should get nothing but unanimous decisions. It would be even more startling if "justice" meant the same to President Kennedy as to Nikita Khrushchev. If we can get deeply into our consciousness the principle that no word ever has the same meaning twice, we will develop the habit of automatically examining contexts, and this will enable us to understand better what others are saying. As it is, however, we are all too likely, when a word sounds familiar, to assume that we understand it even when we don't. In this way we read into people's remarks meanings that were never intended. Then we waste energy in angrily accusing people of "intellectual dishonesty" or "abuse of words," when their only sin is that they use words in ways unlike our own, as they can hardly help doing, especially if their background has been widely different from ours. There are cases of intellectual dishonesty and the abuse of words, of course, but they do not always occur in the places where people think they do.

In the study of history or of cultures other than our own, contexts **25** take on special importance. To say, "There was no running water or electricity in the house," does not condemn an English house in 1570, but says a great deal against a house in Chicago in 1963. Again, if we wish to understand the Constitution of the United States, it is not enough, as our historians now tell us, merely to look up all the words in the dictionary and to read the interpretations written by Supreme Court justices. We must see the Constitution in its historical context: the conditions of life, the state of the arts and industries and transportation, the current ideas of the time—all of which helped to determine what words went into the Constitution and what those words meant to those who wrote them. After all, the words "United States of America" stood for quite a different-sized nation and a different culture in 1790 from what they stand for today. When it comes to very big subjects, the range of contexts to be examined—verbal, social, and historical—may become very large indeed.

26   In personal relations, furthermore, those who ignore psychological contexts often make the mistake of interpreting as insults remarks that are only intended in jest.

The Interaction of Words

27   All this is not to say, however, that the reader might just as well throw away his dictionary, simply because contexts are so important. Any word in a sentence—any sentence in a paragraph, any paragraph in a larger unit—whose meaning is revealed by its context, is itself part of the context of the rest of the text. To look up a word in a dictionary, therefore, frequently explains not only the word itself, but the rest of the sentence, paragraph, conversation, or essay in which it is found. All words within a given context interact upon one another.

28   Realizing, then, that a dictionary is a historical work, we should understand the dictionary thus: "The word *mother* has most frequently been used in the past among English-speaking people to indicate a female parent." From this we can safely infer, "If that is how it has been used, that is what it *probably* means in the sentence I am trying to understand." This is what we normally do, of course; after we look up a word in the dictionary, we reexamine the context to see if the definition fits. If the context reads, "Mother began to form in the bottle," one may have to look at the dictionary more carefully.

29   A dictionary definition, therefore, is an invaluable guide to interpretation. Words do not have a single "correct meaning"; they apply to *groups* of similar situations, which might be called *areas of meaning*. It is for defining these areas of meaning that a dictionary is useful. In each use of any word, we examine the particular context and the extensional events denoted (if possible) to discover the *point* intended within the area of meaning.

EUGENE LINDEN

Man Talks So Oddly!

Eugene Linden was born in 1947 in Vermont and graduated in 1969
from Yale. Formerly on the staff of New York Congressman Richard
Ottinger, Mr. Linden is a free-lance writer living in Connecticut.
His book *Apes, Men and Language* was published in England and
America and won nationwide critical acclaim. His latest book is
The Alms Race (1976). This piece first appeared in *The New York
Times* in 1976. The discovery that chimpanzees have linguistic
capabilities is placed by Mr. Linden in the wider contexts of sci-
entific and technological assumptions. According to his views, "we
[that is, the chimps and us] have a lot to talk about."

In 1966, R. Allen Gardner's and Beatrice Gardner's infant chimpanzee   1
said "more" in Ameslan, the American Sign Language for the deaf. Since
that time, this chimp, named Washoe, has learned 180 other words, and
a number of other chimpanzees have learned to communicate in this
language as well.

Also since that time Washoe and other chimps have taken to using   2
language in many different ways. They swear, invent names, learn signs
from each other, have demonstrated syntactic capabilities, have translated
from spoken to sign language, and have used words to express emotion,
to joke, to converse, to lie.

We could have been watching chimps do all these things 75 years ago.   3
The breakthrough that has enabled us to converse with chimpanzees was
a simple matter of common sense: recognizing that the chimp has trouble
controlling its tongue, lips, and supralaryngeal tract but that it suffers
from no such inhibitions in the use of its hands.

For decades scientists have watched chimps demonstrate different   4
forms of behavior no less propositional than language, and for decades
scientists have ignored the obvious conclusion that chimps have some
linguistic abilities.

Why? What is our stake in language? To start with, our perceptions of   5
other species have been limited by a laboratory tunnel vision in science
that has been part of what the anthropologist Harvey Sarles calls the
cure orientation in science. Operating under Francis Bacon's thesis that
nature best reveals her secrets when tormented, we have tended to
dissect and study animals with the idea of seeing how they might solve
our problems, medical or social, rather than attempting to understand
them in their own right, in their own environment.

6   When we eventually got around to comparing human and animal behavior, we studied animals as if they had no reason or language, while we studied humans knowing we did. Thus the disparate investigations tended to perpetuate the assumptions on which they were based, and our approach to animal and human communication eventually resurfaced as the explanation for the differences between the two: Man is different because that is the way we look at him.

7   The depth of this circular reasoning is evident in our putting men in orbit around the earth before we overcame simple prejudices equating language with speech. This comparison is apt, because the development of technology that permitted us to put people in orbit *depended* on ignorance and insensitivity of the world and animals around us.

8   There is a larger enveloping bias in science that explains its cure orientation and our previous lack of interest in understanding creatures like chimps. That bias is the overarching moral and philosophical traditions we inherit that argue that, because of the divine gift of reason, man is set apart from other animals, and that because man is so blessed the rest of nature is so much raw material at our disposal.

9   Our prerogatives in nature were developed by peoples who were unaware of creatures such as the great apes, creatures that would seem to establish continuity between man and animal. (It is no accident that Western technology did not develop in the jungle.) Eventually, through conquest and exploration, Europeans entered the jungles and came into contact with the great apes, whose existence argued the relatedness of man and nature and the falseness of the underpinnings of our Western world-view.

10   A system of thought that might be suitable to the realities of Europe or the desert had trouble with the tropics.

11   One hundred years after news of the first chimp reached Europe, Darwin argued our ancestral continuity with the other primates. Another hundred years and now scientists are being forced to admit our behavioral continuity with other animals.

12   If chimps and other animals share our gifts of reason and language, what then happens to our prerogatives in nature?

13   It is true that Western thought has been profitable in the short term, but we are now beginning to suffer technology's long-term costs. And we are also discovering that our high, proud loneliness has been achieved at the price of our identity: a sense of place in nature. Jung said once that we lacked self-knowledge because we had no other being with whom we might compare ourselves. Jung expected to find such creatures on other planets. Now we have discovered that they have been here all along. In our ignorance, we have brought the chimp to the point of extinction. It would be unutterably sad to let any of these animals disappear. After so long, we have a lot to talk about.

14   Much as revolutionary experiments with chimpanzees are changing

our view of our place in nature, the experiments are the product of changes themselves: a host of changed relationships in science that indicate that some new *gestalt* is evolving to make better sense of man's place in nature before it is too late. A whole new breed of scientists has shunned the laboratory for the wilds. This breed looks more like back-packers than technicians.

We are beginning to lower our sights from the heavens to the world 15 around us. We are beginning to re-examine the trade-off that enabled us to get to the moon.

Glossary of Rhetorical Terms

Abstract and concrete language. Abstract language presents itself to the mind, which proceeds to enlarge and enliven the experience by providing—if it can—a concrete illustration. Concrete language impresses itself on the senses by helping the mind to recall the sensory experience associated with it. Words: *Military* is abstract, but *aircraft carriers* is concrete, as are *bombers, soldiers,* and *sailors. Military* cannot be pictured in the mind—directly—so the mind must struggle to supply an example; members of the class of military things *can* be pictured because they have visual or other sensory referents. You can thus imagine for yourself which of the two forms of language is easier to "take," so to speak. But both kinds of language are needed in writing because, for example, you couldn't possibly say (in *trying* to say *military strength*) *bombers-aircraft carriers-soldiers-rifles-sailors-missiles . . . strength.* What's needed is a balanced proportion of the two.

A useful point for writers to understand is that some terms are more *specific,* some more *general,* so that we can have a group of words—like a series of Chinese laquered boxes, one fitting into the larger category of the other and taking its companions with it: *Pvt. Mudd, rifleman, infantryman, soldier, military, force, power.* In writing, it is necessary to select the exact Chinese box required—always keeping in mind that vivid (concrete) writing is best. "Corporal Zeiger stayed cool by staying where he was, under a *tree.*" Or should we substitute *"spreading maple"* for "tree" on the grounds that the reader can picture in *spreading maple* the shade that keeps the corporal cool. Still, it is important to note that we sometimes need a more general term like *tree* in order to make an abstract statement; for example, "Volpe can't see the forest for the trees." Clearly, the statement would not be the same if all we had were spreading maples. (For further discussion, see the introduction to Chapter 2.)

Allusion (see *figures of speech*).

Analogy. Analogy is the resemblance in some respects between two things that are otherwise not alike. Thus in some respects, a bird is like (and is thus analogous to) a jet aircraft. Similarly, the spirit that prevails among the players on a winning football team is analogous to what prevails among members of a harmonious family. Making these analogies has the effect of explaining one thing by reference to another, and thus analogy is a useful technique for the writer.

Sometimes a whole essay can be written by means of extended analogy. For example, in explaining the effects of overloading the perceptual apparatus of the human being (unknown, to be explained), the writer can use the analogy of overloading an electrical circuit (the known). Or the finely tuned, harmonious relationship between business partners (unknown) can be explained by analogy to that of marriage partners (known).

Of course, analogies are made on the level of the sentence in many different kinds of writing. (See Mailer, for example; but see also Hutchins's use of analogy in his paragraph 7.)

Argument is one of the forms of discourse. See Chapter 1.

Central idea or central theme (see *subject and unity*).

Classification (see Chapter 4).

Cliché comes from the French word for stereotype plate or printing block. Hence any word or expression whose freshness and clarity have been lost through constant usage is called a cliché or stereotype.

We all use clichés in ordinary conversation. In those circumstances they are forgiven—perhaps because we make up for the tired expression with a lively presence. In any case, whether your writing is formal or informal, you should avoid such expressions as *hot under the collar, neat as a pin, free as a bird, the beginning of the end, pretty as a picture, bigger and better*—and dozens more.

Writers in control of their material can use clichés to make special, fresh points (see, for example, Mannes, paragraphs 6, 7, and 8), but writers who are not in control tend to use clichés unconsciously. They need to devote themselves to the problem. In order to develop a reliable cliché detector, the writer is advised to devote at least one proofreading session to the search for and replacement of clichés.

Coherence is the term we apply to good writing when all its parts hang together in a clear and logical way. When we say that a piece of writing has *unity* (see that entry), we mean that each part of the composition relates to the main point. When we say it has coherence, we mean that each of these parts—sentences and paragraphs—connects smoothly and logically to the ones preceding.

The main component of coherence is logical organization. The writer whose work is carefully planned, especially through use of an outline, is likely to produce coherent work. Devices aiding *transition* are also important and are discussed under that entry.

Colloquial (see *levels of usage*).

Comparison and contrast (see Chapter 3).

Conclusions. Conclusions are the last of the three major parts of an essay (the other two are the introduction and the main body). If the introduction and the main body of your essay have not given the reader a sense of satisfying wholeness and the experience that he or she has read something with a beginning and a middle, then your conclusion is not likely to do the job all by itself. You are in desperate trouble. The function of a conclusion is not to round off the job you've spent most of the essay doing; it is rather to *remind* the reader of the good experience he or she has had reading the other two parts. You can write two good parts and then proceed to use the last part to apologize for what you have just done or for the fact that your typewriter leaks ribbon stain, or you can use the conclusion to occupy the white space of the blank paper (no conclusion) or you can use it to plead for a grade, but if you do any of these you will not be reminding the reader that you have written a splendid introduction and main body. The reader will extrapolate from the disappointment with the end to think that the disappointment is with the beginning and middle. And it's no use making a summary conclusion. Why should readers have paid close attention to the main body of your paper if you are going to summarize it for them in the conclusion? Only longish scientific papers require conclusions because the complex data used to support points made in scientific papers tend to confuse a reader.

Specific techniques for concluding expository prose papers can function to give good papers their due.

For example, you can restate your thesis in the conclusion or in some other way connect the conclusion to a thread running all through your work, a thread that begins in the introduction. (Hemingway, Berman, the O'Neills, as well as Alexander, Herman, and Agee use techniques like these.)

Another technique is to make some climactic point in the conclusion; explaining the significance of your subject is itself a climactic point. One or the other is suitable. Be sure that the climactic point (if it is not explaining the significance) is really a topper and be sure your explanation of the significance—if you choose to do that—is convincing. (Users of this category include Johnson, Selye, Kristol, Mermey, Armour, Medea, and Thompson, Laqueur, and Walker.)

Conclusions that suggest action or change also are forceful and positive. (See the conclusions of "Free the Banks," Thomas, Janeway, Mannes, and Hutchins.)

Conclusions that rely on either verbal devices (metaphors, similes, rhetorical questions, and so forth) or blatant finality signals like *finally* or *in the end* are not really using techniques for concluding since if that is *all* the conclusion can boast then it is likely to have little substance. Nevertheless, some of the writers represented here have used these signals as the central verbal facts of their conclusions. (See Cronin, Lish, Kristol, King, Orwell, Laqueur, Medea, and Thompson.)

Concrete (see *abstract and concrete*).

Connotation and denotation are properties of language. (The reader interested in this entry should also refer to the first page of Chapter 5.)

As we noted earlier, the denotation of a word is simply the thing it names whereas the connotation is the whole range of extra associations that go along with it. A *brick* is a baked-clay building block. But it also connotes strength and solidity to most people (its *general* connotations). To some particular person, this writer for example, bricks also connote the injured finger he sustained while doing an amateur bricklaying job (*personal* connotation).

General and personal connotations are continually being manipulated by the media. By suggesting that some packaged food product is "just like Mom used to make," advertising copywriters play on what "Mom" means to each of us, personally and generally. Connotation is also widely manipulated by political candidates and pressure groups of all persuasions.

Every writer *must* use denotation, and most do so more or less automatically. Some writers manipulate connotation, but every writer should know about it. Although we cannot be responsible for the great range of personal associations any word is likely to invoke, we should be alert to the general connotations. Let us examine just one example in this book of how connotation is manipulated. The last line of Orwell's definition refers to his experience as the *suburbs* of poverty. A more denotative choice would have been, say, *outskirts*. Both words denote a place somewhat removed from the central city—and in this case, city = poverty—but whereas *outskirts* is more or less neutral (with, to my ear, just a connotative shade of the deserted or perhaps sleazy), *suburbs* clearly connotes middle-class affluence. So the point Orwell makes in using *suburbs* is very well-made indeed. By this choice, he establishes the exact distance between the center and the place from which he writes.

Beginning writers should not worry excessively over the matter of connotation, but careful writers who feel confident enough to engage this issue will find that attention to connotation adds precision and emphasis to their writing.

Deduction is the logical process of arguing from a general statement to a particular. Deduction is important in argument and is the basis for various applications of law. It is, in fact, a habit of mind. For example, a child learns at some time that putting his or her hand near a flame will result in pain (a generalization) and on a particular occasion will refrain from doing so (the particular).

Deduction is the process whereby we move from the general to the particular. *Induction,* on the other hand, is the name for the process whereby we *arrive* at the general from particular instances. The child who *knows* that putting his or her hand in the fire will hurt (generalization) knows it because on a number of occasions it has happened to him or her (the particular).

In expository writing, induction and deduction are important logical tools. See Chapter 1.

Diction. Diction means "the use of words." The use of words always involves choice, and the proper choice is governed by the following considerations: (1) Always choose the exact word that will convey your exact meaning. (Do you mean *use* or *utilize?* Do you mean you are *anxious* or you are *fearful?* Do you mean he had *alternatives* or *choices?*) (2) Choose the plainest words and the fewest number necessary to say what you want to say. (What transpired was this: when I made my way home and looked around it occurred to me that somebody had expropriated my car, *or* When I got home, I found my car had been stolen.) Take into account the subject matter, the reader (the kind of audience the writer is speaking to) and the purposes governing the writing. ("The flash that entered Enrico Fermi's head that he was about to unlock the secrets of the atom—it was a real turn on." *No.* Fermi was excited at being so close to the atomic secret. *Yes.*) (4) Choose words for their freshness and clarity; avoid clichés (see that entry in the Glossary) and vague abstractions. Strive to make your writing concrete. ("He had an openness and a sense of possibility about him that made you come to the conclusion that the guy was a real live wire." *Never.* "He was direct, hopefully enthusiastic and ambitious." *Yes.*)

Writers wishing to enlarge their vocabulary have only to pay some attention to their poor diction. The improvement will make it seem that they have suddenly acquired a whole new language.

Division is an aspect of the method known as *classification*. See Chapter 4.

Draft. A draft is the name given to a written-out *version* of a writer's work. A *first draft* is the first written-out version; the *second draft* is the second written-out version; and so forth. Writers do well to understand the necessity of producing several drafts of a writing assignment before submitting a *final draft* to the instructor.

Emphasis. *Unity, coherence,* and *emphasis* are the standards applied to test the value of expository prose. Writing that has all three is very good writing.

Emphasis is the writer's achievement of appropriate attention to each detail of writing, according to the value of that detail to the overall presentation. For example, in an essay arguing *for* gun-control laws, a detail valuable to the argument would be the fact that a great number of small children are either killed or maimed by the accidental discharge of handguns. Since it is a poignant detail and likely to be persuasive—in addition to being true—it should receive an appropriate amount of emphasis; this the writer can do in a number of ways, for the writing techniques for applying emphasis are unusually ample.

The writer could take that detail and place it first in his essay or he could place it last: both places are emphatic *positions*. (See the positional emphasis implied by paragraph 12 in Roger M. Williams and see paragraph 7, "Free the Banks.") In addition, he could allude to this matter more than once, perhaps altering the wording the second or third time to avoid monotony. Thus *repetition and modulation* are also methods of giving emphasis and so attracting the reader's attention. (See Mannes, Gregory, and Runnion.)

The amount of space given to a particular detail of the essay also confers emphasis on that detail; the large *proportion* of his essay that the gun-control man might give over to the statistics for gunshot wounds and deaths would emphasize this portion of the work. (See Kristol and Orwell in particular; see also, in general, the proportional emphases of the writers in Chapter 4.)

Underlinings, quotation marks, ellipses, capital letters, all add emphasis where they are used sparingly. The proponent of our argument might underline his piece of evidence that Massachusetts' stiff gun-control law (with mandatory prison sentences for any possession) has already produced a lower rate of handgun related deaths and injuries. These *typographical* markers require good judgment on the part of the writer. (See Vidal, "Free the Banks," Mermey, and Mannes.)

Of course, the writer can simply *tell the reader* when to pay attention and when not. Again, this is a matter of some delicacy and the student writer is advised to tread carefully here. Perhaps the gun control advocate can get away with "*The most crucial reason to enact gun-control laws—and one that no intelligent reader can ignore is this one:* even if it were true that people and not guns do the killing, why should it be made easier for them to kill?" But be careful. (See Roger M. Williams, paragraph 12; and Medea and Thompson, paragraph 19.)

The particular verbal vitality with which you say something draws the reader's attention to that something. Few of us have *distinctive style*, but see Vidal, Allen, Alexander, Orwell, Walker, and Herman for examples.

A *flavorsome point of view* confers emphasis on a whole piece. (See Vidal and King, for example.) A special case is, of course, the *humorous style,* the comic point of view. Wherever humor erupts, the details are given emphasis. Allen, King, Armour, and Runnion are good examples.

There are even more ways to achieve emphasis, for example by arranging for a structure of suspense in your essay, but these are major techniques and should be carefully studied by the student writer.

Exposition is the kind of writing or speech whose general purpose is to explain. See To the Student at the beginning of this book.

Figures of Speech are turns of phrase that make brief but vivid statements by comparing unlike things. There are literally hundreds of figures of speech, but the following few are likely to prove most useful to the writer:

1. *Metaphor.* In this figure, an indirect comparison is imaginatively made, that is, the wording suggests that the two items being compared are identical. In the phrase "what makes . . . his friends tick" (Selye, paragraph 10), the behavioral springs of a person ("friends") are compared to the inner mechanism of a clock (that produces the "tick"). In "our love affair with big government" (Berman, paragraph 4), the way one feels about a man or woman is being compared to one's attitude toward big government. Other examples of metaphor will be found in Runnion, T. Harry Williams, Hoggart, Woolf, and Mailer.

2. *Simile.* In this figure, a direct comparison is made by employing the word *like* or *as.* For example, "she looks *like* a spider spinning

a web" (Armour, paragraph 23).

3. *Personification.* This is the endowment of inanimate or abstract things with the qualities of a person in order to describe the function of appearance of those things. See Colette's characterization of a room, Woolf's of the sun, and Holt's of the discipline of Nature.

4. *Allusion.* In the ordinary sense, to allude to something is to mention something. In the rhetorical sense, to allude to is to recall the well-known name of a literary or historical figure or event and link it with that of someone else. For example, merely mentioning Hank Aaron's name is a reference. But calling the heaviest hitter on a baseball team "Hank Aaron" is an allusion. Similarly, calling a power-mad person "Napoleon" or referring to his defeat as his "Waterloo" is also an allusion. See Alexander and Holt.

General (see *specific and general*).

Humor is, in one sense, the quality of being laughable or comical. It is funniness. Humor is also something designed to induce laughter or amusement, such as a funny play or movie or TV show or a piece of humorous writing. But humor is also a mystery—maybe the most profound human mystery—and that is why definitions are likely to be scoffed at.

But if you haven't thought much about humor, you should understand that humor appears in writing because it is privately and publicly an initiation to the condition we call civilization. Neither persons nor societies can be said to be in good health if they cannot laugh or be amused. That is because humor results when we look inward—at our selves or our social lives—and see where we have been overreachers; when we see the discrepancy between ideal and actuality, what we want and what we have, what we think and what we do. When we achieve humor, we can say that we have surmounted something, that we have in some way gone beyond the chasm that will always be there. This is a paradox and may be pretty funny besides.

Writers with a sense of humor are rare and should be cherished, but it is not necessarily the case that they are only born and not made. Therefore, it is instructive to examine some of the ways in which writers achieve humor or comical effects. By doing so, you will be able to sharpen your own awareness of humor and begin to try out your own comic wings. Here are a few of the ways in which writers achieve humor:

1. *Exaggeration or hyperbole.* Hyperbole is a figure of speech by which something is exaggerated out of proportion for special or comic effect. Mermey's first two sentences are good examples of comic exaggeration ("I can't eat or drink anything. I can't go anywhere."). In fact, her whole essay is one big hyperbole. Another example is Lish's challenge to the reader to try to spoil his cup of great coffee: "hit it with a hammer."

2. *Understatement.* Used in a certain way, understatement is *irony* (see that entry)—which is also a form of humor. A good example is in Armour's paragraph 20, where he speaks of his grandfather's *ample widow* [ample = sufficient], after describing her very large stature, and then goes on to say that she got *ampler and ampler.*

3. *Satire.* Satire works to expose wickedness, folly, or inappropriate manners or morals by using wit (verbal humor), and derision—frequently also everything else in the humorist's arsenal, including over- and understatement and parody. A good example is the whole of Runnion's first paragraph, where he tries to expose the bad manners of college teachers and administrators who will have little or nothing to do with their students. This he achieves by setting up the students as social outcasts and then pretend-

ing to advise the teachers and administrators how to get friendly with them. Allen's whole essay is satire—as is Runnion's—and one small example of how he achieves the mark is his satire on FBI violence ("several G-men laced my trachea into a reef knot").

4. *Parody.* This is to hold something up to ridicule by broadly mimicking its characteristic style or manner. King parodies newspaper columns giving health advice in his paragraph 7. Armour parodies people proud of their ancestry who invariable say—it is now a cliché—"I come from a *long* line of . . ." by changing the expression to "I come from a *short* line." Allen parodies the solemn and stilted language of the confessional by narrating the fantastic story of Willard Pogrebin mimicking that language.

5. *Reversal of the reader's expectations.* This form of humor is frequently encountered in the essays printed here. Bouton (in paragraph 1) says "what looks like boredom" —and you hold your breath—but he concludes "is usually just that." King gives you what you least expected when he says that kids "rise at an ungodly hour for the sole purpose"—ready for this one?— "of providing their parents a long day."

6. *People seen in a mechanical way.*

Humor is invariably the result when people or social facts are seen as mechanical or treated in a machine-like fashion. Bouton, for example, says that in order to understand what the players are saying to the umpire, the spectator should "bring along a lip reader." Of course, this is also a case of reversed expectations. Armour, in paragraph 14, describes his grandmother in terms that would be suitable for an inanimate object and thus achieves humor in this way.

7. *Striking simile and metaphor.* "A charismatic young woman with a beard like Svengali's" is one of Woody Allen's gems. Another good example is Fleming's characterization of flirting. It is "like trying out a play in Boston before opening on Broadway."

8. *Funny names.* Allen is a master in creating these—"Willard Pogrebin," "Himmelstein's Sausage Factory"—but the titles of Runnion's classes are also examples of this kind of humor.

This by no means exhausts the ways in which authors achieve humor, and the alert student will be able to pick out several more. You should be aware that many of these categories overlap and single humorous effects are sometimes achieved by several different means.

Introductions. The introduction is the beginning of the paper—in the emphatic position—the first of the three major parts of the essay. Wise writers will discipline themselves to compose this part last, waiting until they have a draft (see Glossary entry) completed in order to see what kind of material they have written and what kind of introduction will articulate best to their particular main body.

A slang term for the introduction is *the hook.* With it, you grab the reader's attention (by telling him about your subject and offering him a tough thesis statement); if his attention stays focused, then your introduction also tells him how to read your particular style—not an insignificant educational function and a fair exchange, considering that one of your main purposes is to educate the reader.

But what techniques may be used to dig the hook in deeper and complete this gentle walk into your garden? Below is given a list of these in the order of attention-focusing strength (that is, the first is the most powerful, the second slightly less, and so forth), each accompanied by references to those authors printed in the book who use the particular technique identified:

1. Kicking off with the writer's personal experience. This is most attractive because human beings are most interesting—especially firsthand accounts of their experience. See Fleming, Agee, Allen, Mermey, Vidal, Kristol, and Friedrich.

2. A tie for second place between making an *unusual* statement, as do King, Alexander, Armour, Korda, and "Free the Banks," and making an *ordinary* statement. Unusual statements will focus attention, but ordinary ones will too, in the same way that understatement makes its effect. (See Glossary: *irony*.)

3. Posing a possibility as a challenge. See Berman's introduction.

4. Describing the significance of the subject. This requires a more delicate touch here than in the conclusion because the reader tends to be

skeptical if he is being proselytized at the outset. But it is done by Bouton, Berman, Herman, Thomas, Allen, and the O'Neills.

5. Filling in the background. This may be necessary, but it is not always interesting. See "Free the Banks," Roger M. Williams, Hutchins, and Mermey.

It is worth repeating: catching the reader's attention, getting a hook into the reader, is the writer's most important task in the introduction. Whatever technique you use—do *that* as well as you can.

With these functions in mind, we can look at the various good ways of making an introduction that are illustrated by essays in this book. The writer should bear in mind that several of the following may be used in combination:

1. *Filling in the background* serves to bring the reader up to an important level of knowledge about the subject to be discussed, the issues involved, or the problem to be tackled. See "Free the Banks," Roger M. Williams, Hutchins, Mermey, and others.

2. *Describing the significance or importance of the subject.* See Bouton, Berman, Herman, Thomas, Allen, and the O'Neills.

3. *Stating the central theme.* See Roger M. Williams, "Free the Banks," Bouton, and Medea and Thompson.

4. *Using the writer's personal experience as a kickoff point.* Narrative writing and descriptive writing almost invariably do this, but other kinds of expository writing do it too. See Fleming, Agee, Allen, Mermey, Vidal, Kristol, and Friedrich.

5. *Making an unusual statement* that catches interest and whose explanation a reader wants to follow. See King, Alexander, Armour, Korda, and "Free the Banks."

6. *Making an ordinary statement whose commonness draws interest.* See Kaplan and Schwerner, Hemingway, Runnion, and Thomas.

7. *Using a rhetorical device* of some kind. See Mannes, Runnion, Lierres, and "Free the Banks."

8. *Using a comparison and contrast* to introduce the subject. See Berman.

9. *Posing a possibility as a challenge.* See O'Neills.

10. *Narrowing down from topic to subject.* See Herman.

There are other possibilities, but the writer may wish to experiment with these first.

Irony. This is saying one thing while meaning the opposite. "This is a wild party," said with the proper emphasis, can mean that the party is very dull. In colloquial usage, a *bad* dude is not so bad after all. (For other examples of a similar kind, see Vidal, paragraphs 4 and 5; "Free the Banks," 7; Armour, 3.)

A writer skilled in verbal irony can manipulate the degree with which it bites the way a skilled dentist *seems* to increase or diminish the pain in your tooth. (The dentist doesn't do that, really.) When the ironist is seen to be trying to bite very deeply, we say that he is employing *sarcasm*. (To a recklessly speeding cabdriver, he might say: "How many *other* people have you killed today?") Sometimes, when irony is simple *understatement*, we may think that the ironist is not trying to bite so deep. (To the same cabdriver: "Traffic slows you down around here, doesn't it?") The sarcasm that aims to be caustic can thus inflict *less* damage than the quiet understatement that is devastating. (Lesson: Appearances aren't everything.) The effects are based on the gap between amplitude of the situation it comments on and its own amplitude. Where the gap is greatest (between reckless, noisy, endangering driving, and the mild understatement) the effect is likely to be greatest, the bite deepest, and vice versa. (For a good example of understatement, see Walker's first line.)

But irony can be used in various ways—over a whole passage or in single words or sentences.

Verbal irony needs careful control; otherwise, it degenerates into an expression of mere bad temper. Writers must remember that by saying the opposite of what they really mean, they make their point more forcefully because the reader must come to an intellectual stop. But the purpose is always to *explain* something to your reader; irony is not an appropriate means of expressing personal hostility. Thus, in the hands of a writer who has a sure aim and who understands that it can only be addressed to an alert audience, verbal irony is a very effective instrument.

The irony of situation occurs where the discrepancy is between logical expectation and what actually occurs. An implied irony of this type comes near the end of Vidal's marijuana argument, where he says that nothing will be done about the situation—after his sustained argument. Woody Allen's whole tale is a tissue of situation ironies, and other examples will be found in "Free the Banks," Herman, paragraphs 8 and 12; and Thomas, 1, 2 and 3.

Levels of usage. The old meaning of this phrase suggested a "high" level of usage—appropriate and natural to a "high" socioeconomic class of people—and a "low" level of usage appropriate and natural to a correspondingly "low" socioeconomic class. A better idea is that a good level of English to use is the level appropriate to the audience receiving it and the purpose for which it was written. For our purposes, it is well to recognize the following levels of usage:

Formal writing is appropriate to most college work, writing in business, the professions (for example, the law), and to the whole of scholarly enterprise. It is marked by great precision of expression, expressive complexity of syntax and sentence structure (in other words, the capacity to make complicated, heavily qualified statements), and an elevated kind of diction. Unless otherwise advised by the instructor, students taking this course should strive for this level of usage.

In general, formal usage forbids contractions, prefers the use of a word like *position* to a word like *job* in writing to apply for one, prefers the expression "I understand you are looking for an assistant professor with my qualifications" to one that declares "I heard about the job and it sounds like it fits me." This is not to say that the formal level is all that stuffy, or even uptight, or that you cannot profitably enhance your formal level of writing with an informal, colloquial word or usage. What it does mean is that this level reflects the honor and prestige that accrues to those of us who have struggled to acquire mastery of this most difficult and most honorable enterprise (yourselves included).

Slightly lower, because the purposes are less prestigious and have less urgent significance for large groups of people, is the level we call informal or colloquial. The root of the latter word means "to speak wtih someone" and colloquial simply signifies the kind of English we use in ordinary conversation. *Okay, That'll be fine. How's your wife feeling?* Letters between friends employ the colloquial level and certain kinds of very informal writing assignments, journals, for example. There's nothing wrong with colloquial language —it's plain and serviceable.

Slang, which is a cut below the colloquial, is a mixed blessing. The circumstances and audience for which slang is appropriate are likely to be those that require no writing—perhaps only sign-making. The good thing about slang is that it regularly provides more formal levels of usage with a supply of words and phrases that are fresh, vivid, compelling: useful. The problem with slang is that its formations, the words it invents to form its vocabulary, tend to be too few to express the range of experience of its speakers (although they don't think so). *Cool* and *crazy* and more recently *bad* simply have too much work to do; they serve to symbolize too wide a range of objects, ideas, and actions. When the vivid expressions are invented, therefore, too often and too quickly they are played out and trite (see Glossary: *cliché*) before they have a chance for a useful life. How many of us, for example, still think that *heavy* and *far out* are usable? And who thinks that *a kick in the head* has long to live?

Despite all this, levels of usage are frequently mixed by good writers who want to use slang or colloquial words and phrases to establish special points. (See, therefore, Cronin, King, Bouton, Runnion, Lish, Gregory, and Allen.)

Logic (see Chapter 1).

Main body: one of three parts of the essay; the one that comes between the introduction and the conclusion.

Metaphor (see *figures of speech*).

Paradox is a statement that appears contradictory or absurd on the surface, but upon examination, reveals a truth. Mermey's title, for example, "A Victim of the Consumer Crusades," when we understand that she takes the point of view of a consumer. (For other examples, see King, paragraph 2; Berman, paragraph 2; Tuan, 1; Thomas, 12; Lequeur, 10.)

Parallel structure refers to the use of coordinate form for coordinate elements of writing (for example, series of verbs, prepositions, gerunds, or phrases of one kind or another). Parallel structure affords the writer the opportunity to emphasize parallel ideas in sentences, parts of sentences, paragraphs, or even whole essays. In addition to emphasis; parallel structure gives economy and strength to a writer's prose. For parallelism in paragraph structure, see Orwell;

for parallelism of sentences, see Hutchins, paragraph 1; Bouton, 1; Herman, 2; Williams, 2; for parallel structures within sentences, see Berman, 2; Vidal, 6; Thomas, 15.

Personification (see *figures of speech*).

Point of view. Point of view is the place where the writer stands and looks at his or her work. That *place* is defined by writer's vocation, psychological frame of mind at the moment of writing, his image of himself as someone who knows (in this he can be humble or grandiose) and what he *really* knows. (Good writers cannot fail to disclose their points of view; only inept writers can and in their cases it doesn't matter. This inevitability is good because the reader is entitled to know exactly where the writer stands.)

Example: There is a proposal to cut interstate highways through large tracts of prime farm land. The farmer, the urban planner, the truck driver and the state legislator will all stand differently on this issue. Moreover, where each one stands could be changed, depending on whether one or another thinks *he* can foresee all the consequences and bases his stand on that and not on his natural tendency (based on his occupation).

The student seeking evidence of this point of view should pay close attention to small details—as well as to large ones.

Process analysis (see Chapter 6).

Purpose is a crucial element in controlling any piece of writing because *it* determines how a writer addresses his or her reader. One reason to approach learning to write by practicing the rhetorical categories suggested in this book is that this method gives the writer continual practice in purposeful writing. Thus the writing of an argument has the purpose of "convincing," the writing of a description has the purpose of "making the reader see," the writing of other expository types has the purpose of "explaining," and so on.

Writers should define their purpose clearly, write it down, and work with it through the stages of material gathering, outlining, making the first draft, and revising.

Rhetorical questions. Rhetorical questions are questions that the writer poses but does not answer. The purpose of a rhetorical question is to focus the reader's attention on a particular point and/or to move a discussion along in a particular direction. Rhetorical questions are to be distinguished from ordinary kinds that *are* answered by the writer. The ordinary question and answer is a particular rhetorical technique for organizing small units (usually paragraphs) of the essay and is used especially well by Vidal in paragraphs 6 and 9 of his essay. (See also Kristol, paragraph 10; Thomas, paragraph 18; and Mannes, paragraph 7.)

Simile (see *figures of speech*).

Slang (see *colloquial language*).

Specific and general. These refer to the same qualities of language as *abstract and concrete,* but they are relative terms. See the Glossary entry *abstract and concrete.*

Style and tone. Point of view denotes the place where the writer stands in looking at his subject. Tone is the song that the writer sings as that tune is generated by the nature of the place. Style is the *way* he sings it. These three issues are intertwined so tightly that it's sometimes difficult to disentangle and identify them separately. Still, they are valid tools for rhetorical analysis, and help the student writer to seek out his own trio of point of view, style, and tone.

A writer's tone really says how he feels about or thinks of his subject matter (subject: people's freedom; tone: I love and defend it). A writer's tone may be described as romantic, defensive, liberated, omnipotent, and so on. On the other hand, the writer's style refers to the resources he brings to the task of expressing that tone. How does he do it? With long words, complicated sentences, long paragraphs, tortured arguments, minute details, lots of allusions? One or more of these (or other characteristics) will determine whether his style can be described as hidden, allusive, forceful, formal and lofty, and so on. Style—that is, the exact and characteristic verbal means the writer employs—derives from the writer's history as a student, a reader, and a writer.

Students develop the styles that please themselves and their readers by doing a great deal of writing and reading. (For the great range of styles and tones in this book, read any five, or try Goffman, Vidal, Gregory, Carson, and Allen.)

Subject is what a piece of writing is *generally about*. Love, nuclear energy, friendship, economics, sports—all these are subjects. What a piece of writing is *specifically* about is its *central theme* or thesis statement, or what the writer has to *say* about the subject. *Dogs* is a word (or subject), not a sentence (or central theme). *Dogs bark* is a sentence—and a possible central theme (though, to be sure, *dogs bark* is so simple a central theme that it is virtually a two-word essay all by itself). A writer may state his or her subject in a word or a phrase, but a central theme or thesis statement must be stated in the form of a complete sentence. (See also *unity*.)

Symbols. So adept are we at making symbols—man has been described as a symbol-making animal—that we have made a whole, elaborate set of symbols out of natural experience. Winter and its constituents, ice, snow, cold, gray skies, and so on, symbolize sleep or death; summer and its associated phenomena, warmth, light, sun, radiant skies, and so on, symbolize the opposite. And we have other resources for making symbols useful in everyday life: a red light or sign means danger or stop; thumbs up means victory or something generally positive; the dove symbolizes peace; a political candidate greeting workers at a factory is merely a man shaking hands, but his action symbolizes his candidacy and goodwill; democracy is an idea but it symbolizes our aspirations toward equality. In short, a symbol is an object, man-made or natural, an idea or a pattern of behavior that means something beyond itself.

Of course, each of us has private symbols whether or not we are aware of them. A car is only an automobile to most of us, but the owner you see fussing endlessly with his car's shiny finish, its smoothly purring engine, or its dashing racing stripes, is obviously thinking that the car is something other and quite beyond a mere auto.

Thus all writers make use of symbols, either deliberately or unconsciously. In this book, for example, notice the special symbolic meaning to Mailer of *contests,* or what he conceives as such, that is, the boxing match, the bull-fight, marriage, the dramatic conflict of theatre.

Similarly, Agee's emphatic concentration on the garden hose suggests that object's symbolic nature—in some way personal to him but also available to us. Woolf's special reverence for a natural phenomenon and Colette's recurring reference to colors also seem privately symbolic. But Yi-Fu Tuan makes *place* and *space* take on general symbolic significance.

The student writer who is ambitious for his work should study the possibilities for adding symbolic significance to his or her own work. Sparing and strategic use of an appropriate object or idea can certainly enhance a piece of student writing, but the writer who is unsure of this technique should consult his instructor for assistance.

Syntax. Syntax is the way words are used to form sentences. A sentence that is syntactically correct is one that is a well-formed, standard English sentence, having a subject and a complete predicate. Students who find a good many of the sentences in their writing assignments marked by the instructor to indicate incorrect syntax should consult the instructor about special exercises to eliminate this fault.

In some of the questions following the essays in this book, reference is made to *syntax* and to *unusual syntax.* By these is meant the *deliberate* use of incomplete or nonstandard syntax to achieve a special effect or to enhance a particular style and tone. Consider for example the following paragraph:

Tony walked down the street. *Swaggering.* He tossed a coin in the air as he went, at the same time whistling through tightly clenched lips. *Cool. Not a hair out of place.* The three girls looked him over hungrily. *Six wide eyes.*

The four groups of emphasized words are examples of unusual syntax. Though each begins with a capital letter and ends with a period, none is a standard sentence; strictly speaking, none is syntactically correct. But it is easy to see that they are used for special effect: their use emphasizes the subject's (Tony's) coolness, the abrupt, tense mood of the scene being described, and the action on which no words need be wasted, so to speak. Thus they establish and enhance the particular style and tone of the passage.

There are other examples in the book of unusual syntax. See especially Vidal, paragraphs 5 and 9; "Free the Banks," paragraphs 1, 4, and 5; and King, paragraph 2.

Theme (see *unity*).

Thesis statement is the name we give to a central theme when it is written out as a sentence. A thesis, or theme, is simply the stand you take on an issue (and then it is identical with what we called a *main proposition* in Chapter 1) or the main point you want to make about a subject.

The Decline of American Cities is not a thesis statement but a title. In fact, it isn't a sentence, and a thesis statement must be a complete sentence. "My subject is the decline of American cities" is not a thesis statement, either, but an announcement to the reader of what your subject will be—a job done better by a title. (Notice that it is not an improvement to write "My *thesis* is the decline of American cities.") "The decline of American cities is deplorable" is also not a thesis statement because it needs no essay to support it; it is a fairly obvious statement of fact. A reader would be as interested in reading an essay about it as he would be in reading one that supports the statement, "Hank Aaron holds the major league home run record."

Writers need an effective thesis statement in order to control their writing. A poorly worded thesis statement guarantees a poorly constructed, badly focused, and uninteresting piece of writing. In order to be sure that you have a thesis statement that will help control your writing, you should pay attention to the following criteria of a good thesis statement:

1. *An effective thesis statement is limited* or narrowed down from a larger statement. The idea is to give yourself a manageable, *limited* piece of territory to cover. "College teachers go too fast for the average college student." This is a very broad statement that takes its writer into too large a territory. For example, he or she would have to talk about more than one college teacher and would also have to deal with whatever is an "average college student." The territory can be scaled down considerably if this were changed to "Professor Lucia John goes too fast for her math students." You can see how this limits the territory to one professor in just one class and how it provides real material in the form of actual students. Here are two more examples of large and narrower statements:

Large	*Narrower*
Our tax burdens are too great.	Federal tax rates penalize people for being single.
Baseball is fun.	Nothing matches the excitement of a low-scoring baseball game between evenly matched teams.

2. *An effective thesis statement is singular* in nature. More than one major idea in an essay is one idea too many. The writer with too many major ideas writes diffusely, his or her piece wanders all over the territory, and the reader loses track of what he or she is supposed to be following. "The United Nations has not fulfilled its original purpose of keeping world peace, it's used for narrow political purposes instead, and many countries neglect to pay their share of its unkeep—which is quite expensive." This is a mouthful—enough for at least two and probably three essays. Better would be either "The UN has not fulfilled its original peace-keeping purpose" or "The UN is used for narrow political purposes." Here are two more examples:

Multiple	*Singular*
The social life of a freshman at this college is very limited, the place is so big that you can get lost look-	A freshman at this college has a number of difficult adjustments to make

ing for a classroom, and besides, the professors are an unfriendly bunch.

or

The social life of a freshman at this college is very limited.

or

The professors at this college are an unfriendly bunch.

Our ecological problems are mounting, a situation that is not helped by the energy crunch, the increasing population, and the plans for modern industrial development by the Third World countries.

The energy crisis is contributing to our mounting ecological problems.

or

Plans for industrial development by Third World countries will contribute to our ecology problems.

or

Rapid increases in world population will contribute to our ecology problems.

3. *An effective thesis statement is concrete.* A thesis statement that is limited and singular must also be concrete. An abstract or vague expression can ruin it. "The Olympic Games are a great spectacle" is too vague. "A great spectacle" of futility? "A great spectacle" of athletic prowess? Better would be "The Olympic Games are a great spectacle of people's capacity for friendly competition." Another example: "My mother is some kind of cook" doesn't say *what* kind. Better: "My mother is a versatile cook."

Vague

The Pittsburgh Steelers are a great football team.

Those who stop smoking care about their health.

Concrete

The Pittsburgh Steelers are solid at every position.

Giving up smoking reduces the smoker's chances of contracting lung cancer.

Tone (see *style and tone*).

Transition is the relating of one idea to the next as the essay proceeds from start to finish. Smooth transition contributes to the coherence of sentences, paragraphs, and essays. (See *coherence*.) A tight organizational pattern is usually the best guarantee that the writer will achieve coherence.

The necessity for coherence is based on the reader's need to be led from point to point in the writing by some familiar principle of order. In other words, a reader needs a solid bridge to get from sentence to sentence, paragraph, idea to idea. When such bridges are absent, the reader loses confidence in the writing and distractedly wanders away from what he or she is reading.

Thus unless the organizational pattern is so powerful that the writing has exceptionally smooth flow from part to part, it is a good idea to use what are called *transitional devices* to establish points of references, bridges for the reader's eye and mind. These devices are also useful in that they establish the exact relationship between succeeding parts. In that sense they are useful in *saying* more, and saying is the essential function of expository writing.

The major transitional devices, sometimes used in combination, are as follows:

1. *Repetition.* Repeating a word or a phrase is a most common device. Sometimes a pronoun, referring back to a subject, will also do the trick. Repeating a reference to an idea also comes under this heading.

2. *The whole sentence or brief paragraph.* A sentence can be used as a transition between different ideas following and preceding it. Also, a brief paragraph can serve as a transition between two longer paragraphs.

3. *Standard transitional words or phrases.* All of these are good bridges and most are also useful in indicating relationships. A few of the large number available are listed below:

soon, later, at the same time, afterward, meanwhile, simultaneously, in a little while, subsequently.

nearby, close by, there, here, at the other end.

therefore, thus, hence, consequently.

similarly, likewise, in the same way.

on the other hand, however, but, nevertheless, still, yet, by contrast.

moreover, furthermore, finally, also, in addition.

indeed, in fact, in other words.

Unity. We say that a piece of writing has *unity* when, as we read from beginning to end, we get the distinct impression that what we are reading is reflecting on and developing a *single point*. It isn't that the piece is consistently speaking of one *subject;* you can write consistently about *war* (a subject) and still wander in disunity from the point that (1) war is hell, to the idea that (2) war is a traditional way for nations to settle disputes, to the thesis that (3) war is hardest on civilian populations, to the suggestion that (4) war should be outlawed by the United Nations. An essay that has four main points is not a unified piece of work and can only succeed in distracting and exasperating the reader.

Because a central theme is so central to this most important characteristic of explanatory writing, the student writer is urged to resist all temptations to begin writing before he or she has settled on a central theme (or thesis statement).

The point made in the first paragraph of this entry is, in fact, so important that it is worth repeating with reference to one of the essays in this book, Orwell's definition of poverty in Chapter 5.

The writer may argue, and be partly correct in doing so, that unity is automatically imparted to a piece of narrative writing because the events of the story are naturally related by time and space. In this, he would be only partly correct; the proof would be, say, Gregory's story, "Shame." It takes only a little thought, after reading Gregory, to realize that the *selection* of the related events depended entirely on his central theme; without it, Gregory might have included all kinds of distracting material.

In other words, unity is the *motive* for writing: the writer *wants* to make his singular point and he should therefore continually exercise his skills in becoming proficient at it.

Thematic Table of Contents